Professional French Pastry Series

Creams, Confections, and Finished Desserts

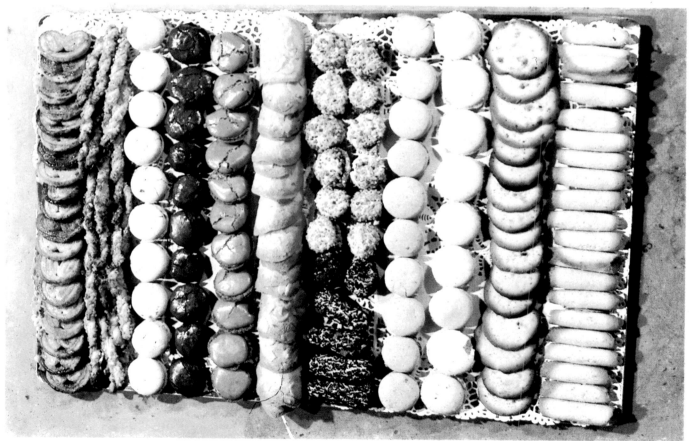

Professional French Pastry Series

Volume 2: Creams, Confections, and Finished Desserts

Roland Bilheux and Alain Escoffier

Under the direction of

Pierre Michalet

Translated by Rhona Poritzky-Lauvand and James Peterson

cicem

A co-publication of
CICEM (Compagnie Internationale
de Consultation *Éducation* et *Media*)
Paris

and

**Van Nostrand Reinhold
New York**

English translation, copyright © 1988 by Van Nostrand Reinhold
for the United States of America and Canada; by CICEM (Compagnie Internationale de Consultation *Education* et *Media*) for
the rest of the world.

Library of Congress Catalog Card Number 88-5537
ISBN 0-442-20567-8

Printed in the United States of America

First published as *Traité de pâtisserie artisanale: Crèmes—Con-
fiserie—Entremets Applications "produits finis"* by Editions St-
Honoré, Paris, France; copyright © 1985

Van Nostrand Reinhold
115 Fifth Avenue
New York, New York 10003

Macmillan of Canada
Division of Canada Publishing Corporation
164 Commander Boulevard
Agincourt, Ontario M1S 3C7, Canada

16 15 14 13 12 11 10 9 8 7 6 5 4 3 2 1

Library of Congress Cataloging-in-Publication Data
(Revised for vol. 2)
Bilheux, Roland, 1944–
  The professional French pastry series.
  Translation of: Traité de pâtisserie artisanale.
  Includes indexes.
  Contents: v. 1. Doughs, batters, and meringues— v. 2.
Creams, confections, and finished desserts—v. 3. Petits fours,
chocolate, frozen desserts, and sugar work—v. 4. Decorations,
borders and letters, marzipan, and modern desserts.
  1. Pastry. 2. Cookery, French. I. Escoffier, Alain, 1947–   .
Michalet, Pierre.
TX773.B49813   1988   641.8′65′0944   88-5537
ISBN v. 1. 0-442-20565-1
       v. 2. 0-442-20567-8
       v. 3. 0-442-20568-6
       v. 4. 0-442-20569-4

The authors
"Savoir et faire savoir"
"To know and to teach"

This expression is perhaps the best way to characterize Roland Bilheux and Alain Escoffier, two **professional** chefs who became **professors** and then **authors**. This natural evolution is attributable to their talent, hard work, ingenuity, and above all their ability to communicate clearly and precisely.

Roland BILHEUX

Roland Bilheux, born in 1944, first apprenticed to become a chef in his childhood province of Mayenne in the west of France. His first formal training was at the famous French culinary school l'Ecole des Métiers de l'Alimentation—known familiarly as "Ferrandi." There, he received the C.A.P. degree in the unusually short period of a year.

After finishing school at the age of eighteen, he worked in a well-respected pâtisserie in Le Mans but was soon sent to Germany to fulfill his military obligation (mandatory in France). There, he cooked for a general of the NATO forces. After his military service, he returned to Le Mans, where he was promoted to pastry chef.

At the age of twenty-three, Roland Bilheux married and opened his own pastry shop and bread bakery in a suburb of Paris. It was here that he perfected many of his skills.

By the age of thirty-one, Roland Bilheux was an experienced pastry chef; he began to work for the "Ferrandi" school in Paris, where he continues to teach today.

Roland Bilheux has won numerous pastry competitions in France and abroad. He is the father of three children and lives in Marly, a suburb outside of Paris.

Alain ESCOFFIER

Born in 1947 in the village of Annonay in Ardèche (a region in southeast France), Alain Escoffier first apprenticed at the Jean Ferrandi cooking school in Paris. At eighteen he obtained his C.A.P. in pastry and bread baking. Over the next two years he continued his training and became a pastry chef's assistant in a well-known Parisian pâtisserie, then an ice-cream specialist in another establishment.

After returning from military service in Germany, he became the chef of a pastry kitchen in a suburb of Paris.

At the age of twenty-six, he became an instructor at the "Ferrandi" school, where he now teaches pastry, ice-cream making, chocolate work, and candy making.

Alain Escoffier is a representative of the French Confederation of Bakers and Pastry Chefs. In this capacity, he often travels abroad, giving lectures and demonstrations on traditional French bread making and on Viennese pastries.

He is married and the father of two children.

The text and photography in the four volumes of *the Professional French Pastry Series* were edited by Pierre Michalet, a specialist in educational materials.
Mr. Michalet is the director of Editions Saint-Honoré.

Contents

Forewords

The *Professional French Pastry Series* consists of four volumes that I would have liked to have owned when I began my training as a professional pastry chef. Now that they are available, they are a resource that I will refer to often. These books are the first available to the serious pastry chef that contain clear and easy-to-follow instructions, which apprentice bakers will also appreciate.

To become a master pastry chef, you need a fine hand, patience, and knowledge. It takes a lot of hard work and perserverance, but the results are well worth the effort. These books show you how to prepare fine pastries using classical methods while allowing the freedom to develop your own ideas, styles, and techniques. Each volume builds upon the skills mastered in the preceding volumes; methods and recipes serve as a continuous source of ideas.

The art of French pastry making is like any art—it is done out of love. Achievements such as the publication of this series help bring respect to pastry making by demonstrating the seriousness of the technique. That's what I particularly like about these volumes—they take you through a precise body of knowledge, step by step, and build your appreciation for it.

I have always hoped that a reference like the *Professional French Pastry Series* would become available to the English-speaking pastry chef as a source to rely on during his or her day-to-day activities. These volumes carefully explain the chemistry of pastry making and include detailed timetables for the recipes. The volumes cover virtually every detail you would need to know in order to learn classical French pastry making. Until now, the only sources available were either in another language or were large collections of recipes without explanations of the methods and techniques. The experience and knowledge of the authors, Roland Bilheux and Alain Escoffier, are apparent throughout all four volumes. The fine abilities of the translators, Rhona Poritzky-Lauvand and Jim Peterson, are also evident.

No one volume or series of volumes can ensure the success of a professional pastry chef. A good resource, however, can help one to develop both the technical and the creative abilities needed for a successful career as a pastry chef. The *Professional French Pastry Series* can assist the chef throughout his or her career. This is truly an encyclopedic work, based on years of professional and teaching experience. To all who are endeavoring to learn the art of French pastry making, as either a professional or a serious amateur, I offer my best wishes for success. It is a wonderful and rewarding experience.

MARKUS FARBINGER
Executive Pastry Chef
Le Cirque Restaurant
New York

When pastry chefs come upon a new book about their craft, their first response is to look for new recipes that can improve their work and inspiring photographs that will enable the creation of more innovative products. The *Professional French Pastry Series* provides both. More important, however, it includes material essential to the day-to-day work of the pastry chef: information about raw ingredients, without which there would be no creation; new and traditional techniques for both making and using pastry; and a historical look at pastry products that enables us to recognize and be a part of the traditions of French pastry making.

In my position as a teacher, I have found this series to be a precious helper; in my position as a chef, an indispensable working tool.

JEAN-MARIE GUICHARD
Director of Instruction
Cacao Barry Training Center
Pennsauken, New Jersey

The Professional French Pastry Series: A guide to the art of French pastry for both the beginner and the experienced professional

The **Professional French Pastry Series** covers a wide range of skills that are useful not only to the pastry chef, but to restaurateurs and caterers as well. Not only does the series provide the essentials to making the basic doughs encountered in traditional French pastry but also teaches the arts of confectionery, ice-cream making, chocolate work, pulling sugar, and a variety of other skills.

The restaurateur will find the **Professional French Pastry Series** extremely valuable, not only for the preparation of desserts, but for any preparation calling for pastry, creams, and sorbets. It will be especially helpful to caterers who are often called upon to prepare hors d'oeuvre and savory baked dishes.

The **Professional French Pastry Series** is a useful resource and reference for anyone interested in learning more about French pastry, regardless of experience.

Diagram of Contents (volumes 1 to 4)

Specialties

Chocolate work	Ice-cream making	Sugar work	Modern specialties
Techniques and methods Vol. 3	Sorbets, ice creams, frozen desserts Vol. 3	All techniques Vol. 3	Vol. 4

Assembled Pastries

Assembled pastries	Finished cakes	Petits fours	Catering specialties
Based on pâte brisée, pâte feuilletée, pâte levée Vol. 2	Finished products Vol. 2	Vol. 3	Vol. 4

Basic Pastry Preparations

Basic doughs and batters	Basic creams	Basic confectionery	Finished cakes
Vol. 1	Vol. 2	Vol. 2	Vol. 2

Precise, clearly explained recipes
Techniques carefully tested by experienced professionals
Carefully explained methods and procedures

Expanding Knowledge of Techniques

Certain recipes and techniques given in the *Professional French Pastry Series* demonstrate specialties in the closely related fields of confectionery, chocolate work, ice-cream making, and catering.

This provides a perfect opportunity for the professional or semiprofessional to develop skills in closely related areas in which he or she may be lacking. Even though it may seem to some degree that these areas are mutually exclusive, developing skills in one area is always helpful in other areas as well.

Even if the professional does not specialize in any of these particular skills, it is important to develop the art of presentation as completely as possible. Decoration enters into French pastry at practically every stage—from making a border on a tart or a spiral design on the top of a Pithiviers to the more elaborate techniques involved in making marzipan roses and writing with a paper pastry cone. Each of these techniques comes into play in the preparation of finished products.

Assembling Finished Pastries

In the assembly of finished pastries, the various basic preparations (dough, batter, cream, candy, ice cream, chocolate) are combined in almost innumerable ways to obtain a wide variety of finished desserts and savory items.

It is this area of the art of French pastry that requires the greatest creativity and skill of the artisan. The pastry chef must also master the self-discipline necessary in working with pastry—constant attention to cleanliness, organization, and knowledge of many different techniques.

Basic Techniques and Preparations

Remember that the quality of a finished dessert depends on the basic batters, doughs, and creams used to create it. Whatever the final presentation of a dish, whether it be simple or elaborate, its intrinsic quality depends on how well each of its components was prepared. Every professional, whether a beginner or a long-experienced professional, must master these basic techniques and preparations before embarking on some of the elaborate methods of assembly and decoration given in this volume.

Translators' Notes

Because these volumes were originally written for a French audience, some changes had to be made in the instructions to make them applicable to American practice. The following notes explain changes that were made, as well as some of the ingredients used in the recipes.

Butter and shortening: Most recipes call for butter because of its superior flavor. Other shortenings may be substituted in part or entirely, according to taste.

Chocolate: The French government strictly controls the quality and appelations of chocolate. The percentage of cocoa butter, cocoa liquor, and sugar are closely controlled. In France, there are various types and qualities of chocolate, which are discussed in detail in volume 3 of this series. Couverture chocolates (the better-quality chocolates) are made with a minimum of 31 percent cocoa butter; no other fats are allowed.

In the United States, what is referred to in this series as white chocolate is actually called white or confectionary coating, as it contains no chocolate, only cocoa butter, sugar, lecithin, and vanilla or other flavoring.

Crème fraîche: Recipes in this series often include crème fraîche. Crème fraîche is thicker than heavy cream but contains the same amount of butter fat. For most recipes, heavy cream can be substituted for crème fraîche.

Flour: Two types of flour are primarily used in the recipes in this series. In general, when products are to be light, such as cake batters, pure cake flour (without baking powder) is called for. When a batter requires more body, all-purpose flour is used. Breads usually require a strong, high-gluten flour, commonly called bread or patent flour. Many of the recipes requiring flour have been tested in the United States by the translators and have been proven to work. As the qualities of flours, as well as the conditions under which they are used (such as humidity and altitude) vary throughout the United States, the amount specified in a recipe may need to be adjusted slightly.

French products: As this series is based on French pastry-making practices, some of the products in it may be unfamiliar. All the products mentioned are available in the United States. Substitutes are given for products that may be difficult to find. All the French products (such as chocolate) can be obtained through wholesale companies that import such products.

Gelatin: In France, gelatin is marketed in 2-gram sheets, whereas in the United States, it is also sold in powdered form. Gelatin sheets vary in weight in the United States, so it is important to weigh them. The equivalent weight of powdered gelatin can be used to replace the gelatin sheets called for in the recipes. Gelatin sheets should always be softened before using them in a recipe by soaking them in cold water for several minutes and then squeezing them to remove the excess water.

Measurements: French professional pastry chefs customarily weigh their ingredients. For this reason, volume measurements are used only for liquids; dry ingredients are difficult to measure accurately by volume. Both metric and U.S. units of measure are given in the text. It is recommended that those who are serious about the profession of pastry making familiarize themselves with the metric system. Because metric measurement is based on units of ten, it is more accurate and easier to use. The metric system is also the most widely used system of measurement, standard almost everywhere but the United States.

Most U.S. conversions have been rounded off to the nearest half unit of measure, except for smaller quantities, when accuracy was important. Quantities less than 15 grams (½ ounce) are given in teaspoons and tablespoons.

Pastry tips: Pastry tip sizes are always indicated by a number. Unfortunately, each manufacturer numbers its tips differently. In this series, the pastry tip numbers are those most commonly used in France. These numbers often correspond to the diameter of the tip in millimeters. French pastry tips are available in the United States.

Sheet pans: Yields given in this series are based on the use of French equipment of standard dimensions. Professional-quality French sheet pans measure 40 x 60 cm (16 x 24 in.) and are made of heavy blue steel. It is always preferable to use the heaviest sheet pans available. If using different-sized sheet pans, be sure to take this into consideration when calculating the number of pastries to place on a pan.

Sugars: Various types of sugars are used in French pastry, each serving a different purpose. Use granulated sugar when no other indication is given.

Confectioners' sugar is sugar that has been finely ground into a powder. It often contains approximately 3 percent cornstarch to prevent caking.

Glucose, also called dextrose, is used along with granulated or cubed sugar when cooking sugar to prevent crystallization. It is also often used for sugar work such as pulled sugar or blown sugar. Corn syrup can be substituted for glucose in the recipes. It is somewhat lighter, however, and so more of it may be required.

Invert sugar, also called trimoline, is 25 to 30 percent sweeter than granulated sugar. It is made by breaking down sucrose into its components, glucose and fructose. Trimoline helps baked goods stay fresher longer because it holds moisture better than granulated sugar does. It is also used in sorbets, as it imparts a smoother texture than granulated sugar alone. Honey is an invert sugar and can be substituted for trimoline in small quantities. Of course, honey is not neutral in flavor, as trimoline is, and can impart an unwanted flavor to the product.

Yeast: The yeast called for in this series is always compressed fresh yeast, not the dry variety. If dry yeast must be substituted, it must be activated at a somewhat higher temperature than fresh yeast. Activate the dry yeast by first moistening it with 43° C (110° F) water. When substituting dry yeast for fresh, use 10 grams or 2 teaspoons of dry yeast for every 20 grams or 2/3 ounce of fresh yeast specified.

Basic creams

Contained in Volume 2

- *the basic creams*

- *basic confectionery*

- *finished cakes prepared using the bases given in volume 1 and the techniques for assembly given in this volume*

Two Main Sections

Basic Preparations

Basic preparations are an important part of volume 2, as they were in volume 1. In this volume they are divided into two categories:

- **basic creams**
- **basic confectionery**

It is important to be familiar with these basic preparations before undertaking the final assembly of certain pastries presented in the section treating finished desserts.

Finished Desserts

The finished desserts presented in this section are classic but lend themselves to modification and adaptation according to the whims of the chef and his or her clientele.

Whatever the finished pastry, it is often necessary to refer back to volume 1 (Doughs, Batters, and Meringues) to check the recipe for a cake, the method of executing a particular technique, organization of the work station, or selection of the raw ingredients.

We strongly recommend that the reader refer back to the section in volume 1 on hygiene, which is especially important when dealing with creams and other extremely perishable preparations.

The organization of the work area and the correct storage of raw ingredients are also extremely important in achieving successful results.

Selecting the Raw Ingredients

In a profession such as that of the French pastry chef, the mastery of certain techniques is imperative to the successful realization of the finished product.

No less important is the understanding and ability to select the appropriate raw ingredients.

Not only is the selection of excellent raw ingredients important, but it is also necessary to choose ingredients that are stable and keep well. This is particularly true in choosing ingredients for creams, which tend to be extremely perishable and need to be stored with great care.

The family of creams

General characteristics

Description

Creamy preparations, of varying richness and lightness, are usually made with a mixture of milk, cream, eggs, sugar, butter or shortening, and natural flavorings (fruit, liquor, liqueurs, extracts).

Creams enter into the preparation of many pastries and cakes and have much to do with determining their final outcome.

Uses

Creams have many uses. Certain creams, such as crème pâtissière (pastry cream) and crème au beurre (butter cream), are well known to pastry chefs and are prepared almost every day. Others, such as crème diplomate and crème mousseline, are less known, while still others, such as crème Saint-Honoré or crème Paris-Brest, have been almost completely forgotten but are nonetheless of interest to the professional.

Most creams are used for frosting and filling cakes. Just as different styles of cakes go in and out of fashion, so do the various creams that enter into their preparation. Mousses and bavarians are examples of creams that in recent years have become increasingly popular.

Whatever the particular cream being prepared, it always requires careful attention. Because of the fragile quality of the raw ingredients and the short cooking times, creams are vulnerable to carelessness and mishandling. Creams are also extremely perishable, which makes it imperative that the pastry chef take extreme care in their preparation and storage.

Selecting the Equipment

It is best to use utensils made of inert materials such as stainless steel when preparing creams. Aluminum can cause the creams to discolor, whereas enameled pots and pans present a danger because of bacterial growth in minute cracks in their surfaces. If copper is used, it must be cleaned at the very last minute with salt and vinegar. If tinned copper is used, it must be checked regularly to make sure the tin has not worn off.

All pastry equipment must be kept perfectly clean.

Selecting the Raw Ingredients

Use only the best and freshest ingredients. Make sure that there is adequate turnover of perishable foods, especially of fruit, milk, eggs, and butter. Discard any questionable ingredients.

Preparation

Always maintain high standards of hygiene, not only in the work area but for the pastry equipment and in dress and personal hygiene (see Pastry Techniques and Skills in volume 1). Since creams are extremely vulnerable to bacterial infestation, government regulations for them are extremely strict and must be closely followed.

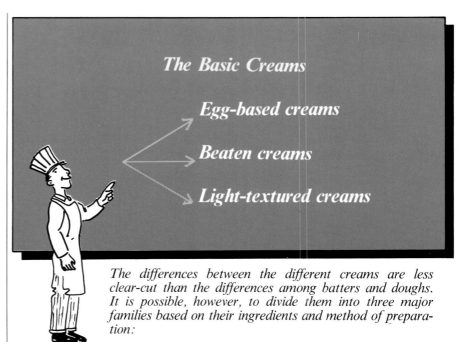

The Basic Creams

Egg-based creams

Beaten creams

Light-textured creams

The differences between the different creams are less clear-cut than the differences among batters and doughs. It is possible, however, to divide them into three major families based on their ingredients and method of preparation:

1. Egg-based Creams

As the name implies, these creams contain a relatively large proportion of eggs. The exact quantity varies with each recipe, but in any case, these creams tend to be extremely perishable. Creams that also contain milk tend to be the most vulnerable to spoilage.

2. Beaten Creams

These are creams that are rapidly beaten with a whisk or an electric mixer to emulsify and lighten them. They are relatively straightforward to prepare, but instructions must be carefully followed and attention must be paid to precautions for cleanliness and hygiene.

Certain of these beaten creams must be used immediately, such as crème de marrons (chestnut cream), crème Paris-Brest, and ganaches montées.

3. Light-textured Creams

These creams obtain their distinctive lightness through the incorporation of beaten egg whites, meringue, or whipped cream. They are consequently delicate and must be prepared carefully. In some cases, these creams involve several different preparations that are carefully folded together to make the final cream. This final folding is delicate and requires experience. The application of these creams also requires considerable care. This is a widely used family of creams and is worth the effort required to master their preparation. These creams are also perishable and must be stored carefully and checked before using.

Using the Creams

Some creams must be used right away, whereas others can be held for several days before their final use.

In either case, creams should be refrigerated, at 5° C (40° F), before use. There are occasional exceptions to this rule, as certain creams lose their consistency and body if too cold.

Storing

Be extremely careful when storing creams. Some are less perishable than others and may be kept for longer periods. A crème Saint-Honoré should be kept no longer than a few hours, whereas a crème pâtissière may be kept for 24 to 48 hours and a crème au beurre (butter cream) for several days.

The recommended limits for storage are specified in the charts in the individual lessons.

As creams sometimes look alike, be extremely careful not to mix them up once they are in the refrigerator—for example, do not confuse crème pâtissière (pastry cream) with crème à flan (flan cream) or a mousse with a bavarian. Labeling the containers to indicate their contents will help prevent these mixups.

Egg-based Creams

	Crème au Beurre aux Oeufs (sucre cuit) Cooked-sugar Butter Cream	Crème au Beurre aux Oeufs (sirop) Sugar-syrup Butter Cream	Crème au Beurre à l'Anglaise Crème Anglaise Butter Cream	Crème au Beurre à Froid Uncooked Butter Cream	Crème Anglaise Crème Anglaise	Crème Pâtissière Pastry Cream	Crème à Flan Flan Cream	Crème Caramel Caramel Custard	Crème Vanille Vanilla Custard
Sugar	1 kg (35 oz.)	—	1 kg (35 oz.)	1 kg (35 oz.)	250 g (9 oz.)	250 g (9 oz.)	250 g (9 oz.)	200 plus 150 g caramel (7 plus 5 oz.)	200 g (7 oz.)
Eggs	4 whole eggs plus 8 yolks or 15 yolks	12 yolks	16 yolks	14 yolks	10 yolks	8 yolks	3 yolks	6 eggs	12 yolks
Butter	1500 g (53 oz.)	750 g (26.5 oz.)	1250 g (44 oz.)	1250 g (44 oz.)	—	100 g (3.5 oz.) (optional)	—	—	—
Sugar Syrup (1260 D)	—	1 L (34 fl. oz.)	1 L (34 fl. oz.)	—	—	—	—	—	—
Milk	—	—	—	—	1 L (34 fl. oz.)	1 L (34 fl. oz.)	1 L (34 fl. oz.)	1 L (34 fl. oz.)	1 L (34 fl. oz.)
Vanilla	—	—	—	—	1 bean	—	—	1 bean	1 bean
Flour	—	—	—	—	—	125 g (4.5 oz.)	—	—	—
Flan Powder	—	—	—	—	—	25 g (1 oz.)	100 g (3.5 oz.)	—	—

Beaten Creams

	Crème d'Amandes Almond Cream	Crème au Fromage Blanc Fromage Blanc Cream	Crème de Marrons Chestnut Cream	Crème Mousseline Mousseline Cream	Crème Paris-Brest Paris-Brest Cream	Ganaches Montées Whipped Chocolate Ganaches
Sugar	500 g (17.5 oz.)	300 plus 100 g (10.5 plus 3.5 oz.)	—	500 g (17.5 oz.)	—	—
Eggs	8	6 yolks	—	4 whole or 8 yolks	—	—
Butter	500 g (17.5 oz.)	—	500 g (17.5 oz.)	500 g (17.5 oz.)	500 g (17.5 oz.)	—
Almond Powder	500 g (17.5 oz.)	—	—	—	—	—
Flour (optional)	100 g (3.5 oz.)	—	—	—	—	—
Flavoring	100 ml rum (3.5 fl. oz.) plus several drops vanilla	several drops vanilla extract	100 ml rum (3.5 fl. oz.)	to taste	100 ml rum or vanilla (3.5 fl. oz.)	to taste
Gelatin	—	20 g (2/3 oz.)	—	—	—	—
Fresh Cheese	—	1 kg (35 oz.)	—	—	—	—
Crème Fraîche or Heavy Cream	—	1 L (34 fl. oz.)	—	—	—	500 ml (17 fl. oz.)
Chestnut Paste	—	—	1 kg (35 oz.)	—	—	—
Water	—	—	150 ml (5 fl. oz.)	—	—	—
Milk	—	—	—	1 L (34 fl. oz.)	—	—
Flan Powder	—	—	—	150 g (5 oz.)	—	—
Crème Pâtissière	—	—	—	—	1 kg (35 oz.)	—
Praline Paste	—	—	—	—	250 g (9 oz.)	—
Chocolate	—	—	—	—	—	1 kg (35 oz.)

Light-textured Creams

	Crème au Beurre aux Blancs Meringue Butter Cream	Crème St-Honoré St-Honoré Cream	Crème Chantilly Chantilly Cream	Crème Fouettée Whipped Cream	Crème Fondante Chocolate Whipped Cream	Crème Diplomate Diplomat Cream	Crème Bavaroise Bavarian Cream	Mousses aux Oeufs Egg-based Mousse	Mousses au Lait et aux Jaunes Milk- and Egg Yolk-based Mousse	Mousses aux Jaunes Egg Yolk-based Mousse	Mousses aux Fruits Fruit Mousse
Sugar	700 plus 300 g (24.5 + 10.5 oz.)	250 g (9 oz.)	150 g (5 oz.)	—	200 g (7 oz.)	350 plus 100 g (12.5 + 3.5 oz.)	400 g (14 oz.)	200 plus 500 g (7 + 17.5 oz.)	300 plus 500 g (10.5 + 17.5 oz.)	400 plus 500 g (14 + 17.5 oz)	200 plus 500 g (7 oz. + 17.5 oz.)
Egg Whites	12	8	—	—	—	—	—	8	8	10	12
Butter	1250 g (44 oz.)	—	—	—	—	—	—	—	—	600 g (21 oz.)	—
Flavoring	to taste	rum or vanilla	vanilla	—	vanilla	—	2 vanilla beans	200 ml liqueur (6.5 fl. oz.)	50 ml coffee + 100 ml rum (1.5 + 3.5 fl. oz.)	50 ml rum (1.5 fl. oz.)	juice of 2 lemons
Milk	—	500 ml (17 fl. oz.)	—	—	—	1 L (34 fl. oz.)	1 L (34 fl. oz.)	1 L (34 fl. oz.)	—	—	—
Eggs	—	8 yolks	—	—	—	6 yolks	14 yolks	4 whole	16 yolks	20 yolks	—
Flour	—	50 g (1.5 oz.)	—	—	—	—	—	—	—	—	—
Gelatin	—	8 g (1/4 oz.)	—	6 g (1/4 oz.)	—	20 g (2/3 oz.)	28 g (1 oz.)	20 g (2/3 oz)	24 g (1 oz.)	—	20 g (2/3 oz.)
Crème Fraîche	—	—	1 L (34 fl. oz.)	1 L (34 fl. oz.)	1.5 L (50.5 fl. oz.)	1.5 L (50.5 fl. oz.)	1.5 L (50.5 fl. oz.)	500 ml (17 fl. oz.)	1 L (34 fl. oz.)	500 ml (17 fl. oz.)	1.5 L (50.5 fl. oz.)
Italian Meringue	—	—	—	450 g (16 oz.)	—	—	—	—	—	—	—
Chocolate	—	—	—	—	1 kg (35 oz.)	—	—	—	—	400 g couverture + 200 g cocoa (14 oz. + 7 oz.)	—
Flan Powder	—	—	—	—	—	80 g (3 oz.)	100 g (3.5 oz.)	—	—	—	—
Glucose	—	—	—	—	—	—	—	—	50 g (1.5 oz.)	100 g (3.5 oz.)	—
Fruit Pulp	—	—	—	—	—	—	—	—	—	—	1 kg (35 oz.)

Cooked sugar and sugar syrups

Sugar Syrups

History

Even though the word *sirop* did not appear in the French language until the twelfth century, syrups had been prepared long before that and were much appreciated by the ancient Greeks and Romans, who made them into a wide variety of exotic drinks. Throughout the Middle Ages, syrups were used in elaborate secret mixtures for medicinal purposes.

Definition

Today the pastry professional uses the term **syrup** to denote a solution of sugar in water. Syrups exist in varying concentrations, from lightly sweetened to fully saturated, which is candying sugar. A sugar/water mixture in which the sugar quantity is beyond the point of saturation is called **cooked sugar.** It is important to remember the different meanings of these two terms.

The chart below gives equivalents between the Baumé system and the international density system :

°B	Dens.	°B	Dens.
5	1 0359	21	1 1699
6	1 0434	22	1 1699
7	1 0509	23	1 1896
8	1 0587	24	1 1995
9	1 0665	25	1 2095
10	1 0745	26	1 2197
11	1 0825	27	1 2301
12	1 0907	28	1 2407
13	1 0989	29	1 2515
14	1 1074	30	1 2624
15	1 1159	31	1 2736
16	1 1247	32	1 2850
17	1 1335	33	1 2964
18	1 1425	34	1 3082
19	1 1515	35	1 3199
20	1 1609	36	1 3319

Sugar syrup concentrations are based upon the amount of sugar added to 1 L (34 fl. oz.) of water. As the chart indicates, the syrups range from extremely light to quite thick and dense.

The density and sugar concentration in a syrup is measured using a **hydrometer.** Until recently, sugar densities were measured using the Baumé system, with hydrometers calibrated accordingly. Since 1963, an attempt has been made to internationalize the system, and density is now measured on a scale from 1000 to 1400 (specific gravity).

Uses

Sugar syrups are used in French pastry, confectionery, and for making ice creams and sorbets. They have a wide range of uses:
- to soak babas and savarins
- to moisten cakes and miniature cakes
- to dilute liquor and food coloring
- to glaze pastries at the end of baking
- to soften and adjust the consistency of fondant
- to prepare recipes for sorbets and macerated fruits

Equipment

Saucepan
Measuring cup
Wooden spatula
Skimmer
Pastry brush

Fine-mesh sieve (china cap)
Hydrometer
Container of water

Approximate Proportions

It is possible to estimate the amount of sugar required for preparing a sugar syrup of a given density using the following chart:

Density of Cool Syrup

1110 D: 1 L water + 450 g sugar
(34 fl. oz. water + 16 oz. sugar)
1130 D: 1 L water + 500 g sugar
(34 fl. oz. water + 17.5 oz. sugar)
1260 D: 1 L water + 1 kg sugar
(34 fl. oz. water + 35 oz. sugar)
1320 D: 1 L water + 1.5 kg sugar
(34 fl. oz. water + 53 oz. sugar)
1350 D: 1 L water + 2 kg sugar
(34 fl. oz. water + 70.5 oz. sugar)

These densities are only approximate because the exact density is influenced by:
- the length of time the syrup has boiled
- the evaporation that is caused by boiling and cooling

The chart is based on syrups that were boiled for one minute.

The density called for in a given recipe is always the density that the syrup should have when it is to be actually used, and it should be at the given temperature. For example:
- 1120-density syrup is used hot for soaking babas and savarins
- 1260-density syrup is used cold for preparing cakes and mokas

Preparation

Always make sure that all the utensils used for preparing sugar syrups are perfectly clean. Use pure water and high-quality sugar.

Procedure

Preparing sugar syrups is relatively straightforward but certain precautions should be kept in mind. When dissolving the sugar in water, the water is always heated to accelerate the process and sterilize the syrup.

Be sure to stir the mixture so that the sugar is completely dissolved before the water comes to a boil. If the sugar is allowed to sit at the bottom of the saucepan while the syrup is being heated, it can caramelize and discolor the syrup.

The sugar can also congeal, which will delay the dissolving and cause the syrup to become overly concentrated.

Skimming the Syrup

When first dissolving sugar in water to make syrup, a gray froth often floats to the surface. This is caused by the impurities in the sugar, which separate and float to the top. The amount of froth depends on the concentration of the syrup and the purity of the sugar.

It is important to remove this froth with either a clean pastry brush or a skimmer dipped in cold water as soon as the syrup comes to a boil. Do this several times, rinsing the brush or skimmer after each use.

Clarifying the Syrup

Sometimes a sugar syrup remains cloudy even after careful skimming. If this occurs, the syrup should be clarified with egg whites. To do this, beat several egg whites and place them in the boiling syrup.

The impurities contained in the syrup will adhere to the coagulating protein contained in the whites. Remove the egg whites with a skimmer and strain the syrup through a fine-mesh strainer or through cheesecloth.

Using this method, it is possible to obtain a perfectly clear syrup. In the case of a sugar syrup with lots of impurities (such as used baba syrup), the syrup should be strained before skimming and clarifying.

Storage

A sugar syrup should always be brought to a boil in order to sterilize it and help it keep longer. The more concentrated a syrup is, the longer it will keep. For example:

Syrup at density 1100 will keep for 24 hours (refrigerated)

Syrup at density 1150 will keep for 2 to 3 days (refrigerated)

Syrup at density 1240 will keep for 8 to 10 days (refrigerated)

Syrup at density 1260+ will keep for 10 to 15 days at room temperature

---

Cooked Sugar

Familiarity with cooked sugar is important, as it is often used in pastry, confectionery, and ice-cream making.

Unlike sugar syrups, which call for a certain proportion of sugar per L water, cooked sugar is reversed—water is added to a given quantity of sugar (usually 30 to 40 percent water to sugar).

Definition

Cooked sugar is a solution of sugar and water in which the concentration of sugar is very high. Solutions ranging from 1350 density to actual caramel are referred to as cooked sugar.

Care must be taken in the preparation of cooked sugar. The success of many preparations depends on its being correctly prepared.

It is particularly important that the temperature of the cooked sugar be accurately determined.

Uses

Cooked sugar is used for creams, meringues, fondant, caramel, and nougatines, as well as for glazing and special decorations such as pulled-sugar flowers.

Equipment

Copper sugar pan

Pastry brush
Metal spatula or skimmer
Bowl (larger than the sugar pan)
Clean, cold water
Sugar thermometer
White plate (sometimes needed)
Tart baking sheet

Recipe

1 kg sugar (35 oz.), chunks or granulated
300 to 400 ml water (10 to 13.5 fl. oz.)
glucose or cream of tartar (optional)

Preparation

Whenever possible, use a copper sugar pan. Be sure to clean it with salt and

vinegar and rinse it with cold, running water.

To avoid leaving traces of lint or grease, do not wipe it dry.

All utensils used for cooking sugar must be extremely clean—pastry brush, thermometer, and others—especially for very delicate preparations such as glazes and pulled sugar.

There is no individual recipe for cooked sugar, because the proportions and ingredients vary depending on the final use. Sometimes regular sugar is used (sucrose) and at times a mixture of glucose, sucrose, and cream of tartar is used.

In any case, make sure the sugar being used is pure and free of foreign particles. Make sure that the weighing pan on the scale is perfectly clean.

Crystallized or cubed sugar is preferable to granulated sugar because it is less likely to contain impurities.

Be sure that the water used to wash the sugar pan and the utensils are also perfectly clean.

Choose a sugar pan that corresponds to the amount of cooked sugar being prepared. The syrup should come two-thirds up the sides of the pan.

When very small amounts of sugar are being prepared, the cooking times are even more critical because the sugar cooks more quickly.

With small amounts it is also more difficult to control the temperature, and the sugar may caramelize. The sugar mixture should be at least 3 cm (1.5 in.) deep in the copper sugar pan for the thermometer to be effective.

Fill a bowl two-thirds full with water and keep it next to the cooking sugar.

The thermometer and pastry brush may be kept in the bowl during the preparation of the sugar. The bowl should be large enough so that the bottom of the sugar pan can be plunged in the water to stop its cooking immediately when the right temperature has been reached.

Procedure

Put the sugar and water in the clean sugar pan. Stir with a spatula or skimmer and place the pan on a high flame. Make sure, however, that the flame does not wrap around the sides of the pan.

Stir from time to time to ensure that the sugar dissolves quickly. Brush the inside walls of the pan with the pastry brush to prevent the formation of sugar crystals. Watch the mixture closely as it comes to a boil. Sometimes the presence

of impurities, especially calcium carbonate, will cause the sugar solution to froth up in much the same way as boiling milk. Usually this froth quickly dissipates but sometimes it leaves a gray precipitate at the bottom of the pan, which should be removed with a pastry brush or skimmer.

Make sure to rinse the brush or skimmer continually in cold water between uses.

This skimming should be continued until the sugar is perfectly clear.

Continue to rinse the insides of the copper sugar pan with the moistened pastry brush. This prevents the formation of crystals, which could fall into the syrup and cause the entire mass to crystallize and form lumps. Make sure that

the thermometer has been well rinsed before plunging it into the syrup. It is also possible to cover the sugar pan

with a plate or a tart sheet pan to prevent crystallization of the sugar.

Reversing the Cooking of the Sugar

If the sugar is cooked too long and the appropriate temperature is exceeded, water can be added to the syrup to reverse the cooking process. It is then necessary to cook the sugar again to arrive at the proper point.

For example, if the desired temperature is 117° C (242° F) and the temperature reaches 120° C (248° F), add a small amount of cold, clean water and continue cooking until the temperature returns to 117° C (242° F). If, however, the sugar has cooked to the point where it has caramelized and discolored, this method will not work.

Stopping the Cooking

As the sugar approaches the desired temperature—the last 5 degrees Celsius (10 degrees Fahrenheit)—turn down the flame. This helps to determine the exact point at which the sugar is cooked.

As soon as the sugar reaches the appropriate temperature, dip the bottom of the copper sugar pan into the bowl of cold water. This immediately stops the cooking of the sugar and prevents it from coloring or becoming too hard. Cooked sugar should be used almost immediately once its cooking is complete. In some situations, cooked sugar may be reheated (as for glazes and fondants). It should be reheated very gently in the oven or over a low flame; if not, it may caramelize or burn.

Checking Cooked Sugar by Hand

Some pastry chefs like to judge the cooking of sugar with their hands. This requires experience, and certain precautions should be followed. Always have a bowl of cold, clean water next to the sugar (do not use the water being used to rinse the pastry brush or skimmer). A bit of sugar is taken from the sugar pan with the fingers and dipped into the cold water (the water is used to avoid burns). It is also important to avoid introducing water into the sugar syrup, which would reverse the cooking process and give an inaccurate reading. This process should be carried out in three stages:

1. Dip the hand in cold water and give it a quick shake to remove excess water. This will leave the finger moist but not dripping.

2. Quickly pinch the sugar between the thumb and forefinger in the middle of the sugar pan, as if to remove a little chunk.

3. Remove the hand quickly from the hot sugar and dip it in the cold water. Pull the hand immediately out of the water. Judge the consistency (see chart on page 17).

Note:

The cooking of the sugar can also be checked by using a skimmer. This avoids introducing too much water into the syrup, which can slow the cooking of the syrup.

Checking Cooked Sugar with a Candy Thermometer

This technique is extremely reliable and is becoming the method of choice. Its main disadvantage is that it is easy to break the thermometer if certain precautions are not followed.

At no point should the thermometer come in direct contact with the flame. When using a thermometer, make sure that it does not reach over the sides of the sugar pan: arrange it so that it leans over the handle of the pan. In this way, it will be protected from the flame. It can also be wrapped with a sheet of aluminum foil.

Candy thermometers are graduated from 80° to 200°C (155° to 390°F).

Since 1948, pastry chefs in France have used the Celsius system of temperature measurement. It was invented by the Swedish physicist Anders Celsius at the beginning of the eighteenth century. It is based on a hundred-degree scale, with 0°C being the freezing point of water and 100°C being the boiling point of water. Americans continue to use the Fahrenheit scale, in which 32°F is the freezing point and 212°F, the boiling point of water.

Coating

Thread

Cooked Sugar

Type	Temperature	Consistency	Uses	Concentration (weight of sugar per L)
Coating (Nappé)	105° C (221° F)	A thin film of syrup covers the surface of the skimmer. Large drops form on its surface before rolling off.	Jellied fruits Candied fruits Fruit preserves Liqueur candies	750 g (26.5 oz.)
Thread (Filet)	110° C (230° C)	The syrup forms a thread, 2 to 3 cm (3/4 to 1.5 in.) long when two fingers are dipped in the syrup and pulled apart.	Butter creams Candied fruits Jellies	850 g (30 oz.)
Soft Ball (Petit Boulé)	115° to 117° C (239° to 243° F)	A soft ball forms between the fingers when the syrup is rolled.	Almond paste Butter cream Meringues Fondant (for glazing) Glazed chestnuts	950 g (33.5 oz.).
Firm Ball (Boulé)	120° C (248° F)	A firm ball forms between the fingers when the syrup is rolled. The ball should remain malleable.	Meringues Butter cream Marzipan Fondant (for candy fillings)	975 g (34 oz.)
Hard Ball (Gros boulé)	125° to 130° C (257° to 266° F)	The ball is firm and holds its shape when rolled.	Almond paste (for candy fillings) Soft caramels	985 g (34.5 oz.)
Soft Crack (Petit Cassé)	135° to 140° C (275° to 284° F)	A ball cannot be formed between the fingers. The sugar breaks when folded quickly. It stick to the teeth.	Nougat Montelimar (soft) Caramel candy	995 g (35 oz.)
Hard Crack (Grand Cassé)	145° to 150° C (293° to 302° F)	Breaks the same way as soft crack but no longer sticks to the teeth.	Hard nougat Jams and preserves Jellied fruits Pulled and blown sugar Rock candy	1 kg (35 oz.)
Pale Caramel (Petit Jaune)	155° C (311° F)	Same as hard crack but with a yellow tint.	Glazing Decorated fruits Pulled sugar Spun sugar Blown sugar	Dehydrated (melting begins)
Golden Caramel (Jaune)	160° C (320° F)	Same as pale caramel but with darker color.	Glazing salambos, Saint-Honoré, choux Pièces montées Nougatine	Melted
Caramel (Grand Jaune)	165° C (329° F)	Hard as golden caramel but dark yellow.	Nougatine Praline Light caramel	Melted
Dark Caramel (Caramel)	180° C (356° F)	Progressively darker than caramel.	Crème caramel Dark caramel Caramel glaze Coloring Coffee flavoring	Melted

Soft Ball

Firm Ball

Hard Ball

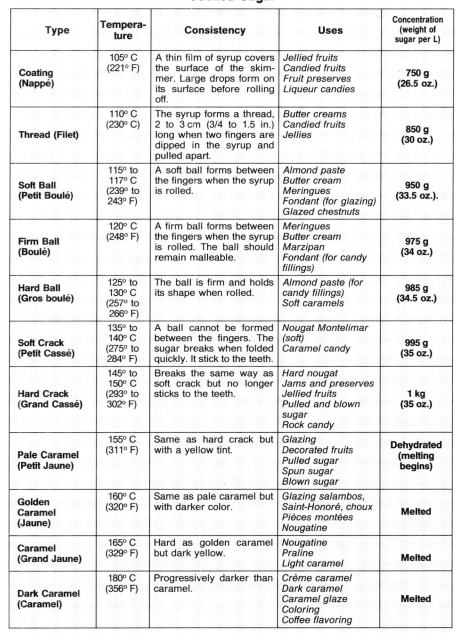

Soft Crack

Hard Crack

Golden Caramel

Pale Caramel

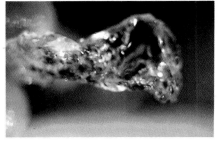

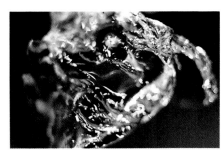

Chapter 1 Egg-based creams
La crème au beurre aux œufs (Cooked-sugar butter cream)

History

As the name indicates, this cream is based on butter. Even though butter has been known since biblical times, it was the Greeks who first incorporated it into cuisine. When French pastry was first being developed, butter cream was simply butter that had been worked with sugar.

Butter cream was perfected after a great deal of research by Antonin Carême in the nineteenth century.

Auguste Escoffier developed the modern recipe we use today. In fact, the development of French pastry and cooking in the nineteenth and twentieth centuries is largely due to their contributions.

The quality of butter cream is an important factor in determining the success of finished pastries such as mokas and génoise.

Butter cream requires great care and attention during its preparation. Unfortunately, shortcuts are often taken, and butter cream is sometimes simply a mixture of sugar and a questionable shortening. Anyone familiar with the genuine product will not be fooled by these imitations.

The outcome of butter cream is especially dependent on the quality of the raw ingredients. It is extremely important that the pastry chef pay close attention to their quality.

Careful working, not just careless mixing of the ingredients, is also essential.

Butter cream is not extremely difficult to prepare but requires close attention, especially in cooking the sugar and adding it to the eggs.

Frequently used by pastry chefs, it requires traditional pastry equipment.

Allow 30 minutes for its preparation.

It freezes well.

Procedure

Several different methods are used to prepare butter cream. Choosing the best one often simply depends on working conditions, personal taste, and the tastes of the clientele.

Butter creams are always based on a preliminary mixture (French, *appareil*). It is this mixture that will determine the final quality of the cream.

The methods for preparing butter creams are broken into the following categories:

- method using **eggs and cooked sugar** similar to the preparation of **bombes**

- method using **eggs and sugar syrup** also similar to the preparation of **bombes**

- method "**à l'anglaise**"

- "**uncooked method**"

- method using **Italian meringue**

- method using **Swiss meringue**

The most commonly used method for preparing butter cream is the first, which uses eggs and cooked sugar. It gives excellent results provided it is correctly carried out. The heat of the cooked sugar pasteurizes the eggs, giving the butter cream greater stability and shelf life.

The choice of raw ingredients is extremely important in the preparation of butter cream.

Always use the freshest eggs available. No margarine or shortening is allowed in the preparation of butter cream. If these substitutes are used, the result should be called by another name such as frosting or filling.

In a preparation of this type, where the quality of the finished product depends on the flavor of the ingredients, it is necessary to use only butter.

Uses

Butter cream is used to fill a large variety of different cakes, including mokas, wedding cakes, and yule logs.

It is also used for filling and glazing miniature cakes and petits fours, as well as for their final decoration.

Making Butter Cream with Eggs and Cooked Sugar

Equipment

Using the Electric Mixer

Mixing bowl and whisk attachment
Saucepan or copper sugar pan
Skimmer, pastry brush, water
Bowl for the eggs - Pastry scraper
Fine-mesh sieve (china cap)
Candy thermometer (optional)
Bowl for the butter
Bowl for storing the butter cream

Hand Method

Bowl (should contain six times the volume of the cooked sugar)
Hand whisk
Copper sugar pan - Bowl for the eggs
Skimmer, pastry brush, water
Fine-mesh sieve (china cap)
Pastry scraper - Bowl for the butter
Bowl for storing the butter cream
Candy thermometer (optional)

Professional Recipe

1 kg sugar (35 oz.), cooked to 118°C (244°F) when using 8 yolks, or 114°C (237°F) when using 4 whole eggs and 8 yolks, or 110°C (230°F) when using 15 yolks
1500 g butter (53 oz.)
flavoring

Alternative Recipe

1 kg sugar (35 oz.), cooked to 117° to 120°C (242° to 248°F) when using 8 to 10 eggs, or 113° to 116°C (235° to 240°F) when using 3 to 6 eggs and 6 to 10 yolks, or 110° to 112°C (220° to 231°F) for 14 to 16 yolks
1250 to 1500 g butter (44 to 53 oz.)
flavoring

Recipe for a Small Quantity

250 g sugar (9 oz.), cooked to 117°C (242°F)
2 whole eggs - 300 g butter (10.5 oz.)
flavoring

Preparation

Follow the precautions for cooking sugar (see pages 14 to 17), regardless of the degree of cooking required.

As noted above, the temperature of the cooked sugar is very important to the final outcome of the butter cream. In general, the temperature of the sugar depends on whether whole eggs or egg yolks are being used:

- *whole eggs:* since egg whites contain considerable liquid, the temperature of the sugar should be somewhat higher

- *egg yolks:* since egg yolks contain less liquid than whole eggs, the temperature of the syrup should be somewhat lower

As discussed in the lesson on cooking sugar, the temperature of the sugar may be reversed by simply adding a small amount of water while it is cooking. Egg whites function in the same way when whole eggs are used for butter cream.

The temperature of the cooking sugar should also be a function of the type of butter being used. With a wet butter, raise the temperature of the sugar by 2 to 3 degrees Celsius (4 to 5 degrees Fahrenheit).

It is important that the butter be softened before it is used in the recipe. If it is too hard, it might form grains in the cream that are difficult to remove.

Also be sure that the eggs have been prepared and beaten ahead of time.

Procedure

Cooking the Sugar

Cook the sugar to the desired temperature. Take the standard precautions.

19

Preparing the Eggs

Depending on the recipe being used, place in a bowl:

- whole eggs
- whole eggs and egg yolks
- egg yolks alone

Beat vigorously using either a hand whisk or an electric mixer until the mixture is smooth. This facilitates the incorporation of the sugar.

Adding the Cooked Sugar

Whole Eggs

Cook the sugar to the soft ball stage, 118°C (244°F), and pour it into the eggs while beating.

Avoid pouring the cooked sugar on the whisk. This causes it to splatter on the walls of the bowl and harden, forming hard crystals that remain in the butter cream.

When all the sugar has been added to the eggs, strain it through a fine-mesh sieve (china cap) to remove bits of coagulated egg white or yolks and any particles of sugar.

Once the mixture has been strained, continue beating energetically either by hand or in the electric mixer at medium or high speed.

Beat until the mixture is completely cool.

The egg mixture is ready when it has completely cooled. It should be light and smooth.

Whole Eggs Combined with Yolks

Cook the sugar to the thread stage, 114°C (237°F), and pour it slowly over the egg/egg yolk mixture. Beat vigorously as described for using whole eggs alone.

Egg Yolks Alone

Cook the sugar to a slightly lighter thread stage, 110°C (230°F), and pour it slowly in a stream over the egg yolks. Beat the mixture energetically until cool.

It is important that the syrup be poured into the yolks slowly while beating. If it is poured in too quickly, it can cause the yolks to coagulate or even burn.

Adding the Butter

When any of the above mixtures has been completely beaten and has cooled to room temperature, the butter can be incorporated.

The butter should be softened before being added to the egg mixture. Work it in a bit at a time, either by hand or with the electric mixer at slow speed.

Be sure to scrape the sides of the mixing bowl from time to time with a plastic pastry scraper.

Once all the butter has been added, continue to beat rapidly (if using the electric mixer, turn it up to high speed) for 4 to 5 minutes or until the butter cream is smooth and light.

Flavoring the Butter Cream

Butter cream may be flavored at any stage in its preparation. A wide variety of natural flavorings can be used—vanilla, coffee, pistachio, praline, caramel, or chocolate, for example. Liquors and liqueurs such as Grand Marnier, Cointreau, rum, or Kirsch may also be used. Occasionally butter cream is colored with food coloring.

Always use coloring sparingly and aim for pastel rather than bright colors, which look unnatural.

Storage

Butter cream can be stored for up to 10 days in the refrigerator, 5°C (40°F), if it is well covered in a plastic or stainless steel container. It can also be frozen.

Making Butter Cream with Eggs and Sugar Syrup

This is an excellent method for preparing butter cream. It should, however, be avoided in hot weather, as this butter cream tends to be more delicate and to melt easier than that made with cooked sugar.

Equipment

Mixing bowl and whisk attachment
Bowls
Fine-mesh sieve (china cap)
Pastry scraper
Saucepan
Wooden spatula

Recipes

Professional Recipe

1 L syrup (34 fl. oz.) at 1260 D
12 egg yolks
750 g butter (26.5 oz.)
flavoring

Alternative Recipe

1 L syrup (34 fl. oz.) at 1260 D
10 to 12 egg yolks or 6 to 8 whole eggs
700 to 800 g butter (24.5 to 28 oz.)
flavoring

Recipe for a Small Quantity

500 ml syrup (17 fl. oz.) at 1260 D
6 egg yolks
350 g butter (12.5 oz.)
flavoring

Preparation

Prepare and measure the sugar syrup. Separate the eggs. Soften the butter.

Procedure

Preparing the Yolk/Sugar Mixture

Bring the syrup to a boil and pour it in a steady stream over the yolks. Beat energetically until the mixture is completely cool.

Cooking the Yolk/Sugar Mixture

One of two methods can be used:
- place the mixture into a saucepan and cook over a low flame while stirring with a wooden spatula or a whisk

- cook the mixture in a double boiler or over a pan of hot water (bain-marie), stirring from time to time with a wooden spatula or whisk

Whichever method is used, the temperature of the mixture should never exceed 85°C (185°F).

Strain the yolk/sugar mixture into the mixing bowl. Beat the mixture until it is light, smooth, and frothy. It should be at room temperature when finished.

Adding the Butter

Once the yolk/sugar mixture is smooth and cool, add the softened butter in small quantities. Continue to beat the mixture until the butter is completely worked in and the mixture is perfectly smooth and homogeneous. Be sure to scrape the sides of the mixing bowl from time to time with the pastry scraper during the final beating.

Place the finished butter cream in a plastic or stainless steel container and cover it with plastic wrap.

Storage

Butter cream can be kept for up to 8 days in the refrigerator, 5°C (40°F), provided it is kept in a plastic or stainless steel container and well covered with plastic wrap.

La Crème au Beurre aux Oeufs et au Sucre Cuit
Cooked-Sugar Butter Cream

	Time	
PREPARATION **Assemble** the Equipment **Prepare, Weigh and Measure** the Raw Ingredients	**0** min	• Make sure all the equipment is extremely clean. • Break the eggs and separate them if necessary. • Soften the butter.
PROCEDURE	**5** min	
Cook the Sugar		• Cook the sugar to the desired temperature, taking the usual precautions.
Prepare the Eggs		• Beat the eggs energetically for a few seconds to facilitate the incorporation of the cooked sugar.
Add the Sugar	**18** min	• Pour the cooked sugar over the eggs; do not stop beating.
Strain the Mixture **Beat** the Mixture	**20** min	• Strain the egg/sugar mixture directly into the bowl to be used for the addition of the butter. • Beat until completely cool.
Check the Beating	**27** min	• Beat until the mixture is cool, smooth, and light.
Add the Butter	**30** min	• Add the butter in several stages, a bit at a time. • Continue beating vigorously until the cream is smooth and homogeneous.
Add Flavoring		• Add desired flavorings either at the beginning or at the end of beating.
HOLDING THE CREAM	**35** min	• The cream can be kept in a stainless steel or plastic container.
STORAGE		Cooked-sugar butter cream can be kept for up to 10 days in the refrigerator, 5°C (40°F) in a plastic or stainless steel container if covered with plastic wrap. Butter cream can also be frozen.

La crème au beurre à l'anglaise (Crème anglaise butter cream)

Butter cream based on crème anglaise is a light version of butter cream with an agreeable consistency. It is rather delicate and does not keep as well as butter creams made from cooked sugar.

When used for preparing cakes, this type of butter cream must be warmed from time to time to smooth it out.

Equipment

Machine Method

Mixing bowl with whisk attachment
Stainless steel saucepan
Measuring cup - Pastry scraper
Wooden spatula - Hand whisk
Bowls for the yolks, for the butter, and for the finished cream

Hand Method

Mixing bowl
Whisk
Stainless steel saucepan
Measuring cup
Pastry scraper
Wooden spatula
Bowls for the yolks, for the butter, and for the finished cream

Professional Recipe

1 L milk (34 fl. oz.)
1 kg sugar (35 oz.)
16 egg yolks
1250 g butter (44 oz.)

Alternative Recipe

1 L milk (34 fl. oz.)
1 kg sugar (35 oz.)
14 to 18 egg yolks
1 kg to 1500 g butter (35 to 53 oz.)

Recipe for a Small Quantity

250 ml milk (8.5 fl. oz.)
250 g sugar (9 oz.)
4 egg yolks
300 g butter (10.5 oz.)

Preparation

Use only the freshest ingredients. Separate the eggs. Work the butter to warm it to room temperature and soften it.

Procedure

See crème anglaise (pages 24 to 26).

Preparing the Yolk/Sugar/Milk Mixture

Bring the milk to a boil with one-half of the sugar. Whisk together the yolks and remaining sugar until the mixture becomes pale yellow or almost white. Pour some of the boiling milk into the yolk/sugar mixture and return this mixture to the saucepan. Heat the mixture

while stirring with a wooden spatula. When the crème anglaise is cooked, strain it into the mixing bowl.

Beating the Mixture

Beat the mixture until it is almost completely cool. Use either a hand whisk or the whisk attachment to the electric mixer. The mixture is ready when airy and almost at room temperature.

Adding the Butter

Once the yolk/milk/sugar mixture has completely cooled, add the softened but-

ter bit by bit while beating. Continue beating until the cream is smooth and homogeneous. Scrape the sides of the mixing bowl with the pastry scraper from time to time during the beating.

Transfer the finished butter cream to a plastic or stainless steel container and cover it with plastic wrap.

Storage

This type of butter cream keeps for 3 to 4 days in the refrigerator, 5°C (40°F) if well covered with plastic wrap.

La crème au beurre à froid (Uncooked butter cream)

This is one of the simplest methods for preparing butter cream, but the finished product is not as fine as butter cream prepared with cooked sugar. It also can only be stored for a short time.

Equipment

Machine Method

Water bath (bain-marie)
Mixing bowl with whisk attachment
Bowl for the eggs
Bowl for the butter
Hand whisk
Pastry scraper
Bowl for finished butter cream

   This butter cream requires careful attention, especially in the preparation of the crème anglaise.

It uses traditional pastry equipment and can be prepared in one hour.

It can be stored for a short time only.

La crème au beurre à froid (Uncooked butter cream)

Hand Method

Equipment is the same as for machine method except that a stainless steel mixing bowl is used instead of the attachment to the electric mixer.

Professional Recipe

1 kg granulated sugar (35 oz.)
14 egg yolks
1250 g butter (44 oz.)

Alternative Recipe

1 kg granulated sugar (35 oz.)
10 to 16 eggs
1 kg to 1500 g butter (35 to 53 oz.)

Recipe for a Small Quantity

250 g sugar (9 oz.)
4 eggs
300 g butter (10.5 oz.)

Procedure

See génoise, volume 1, pages 72 to 75.

Heating the Mixture

Beat together the eggs and sugar over a water bath (bain-marie) until they

are lukewarm, 40° to 45°C (104° to 113°F), and the sugar has dissolved.

Beating the Egg/Sugar Mixture

Beat the mixture off the heat until it has completely cooled and expanded to its maximum volume. The mixture should be completely cool and form a ribbon when held up with the whisk.

Adding the Butter

When the mixture is almost cool, the softened butter can be added. It should be added in several stages instead of all at once.

After adding the butter, continue beating the mixture until it is smooth and homogeneous. Scrape the sides of the mixing bowl during beating using a plastic pastry scraper.

Place the finished butter cream in a plastic or stainless steel container.

Storing Butter Cream

Butter cream keeps well in the refrigerator, 5°C (40°F), provided it is stored in a plastic or stainless steel container and is well covered with plastic wrap or wax paper:

- crème anglaise–based butter cream and uncooked butter cream will keep for 2 to 3 days

- butter cream based on syrup and cooked sugar will keep for 6 to 10 days

- meringue-based butter cream will keep for 10 days (see pages 48 to 50).

When using refrigerated butter cream, remove it from the refrigerator a few hours before using to allow it to warm up. It should be warmed slightly in a water bath (bain-marie) and worked with a whisk to restore its smooth texture.

Butter cream will freeze well, −30°C (−20°F), for several weeks, provided it is protected from frost. When using frozen butter cream, take it out of the freezer 24 to 48 hours before using.

Do not store butter cream with strong-smelling foods, as it has a tendency to absorb odors.

Flavoring Butter Creams

Butter cream can be prepared with practically any natural flavoring including liquors, liqueurs, and extracts.

When using liqueurs or other alcoholic flavorings, be careful not to add too much, or the butter cream may break up and become granular. The flavoring recommendations given here are only parameters; the quantities can be adjusted as desired.

Flavorings should be added to butter cream only when it is smooth and at room temperature; otherwise they may be difficult to work in.

The quantities given below are designed to flavor 1 kg (35 oz.) of plain butter cream.

Solid Flavorings

Chocolate: about 100 to 150 g bitter baking chocolate (3.5 to 5 oz.), which should first be melted in a double boiler; or 200 to 300 g melted semisweet chocolate (7 to 10.5 oz.). A few drops of red food coloring can be added to give the butter cream a warmer color.

Praline: about 300 to 400 g praline paste (10.5 to 14 oz.). To facilitate the incorporation of the praline paste, work it on a marble with one-fourth the butter cream, using a metal spatula or a flat triangle. Once this mixture is smooth, add it to the rest of the butter cream and work the whole batch. The flavor can be reinforced by adding 20 to 40 ml rum or Kirsch (2/3 to 1.5 fl. oz.).

Chestnut: about 400 to 500 g chestnut puree (14 to 17.5 oz.). Mix using the method given for praline. For chestnut cakes, chestnut cream (crème de marrons) is recommended.

Liquid Flavorings

Coffee extract: about 30 to 50 ml of the best quality (1 to 1.5 fl. oz.).

Liquors and liqueurs:

Kirsch: 80 to 100 ml (2.5 to 3.5 fl. oz.)
Rum: 80 to 100 ml (2.5 to 3.5 fl. oz.)
Grand Marnier: 60 to 80 ml (2 to 2.5 fl. oz.)

Extracts and concentrates:

Use with moderation, being careful to follow the recommendations given by the manufacturer. Usually 50 to 80 ml (2 to 2.5 fl. oz.) are sufficient.

  This butter cream is easy to prepare if precautions are observed. Be especially careful of the temperature of the egg/sugar mixture before beating.

It requires traditional pastry equipment and can be prepared in 30 minutes. It may be stored for a short time, 48 hours at 5°C (40°F).

La crème anglaise
(Crème anglaise)

History

The origin of crème anglaise can be traced to the beginning of the nineteenth century. Recipes written by Antonin Carême in 1828 reveal a custard-based ice cream, with ingredients similar to those used in ice creams today. However, Carême added starch to his ice cream, giving it a thick consistency. He called this cream *crème française* (French cream).

While working in England, Auguste Escoffier revised this recipe by removing the starch, creating a lighter and more delicate cream, and he renamed the cream *crème anglaise* (which can be literally translated as English cream, though it is more commonly called crème anglaise). This cream is also used as the base for many egg-based ice creams.

Definition

The basic difference between crème anglaise and the mixture for ice cream is that the latter must be pasteurized. This is not necessary when the mixture is used as a sauce.

Crème anglaise can be lightly thickened only when used for a sauce, by adding a small amount of cornstarch or gelatin.

Usage

Crème anglaise is used as a sauce to accompany such desserts as œufs à la neige (snow eggs), île flottante (floating islands), and charlottes. It is also served with desserts such as pain de Gênes (almond cake), gâteaux de riz (rice pudding), and other English-style puddings (such as plum pudding). It is also used as a base for fillings such as crème au beurre (butter cream), charlotte, and bavarois (bavarian cream), to name a few.

Equipment

Heavy-bottomed 2-quart saucepan
Whisk, plastic scraper
Wooden spatula
Mixing bowls (2)
Fine-mesh sieve (china cap)

    Difficult to make, crème anglaise requires constant attention during its preparation. Carefully follow all given precautions.

An often-used cream, it requires no special equipment. Allow approximately 30 minutes to prepare it. The milk should be pasteurized at a high temperature.

Storage is limited to 48 hours maximum in the refrigerator at 5°C (40°F).

Recipes

Professional Recipe

1 L milk (34 fl. oz.)
250 g sugar (9 oz.)
10 egg yolks
1 vanilla bean

Alternative Recipe

1 L milk (34 fl. oz.)
200 to 300 g sugar (7 to 10.5 oz.)
8 to 14 egg yolks
1 to 2 vanilla beans or 1 tsp. to 1 Tbsp. vanilla extract

Recipe for a Small Quantity

500 ml milk (17 fl. oz.)
125 g sugar (4.5 oz.)
6 egg yolks
several drops of vanilla extract

Preparation

Crème anglaise is not really cooked: it cannot be brought to a boil once the egg yolks are added. This makes checking all raw ingredients for freshness extremely important, as the heat is not sufficient to kill bacteria. Also verify the cleanliness of the equipment.

Separate the eggs. Cut the vanilla bean in half lengthwise. Prepare an ice bath for cooling the cream.

Procedure

Boiling the Milk

Pour the milk into a saucepan large enough to hold three times the quantity used. Add half to three-quarters of the sugar and the split vanilla bean, and bring the mixture to a boil.

Mixing the Eggs and Sugar

While the milk is coming to a boil, vigorously mix the egg yolks with the remaining sugar with a whisk until the mixture lightens in color and thickens in consistency (this is called *blanchir* or

bringing the mixture to ribbon stage). It is important to whisk the yolks as soon as the sugar is added to prevent a stiff film from forming on the yolks. This can also be prevented by mixing a few tablespoons of milk from the recipe into the yolks.

The yolks and sugar are whisked to the ribbon stage to facilitate the incorporation of the milk and to prevent the eggs from curdling when the mixture is poached.

Adding the Milk to the Eggs

Once the milk has come to a boil, slowly pour half the milk into the egg/sugar mixture, following the same technique as for pastry cream (see pastry cream, pages 27 to 29). Pour this mixture back into the saucepan with the remaining milk. Place over low heat, stirring constantly with a wooden spatula.

Poaching the Mixture

Continue to stir the cream gently in a figure eight pattern so that it is in constant motion and does not stick to the bottom of the pan. Watch the consistency carefully. The mixture is actually

poached, not cooked. Depending on the number of yolks used, the final temperature should be 85° to 90°C (185° to 194°F); this temperature should not be exceeded. This heating is done to eliminate as much of the bacteria as possible, as well as to thicken the cream. It is the yolks that thicken the cream when heated.

Be careful!

At no point should the mixture come to a boil, or the yolks will coagulate, curdle, and separate from the milk, breaking down the smooth texture of the cream.

Obtaining the Proper Consistency

When the mixture is first placed on the stove, a foam will form on the surface.

As the cream is poaching, the foam will slowly disappear, indicating that the cream is almost ready to be removed from the heat.

It is important to watch the cream very carefully at this point.

As the cream thickens, a film will cover the wooden spatula. Angle the spatula at 45 degrees and run a finger

through the film lengthwise. If the cream does not flow over the line traced, it is ready. Immediately remove the saucepan from the heat.

Strain the cream through the china cap directly into a bowl set over an ice bath. Straining the cream removes any bits of cooked yolk, umbilical cord, or shell that might remain. If the cream

started to boil or break, it is possible to save it once it is over the ice bath by throwing a few ice cubes into the cream and whisking vigorously.

Cooling the Crème Anglaise

Briskly stir the cream occasionally, as it cools with a wooden spatula or whisk to prevent a film from forming on the surface.

Repeat this procedure often until the cream is cool. Once the cream is tepid, 35° to 40°C (95° to 104°F), remove it

from the ice bath and place it into a refrigerator at 5°C (40°F).

Storage

Crème anglaise is usually served chilled, at 5° to 10°C (40° to 50°F). It can be kept at this temperature for up to 24 hours.

Crème anglaise stores best when it is cooled over an ice bath immediately after it is taken off the heat.

Variations on Crème Anglaise

Coffee Crème Anglaise

1 L milk (34 fl. oz.)
250 g sugar (9 oz.)
25 ml coffee extract (1 fl. oz.) *or* 100 g coarsely ground coffee beans (3.5 oz.)
10 egg yolks

Chocolate Crème Anglaise

1 L milk (34 fl. oz.)
250 g sugar (9 oz.)
50 g unsweetened chocolate (1.5 oz.) *or* 50 g cocoa powder (1.5 oz.) *or* 100 g couverture chocolate (3.5 oz.)
8 egg yolks

Praline (Hazelnut) Crème Anglaise

1 L milk (34 fl. oz.)
200 g sugar (7 oz.)
150 g praline paste (5 oz.)
9 egg yolks

Caramel Crème Anglaise

1 L milk (34 fl. oz.)
150 g sugar (5 oz.)
150 g caramel (5 oz.)
12 egg yolks

Pistachio Crème Anglaise

1 L milk (34 fl. oz.)
250 g sugar (9 oz.)
25 g pistachio paste (1 oz.)
10 egg yolks

Liqueur Crème Anglaise

1 L milk (34 fl. oz.)
250 g sugar (9 oz.)
12 egg yolks
50 to 55 ml liqueur (1.5 to 2 fl. oz.)

Liquor Crème Anglaise

1 L milk (34 fl. oz.)
250 g sugar (9 oz.)
12 egg yolks
65 to 70 ml liquor (2 to 2.5 fl. oz.)

Nonalcoholic flavorings such as vanilla, coffee, chocolate, caramel, hazelnut, and pistachio are infused in the milk and sugar.

Liqueur and liquor flavorings are always added to the crème anglaise after it has cooled, to prevent evaporation of the alcohol.

Crème Anglaise

PREPARATION	0 min	
Assemble the Equipment Prepare, Weigh, and Measure the Raw Ingredients		● Verify the cleanliness of the equipment. ● Check the freshness of the raw ingredients. ● Separate the eggs. ● Split the vanilla bean lengthwise. ● Set up the ice bath.
PROCEDURE	10 min	
Boil the Milk		● Add half the sugar and the split vanilla bean to the milk and bring to a boil.
Whisk the Eggs and Sugar		● Use a whisk to facilitate incorporating the milk.
Add the Hot Milk	15 min	● Slowly add half of the boiling milk to the egg/sugar mixture, whisking constantly, then place the mixture in the saucepan with the remaining milk.
Poach the Mixture		● Use a low flame and stir with a wooden spatula.
Check the Consistency	17 min	● The cream will begin to thicken. ● Angle the spatula at 45 degrees and coat it. Draw a horizontal line with a finger through the cream, which will not cover over if the cream is ready.
Strain the Cream	20 min.	● Immediately strain the cream into a bowl. Set in an ice bath.
Cool the Cream	22 min	● Stir with a wooden spatula over the ice bath.
STORAGE		Crème anglaise can be stored for up to 24 hours maximum in the refrigerator at 5°C (40°F).

La crème pâtissière (Pastry cream)

Equipment

Saucepan
Drum sieve with parchment paper
Measuring cup
Pastry scraper
Bowls
Whisk
Clean sheet pan

History

As amazing as it may seem, the exact origin and inventor of pastry cream is unknown.

This is particularly surprising since pastry cream is probably the most popular of all creams.

It is probably safe to assume that it was invented near the end of the nineteenth century, when much development of the arts of both French cooking and French pastry making was taking place.

Originally, pastry cream probably resembled roux with sugar added to it rather than the modern version that we know today.

For the professional pastry chef, it is the most frequently used of all the creams.

Uses

In Finished Products:

For filling large and individual cakes made out of pâte à choux; for filling napoleons and fruit tarts with precooked shells; for filling cakes and savarins.

In Cooked Products:

For filling cooked fruit tarts, cream-filled brioches, raisin breads, and schnecks; for special cakes such as polonaises and gâteaux basques.

Combined with Other Mixtures:

Pastry cream plus almond cream
Pastry cream plus pâte à choux (cream puff pastry)

Recipes

One liter (34 fl. oz.) of pastry cream will fill 25 to 30 individual-size pâte à choux (cream puff) pastries or 2 kg (70.5 oz.) of petits fours.

Professional Recipe

1 L milk (34 fl. oz.)
250 g granulated sugar (9 oz.)
8 egg yolks
125 g cake flour (4.5 oz.), sifted with 25 g powdered flan mix (1 oz.)
100 g butter (3.5 oz.), optional

Alternative Recipe A

1 L milk (34 fl. oz.)
300 g granulated sugar (10.5 oz.)
5 eggs or 8 egg yolks
150 g cake flour (5 oz.)
100 g butter (3.5 oz.), optional

Alternative Recipe B

1 L milk (34 fl. oz.) or 1 L water plus 100 g powdered milk (34 fl. oz. plus 3.5 oz.)
200 to 300 g sugar (7 to 10.5 oz.)
2 to 6 eggs or 4 to 10 egg yolks
120 to 160 g cake flour (4 to 5.5 oz.) or 50 g cake flour sifted with 50 g powdered flan mix (1.5 oz. plus 1.5 oz.)
100 g butter (3.5 oz.), optional

Pastry cream is often used in French pastry.
It is easy to prepare if done properly. Watch the cooking carefully.
It requires traditional pastry equipment.
Allow 30 minutes for its preparation.
Pastry cream must be used the same day it is prepared.

Recipe for a Small Quantity

500 ml milk (17 fl. oz.)
125 g sugar (4 oz.)
2 eggs
75 g cake flour (2.5 oz.)
50 g butter (1.5 oz.), optional

This recipe will fill 12 to 15 pâte à choux (cream puff) pastries.

Preparation

Because of its composition, considerable care must be taken in the preparation of pastry cream to avoid bacterial contamination:

- Use only fresh raw ingredients.

- Make sure the equipment is perfectly clean.

- Clean work habits are important, as is personal hygiene.

Have either a plastic tub or stainless steel bowl ready to hold the finished cream.

Procedure

Preparing the Milk

Bring the milk and half the sugar to a simmer in a saucepan that can hold three times their volume. This kills harmful bacteria.

When using powdered milk, make sure that it is well combined with the water and does not precipitate to the bottom of the saucepan and burn.

Avoid preparing too much pastry cream at once.

Preparing the Egg/Sugar/Flour Mixture

Beat the eggs and remaining sugar

together until the mixture becomes pale yellow or white and forms a ribbon.

This initial beating facilitates the incorporation of the flour.

Add the flour and powdered flan mix all at once to the egg/sugar mixture.

Stir the mixture with a whisk to eliminate lumps and obtain a smooth consistency.

Do not overbeat the mixture at this stage, or it will become elastic and tend to be pasty and sticky.

Adding the Milk

Once the milk/sugar mixture has come to a boil, turn the heat down to low. Gradually add half the hot milk/sugar mixture to the egg/sugar mixture. Stir continuously with a whisk.

The purpose of this is to avoid overheating and coagulating the yolks,

which would create a granular texture in the final cream, as well as to prevent the cream from congealing when it comes in contact with the heat, which would create lumps in the final mixture.

Once the first half of the milk has been added, the mixture should be completely liquid. Off the fire, pour the milk/egg/sugar mixture into the remaining milk.

Beat continuously to avoid the formation of lumps. Scrape the sides of the saucepan and place it back on the stove.

It is advisable to add the mixture to the hot milk *off the fire* for two reasons:

the cream will thicken less quickly and is less likely to stick to the bottom of the saucepan; and it is easier to prepare a homogeneous mixture because the cream can be well mixed and the sides of the saucepan can be scraped.

Mixing and Cooking the Pastry Cream

The cream should be brought back to a boil; stir constantly. If the mixture is not stirred, it will stick to bottom and corners of the saucepan.

Make sure that the flame does not wrap around and come up the sides of the saucepan. On the other hand, the flame should be high enough to heat the entire bottom of the saucepan evenly.

Stir slowly, making sure that the whisk scrapes gently on the bottom and in the corners of the saucepan.

The cream is cooked once it has boiled for a minimum of 3 minutes. If a large quantity of cream is being prepared, it should be boiled for at least 5 minutes.

When the cream is ready, it will be smooth and shiny.

Adding the Butter

Adding butter to pastry cream gives it a smoother texture and a finer taste. The butter should be incorporated in chunks, which should be added off the heat.

When it is added to the hot cream, it melts extremely quickly.

Holding the Cream

Transfer the cream immediately to a large plastic tub or a clean baking sheet.

Spread it over the surface of a baking sheet so that it cools more quickly. It is important to cool the cream as quickly as possible to help prevent the growth of bacteria.

Spread the surface of the cream with butter to prevent the formation of a crust and then cover with plastic wrap.

It is also possible to prevent the cream from forming a crust by stirring it constantly while it cools.

Pastry chefs often sprinkle the surface of cooling pastry cream with confectioners' sugar to avoid the formation of a crust. When the sugar comes in contact with the warm pastry cream, it forms a protective layer of syrup.

This method, however, is not recommended because once the cream is stirred, the syrup that has formed on the surface enters the cream. Because raw sugar contains dust and bacteria, it can contaminate the finished pastry cream.

Storage

Pastry cream should always be stored in the refrigerator, 5°C (40°F). It can be stored for only 24 to 36 hours maximum after it is prepared.

Pastry cream may be flavored using natural flavors, and with liquors and liqueurs: Kirsch, rum, Cointreau, Grand Marnier, vanilla, coffee, chocolate, or pralines, for example.

La Crème Pâtissière
Pastry Cream

Step	Time	Details
PREPARATION	**0** min	
Assemble the Equipment **Prepare, Weigh, and Measure** the Raw Ingredients		• Make sure all equipment is clean. • Make sure all the raw ingredients are perfectly fresh.
PROCEDURE	**5** min	
Prepare the Milk/Sugar Mixture		• Add half the sugar to the milk in a saucepan. • Bring the mixture to the boil.
Prepare the Egg/Sugar Mixture		• Whisk the eggs with the sugar. • Add the flour and the powdered flan mix. • This facilitates the eventual incorporation of the sugar and helps produce a smooth mixture.
Add the Boiling Milk	**10** min	• Pour half the boiling milk gradually over the egg/sugar mixture. • The consistency of the thinned mixture should be about the same as milk, which helps the final mixing.
Add the Milk/Egg Mixture to the Rest of the Milk	**12** min	• Stir continuously, off the heat.
Return the Mixture Back to the Heat	**15** min	• Continue stirring the cream with a whisk • Cook and stir for several minutes after the cream comes to a boil. • This helps the consistency and shelf life of the cream.
Add the Butter		• Add chunks of butter off the heat. • Mix with a whisk.
Transfer the Cream	**20** min	• Transfer the Cream immediately after cooking to a sheet pan or large tub so that it cools quickly. • Never allow the cream to cool in the saucepan used for its preparation. • This is important to avoid bacterial growth.
STORAGE		Store in the refrigerator for 12 hours maximum before use in a pastry, 24 hours before serving.

La crème à flan (Flan cream)

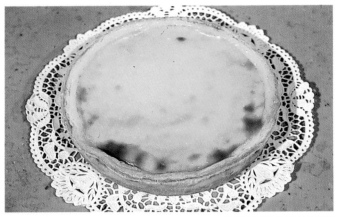
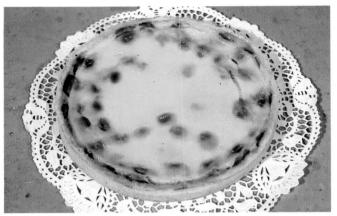
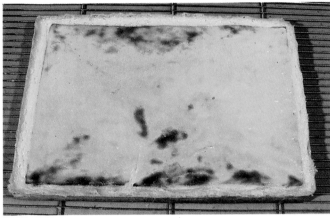

History

In fourteenth-century France, the word *flan* was used to describe a particular type of cake, quite popular at the time, that had none of the finesse or lightness of the modern version. The original flan was heavily spiced, as was typical of most medieval pastries and cakes.

To some degree, the meaning of the word *flan* remains somewhat ambiguous. In certain regions of France, a flan is similar to a crème renversée and is usually flavored with vanilla, chocolate, or coffee. In other regions, it is a kind of tart, usually filled with a stiff cream similar to pastry cream and garnished with different kinds of fruit.

Because of these various interpretations, it is difficult to give an all-encompassing, basic recipe. However, the recipes given here for flan cream have a consistency between that of crème anglaise and of pastry cream (crème pâtissière). Today flan cream is usually prepared using powdered flan mix, which helps in its preparation and gives it a longer shelf life.

Although the finished flans are of good quality and keep better, a flan made with powdered flan mix will never have as good a consistency as one made using the traditional ingredients.

The preparation of flan cream is very similar to that of pastry cream (crème pâtissière).

Uses

Plain

Flan cream is used to fill a variety of pastry shells and bases, including pâte feuilletée rognures (puff pastry trimmings), basic pie and tart dough (pâte à foncer), and sweetened tart dough (pâte sucrée), as well as in a variety of large and individual molds and tart rings.

With Fresh or Canned Fruits

Flan is mixed with fresh or canned fruit to create apricot flans, cherry flans, pear flans, banana flans, blueberry flans, and many others.

With Dried or Candied Fruits

With Meringue

Meringue flans are flavored with fruit, including raspberries, strawberries, blueberries, red currants, and lemon.

These pastries are popular because of their variety and agreeable texture.

Equipment

The utensils for flan are the same as for crème pâtissière (pastry cream).

Professional Recipe

1 L milk (34 fl. oz.)
250 g sugar (9 oz.)
3 egg yolks
100 g powdered flan mix (3.5 oz.)

Alternative Recipe A

1 L milk (34 fl. oz.)
300 g sugar (10.5 oz.)
4 to 6 egg yolks
130 g cornstarch or flour (4.5 oz.)
fruit (optional)

Flan cream is often used in French pastry making.

Its preparation does not require much experience.

Use traditional pastry equipment.

Allow 15 minutes for its preparation.

Alternative Recipe B

1 L milk (34 fl. oz.) *or* 1 L water combined with 100 g powdered milk (34 fl. oz. plus 3.5 oz.)
200 to 300 g sugar (7 to 10.5 oz.)
2 to 4 eggs
80 to 100 g powdered flan mix (3 to 3.5 oz.)

Alternative Recipe C

1 L milk (34 fl. oz.) *or* 1 L water combined with 100 g powdered milk (34 fl. oz. plus 3.5 oz.)
200 to 300 g sugar (7 to 10.5 oz.)
2 to 4 eggs *or* 2 to 6 egg yolks
120 to 150 g flour or cornstarch (4 to 5 oz.)
fruit (optional)

Recipe for a Small Quantity

500 ml milk (17 fl. oz.)
150 g sugar (5 oz.)
2 eggs
75 g flour (2.5 oz.)
fruit (optional)

Preparation

Follow the instructions given for crème pâtissière (pastry cream; see pages 27 to 29). When using fruit:

● *Fresh fruit:*
prepare by pitting, washing, and draining

● *Canned fruit:*
prepare by draining

● *Dried fruit:*
prepare by washing and draining

The amount of fruit to use varies, depending on its size. Use enough to cover the bottom of the tart lightly.

Procedure

The method used for preparing flan cream is almost the same as for crème pâtissière.
Heat three-fourths of the milk in a saucepan with half the sugar. Combine the remainder of the milk with the sugar, powdered flan mix, and the eggs. Combine well to smooth out any lumps in the flan mix.
Continue in the same way as for pastry cream. It is not necessary, however, to continue cooking the cream once it has come to a boil, because it will cook again in the oven.

Filling the Pastry Shells

As soon as the flan cream is ready, fill half-baked pastry shells or molds. If fruit is being used, place it in the shells before adding the cream. Pour the cream into the shells while it is still boiling hot. Tart shells should be filled nine-tenths of the way up the sides.
The cream can be poured directly, or it can be spooned with a ladle.
Once the pastry shells or molds have been filled, allow the cream to cool completely before baking.

Baking

After the flans have cooled, place them in a medium oven, 200° to 220°C (375° to 425°F), or a slow oven, 180°C (350°F), if they are particularly large.
To obtain an attractive sheen, the flans may be brushed with a light egg wash before baking.
If the flans are being baked directly in molds, without pastry shells, they should be placed directly on the oven floor. Pastry-lined flans should be placed on baking sheets.

Checking the Baking

The tart's crust should be pale brown and should pull away slightly from the sides if baked in a ring or mold.
If the flans have been cooked in tart shells on sheet pans, remove the rings and transfer them to cake racks to cool. When they have completely cooled, refrigerate at 5°C (40°F).
If the flans have been cooked directly in molds, wait for them to cool completely before unmolding them. Once they are unmolded, place them on a rack in the refrigerator, 5°C (40°F).

Storage

Flans may be kept for up to two days in the refrigerator, 5°C (40°F).

Flans may be frozen but this is not advised because it causes them to release too much moisture once they are thawed. Their quality suffers considerably.

La Crème à Flan
Flan Cream

Step	Time	Notes
PREPARATION	**0** min	
Assemble the Equipment Prepare, Weigh, and Measure the Raw Ingredients		● Make sure to assemble tart rings or molds. ● All the equipment must be perfectly clean.
PROCEDURE	**5** min	
Prepare the Milk/Sugar Mixture		● Put three-fourths of the milk in a saucepan with one-half the sugar. ● Bring to a boil.
PREPARATION OF EGG MIXTURE Whisk the Eggs with the Remaining Sugar		● This helps to incorporate the powdered flan mix.
Add the Powdered Flan Mix		● Add the powdered flan mix along with the remaining milk to the egg/sugar mixture.
Add the Boiling Milk	**10** min	● Add the boiling milk in two stages, stirring each time.
Add the Rest of the Milk		● Add the remaining milk to the mixture off the heat. ● Stir constantly.
Return Mixture to the Stove	**12** min	● Simmer the mixture while stirring rapidly, until the cream is smooth.
FILLING TARTS OR MOLDS	**15** min	● Fill molds or half-baked tart shells with the boiling hot cream, nine-tenths full. ● Fill the molds immediately, before the cream congeals.
Cooling		● Allow the filled tarts or molds to cool completely before baking.
STORAGE		Flan can be stored for 48 hours in the refrigerator after baking. It does not freeze well.

La crème caramel (Caramel custard)

Crème caramel and its derivatives (such as crème renversée, crème aux œufs, and crème au lait) are prepared in pastry shops more than ever before, primarily because of the development of disposable aluminum molds that make the creams easy to send out or sell in the shop. The creams are increasingly popular in France as an afternoon accompaniment to tea or coffee.

Uses

Crème caramel and its derivatives may be served:
- plain
- with petits fours
- molded in a savarin mold and accompanied by fresh fruits such as strawberries, raspberries, peaches, pears, or cherries
- occasionally, with crème Chantilly (Chantilly cream).

Equipment

Saucepan - Whisk
Pastry scraper

Fine-mesh sieve (china cap) or cheese-cloth
Mixing bowl - Ladle
Bain-marie (water bath) and paper

Professional Recipe

Serves twelve: three molds, 12 cm (4.5 in.) in diameter; or two molds, 14 cm (5.5 in.) in diameter

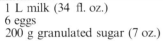
1 L milk (34 fl. oz.)
6 eggs
200 g granulated sugar (7 oz.)

vanilla
caramel

Alternative Recipe

1 L milk (34 fl. oz.)
6 eggs or 4 eggs plus 4 egg yolks
150 to 250 g granulated sugar (5 to 9 oz.)
vanilla
caramel

Vanilla: one vanilla bean split lengthwise down the middle and infused in the hot milk, or 1 Tbsp. vanilla extract added to the mixture before straining. Use 150 g of sugar (5 oz.) and 50 ml water (1.5 fl. oz.) for the caramel.

Procedure

Preparing the Caramel

Prepare the caramel with 150 g (5 oz.) sugar and 50 ml (1.5 fl. oz.) water (see *Cooked Sugar*, pages 14 to 17). Cook to the caramel (grand jaune) stage. Stop the

Crème caramel is not difficult to prepare, except possibly the caramel, which requires close attention.
Closely watch the cooking of the sugar and the temperature of the bain-marie.
Use traditional pastry equipment.
Allow approximately 2 1/2 hours to prepare.

cooking immediately.

Line the molds or individual ramekins with the caramel by pouring enough in the bottom to cover about half the surface. Quickly pick up the mold or ramekin and rotate it so that the entire bottom surface is evenly covered with the caramel. The layer of caramel should be from

1 to 2 mm (1/32 to 1/16 in.) thick. Let cool.

Note

The caramel that remains in the copper sugar pan can be deglazed with a small amount of water, to create a thick syrup that can be used as a sauce served on the side.

Preparing the Mixture

Boil the milk with the sugar and the vanilla bean (if used). Beat the yolks rapidly with a whisk and slowly pour the boiling milk into the yolks. Do not add the milk too quickly at first or the yolks could coagulate.

Strain the mixture through cheesecloth or a fine-mesh sieve.

Add vanilla extract if a vanilla bean was not used, or flavor the crème in another way.

Pour the mixture into the caramel-lined molds. Fill the molds or ramekins to 1 cm (1/2 in.) below the rim, and

place them in the bain-marie (water bath). Make sure the bottom of the bain-marie is lined with paper to prevent the water from splashing if it boils, which in any case should be avoided. The paper (a metal rack can also be used) also protects the crème caramel from the direct heat of the oven.

Fill the bain-marie with boiling water until the water reaches halfway up the sides of the molds. Be careful not to let any of the water splash into the crèmes.

Slide the bain-marie into the oven carefully so that none of the water splashes into the molds or ramekins.

Baking

Bake the crème caramels in a slow oven, 160°C (325°F) with vents open (if available) and the door ajar. It is imperative that neither the water in the bain-marie nor the crèmes themselves come to a boil. If the water in the bain-marie comes to a boil, the eggs will coagulate and separate from the milk. This results in a mixture that is grainy and runny at the same time. It becomes difficult to unmold and has an unpleasant texture.

The baking time varies, depending on the size of the molds but usually ranges from 25 to 45 minutes. The crème caramels should be checked regularly to make sure that they are not coloring too rapidly and that the bain-marie water is not boiling. If the water in the bain-marie begins to boil, remove the crèmes and lower the oven temperature. Once the oven and water bath have cooled somewhat, return the crèmes to the bain-marie and continue baking.

Verifying Doneness

The crème caramels have set when a knife inserted in the center remains clean when pulled out. The surface of the crèmes should tremble slightly when jiggled.

Cooling and Unmolding

When the crèmes are done, they should be removed from the bain-marie and placed on cooling racks. They may also be put directly on crushed ice if they need to be quickly cooled.

La Crème Caramel

PREPARATION	**0** min	
Assemble the Equipment **Prepare**, Weigh, and Measure the Raw Ingredients		● Use appropriately sized molds or ramekins. ● Do not forget the ingredients for the caramel.
PROCEDURE	**5** min	
Prepare the Caramel		● Cook the sugar until caramel. ● Stop the cooking as soon as the caramel is at the correct stage.
Line the Molds		● Pour enough hot caramel into the molds or ramekins to create a layer 1 to 2 mm (1/32 to 1/16 in.) thick.
Prepare the Sugar/Milk Mixture	**15** min	
		● Combine the milk and sugar in a saucepan and bring to a boil. ● Stir the mixture continuously to help dissolve the sugar.
Add to the Yolks **Strain** **Fill** the Molds	**18** min	● Pour the boiling milk over the beaten yolks. ● Strain the mixture through a fine-mesh sieve or through cheesecloth. ● The molds should be already lined with caramel.
Bake	**20** min	● Place the filled molds or ramekins in a bain-marie. ● Carefully place the bain-marie into a 160°C (325°F) oven with vents opened and door ajar.
Verify Doneness	**45** min	● The crèmes are done when a knife is inserted and comes out clean.
TRANSFERRING THE CREAMS	**1** hr	● Remove the crème caramels from the bain-marie and place them on a cooling rack or in crushed ice to cool.
UNMOLDING	**2 hr 30**	● The creams should be completely cool. ● Insert a knife around the insides of the molds to detach the crèmes. ● Turn out onto a plate or platter. ● Shake to help unmold if necessary.
STORAGE	Crème caramels can be kept in their molds, refrigerated, for 48 hours; out of their molds, refrigerated, for 24 hours.	

Once the molds have completely cooled, all the way through (usually after about an hour in the refrigerator), they can be unmolded either onto a platter or directly onto the serving plate. Proceed as follows:
a. Separate the crème caramel from the sides of the molds using the fingers or by shaking. If the crèmes do not pull away from the sides, run a knife or pastry scraper around the inside to detach them.
b. Place the plate or platter on top of the crème and quickly flip both over. When the mold is inverted onto the plate, quickly move the mold and plate together using a back-and-forth motion.

This allows air to enter into the mold and releases the suction holding the crème.

If a sauce is being served, it may be poured around the crème caramel at this point.

Note: Crème renversée is the same as crème caramel but has no caramel. It may be flavored with coffee, chocolate, or vanilla (see crème vanille, below).

Storage

It is best to store crème caramel while it is still in the molds. It will keep in this way for 48 hours in the refrigerator. If unmolded, it will keep safely for only 24 hours, refrigerated.

La crème vanille (Vanilla custard)

Equipment

Same as for crème caramel.

Professional Recipe

1 L milk (34 fl. oz.)
12 egg yolks
200 g sugar (7 oz.)
vanilla bean and/or other flavoring

Alternative Recipe

1 L milk (34 fl. oz.)
10 to 12 egg yolks
200 to 300 g sugar (7 to 10.5 oz.)
vanilla bean and/or other flavoring

Vanilla: one vanilla bean, split lengthwise down the middle and infused in the hot milk, or 1 Tbsp. vanilla extract added to the mixture before straining.

Coffee: use 15 g (1/2 oz.) instant coffee dissolved in the milk. It is also possible to use coffee extract or to infuse 50 g (1.5 oz.) coarsely ground coffee beans in the milk as it is brought to a boil.

Chocolate: use 40 to 60 g (1.5 to 2 oz.) cocoa powder or unsweetened chocolate infused in the milk. When using unsweetened chocolate or cocoa, add 50 g (1.5 oz.) additional sugar to the mixture

to compensate for the bitterness. The unsweetened chocolate or cocoa powder can be replaced with 100 to 120 g (3.5 to 4 oz.) semisweet chocolate without increasing the quantity of sugar.

Praline: infuse 100 to 120 g (3.5 to 4 oz.) praline paste in the milk

Procedure

Preparing the Milk/Egg/Sugar/Flavoring Mixture

Follow the procedure for crème caramel (see pages 32 to 34).

Baking

The method of baking these creams is the same as for crème caramel.
It is best to cover the creams with a sheet of aluminum foil or a sheet pan to prevent the surface from forming a crust and coloring. Bake for about 30 minutes.

Checking the Baking

The cream should be firm (a knife should come out clean) but at the same time tremble slightly when jiggled.

Cooling

Cool the creams on cooling racks or in the refrigerator. These creams are not unmolded but are served directly in the mold or ramekins.

Storage

Vanilla custard will keep for 48 hours in the refrigerator, 5°C (40°F).

  Vanilla custard is easy to prepare, but careful attention should be paid during the baking. No special equipment is required. Allow about 2 hours for its preparation.

Chapter 2   Beaten creams

La crème d'amandes
(Almond cream)

History

As its name indicates, almond cream is made from a base of almonds. Desserts based on almonds mixed with various spices have been made since the time of ancient Greece.

The first almond jellies were created during the Middle Ages, after which various recipes and presentations were developed. These jellies were presumably not very attractive, so coloring such as yellow, red, and green was used to improve their appearance and render them more appetizing.

The almond jelly during this period was more a paste than a cream. Eventually, the almonds were skinned and ground with honey, sugar, water, orange flower water, and spices.

It was from this somewhat creamy mixture that almond cream was derived at the beginning of the seventeenth century.

The Comte Frangipani gave Marie de Médicis, the future queen of France, a recipe invented by his chef based on a variation of almond cream. This cream so pleased the court of France that it quickly became popular and was called crème frangipane.

Almond cream is used in numerous dessert preparations.

Uses

Almond cream is used exclusively to garnish desserts:

● *full-sized cakes:* Pithiviers (almond-cream-filled puff pastry), dartois (almond-cream-filled strips), conversations (almond-cream-filled pastries covered with royal icing), pains complets, and amandines.

● *individual desserts:* conversations, amandines, pains complets, the bases of small butter cream pastries, and chestnut barquettes.

Equipment

By Hand

Stainless steel bowl, wooden spatula
Whisk
Stainless steel bowl for the eggs
Pastry scraper
Drum sieve and paper for sifting

    Almond cream is easy to prepare. Bring all raw ingredients to room temperature, to facilitate making a smooth batter.

It is best to use an electric mixer for its preparation, which takes approximately 15 minutes. Almond cream can be stored for one week refrigerated at 5°C (40°F).

By Machine

Mixing bowl and paddle attachment
Bowl for the eggs
Pastry scraper
Bowl for the finished product
Drum sieve and paper for sifting

Professional Recipe

500 g butter (17.5 oz.)
500 g granulated sugar (17.5 oz.)
8 eggs
500 g almond powder (17.5 oz.)
100 g cake flour (3.5 oz.), optional
150 ml flavoring: rum and vanilla
(5 fl. oz.)

Alternative Recipe A

1 kg almond tant pour tant* (35 oz.)
500 g butter (17.5 oz.)
500 g eggs (17.5 oz.)
100 g cake flour (3.5 oz.), optional
150 ml flavoring: rum and vanilla
(5 fl. oz.)

Alternative Recipe B

900 to 1100 g of almond tant pour tant*
(31.5 to 39 oz.) *or*
450 to 550 g granulated or confectioners'
sugar (16 to 19.5 oz.) plus 450 to
500 g almond powder (16 to 19.5 oz.)
450 to 550 g butter (16 to 19.5 oz.)
8 to 12 eggs
80 to 140 g cake flour (3 to 5 oz.),
optional
100 to 200 ml flavoring: rum and vanilla
(3.5 to 7 fl. oz.)

Recipe for a Small Quantity

250 g butter (9 oz.)
250 g sugar (9 oz.)
4 eggs
250 g almond powder (9 oz.)
50 g cake flour (1.5 oz.)
50 ml rum (1.5 fl. oz.)

*Tant pour tant consists of equal amounts
of almond and granulated or confectioners'
sugar ground into a powder or almond
powder and granulated or confectioners'
sugar mixed together (see volume 1,
page 89, succès/progrès).

Preparation

Almond cream can be made by hand
or machine; in either case the instructions
remain the same. Either almond powder
or tant pour tant can be used. All other
raw ingredients are the prepared in the
same way as for all recipes.

When **working by hand,** combine the
sugar and almond powder separately to
make blending the ingredients easier. The
final result is the same when using tant
pour tant.

Cream the butter, after bringing it
to room temperature, to give a creamy
consistency to the batter. If the butter
has just come out of the refrigerator or
is very firm, it is especially important to
soften it.

If necessary, the butter can be softened
by tapping it with a rolling pin or the
hands. This softens the butter, preventing
the batter from becoming grainy.

Procedure

By Hand

Creaming the Butter and Sugar

Cream the butter alone in a bowl with
a wooden spatula. Do not use a whisk
for this procedure, as, when the butter is
cold, it can stick inside the wires of the
whisk. This makes the butter impossible
to work, and wastes time.

To make this step easier, warm the
butter over a warm water bath (bain-
marie) or directly over a low flame.

Once the butter is soft (to pommade
consistency), add the sugar, and cream
the two ingredients together with a
whisk.

Whisking in the Eggs

Add the eggs slowly, whipping the
batter so that it increases in volume. This
procedure should be done slowly, adding
the eggs one by one (or in small quantities at a time) so that the egg is emulsified

as it is added, maintaining a homogeneous consistency.

With a pastry scraper, scrape any batter sticking to the sides of the bowl as the
eggs are added to ensure a homogeneous
mixture. At this point the batter should
be light and fluffy.

Incorporating the Almond Powder

Once all the eggs have been added,
add the almond powder all at once and
mix. Do not overwork the batter.

Finish by adding the flour, again being
careful not to overwork the batter. If

flour is used, it can be added along with
the almond powder. In this case, sift the
two together before adding them to the
batter.

Flavoring the Batter

Almond cream can be flavored with
either liquor and/or vanilla. Most pastry
chefs do not add any flavoring until the
cream is to be used, so that the flavoring
does not evaporate during storage.

It is possible, however, to flavor the
cream while it is being made. If that is
done, the flavoring is added last.

By Machine

Cream the Butter with the Tant Pour Tant or the Sugar and Almond Powder

Place the butter and tant pour tant

(or sugar and almond powder) in the mixing bowl. Start the machine on slow speed, working the mixture for a few moments, then turn the machine to medium speed and mix until the batter is creamy and homogeneous.

Incorporating the Eggs

Slowly add the eggs, allowing the batter to absorb them as they are added.

During this step, scrape the sides and bottom of the bowl as well as the paddle once or twice throughout the procedure.

Once all the eggs have been added, finish by adding the flour and rum. Place the cream in a container or bowl

Choosing the Hand or Machine Procedure

Almond cream can also be made in the electric mixer following the procedure for the hand method.

The procedures presented are intended to save time and make the work easier, and in no way compromise the quality of the final result.

Storage

Almond cream can be stored in the refrigerator for approximately 6 days at 5°C (40°F) in a plastic or stainless steel container.

Almond cream can be frozen for several weeks if protected from frost.

Frangipane Cream

Frangipane cream is made by adding pastry cream and flavoring to a plain almond cream.

Generally, the proportions are two-thirds almond cream to one-third pastry cream plus flavoring. This mixture is called crème frangipane (frangipane cream), not almond cream.

La Crème d'Amandes
Almond Cream

PREPARATION **Assemble** the Equipment **Prepare, Weigh, and Measure** the Raw Ingredients	**0** min	• *Verify the cleanliness of the equipment.* • *Bring the butter to room temperature and soften it.* • *Use high-quality almond powder.* • *Use very fresh eggs.*
PROCEDURE 1. *By hand* **Cream** the Butter and Sugar	**5** min	• *Cream the mixture until it is light and fluffy.*
Incorporate the Eggs	**10** min	• *Slowly and steadily add the eggs while mixing constantly, so that the batter increases in volume.*
Add the Almond Powder	**18** min	• *Add the almond powder all at once with a wooden spatula, being careful not to overwork the batter.*
Add the Flour	**19** min	• *This step is optional.*
Flavor the Cream	**20** min	• *Flavor as the last step, or wait until the cream is to be used.*
2. *By machine* **Cream** the Butter with the Tant Pour Tant or Sugar and Powder Almonds	**5** min	• *In the bowl of the mixer, with a paddle attachment, start creaming on slow speed and then increase to medium speed until the batter is very creamy.*
Incorporate the Eggs	**10** min	• *Slowly add the eggs so the batter can absorb them and increase in volume.*
Add the Flour (optional). **Flavor** the Cream	**15** min	• *Add flavoring as the last step, or wait until just before the cream is to be served.*
TRANSFER		• *Place the cream in either a stainless steel or plastic bowl.*
STORAGE	Almond cream can be refrigerated for approximately 6 days at 5°C (40°F). If protected from frost, it freezes well for several weeks.	

La crème au fromage blanc
(Fromage blanc cream)

History

Fromage blanc cream is the most recently developed of the beaten creams, very much an example of the new, light desserts, although it is made from rich ingredients.

Fromage blanc cream is a very light preparation, made primarily with fromage blanc (a soft, white, smooth fresh cheese with a texture similar to sour cream), and heavy cream, sugar, and egg yolks.

These ingredients are blended together to obtain a delicate, smooth, light cream.

Uses

Fromage blanc cream is most often used to garnish or fill various individual cakes and desserts made with génoise, sponge cake, meringue, succès, and progrès.

Equipment

Electric mixer with bowl and whisk attachment
Bowl for the gelatin plus a small saucepan
Bowl for the egg yolks
Equipment for cooking the sugar
Fine-mesh sieve (china cap)
Plastic scraper
Bowl plus whisk for whipping the heavy cream

Fromage blanc cream is easy to prepare. Careful attention should be given to cooking the sugar and mixing it with the egg yolks.

No special equipment is required.

Allow 30 minutes to prepare the batter. Fromage blanc cream freezes well.

Recipes

Professional Recipe

300 g sugar (10.5 oz.) plus 100 ml water
    (3.5 fl. oz.), cooked to 120°C (248°F)
6 egg yolks
10 leaves (20 g) of gelatin (2/3 oz.)
1 kg fromage blanc (35 oz.)
1 L heavy cream (34 fl. oz.)
100 g sugar (3.5 oz.)
several drops of vanilla extract

Alternative Recipe

250 to 300 g sugar (8.5 to 10.5 oz.) plus
    100 ml water (3.5 fl. oz.)
6 to 8 egg yolks
8 to 12 leaves (16 to 24 g) gelatin (2/3
    to 3/4 oz.)
800 g to 1 kg fromage blanc (28 to
    35 oz.)
1 L heavy cream (34 fl. oz.)
several drops of vanilla extract
250 to 300 g Italian meringue (9 to
    10.5 oz.)

Recipe for a Small Quantity

125 g sugar (4.5 oz.) plus 40 ml water
    (1.5 fl. oz.)
3 egg yolks
5 leaves (10 g) gelatin (1/4 oz.)
400 g fromage blanc (14 oz.)
500 ml heavy cream (17 fl. oz.)
50 g sugar (1.5 oz.)
vanilla extract

Preparation

Assemble all necessary equipment.

Place the heavy cream in a bowl and refrigerate.

Soften the gelatin by soaking the leaves in cold water.

Separate the eggs.

Procedure

Cooking the Sugar and Water

Cook the sugar with 30 percent of its weight in water to 120°C (248°F). Follow the necessary precautions: see Cooking Sugar, pages 14 to 17.

Combining the Cooked Sugar with the Egg Yolks

While the sugar is cooking, lightly beat the egg yolks to facilitate adding the

cooked sugar. Stop the sugar from cooking when it reaches 120°C (248°F), and slowly pour it over the yolks, stirring constantly and vigorously with a whisk.

Straining the Mixture

After all the cooked sugar has been added, strain the yolk/sugar mixture (which is also called a *bombe* mixture, used for frozen desserts) to remove any bits of cooked yolk, shell, or umbilical cord.

Beating the Batter

Once strained, place the batter in a mixing bowl. Using the whisk attachment, beat it on high speed until cool.

Adding the Gelatin

Melt the gelatin over a double boiler (do not allow it to get too hot); then add it to the mixture while both are still warm. Beat the batter in the electric mixer on high speed until it is completely cool.

Adding the Fromage Blanc

Incorporate the fromage blanc into the batter, mixing with the whisk by hand.

Whipping the Heavy Cream

Follow the same procedure given for whipping heavy cream or Chantilly cream (see pages 54 to 57). Include the remaining sugar in the whipped cream.

Incorporating the Whipped Cream

Slowly and carefully pour the batter into the whipped cream, and fold it in with either a rubber spatula or whisk.

Finishing

The cream is now ready to be used. Because of the gelatin, which sets up the cream, it is best to immediately fill or dress the cake or dessert for which the cream is intended. Once the cream sets, it is more difficult to use.

Storage

Fromage blanc cream can be refrigerated for 4 to 5 days at 5°C (40°F), or stored in the freezer for 3 weeks at −30°C (−20°F).

La Crème au Fromage Blanc
Fromage Blanc Cream

PREPARATION	**0** min	
Assemble the Equipment **Prepare, Weigh and Measure** the Raw Ingredients		• Chill the bowl to be used for whipping the heavy cream. • Soak the gelatin leaves in cold water. • Separate the eggs.
PROCEDURE	**5** min	
Cook the Sugar **Incorporate** the Cooked Sugar		• Cook the sugar to 120°C (248°F), following the necessary precautions. • Pour the cooked sugar slowly over the beaten yolks.
Strain the Mixture **Add** the Gelatin	**10** min	• Strain the mixture through a china cap into the mixing bowl. • After melting the gelatin, add it to the warm yolk/sugar mixture.
Whip the Mixture	**12** min	• Beat the batter at high speed with the whisk attachment.
Add the Fromage Blanc	**17** min	• Combine the cheese with the whipped, cold mixture.
Whip the Heavy Cream	**20** min	• Follow the necessary precautions.
Incorporate the Whipped Batter	**25** min	• Delicately fold the batter into the whipped cream with a rubber spatula or whisk.
TRANSFERRING	**30** min	• Put the cream to use immediately.
STORAGE:		• Fromage blanc cream can be stored for 4 to 5 days at 5°C (40°F). It can be frozen for 3 weeks at −30°C (−20°F).

La crème de marrons (Chestnut cream)

Definition

Chestnut cream is a creamy, light, preparation based on chestnut paste and often flavored with rum and vanilla.

Uses

Chestnut cream is used like butter cream to fill and garnish various desserts and individual cakes.

It is not often used in pastry making, perhaps because it is often made by home cooks.

Equipment

By Hand

Bowl
Rubber spatula
Pastry scraper
Small saucepan

By Machine

Mixing bowl and whisk or paddle attachment
Small saucepan
Pastry scraper
Bowl for storage

Professional Recipe

1 kg chestnut paste (35 oz.)
500 g butter (17.5 oz.)
150 ml water (5 fl. oz.)
100 ml rum (3.5 fl. oz.)

Alternative Recipe A

1 kg chestnut paste or ground chestnut pieces (35 oz.)
400 to 600 g butter (14 to 21 oz.)
120 to 180 ml water (4 to 6 fl. oz.)
80 to 120 ml rum (2.5 to 4 fl. oz.)

Alternative Recipe B

1 part butter cream
1 part chestnut puree or paste
rum

Recipe for a Small Quantity

250 g chestnut puree (9 oz.)
125 g butter (4.5 oz.)
50 ml water (1.5 fl. oz.) plus 25 ml rum (1 fl. oz.)
several drops of vanilla extract

Preparation

Chestnut cream should not be reheated; make only the quantity needed.

 Chestnut cream is fairly easy to prepare. Bring all raw ingredients to room temperature, to facilitate the emulsion of the cream.

No special equipment is required.

Allow approximately 15 minutes for its preparation.

Chestnut cream should be used soon after being made.

For this reason it is important to have the bases to be garnished ready, such as génoise sheets for a yule log or other cakes, or sweetened pie dough for the chestnut barquettes.

Chestnut cream sold commercially lacks the quality of the cream made by pastry chefs. Nor can it replace chestnut paste in texture and quality of ingredients.

There are many procedures for making chestnut cream; many offer only fair results.

Procedure

Softening the Chestnut Paste

By Hand

Scrape (fraise) the chestnut paste with a pastry cutter on a clean work surface. Place it in a bowl.

By Machine

Break up the chestnut paste into small pieces. Place it in a mixing bowl and mix at low speed with the paddle attachment. As the paste softens, scrape the bowl.

Creaming the Butter

With both the hand and machine methods, it is important that the butter be creamed to the same consistency as the chestnut paste, to make it easier to blend ingredients. The butter can be softened by tapping it with the rolling pin or by hand.

Incorporating the Butter

By Hand

Break up the softened butter into small pieces and slowly add them to the chestnut paste. Work the two with a wooden spatula or pastry scraper until the mixture becomes creamy. Working the mixture over a warm water bath makes blending the two ingredients easier.

By Machine

Add small pieces of the softened butter, a bit at a time, to the chestnut paste, while mixing on medium speed. Continue mixing until the batter becomes creamy.

Scrape the bowl and paddle occasionally to be sure the ingredients are well blended.

Heating the Water and Rum

The water and rum must be boiling when added to the batter.

Whipping the Chestnut Cream

By Hand

Incorporate the hot water and rum bit by bit to lighten the cream as it is whipped with the whisk. Scrape the sides of the bowl with a pastry scraper during this procedure.

By Machine

On medium or high speed, add the hot water and rum gradually.

It is very important that the water is as hot as possible when added to the mixture. It is the steam of the water

that causes the emulsion and creates the airiness of the cream.

Scrape the bowl occasionally to ensure a good blending of ingredients. The rum can be mixed with the water or added separately, after the water.

As the cream begins to lighten in color and become fluffy, increasing in volume, the paddle can be replaced with the whisk attachment.

The cream should be whipped until it is a light color and very creamy.

Storage

Chestnut cream can be refrigerated for 4 to 6 days at 5°C (40°F). It will also freeze well for several weeks.

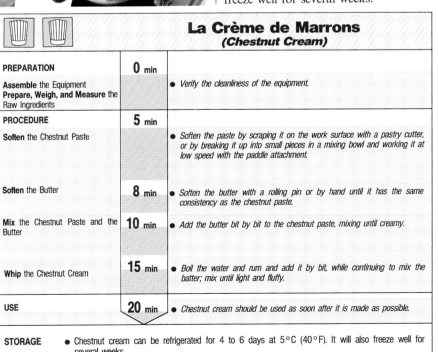

La Crème de Marrons
(Chestnut Cream)

PREPARATION	**0** min	
Assemble the Equipment **Prepare, Weigh, and Measure** the Raw Ingredients		• Verify the cleanliness of the equipment.
PROCEDURE	**5** min	
Soften the Chestnut Paste		• Soften the paste by scraping it on the work surface with a pastry cutter, or by breaking it up into small pieces in a mixing bowl and working it at low speed with the paddle attachment.
Soften the Butter	**8** min	• Soften the butter with a rolling pin or by hand until it has the same consistency as the chestnut paste.
Mix the Chestnut Paste and the Butter	**10** min	• Add the butter bit by bit to the chestnut paste, mixing until creamy.
Whip the Chestnut Cream	**15** min	• Boil the water and rum and add it by bit, while continuing to mix the batter; mix until light and fluffy.
USE	**20** min	• Chestnut cream should be used as soon after it is made as possible.
STORAGE		• Chestnut cream can be refrigerated for 4 to 6 days at 5°C (40°F). It will also freeze well for several weeks.

La crème mousseline (Mousseline cream)

History

The French word *mousse* means foamy and light. In pastry making, the word *mousseline* describes preparations that are light and delicate.

Mousseline cream is a derivative of crème pâtissière (pastry cream). It is more buttery yet lighter, between crème pâtissière and crème au beurre (butter cream). It is an excellent garniture or filling for certain desserts.

Uses

Mousseline cream is not used as often as pastry cream. This cream does not hold up well under warm conditions and cannot be baked.

For certain preparations, mousseline cream can replace pastry cream; for example, it can be used as a lighter cream for mille-feuilles (napoleons).

Mousseline cream can also be used to garnish and decorate desserts. With a pastry bag with a fluted tip, this cream can fill and decorate savarins and all pâte à choux (cream puff pastry) such as swans and baskets.

Equipment

Heavy-bottomed saucepan
Bowls (2)
Whisk
Pastry scrapers (2)
Drum sieve and paper for sifting
Plastic container
Electric mixer with mixing bowl and whisk attachment *or*
Bowl and whisk or hand mixer

Professional Recipe

1 L milk (34 fl. oz.)
500 g sugar (17.5 oz.)
4 eggs or 8 egg yolks
150 g flan powder (5 oz.)
500 g butter (17.5 oz.), softened
flavoring

Alternative Recipe

1 L milk (34 fl. oz.)
400 to 600 g granulated sugar (14 to 21 oz.)
3 to 6 eggs or 6 to 10 egg yolks
130 to 160 g flan powder (4.5 to 5.5 oz.) *or* 160 to 180 g flour (5.5 to 6.5 oz.)
500 to 600 g butter (17.5 to 21 oz.), softened
flavoring

Mousseline cream is somewhat difficult to prepare. Careful attention should be given to cooking the cream.

Soften the butter before it is incorporated.

Beating the cream is an important step.

No special equipment is required. Allow approximately 45 minutes for its preparation.

Mousseline cream should be used soon after it is made.

Recipe for a Small Quantity

250 ml milk (8.5 fl. oz.)
125 g granulated sugar (4.5 oz.)
1 egg or 2 egg yolks
40 g flan powder (1.5 oz.) *or* 50 g flour
  (1.5 oz.)
125 g butter (4.5 oz.), softened
flavoring

Preparation

Mousseline cream, like pastry cream, requires careful preparation and storage.
Be sure to use a heavy-bottomed saucepan, as this cream tends to burn easily because of its high sugar content.
The butter should be very soft, to prevent it from becoming grainy when beaten with the cool cream.

Procedure

Follow the same procedure as for pastry cream (see pages 27 to 29).

Preparing the Milk

See pastry cream.

Preparing the Batter

See pastry cream.
Heat and cook the mixture as for pastry cream.

Mixing and Cooking the Cream

Follow the procedure for pastry cream *but* cook the cream over lower heat. Because of its high sugar content, mousseline cream tends to stick more easily to the saucepan. For the same reason it is important to stir the cream constantly while it is cooking.
To verify doneness, follow the guidelines for pastry cream.
Off the flame, add half of the butter, then quickly cool the cream as for pastry cream.

Beating the Cream

Place the cooled cream in the bowl of the mixer (capable of holding four times the quantity of cream added). On low speed with the whisk attachment, incorpo-

rate the remaining softened butter Turn the machine up to medium speed for a few moments to ensure a complete blending of ingredients.

Then turn the machine to high speed for approximately 5 minutes and whip until the cream is light and fluffy.

When the butter is beaten into the cream, it forms an emulsion with the cream, which makes it fluffy and doubles its volume. The flan powder is made mostly of starch and helps to set up the cream after it has doubled in volume.

The flavoring should be added after the cream is finished to avoid evaporation of the liquor during the beating. If the liquor is added while the cream is being whipped, it will also make the mixture heavy and prevent it from rising fully.

As with pastry cream, mousseline cream can be flavored with any natural flavoring or liquor. Coloring is almost never added.

Storage

Mousseline cream can be refrigerated for up to, but not exceeding, 48 hours.

Note:

Mousseline cream can be finished (beaten) in small quantities at a time, following the same procedure given for larger quantities. This can be done by hand or using a hand-held mixer.

La Crème Mousseline
(Mousseline Cream)

PREPARATION	0 min	
Assemble the Equipment **Prepare, Weigh, and Measure** the Raw Ingredients		• Verify the cleanliness of the equipment. • Soften the butter. • Separate the yolks, if used.
PROCEDURE	5 min	
Prepare Pastry Cream		• Heat the milk and sugar together. • Whisk the yolks and sugar until a ribbon is formed. • Add the flan powder or flour and blend. • Temper the mixture with the hot milk. • While the mixture is cooking, carefully watch the bottom of the saucepan to prevent the mixture from sticking.
Incorporate Half the Butter	20 min	• Using a whisk, add half the butter to the hot cream, off the heat.
Cool the Cream	22 min	• Transfer the cream to a stainless steel sheet pan. • Butter the surface of the cream to prevent a skin from forming.
Incorporate the Remaining Butter	50 min	• Add the rest of the butter and, with a mixer, using the whisk attachment, beat at medium speed, until the butter and cream are well blended.
Beat the Cooled Cream	55 min	• Beat the cream at high speed until it doubles in volume.
Flavor the Cream	1 hr	• After the cream has doubled in volume, flavor to taste.
STORAGE:		• Mousseline cream can be stored up to 48 hours in the refrigerator at 5°C (40°F). It freezes well for up to several weeks.

La crème Paris-Brest (Paris-Brest cream)

History

The Paris-Brest cake was invented before the cream of the same name. The Paris-Brest cake, named for a popular French bicycle race, is usually shaped in circles, to represent bicycle wheels, and in strips or zigzags, to represent the roads traveled in the race.

Originally, the pastry was filled with Saint-Honoré cream, plain or flavored with praline (hazelnut) paste, or with crème Chantilly (sweetened, flavored whipped cream). Then a pastry chef of the Basse-Normandie region of France decided to show his support of the cyclists by making them a cream high in calories to fortify them for this famous race.

Paris-Brest cream is high in sugar and rich with butter.

Uses

This is the cream now most commonly used to garnish the Paris-Brest cake, regardless of the size or shape of the pastry.

It can also be used to fill other desserts as well as individual cakes.

Equipment

Mixing bowl and whisk or paddle attachment
Bowl for the pastry cream
Bowl for the butter
Bowl for the praline (hazelnut) paste
Pastry scraper
Pastry bag and medium-sized fluted tip (to fill pastries)

Professional Recipe

1 kg pastry cream (35 oz.), cold
500 g softened butter (17.5 oz.)
250 g praline paste (9 oz.)
100 ml rum (3.5 fl oz.), or to taste
1 Tbsp. vanilla extract

Alternative Recipe

1 kg pastry cream (35 oz.)
400 to 600 g butter (14 to 21 oz.)
200 to 300 g praline paste (7 to 10.5 oz.)
flavoring to taste

Recipe for a Small Quantity

To fill one Paris-Brest cake serving eight, or ten individual cakes

250 g pastry cream (9 oz.)
150 g butter (5 oz.)
75 g praline paste (2.5 oz.)
rum, to taste

Preparation

Weigh and place each item in a separate bowl. The pastry cream should be cooled to room temperature.

Soften the butter so it is the same consistency as the pastry cream. The praline paste (see praline paste, pages 114 to 117) should be smooth, without lumps, and not grainy. It can be scraped on the marble (fraised) if necessary, to smooth it out.

Note:

Use only butter for Paris-Brest cream; any other shortening will produce poor results.

Procedure

Mixing the Butter and Praline Paste

Blend the softened butter and the praline paste. Do not overwork the mixture to obtain a perfect blending of ingredients.

Paris-Brest cream is easy to prepare.

Be sure to soften the praline paste so it will easily mix into the cream, ensuring an homogeneous mixture.

No special equipment is required.

Allow 20 minutes to make Paris-Brest cream, which should be used soon after it is made.

It is normal to find streaking of the two ingredients.

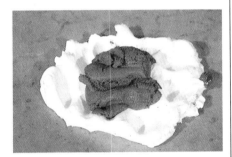

If overworked, the butter will become too soft and the cream will not properly increase in volume when the butter/praline mixture is added to the pastry cream.

Combining the Butter/Praline Mixture with the Pastry Cream

Place the butter/praline mixture and pastry cream into a mixing bowl.

When working with a large amount, or if the butter is too firm, begin mixing with the paddle attachment. When using a small quantity or when the mixture is easy to work, use the whisk attachment. In either case, blend the ingredients at slow speed, then finish beating at medium speed.

Whipping the Cream

Beat the cream at high speed for 4 to 6 minutes. The cream should double in volume and be smooth and creamy.

Flavoring the Cream

Slow the mixer to add the flavoring; this will prevent air bubbles.

The flavoring is always added at the end of the mixing step for two reasons:

- liquor evaporates during beating

- liquor can make creams heavy, preventing the cream from fully increasing in volume.

Transferring the Cream

Transfer the cream into a bowl. It is best to use Paris-Brest cream immediately after its completion.

If the cream cannot be used right away, cover the bowl with plastic wrap and refrigerate at 5°C (40°F).

Storage

Paris-Brest cream has a limited storage time, 48 hours at 5°C (40°F). If added to a dessert and well wrapped, it can be stored for 3 to 4 days maximum in the refrigerator, 5°C (40°F).

La Crème Paris-Brest (Paris-Brest Cream)

PREPARATION	0 min	
Assemble the Equipment Prepare, Weigh, and Measure the Raw Ingredients		● Verify the cleanliness of the equipment. ● Have the pastry cream ready.
PROCEDURE	5 min	
Blend the Butter and the Praline Paste		● Blend by hand or with the pastry scraper. ● Do not overwork the mixture.
Mix the Cream	10 min	● Add the butter/praline mixture to the pastry cream in a mixing bowl. ● With the paddle or whisk attachment, blend the ingredients at low speed, then increase to medium speed.
Beat the Cream		● Beat the cream at high speed for 4 to 6 minutes. ● The cream should double in volume.
Add Flavoring	15 min	● At reduced speed, add the flavoring.
TRANSFERRING	20 min	● Transfer the cream to a bowl and use immediately if possible.

STORAGE: ● Paris-Brest cream can be refrigerated for 24 to 48 hours at 5°C (40°F). If filled in cakes, it can be stored for 3 to 4 days maximum.

Les ganaches montées
(Whipped chocolate ganache)

History

Ganache, it is assumed, originated in the southwest of France, where the word *ganacher* stands for *patauger*. In English, *patauger* means to wade or splash through something, which describes the chocolate when a hot liquid is poured over and mixed into it.

No eggs are used in recipes for ganache; if they were, this cream would be in the family of mousses.

Uses

Ganaches have been used for a long time in chocolate making. They are used for various candy fillings, the most well known of which are for truffles.

Ganaches can also be beaten with a whisk to lighten them for filling and frosting various desserts and cakes of all sizes.

In a semiliquid state, without being whipped, they can be used to glaze cakes.

Easy to prepare, many varieties of flavors and colors exist:

- *blonde* **ganaches** made with milk chocolate
- *brown* **ganaches** made with dark chocolate
- *white* **ganaches** made with white chocolate
- ganaches flavored with *tea, coffee, honey,* or *mint.*

Equipment

Saucepans (1 or 2, depending on the recipe)
Bowl, whisk, pastry scraper
Cutting board and chef's knife
Mixer with bowl and whisk attachment
Bowl for the finished ganache

Professional recipe

1 kg chocolate (35 oz.)
500 ml crème fraîche or heavy cream (17 fl. oz.)
flavoring

Alternative Recipe

1 kg chocolate (35 oz.)
250 ml unsweetened evaporated milk (8.5 fl. oz.)
250 g butter (9 oz.)
flavoring

Other Alternative Recipes

See recipes for *ganaches confiseur* (ganache fillings), pages 124 to 125.

Beaten ganaches are easy to make.

Carefully observe the consistency of the ganache when it is beaten.

Allow 1 hour for preparation.

Preparation

With the chef's knife, chop the chocolate into small pieces on a cutting board. Place the chocolate pieces in a clean, dry bowl.

Melt the chopped chocolate in the bowl over a warm water bath, approximately 50°C (120°F), or soften the chocolate in a proofing box for 1 hour at 50°C (120°F).

Prepare the crème fraîche (or heavy cream), evaporated milk, or butter. In France (where raw creams are available), it is preferable to use pasteurized crème fraîche or heavy cream from an unopen container for sanitary reasons. These creams need only be heated to 80° to 85°C (175° to 185°F). If the cream is unpasteurized, or from a container open for more than 24 hours, it must be brought to a full boil to eliminate any acid taste. If the cream is not very fresh, the storage time of the ganache will be limited.

If butter is being added, it should be melted with the crème fraîche or evaporated milk, or it can be softened and mixed into the melted chocolate.

Ganaches can be flavored in two ways. Flavorings such as tea or coffee should be infused in the evaporated milk or cream by adding them to the liquid and then boiling. Cool the liquid with the flavoring, strain, and reheat. If liquors are used as flavoring, they are added after the ganache is made.

Procedure

Making the Mixture

Pour the hot liquid (crème fraîche, evaporated milk, butter) over the melted or softened chocolate.

Mix with a whisk until the chocolate is completely melted and the mixture is homogeneous.

Cooling the Mixture

Cool at room temperature. Stir occasionally so the ganache will thicken and cool evenly. Stirring will help cool it more quickly.

The ganache can also be cooled in the refrigerator, 5°C (40°F). In this case, do not let the ganache become too firm.

Whipping the Ganache

The ganache is ready to be whipped once it has cooled. To test for this, stir the ganache with a whisk, then hold the whisk up. If the ganache sticks to and does not run off the whisk, it is ready to be whipped.

Place the cooled ganache in the mixing bowl with the whisk attachment. Turn the mixer to high speed and whip for 4 to 6 minutes until the ganache reaches the desired consistency.

Flavoring

Liquors should be added at the end of beating; otherwise, their flavor might evaporate and the cream will not fully rise.

Ganaches that are not beaten are flavored as they begin to thicken.

Using the Ganache

It is best to use the ganache immediately, or it may become too firm and harden. If this happens, it can be warmed, but it will fall and lose its lightness.

Storage

Ganaches can be stored in the refrigerator at 5°C (40°F). Length of storage depends on the ingredients used. Ganache made with heavy cream can be stored for up to one week. Ganaches can also be frozen for several weeks at −30°C (−18°F).

Les Ganaches Montée (Whipped Chocolate Ganaches)		
PREPARATION **Assemble** the Equipment **Prepare, Weigh, and Measure** the Raw Ingredients	**0** min	• Chop the chocolate and soften or melt it. • If necessary, add flavoring to be infused in the evaporated milk or cream.
PROCEDURE **Heat** the Liquid	**5** min	• The heavy cream should be heated to 80° to 85°C (175° to 185°F) if pasteurized. • Bring the liquid to a boil; add the butter if used.
Make the Batter	**10** min	• Pour the hot liquid over the softened or chopped chocolate and mix until well blended.
Cool the Batter		• Stir the batter occasionally with the whisk as it cools.
Beat the Ganache	**45** min	• Once the batter is cool and firm, it can be beaten. • Beat at high speed in the electric mixer with the whisk attachment.
Flavor	**50** min	• Add the flavoring (liquor) at the end of beating.
APPLICATION	**1** hr	• Use immediately, or keep at room temperature until needed.
STORAGE:		• Beaten ganaches have limited storage in the refrigerator, depending on the recipe made. They can be frozen for several weeks once filled in cakes.

Chapter 3 Light-textured creams

La crème au beurre aux blancs
(Meringue butter cream)

A. Using Italian Meringue

This cream is particularly light because it includes Italian meringue.

It keeps well even during the hot season, but its texture is not as smooth as butter cream made with cooked sugar and egg yolks.

Equipment

Machine Method

Mixing bowl and whisk attachment
Copper sugar pan
Skimmer
Pastry brush
Water for rinsing pastry brush
Bowl for butter
Pastry scraper
Thermometer (optional)
Bowl for finished cream

   Butter cream with egg whites is not difficult to prepare, provided that correct procedures are followed.
Be especially careful cooking the sugar and beating the egg whites. Adding the cooked sugar to the beaten egg whites is somewhat difficult.
Use traditional pastry equipment. Allow about 30 minutes for its preparation.
This cream can be frozen.

Hand Method

Mixing bowl
Whisk
Copper sugar pan
Skimmer
Pastry brush
Water for pastry brush
Pastry scraper
Thermometer (optional)
Bowl for finished cream

Recipes

Professional Recipe

700 g sugar (24.5 oz.), cooked to firm ball
    stage, 118° to 120°C (244° to 248°F)
12 egg whites, beaten to stiff peaks
300 g sugar (10.5 oz.), to stiffen the
    whites
1250 g butter (44 oz.)
flavoring

Alternative Recipe

700 g sugar (24.5 oz.), cooked to firm
    ball stage, 118° to 120°C (244° to
    248°F)
10 to 14 egg whites
200 to 400 g sugar (7 to 14 oz.), to stiffen
    the whites
1250 g butter (44 oz.)
flavoring

Recipe for a Small Quantity

200 g sugar (7 oz.), cooked to firm ball
    stage, 120°C (248°F)
3 egg whites
100 g sugar (3.5 oz.), to stiffen the whites
300 g butter (10.5 oz.)
flavoring

Preparation

Use fresh egg whites from recently
separated eggs. Gather all the necessary
equipment for cooking the sugar. Soften
the butter.

Procedure

Prepare Italian meringue (see volume 1,
pages 82 to 83).

Cooking the Sugar

Cook the sugar with 30 percent of its
weight in water to a temperature of
120°C (248°F). Take the necessary precautions (see Cooking Sugar, pages 14
to 17).

Beating the Egg Whites

Get the egg whites ready for the addition of the sugar. See Beating Egg Whites
in volume 1, pages 78 to 80.
- hand method: start beating the whites
  as soon as the sugar starts to boil
- machine method: start beating the
  whites when the sugar reaches the
  thread stage, 110°C (230°F)
Once the eggs have been beaten to
stiff peaks, add the sugar needed for
stiffening.

Adding the Cooked Sugar

When the sugar has cooked to the
right stage, pour it in a thin, steady
stream over the beaten and stiffened egg
whites while continuing to beat. Be careful not to let any of the cooked sugar
fall onto the whisk.

When all the cooked sugar has been
added, scrape the sides of the mixing
bowl with the pastry scraper. Continue
beating the whites at medium speed until
they have completely cooled.

Adding the Butter

When the beaten egg whites have
cooled to the point where they are lukewarm, add the softened butter in chunks,
adding a bit at a time.

Once the butter has been added, continue mixing at slow speed until the

cream is perfectly smooth. Scrape the
sides from time to time with the pastry
scraper.

When the cream is finished, transfer it
to a stainless steel bowl or a plastic tub.

Storage

This butter cream can be kept refrigerated at 5°C (40°F), in a covered plastic
or stainless steel tub for up to 8 days.

B. Using Swiss Meringue

This is a good, quick method for preparing a light and appealing cream that keeps well even in summer. Like butter cream prepared with Italian meringue, however, it does not have the finesse of butter cream made with eggs and cooked sugar.

Equipment

Mixing bowl and whisk attachment
Pastry scraper
Measuring cup
Bowl for holding finished butter cream

Recipes

Professional Recipe

12 egg whites
1 kg granulated sugar (35 oz.)
1250 g butter (44 oz.)
flavoring

Alternative Recipe

12 egg whites
900 g granulated sugar (32 oz.)
50 g trimoline (1.5 oz.)
1 kg to 1300 g butter (35 to 45 oz.)
flavoring

Recipe for a Small Quantity

3 egg whites
250 g sugar (9 oz.)
300 g butter (10.5 oz.)
flavoring

Preparation

Separate the eggs and soften the butter.

Procedure

Prepare Swiss meringue (see volume 1, pages 84 to 85).

Combine the egg whites and sugar.

Heat the mixture to 45° to 50°C (113° to 122°F) by placing the mixing bowl directly over the flame. Beat rapidly without stopping, until the mixture has a thick, smooth texture. The bottom of the bowl should be lukewarm.

Adding the Butter

When the meringue has been beaten until thick but is still warm, add the softened butter in small pieces in several stages. Continue beating, scraping the sides of the bowl from time to time with the pastry scraper, until the mixture is smooth and homogeneous.

Transfer the cream to a stainless steel

bowl or a plastic tub.

Storage

This butter cream can be kept refrigerated, 5°C (40°F) in a covered plastic or stainless steel container for up to 8 days.

La Crème au Beurre aux Blancs
(Meringue Butter Cream)

PREPARATION	**0** min	
Assemble the Equipment Prepare, Weigh, and Measure the Raw Ingredients		● Make sure that all equipment is clean. ● Separate the eggs. ● Soften the butter.
PROCEDURE	**5** min	
1. Using Italian Meringue		
Cook the Sugar		● Take recommended precautions and cook to 120°C (248°F).
Beat the Egg Whites	**15** min	● By hand, start beating when the cooked sugar comes to a simmer. ● By machine, start beating the whites when the sugar reaches the thread stage, 110°C (230°F).
Add Sugar to Stiffen the Whites	**20** min	
Add the Cooked Sugar	**22** min	● Add the cooked sugar to the beaten whites in a thin stream while beating. Continue beating until the mixture is lukewarm.
Add the Butter	**30** min	● While the meringue is still lukewarm, add the softened butter a bit at a time.
Scrape the Bowl	**32** min	
Smooth the Cream	**38** min	● Beat the cream until it is perfectly smooth and homogeneous.
2. Using Swiss Meringue		
Heat the Egg White/Sugar Mixture	**5** min	● Beat over the flame until the mixture reaches 45° to 50°C (113° to 122°F).
Beat the Warm Mixture	**13** min	● Continue beating until the mixture is dense and smooth. ● Remove from the heat and, with mixer and whisk attachment, beat on medium or high speed.
Add the Butter	**20** min	● When the meringue is thick and lukewarm, add the butter a bit at a time.
Scrape the Bowl	**22** min	
Continue Beating	**28** min	● Continue beating until the cream is smooth and homogeneous.
TRANSFERRING		● Place the cream in a stainless steel or plastic container.
STORAGE:		● Up to 8 days in the refrigerator, 5°C (40°F) in a plastic or stainless steel container

La crème Saint-Honoré
(Saint-Honoré cream)

History

Saint-Honoré cream is derived directly from crème pâtissière (pastry cream). Beaten egg whites are simply added to crème pâtissière to lighten it.

This cream is sometimes called *crème légère* or *crème Chiboust,* after Chiboust, who invented the gâteau Saint-Honoré around 1840.

Originally, the border of the gâteau Saint-Honoré was made with pâte à brioche.

Not until the beginning of the twentieth century was the modern method of using pâte à choux used.

Warning

It is essential that certain precautions be followed in the preparation of this cream.

Because of the addition of raw egg whites, crème Saint-Honoré has frequently been a cause of food poisoning.

In each case of food poisoning that has been studied, the egg whites have been the cause because of contamination of the hen's oviduct before laying.

This was primarily true in old-style egg hatcheries, where the hens would search for food in dung and garbage.

The principal causes of this food poisoning have been greatly reduced in modern hatcheries.

Food poisoning may also be caused by careless handling of the cream and storage for excessively long periods.

Crème Saint-Honoré is an excellent cream and may be safely prepared and served provided that the necessary precautions are scrupulously adhered to.

It is especially important that the cream be stored only for the recommended period.

The maximum storage time also depends on the chosen method of preparation.

   Crème Saint-Honoré requires constant attention and careful organization during its preparation.

It consists of two preparations, crème pâtissière and Italian or French meringue, which are made simultaneously.

Be extremely careful in following all instructions regarding storage and cleanliness.

Use traditional pastry equipment.

This cream requires about 30 minutes to prepare.

Do not store for longer than 12 hours under any circumstances.

Uses

Crème Saint-Honoré is used primarily as a decorative garniture for large and miniature gâteaux Saint-Honoré, as a filling for pâte à choux preparations (such as pastry swans), and as cake decoration.

Crème Saint-Honoré is rarely used in modern French pastry, primarily because it is difficult to prepare and store. Numerous precautions must be followed.

Equipment

For the Pastry Cream

Saucepan
Mixing bowl
Whisk
Drum sieve
Parchment paper
Plastic pastry scrapers
Large mixing bowl with water bath for transferring the cream
Clean kitchen towel

For Beating the Egg Whites

Stainless steel mixing bowl and whisk *or* Mixing bowl and whisk attachment
Plastic pastry scraper

For Mixing

Rubber spatula
Plastic pastry scraper

For Applying Cream

Large pastry bag with star tip or a special gâteau Saint-Honoré tip
Plastic pastry scraper

Recipes

Professional Recipe

500 ml milk (17 fl. oz.)
250 g sugar (9 oz.)
8 egg yolks
50 g flour (1.5 oz.)
4 leaves (8 g) gelatin (1/4 oz.)
8 egg whites, beaten to stiff peaks and stiffened with 100 g sugar (3.5 oz.) taken from the recipe
vanilla/rum

Alternative Recipe

500 ml milk (17 fl. oz.)
200 to 300 g sugar (7 to 10.5 oz.)
8 to 12 egg yolks
50 to 80 g flour or cornstarch (1.5 to 2.5 oz.)
3 to 6 leaves (6 to 12 g) gelatin (1/4 to 1/2 oz.)
8 to 12 egg whites, beaten to stiff peaks
vanilla/rum

Recipe for a Small Quantity

For a gâteau Saint-Honoré serving eight to ten people

250 ml milk (8.5 fl. oz.)
130 g sugar (4.5 oz.)
4 egg yolks
25 g flour (1 oz.)
3 leaves (6 g) gelatin (1/4 oz.)
4 egg whites, beaten to stiff peaks

Preparation

Always try to prepare this cream just before it is needed so that it does not sit for long periods before being served. Make sure that the other components for the gâteau Saint-Honoré are ready before preparing the cream so that it can be used right away. The pastry base with its surrounding miniature cream puffs should be ready before preparation of the cream begins.

Make sure that all the pastry equipment is perfectly clean. This is one situation where a stainless steel bowl should be used instead of a copper one for beating the egg whites: traces of copper can oxidize and form toxic compounds in the cream.

Carefully check the freshness of the raw ingredients, especially the egg whites, which should have no odor. It is also important to avoid running the finger around the inside of the egg to push the remaining egg white out. The area just under the shell usually contains bacteria, which could cause the cream to turn.

Soften the gelatin in cold water and gently squeeze out the excess water before incorporating it into the cream.

Procedure

There are several methods used for preparing crème Saint-Honoré. Some are easier than others but will not produce the finesse and texture of a perfectly prepared classic cream.

Hand Method

Preparing the Pastry Cream

Prepare a pastry cream with the yolks, the flour, and 150 g (5 oz.) of sugar (see pastry cream, pages 27 to 29).

When the pastry cream has boiled for at least 3 minutes, remove it from the

flame and stir in the softened gelatin leaves. Continue stirring until the gelatin has completely dissolved in the cream; then transfer the finished cream to a clean bowl.

If working alone, keep this finished cream in a hot water bath (bain-marie) while preparing the whites. The cream can also simply be covered with a clean towel to keep it warm.

It is preferable for two people to work at a time so that one can beat the egg whites while the other prepares the cream. Holding the cream in a bain-marie increases the risk of bacterial growth.

Beating the Egg Whites

If two people are working at once, one should beat the whites while the other prepares the cream. In this way, both the whites and the pastry cream can be used immediately. The egg whites, once beaten to stiff peaks, should be stiffened further with the remaining sugar.

Combining the Egg Whites with the Pastry Cream

Flavor the pastry cream with rum, vanilla, or other flavoring before adding the egg whites. The whites should be folded quickly into the hot cream using the same method as for making ladyfingers (see volume 1, pages 68 to 71).

Note: When folding egg whites with a heavier mixture, remember to mix one-fourth of the whites into the mixture first, to lighten it. The remaining egg whites can then be carefully folded into the mixture.

To fold, use either a whisk or a spatula. Give a final beating with the whisk to eliminate any unincorporated

egg white, which would give the cream an unappealing appearance and would make the cream more perishable.

Machine Method

a. Prepare the pastry cream as described above, but use only 125 g (4.5 oz) of sugar.

b. Beat the egg whites with the electric mixer. When they have stiff peaks, add the second half of the sugar to stiffen them further.

c. Add the gelatin and flavoring to the pastry cream. Turn the mixer to medium speed and pour the still-hot pastry cream mixture over the egg whites.

d. Do not continue to beat the mixture once the pastry cream has been added. If necessary, the mixture can be smoothed with either a skimmer or a rubber spatula.

Piping Out the Cream

Whether the crème Saint-Honoré has been prepared by hand or in the electric mixer, it must be used before it cools. If not, it tends to break apart, fall, and become runny. The gelatin also sets, making it nearly impossible to pipe out the cream with a pastry bag.

Once the crème Saint-Honoré has been piped out onto the finished gâteau, it should be placed in the refrigerator, 5°C (40°F), until it has completely cooled and set.

This is the classic method for preparing the cream and also gives the best results.

Storage

Crème Saint-Honoré should be served within 6 to 8 hours after completion. It cannot be frozen.

Flavoring Crème Saint-Honoré

Crème Saint-Honoré can be flavored with coffee or chocolate, which should be added to the pastry cream after it is cooked, or to the hot milk, at the beginning.

Coffee: use an extremely concentrated mixture of coffee extract that has been strengthened with additional instant coffee granules.

Chocolate: add 50 g (1.5 oz.) melted unsweetened chocolate or cocoa powder to the milk used for making the pastry cream.

Alternative Methods

Prepare an Italian meringue by adding three-quarters of the sugar cooked to 120°C (248°F) to the beaten whites.

Prepare a pastry cream using the rest of the sugar, but do not use any gelatin.

Pour the hot pastry cream over the hot Italian meringue.

When this method is used, the crème Saint-Honoré can be stored for up to 12 hours before serving.

The professional chef who sells gâteaux Saint-Honoré in a retail establishment should inform his clientele that the cake must be served soon after purchase.

				La Crème Saint-Honoré *(Saint-Honoré Cream)*		
PREPARATION		**0** min				
Assemble the Equipment Prepare, Weigh, and Measure the Raw Ingredients			• Make sure all equipment is clean. • Put the gelatin in cold water to soften. • Make sure the pâte à choux bases are ready to use.			
PROCEDURE		**5** min				
Prepare the Pastry Cream			• The preparation is the same as for pastry cream used for other purposes.			
Add the Gelatin		**20** min	• Add the soaked and drained gelatin leaves. • Mix with a whisk.			
Hold the Pastry Cream/Gelatin Mixture		**21** min	• Cover with a clean towel. • Do not allow the mixture to cool too much.			
Beat the Egg Whites		**22** min	• Beat by hand or with an electric mixer, taking the usual precautions.			
Stiffen the Whites		**28** min	• Use the sugar reserved for this purpose.			
Fold in the Cream		**30** min	• Fold one-quarter of the volume of the whites into the pastry cream to lighten it. The remainder of the whites should then be added all at once and folded in with a spatula.			
PIPING OUT THE CREAM		**35** min	• Pipe out the cream immediately, before it has time to cool. • Use a pastry bag.			
STORAGE: • Crème Saint-Honoré has very limited storage: a maximum of 6 to 8 hours in the refrigerator, 5°C (40°F).						

La crème Chantilly (Chantilly cream)

Uses

Crème Chantilly is used for frosting a wide variety of cakes and ice creams. It is also a good accompaniment to fresh and canned fruits and berries. It is used:

- as a filling: strawberry, red currant, blueberry, black currant tarts
- as a filling and decoration: Saint-Honoré, choux (cream puffs), cygnes (cream puff pastry swans), paniers, savarins, Mont-Blanc
- to decorate ice creams: ice-cream specialties, such as vacherins, for which a soft center is desirable; parfaits; frozen soufflés

Crème Chantilly should always be eaten as soon as it is prepared. It is sensitive to warmth and the slightest changes in temperature. Because it tends to melt, it must always be prepared at the last minute, just before serving.

History and Definition

Louis XIV first tasted crème Chantilly when it was served to him in 1665 by his former chef, Vatel. Vatel was by then in the service of the Prince de Condé, who had his palace in Chantilly, outside Paris.

In France, crème Chantilly is usually prepared with crème fraîche, which is thicker than American heavy cream and has an agreeable sour taste. Although it is thicker, it does not have a higher butterfat content than heavy cream. American heavy cream may be substituted for crème fraîche when making crème Chantilly.

Crème Chantilly is simply crème fraîche or heavy cream that is whipped with sugar and vanilla.

Whichever cream is used, it should contain at least 30 percent butterfat.

Note: Other creams, such as those based on Italian meringue, cannot be called crème Chantilly, but should be referred to simply as whipped creams.

Equipment

Machine Method

Mixing bowl and whisk attachment
Plastic pastry scraper
Measuring cup
Drum sieve
Parchment paper for the sugar
Bowl to hold finished cream

Hand Method

Stainless steel mixing bowl
Flexible whisk
Plastic pastry scraper
Measuring cup
Drum sieve
Parchment paper for the sugar

Professional Recipe

1 L heavy cream (34 fl. oz.)
150 g confectioners' sugar (5 oz.)
1 Tbsp. vanilla extract

Alternative Recipe

1 L heavy cream or crème fraîche (34 fl. oz.)
200 to 300 ml cold water or milk (7 to 10 fl. oz.)
120 to 180 g granulated or confectioners' sugar (4 to 6 oz.)
several drops vanilla extract (optional)

Recipe for a Small Quantity

250 ml heavy cream (8.5 fl. oz.)
40 g confectioners' sugar (1.5 oz.)
several drops vanilla extract or 1 tsp. Kirsch

Crème Chantilly is easy to prepare, provided that correct procedures are followed. Always use cream that has been well chilled; 5°C (40°F) is best.

Confectioners' sugar is preferable to granulated.

The cream may be prepared either by hand or with an electric mixer. This cream requires 10 minutes to prepare.

It will not keep longer than 24 hours.

Preparation

When making crème Chantilly, the choice of cream is extremely important for the final result.

In France, two types of cream are available (see above):

- crème fraîche
- crème fleurette (heavy cream)

French-style crème fraîche is more difficult to store than American-style heavy cream because it has undergone a partial fermentation before pasteurization. In France, however, it is often preferred because of the distinctive flavor it lends to the finished crème Chantilly.

Whatever cream is being used, it is important that all the utensils and the cream itself be well chilled, 5°C (40°F), and clean before beating.

It is often helpful to put the mixing bowl used for beating the cream into the freezer a few minutes beforehand. This keeps the cream cool during beating and will help the finished cream hold its shape.

Procedure

Crème Chantilly can be prepared either by hand or with an electric mixer. There are also special machines that are used to prepare crème Chantilly to order.

Hand Method

Put the cream into a chilled bowl that can hold seven to eight times the amount of cream to be beaten. Make sure the cream is well chilled, 5°C (40°F).

If using crème fraîche, add cold water or milk until the cream lightly coats a finger or spoon.

Flavorings such as vanilla or Kirsch can be added to the cream before or after beating.

If granulated sugar is being used, it must be added before beating. Sugar that dissolves during the beating of the cream gives the crème Chantilly a thicker, stiffer texture and somewhat limits the incorporation of air into the cream.

The movement of the whisk causes the particles of butterfat contained in the cream to break up and form an emulsion with the air being beaten into the cream.

It is preferable to beat confectioners' sugar into the cream after it is stiff.

Beating

Use a flexible whisk. Start with a slow, regular movement and build up speed as the cream begins to stiffen.

Checking the Consistency

Stop beating as soon as the cream forms a point on the end of the whisk. The cream should hold the shape of the tracks left by the whisk and should have doubled in volume.

Warning! Do not overbeat the cream or it will turn into butter. This is especially true when using crème fraîche.

Final Stiffening of the Cream

If the sugar has been added to the cream before beating, beat it with the whisk using a rapid, circular movement. Do not beat it too long. Whip it quickly and energetically to avoid overbeating.

When beating unsweetened cream, add the sifted confectioners' sugar all at once and mix it in gently with the whisk.

Applying the Cream

Once the crème Chantilly is ready, it should be used as quickly as possible. The finished pastries should be kept in the refrigerator until served, 5°C (40°F).

If the cream has been kept waiting and has become runny, it can be stiffened by quickly beating it for a short time with a whisk.

Machine Method

The same precautions apply when using the electric mixer as when preparing the cream by hand. Careful attention must be paid to the cream when beating in the machine because it is very easy to overbeat and turn the cream into butter. A few seconds too long on high speed will ruin the cream.

When preparing crème Chantilly in the electric mixer, lightly beat the sugar into the cream by hand in order to dissolve the sugar without overbeating the cream. Once the sugar has dissolved, the bowl should be chilled for a few minutes before starting the final beating.

Storage

Crème Chantilly should be stored at all times in the refrigerator in a cool place. Once prepared, it should never be stored for longer than 24 hours. Crème Chantilly may be frozen, provided it has already been applied to a finished pastry.

La Crème Chantilly
(Chantilly Cream)

PREPARATION	**0** min	
Assemble the Equipment **Prepare, Weigh, and Measure** the Raw Ingredients		• Make sure that all the equipment is clean. • Chill the mixing bowl in the refrigerator. • Add milk or water to the cream if crème fraîche is being used. • Sift the confectioners' sugar if used.
PROCEDURE	**5** min	
Whip the Cream		• Use a hand whisk to dissolve granulated sugar (if used) in the cream before beating.
Check the Cream	**12** min	• The cream should double in volume. • It should be stiff and form a point on the end of the whisk.
Add Sugar and Stiffen the Cream	**13** min	• Add the sugar after the cream is beaten if confectioners' sugar is used. • Use a whisk. • Stiffen the cream using a rapid circular motion.
APPLYING THE CREAM	**15** min	• Use the cream immediately if possible. • If the cream must wait, keep it in the refrigerator, 5°C (40°F). Cream that has been stored before use often requires a quick, final beating to restore it to the desired consistency.

STORAGE:
- Crème Chantilly can be stored in the refrigerator, 5°C (40°F), after it has been applied to the finished pastry. Never hold it longer than 24 hours. It may be frozen after being applied to the final pastry.

Les crèmes fouettée et fondante

(Whipped and chocolate whipped creams)

Whipped Cream

Definition

Whipped cream (crème fouetée) is chilled crème fraîche or heavy cream that has been beaten until it becomes stiff and airy.

Whipped cream can be flavored in any way—using extracts, liqueurs, or fruit purees, for example. It can also be sweetened in the same way as crème Chantilly, using granulated sugar, confectioners' sugar, or Italian meringue.

Occasionally, professional pastry chefs add gelatin to whipped cream to help it remain stiff longer.

Uses

Whipped cream is often combined with other creams to lighten their texture and give them more delicacy.

It is also used in frozen preparations such as parfaits and frozen soufflés.

Whipped cream is also used to lighten bavarian creams and diplomates.

Finally, whipped cream serves to lighten frozen mousses, frozen sabayons, and frozen cakes.

Equipment

Machine Method

Mixing bowl and whisk attachment
Measuring cup
Plastic pastry scraper
Drum sieve
Parchment paper for the sugar
Copper sugar pan
Thermometer
Pastry brush
Skimmer
Bowl for the finished cream

Hand Method

Copper or stainless steel bowl for beating the whites
Flexible whisk
Measuring cup
Plastic pastry scraper
Drum sieve
Parchment paper for the sugar
Copper sugar pan
Pastry brush
Skimmer
Bowl for the finished cream
Thermometer

Professional Recipe

1 L heavy cream (34 fl. oz.)
400 to 500 g Italian meringue (14 to 17.5 oz.) *or* 150 g confectioners' sugar (5 oz.)
2 to 4 leaves (4 to 8 g) gelatin (1/8 to 1/4 oz), optional
flavoring

Other Recipes

Coffee-flavored Whipped Cream
1 L heavy cream (34 fl. oz.)
40 ml coffee extract (1.5 fl. oz.)
450 g Italian meringue (16 oz.) *or* 150 g confectioners' sugar (5 oz.)
gelatin (optional)

Chocolate-flavored Whipped Cream
1 L heavy cream (34 fl. oz.)
100 g sifted cocoa powder (3.5 oz.)
450 g Italian meringue (16 oz.) *or* 150 g confectioners' sugar (5 oz.)
gelatin (optional)

 Both these creams are easy to prepare. Be careful when melting the chocolate; it should be carefully folded into the whipped cream.

These creams require traditional pastry equipment.

Allow 20 minutes for their preparation.

These creams should be used soon after preparation. Once applied to a final pastry, they freeze quite well.

Praline-flavored Whipped Cream

1 L heavy cream (34 fl. oz.)
60 g confectioners' sugar (2 oz.)
gelatin (optional)
250 g praline paste (9 oz.)

After the cream has been whipped, lighten the praline paste with about one-fourth of the cream before the final folding.

Vanilla-flavored Whipped Cream

1 L heavy cream (34 fl. oz.)
5 to 10 ml vanilla extract (1 to 2 tsp.)
450 g Italian meringue (16 oz.) *or* 150 g confectioners' sugar (5 oz.)

Liquor-flavored Whipped Cream

1 L heavy cream (34 fl. oz.)
50 ml liquor (1.5 fl. oz.), such as whiskey, Cognac, or Kirsch
450 g Italian meringue (16 oz.) *or* 150 g confectioners' sugar (5 oz.)
gelatin (optional)
several drops vanilla extract (optional)

Liqueur-flavored Whipped Cream

1 L heavy cream (34 fl. oz.)
50 ml liqueur (1.5 fl. oz.), such as Grand Marnier or Cointreau
gelatin (optional)
several drops vanilla extract (optional)
450 g Italian meringue (16 oz.) *or* 150 g confectioners' sugar (5 oz.)

Fruit-flavored Whipped Cream

1 L heavy cream (34 fl. oz.)
50 to 100 ml fruit puree (1.5 to 3.5 fl. oz.), depending on desired consistency
juice of one lemon
400 g Italian meringue *or* 150 g confectioners' sugar (5 oz.)

Preparation

See instructions for crème Chantilly (volume 2, pages 54 to 55) and Italian meringue (volume 1, pages 82 to 83).

Procedure

Assemble all the equipment for beating the cream and place it in the freezer to chill.

Prepare, weigh, and measure the raw ingredients. Make sure that the cream is well chilled—less than 5°C (40°F)—before beating.

If confectioners' sugar is being used, it should be added after the cream has been beaten.

Flavorings such as extracts, liqueurs, and liquor should be added before the cream is beaten.

Gelatin should be added before beating. Italian meringue should be added after beating.

Flavorings such as praline paste, chestnut cream, and pistachio puree should be added after beating.

Always be sure that the bowl used for whipping the cream is well chilled, 4° to 6°C (39° to 42°F).

Start by whipping the cream slowly to make it frothy; then gradually increase speed until it becomes quite thick.

Finish beating the cream by stiffening it with a rapid, circular movement of the whisk.

Constantly check to make sure that the cream is not overbeaten.

Storage

Whipped cream should be used as soon as possible after beating. This is especially important if gelatin has been used. It should always be kept refrigerated, 5°C (40°F) and should never be held for longer than 24 hours.

Whipped cream can be frozen once it has been applied to a final pastry preparation.

La Crème Fondante (Chocolate Whipped Cream)

Crème fondante is a variation of whipped cream. It has a fine, melting texture.

Chocolate whipped cream is used primarily as a filling for specialized cakes.

Professional Recipe

1 kg chocolate (35 oz.)
1.5 L heavy cream (50.5 fl. oz.), whipped
vanilla extract
200 g sugar (7 oz.)

Alternative Recipe

500 g semisweet chocolate (17.5 oz.)
500 g chocolate (17.5 oz.)
1.5 to 2 L heavy cream (50.5 to 67.5 fl. oz.), whipped
vanilla extract

Recipe for a Small Quantity

350 g semisweet chocolate (12.5 oz.)
500 ml heavy cream (17 fl. oz.), whipped
vanilla extract

Preparation

(see crème fouettée)

Carefully melt the chocolate over a pan of warm water, 35°C (95°F). Whip the heavy cream with the sugar; add vanilla extract as desired to flavor.

Procedure

Allow the chocolate to cool slightly and add one-fifth of the whipped cream to it to lighten it. Combine this mixture until smooth and then incorporate the rest of the whipped cream.

Applying and Storing the Cream

(see crème fouettée)

La crème diplomate (Diplomat cream)

History and Definition

Diplomat cream is derived from a popular nineteenth-century French pudding called pudding à la Châteaubriand.

It was first introduced to Parisians by a well-known diplomat's pastry chef and soon it was called pudding à la diplomate. The cream filling for the pudding was then called crème à la diplomate.

Diplomat cream is a light but still smooth cream that is prepared by adding gelatin and whipped cream to pastry cream. It can be flavored with any natural flavoring, including extracts, liqueurs, liquors, and fruit purees.

Uses

Diplomat cream is used primarily for filling diplomat tarts, of course, but it may also be used as a filling for miniature cakes and petits fours.

Equipment

Saucepan
Mixing bowls
Whisk
Drum sieve
Parchment paper for flour
Measuring cup
Plastic pastry scrapers
Equipment used to prepare whipped cream

Professional Recipe

1 L milk (34 fl. oz.)
6 egg yolks
350 g sugar (12.5 oz.)
80 g powdered flan mix (3 oz.)
10 leaves (20 g) gelatin (2/3 oz.)
flavoring
1.5 L heavy cream (50.5 fl. oz.)
50 to 100 g confectioners' sugar (2 to 3.5 oz.)

Alternative Recipe

1 L milk (34 fl. oz.)
3 to 4 eggs
80 to 100 g powdered flan mix or cornstarch (3 to 3.5 oz.)
8 to 12 leaves (16 to 24 g) gelatin (1/2 to 3/4 oz.)
flavoring
1 to 1.5 L heavy cream (34 to 50.5 fl. oz.)
50 to 150 g confectioners' sugar (1.5 to 5 oz.)

  Diplomat cream is not difficult to prepare but demands constant attention. Be sure to follow directions carefully to prepare both pastry cream and whipped cream.
Use traditional pastry equipment. Allow about 30 minutes to prepare this cream.
It should be used immediately.

Recipe for a Small Quantity

250 ml milk (8.5 fl. oz.)
1 egg
100 g sugar (3.5 oz.)
25 g cornstarch (1 oz.)
2 leaves (4 g) gelatin (1/8 oz.)
flavoring
400 ml heavy cream or crème fraîche
   (14 oz.)
25 g confectioners' sugar (1 oz.)

Preparation

Assemble all the equipment, making sure that it is clean and dry.
Prepare, weigh, and measure the raw ingredients.
Chill the bowl to be used for whipping the cream in the refrigerator or freezer.
Prepare the gelatin by soaking it in cold water.
Separate the eggs.

Procedure

Prepare the Pastry Cream

Carefully follow the directions given for the preparation of this cream (see pages 27 to 29):

- heat the milk containing the sugar

- combine the sugar and egg yolks, then whisk in the flour

- thin the yolk/flour/sugar mixture with the hot milk

- place the cream back on the stove and finish cooking

Adding the Gelatin

Add the gelatin, which has been

soaked in cold water and drained, to the hot pastry cream. Combine well, using a whisk.

Cooling the Pastry Cream

Transfer the cream from the saucepan

to a stainless steel bowl.

Continue to stir the mixture to prevent a skin from forming on the surface of the cream while it is cooling.

Preparing the Whipped Cream

Beat the heavy cream or crème fraîche, which should be well chilled beforehand.

Folding in the Whipped Cream

When the pastry cream is almost completely cool, smooth it out with a whisk and carefully fold in the whipped cream

Storage

Diplomat cream should be used as soon as it is prepared.
Cakes and tarts that have been prepared with this cream should be immediately refrigerated, 5°C (40°F), until served. The finished pastries should not be kept for more than 2 days before serving.
Cakes and tarts using diplomat cream freeze well. Do not freeze the cream unless it is already a part of a finished preparation.

La Crème Diplomate
(Diplomat Cream)

PREPARATION	**0** min	
Assemble the Equipment **Prepare, Weigh, and Measure** the Raw Ingredients		• Make sure that the equipment is clean. • Chill the bowl for whipping the cream in the refrigerator or freezer. • Soften the gelatin. • Separate the eggs.
PROCEDURE	**5** min	
Prepare the Pastry Cream		• Heat the milk containing the sugar. • Work the yolks with the sugar, and add the flour. • Thin the flour/yolk mixture with the hot milk. • Cook the pastry cream.
Add the Gelatin	**20** min	• Add the soaked and drained gelatin to the hot pastry cream.
Cool the Pastry Cream Mixture	**22** min	• Transfer the cream to a stainless steel bowl. • Stir the pastry cream from time to time while the heavy cream is being beaten.
Beat the Heavy Cream	**25** min	• Use a whisk and be careful not to overbeat.
Fold in the Cream	**30** min	• Use a whisk to fold together carefully the pastry cream and the whipped cream.
USING THE FINISHED CREAM	**35** min	• Use immediately.

STORAGE: • Once tarts and cakes are filled with diplomat cream, they are either refrigerated for up to 48 hours at 5°C (40°F) or frozen.

La crème bavaroise (Bavarian cream)

History and Definition

Bavarian cream was originally a drink that was popular with the Bavarian aristocracy.

It was introduced in Paris by a Bavarian prince who frequented the famous café Procope, whose clientele included Buffon, Voltaire, Diderot, d'Alembert, Piron, Mermontel, Gilbert, and many others.

Originally, bavarian cream was a kind of infusion made from ferns. Soon other ingredients were added, such as egg yolks, milk, and Kirsch.

The mixture was then beaten to a froth. This same technique was also used for preparing hot chocolate and coffee.

Over the years, bavarian cream has changed so much that it has little if anything in common with the drink of the Bavarian princes.

Today it is used primarily as a component in cold pastry preparations such as cakes and charlottes.

It is a light and delicate cream with a lovely texture. It is prepared with crème anglaise, gelatin, and whipped cream.

Bavarian cream may be flavored with practically any flavoring or extract:

- chocolate, coffee, tea, chestnut cream, praline, pistachio, caramel, and other flavorings can be added during the preparation of the crème anglaise

- liqueurs and liquors can be added to the crème anglaise after it has cooled

There are two major categories of bavarian cream:

- bavarian creams based on *crème anglaise*

- bavarian creams based on *fruits and syrup*

Uses

Bavarian cream is used for a wide variety of cakes, charlottes, and cold desserts.

Equipment

Heavy-bottomed saucepan
Whisk
Plastic pastry scrapers
Wooden spatula
Strainer
Measuring cup
Mixing bowls
Copper or stainless steel bowl for beating
   the whites
Flexible whisk
Bowl for the finished cream

 Bavarian cream is difficult to prepare and requires constant attention at all stages. It is important to follow directions very carefully.
It is used often as the base for cakes and charlottes.
Use traditional pastry equipment.
Allow about 1 hour to prepare it.
It should be used as soon as prepared.
It may be frozen once used in finished pastry.

Professional Recipe

1 L milk (34 fl. oz.)

400 g sugar (14 oz.)
14 egg yolks
2 vanilla beans
14 leaves (28 g) gelatin (1 oz.)
1.5 L heavy cream or crème fraîche (50.5 fl. oz.), whipped

Alternative Recipe

1 L milk (34 fl. oz.)
400 to 500 g sugar (14 to 17.5 oz.)
12 to 16 egg yolks
flavoring (such as chocolate, coffee, or vanilla)
12 to 15 leaves (25 to 30 g) gelatin (about 1 oz.)
1250 to 1500 ml heavy cream or crème fraîche (42.5 to 50.5 fl. oz.), whipped

Recipe for a Small Quantity

250 ml milk (8.5 fl. oz.)
100 g sugar (3.5 oz.)
4 egg yolks
1/2 vanilla bean
4 leaves (8 g) gelatin (1/4 oz.)
400 ml heavy cream (13.5 fl. oz.), whipped

Preparation

Assemble all the necessary equipment and make sure that it is perfectly clean.
Prepare, weigh, and measure all the raw ingredients.
Carefully separate the eggs.
Soak the gelatin leaves in cold water.
Chill the bowl for beating the cream in the refrigerator or freezer.

Procedure

Preparing the Crème Anglaise

See instructions for crème anglaise (pages 24 to 26):

- boil the milk with half the sugar

- work the remaining sugar with the egg yolks

- add some of the boiling milk to the egg yolk/sugar mixture

- return the mixture to the saucepan

- cook until done

Adding the Gelatin to the Cream

When the crème anglaise is cooked, add the leaves of gelatin, which have been soaked in cold water and dried. Combine well, using a whisk.

Straining and Cooling the Cream

Strain the mixture into a cool bowl.
Stir the cream while it is cooling to prevent a skin from forming on its surface and to help it cool evenly.

Beating the Heavy Cream or Crème Fraîche

While the crème anglaise is cooling, prepare the whipped cream (see whipped cream, pages 56 to 57).

Flavoring the Cool Crème Anglaise

Use liquors and liqueurs as desired to flavor the cream.

Folding the Creams Together

Once the crème anglaise has completely cooled, add it bit by bit to the

whipped cream. Fold it carefully, using a whisk. Stop folding as soon as the mixture is completely homogeneous.

Storage

Bavarian cream should be used as soon as it is prepared.

Cakes and other preparations that use bavarian cream can be stored for up to 48 hours in the refrigerator, 5°C (40°F).

More often, they are frozen and may be stored for up to 2 weeks.

La Crème Bavaroise à l'Anglaise
(Crème Anglaise–based Bavarian Cream)

PREPARATION	**0** min	
Assemble the Equipment Prepare, Weigh, and Measure the Raw Ingredients		● Make sure that all equipment is clean and dry. ● Separate the eggs. ● Soak the gelatin leaves in cold water. ● Chill the bowl for beating the cream in the refrigerator or freezer.
PROCEDURE	**5** min	
Prepare the Crème Anglaise		● Boil the milk with half the sugar. ● Work together the yolks with the remaining sugar. ● Add the hot milk mixture to yolk mixture. ● Return the cream to the saucepan. ● Carefully oversee the cooking.
Add the Gelatin to the Crème Anglaise	**20** min	● Add the leaves of gelatin to the hot crème anglaise; combine with a whisk.
Strain and Cool	**22** min	● Immediately strain the cream into a cool bowl. ● Stir from time to time to prevent the formation of a skin and to help the cream cool evenly.
Whip the Heavy Cream or Crème Fraîche	**25** min	● Whip the cream with a whisk while the crème anglaise is cooling.
Fold the Creams Together	**30** min	● Add the creme anglaise bit by bit to the whipped cream, using a whisk.
USING THE FINISHED CREAM	**35** min	● Use immediately.

STORAGE: Cakes, charlottes and other cold preparations containing bavarian cream can be:
● immediately placed in the refrigerator, 5°C (40°F), and stored for up to 48 hours
● frozen and stored for up to 2 weeks. Freezing in this way is recommended for this cream.

B - Bavarian Cream Based on Fruit and Syrup

The basic recipe for this bavarian cream remains the same regardless of the kind of fruit used—strawberries, raspberries, red currants, blueberries, black currants, peaches, apricots, or other fruit purees.

Equipment

Saucepan
Skimmer
Measuring cup
Strainer
Mixing bowl
Whisk
Plastic pastry scrapers

Professional Recipe

1 L sugar syrup (34 fl. oz.), at 1260 D
1 L fruit puree (34 fl. oz.)
juice of two lemons (optional)
16 leaves (32 g) gelatin (1 oz.)
2 L heavy cream (67.5 fl. oz.)

Alternative Recipe

1 L sugar syrup (34 fl. oz.), at 1260 D
1 L fruit puree (34 fl. oz.)
juice of two to four lemons (optional)
14 to 20 leaves (28 to 40 g) gelatin (1 to 1.5 oz.)
1.5 to 2 L heavy cream or crème fraîche (50.5 to 67.5 fl. oz.)

Recipe for a Small Quantity

250 ml sugar syrup (8.5 fl. oz.), at 1260 D
250 ml fruit puree (8.5 fl. oz.)
juice of one lemon
4 leaves (8 g) gelatin (1/4 oz.)
500 ml heavy cream (17 fl. oz.)

Preparation

Assemble all the pastry equipment and make sure that it is clean and dry.
Prepare, weigh, and measure all the raw ingredients.
Soak the leaves of gelatin in cold water.
Chill the bowl for beating the heavy cream in the refrigerator or freezer.

Procedure

Preparing the Sugar Syrup, 1260 D

Measure the ingredients for the syrup and boil for 1 minute.

Adding the Gelatin to the Syrup

Transfer the hot syrup to a stainless steel bowl. Add the gelatin, which should have been soaked in cold water and drained. Stir the syrup with a whisk until the gelatin has completely dissolved.

Adding the Fruit Puree and the Lemon Juice

Add the fruit puree and the lemon juice to the sugar syrup/gelatin mixture. Combine well with a whisk.

Straining and Cooling the Mixture

Strain the mixture into a cool bowl. Stir it from time to time so that it cools evenly.

Whipping the Heavy Cream

Whip the cream while the syrup/fruit mixture is cooling.

Folding in the Whipped Cream

When the syrup/fruit/gelatin mixture has almost completely cooled, add it bit

by bit to the whipped cream, stirring with a whisk. Stop mixing as soon as the cream is smooth and homogeneous.

Using and Storing the Finished Cream

Use and storage are the same as for crème anglaise–based bavarian cream.

La Crème Bavaroise au Sirop
(Fruit-and-syrup-based Bavarian Cream)

	Time	
PREPARATION	**0** min	
Assemble the Equipment Prepare, Weigh, and Measure the Raw Ingredients		• Make sure that all equipment is clean and dry. • Soak the gelatin leaves in cold water. • Chill the bowl for whipping the cream in the refrigerator or freezer.
PROCEDURE	**5** min	
Prepare the Sugar Syrup, 1260 D		• Simmer the syrup for 1 minute; measure the necessary quantity into a stainless steel bowl
Add the Gelatin to the Syrup	**10** min	• Add the gelatin to the hot syrup.
Add the Fruit Puree and Lemon Juice	**12** min	• Combine well with a whisk.
Strain	**14** min	
Cool the Mixture	**15** min	• After straining, stir the mixture from time to time to help the mixture cool evenly.
Whip the Heavy Cream	**20** min	• Whip the cream with a whisk while the fruit/gelatin mixture is cooling.
Fold into the Whipped Cream	**23** min	• Slowly add the cooled fruit/gelatin/syrup mixture to the whipped cream.
USING THE FINISHED CREAM	**25** min	• Use immediately.

STORAGE: This bavarian cream can be stored for:
• 48 hours maximum in the refrigerator, 5°C (40°F)
• 2 weeks in the freezer

Les mousses (Mousses)

History and Definition

The first recipe for fruit mousse is credited to Alexandre Dumas, who mentioned it in one of his stories brought back from the New World: *"a mixture of sweetened fruit puree and whipped cream is chilled over crushed ice combined with salt and saltpeter."*

Soon after, pastry chefs who worked in restaurant kitchens and in private homes perfected extremely light, frozen, sweet mousses based on what they knew of savory mousses.

Today, sweet mousses used in various cakes and charlottes owe their popularity to their great diversity and lightness.

Modern mousses are extremely light and creamy. They may be lightened in several ways:

● by adding Italian meringue

● by adding whipped cream

● most frequently, by adding both whipped cream and Italian meringue

Mousses are usually based on one of four thick base mixtures:

Whole-egg base: this mixture is similar to pastry cream. It also includes gelatin, Italian meringue, flavoring, and whipped cream.

Milk and egg-yolk base: this mixture is based on crème anglaise to which gelatin has been added. It also contains Italian meringue, whipped cream, and flavoring.

Egg-yolk base: this mixture is based on a bombe mixture to which gelatin has been added. It also contains Italian meringue, whipped cream, and flavoring.

Fruit base: This mixture contains whipped cream, Italian meringue, fruit puree, and gelatin.

  Mousses are not extremely difficult to prepare provided that key points are followed. They do, however, need to be prepared with great care and precision. They form the base for a wide variety of cakes and pastries. Several methods can be used for their preparation. Be sure to use the mousse in the finished product as soon as it is completed.

The time required to prepare mousse varies, depending on the recipe, but is usually about an hour.

Mousses freeze very well once applied to a finished pastry.

Preparation

Assemble the necessary equipment, depending on which type of mousse is being prepared.

Prepare, weigh, and measure all the raw ingredients.

Carefully separate the eggs.

Prepare the heavy cream or crème fraîche in a chilled mixing bowl and keep in the refrigerator.

Soak the leaves of gelatin in cold water.

A - Whole-egg-based Mousses: Pastry Cream Method

Equipment

Saucepan
Whisk
Plastic pastry scraper
Mixing bowls (for base mixture, gelatin, and separating the eggs)
Bowl for beating the egg whites or mixing bowl for electric mixer
Hand whisk or whisk for electric mixer
Equipment for cooking sugar
Bowl for the final mixing of the finished mousse
Whisk

Liquor-flavored Mousses

1 L milk (34 fl. oz.)
200 g sugar (7 oz.)
4 eggs
100 g powdered flan mix (3.5 oz.)
10 leaves (20 g) gelatin (2/3 oz.)
200 ml liquor or liqueur (6.5 fl. oz.), or 2 vanilla beans
8 egg whites plus 500 g sugar (17.5 oz.) plus 150 ml warm water (5 fl. oz.), 120°C (248°F)
food coloring, optional
500 ml heavy cream (17 fl. oz.)

Fruit Mousses

1 L fruit puree or fruit juice (34 fl. oz.)
250 g sugar (9 oz.)
6 eggs
100 g powdered flan mix (3.5 oz.)
10 leaves (20 g) gelatin (2/3 oz.)
several drops vanilla extract
8 egg whites plus 500 g sugar (17.5 oz.) plus 150 ml warm water (5 fl. oz.), 120°C (248°F)
food coloring, optional
500 ml heavy cream (17 fl. oz.)

Procedure

Preparing the Pastry Cream

Bring either the milk, the fruit juice, or the fruit puree to a boil.

Prepare the egg/sugar/flan powder mixture.

Thin the egg mixture with the boiling liquid.

Cook the final mixture for at least 2 minutes after it comes to a boil.

Adding the Gelatin

Remove the hot pastry cream from the stove and add the gelatin leaves, which should have first been soaked in cold water and drained. Stir them in with a whisk.

Cooling the Cream

Stir the cream from time to time while it is cooling to prevent the formation of a skin and to help it cool evenly.

Preparing the Italian Meringue

See instructions for Italian meringue in volume 1, pages 82 to 83:

- cook the sugar to 120°C (248°F)

- beat the egg whites

- add the cooked sugar to the whites

- continue beating until the meringue is cool

Flavoring the Cream

Add the flavoring (liquor, liqueur, extract) to the warm cream. Smooth the mixture with a whisk.

Combining the Pastry Cream with the Italian Meringue

This step is delicate and must be done carefully. If the pastry cream is overworked when added to the Italian meringue, the resulting mixture may fall, making the mousse heavy and too thin. If, on the other hand, the Italian meringue is insufficiently combined with the cream, the mousse will not have an homogeneous texture.

Two methods can be used for combining the Italian meringue with the cream:

Method 1 (best)

Lighten the pastry cream containing the gelatin with a small amount of the Italian meringue.

Place the rest of the Italian meringue in a large mixing bowl.
Add the pastry cream/meringue mixture to the Italian meringue in the large mixing bowl.

Carefully fold the two mixtures together using a whisk. The movements for this are similar to those used in the preparation of soufflés and génoise (see volume 1, pages 92 to 95, 72 to 75).

Stop folding when the mousse is smooth and homogeneous.

Method 2

Pour the warm pastry cream directly into the Italian meringue, carefully combining with a whisk.

Incorporating the Whipped Cream

Carefully fold in the whipped cream, using a whisk.

Finish combining the whipped cream with the pastry cream/meringue mixture, using a quick circular motion with the whisk. This completes the mixture without causing the mousse to fall.

Whole-egg-based Mousses: Pastry Cream Method

PREPARATION **Assemble** the Equipment **Prepare, Weigh, and Measure** the Raw Ingredients	**0** min	● Assemble the equipment needed to prepare pastry cream. ● Soften the gelatin in cold water. ● Keep the ingredients for each base mixture separate.
PROCEDURE **Prepare** the Pastry Cream	**20** min	● See instructions for pastry cream, pages 27 to 29.
Add the Gelatin to the Hot Pastry Cream **Cool** the Pastry Cream	**30** min	● Add the gelatin, which should have been soaked in cold water and drained. ● Combine with a whisk. ● Cover the cream with a towel or stir from time to time, to prevent a skin from forming.
Prepare the Italian Meringue **Beat** the Meringue until Cool	**35** min	● Follow instructions for Italian meringue, volume 1, pages 82 to 83. ● Beat at medium speed in the electric mixer; coloring may be added at this time.
Flavor the Pastry Cream	**45** min	● Add the desired flavoring. ● Work it in completely with a whisk.
Combine the Pastry Cream with the Meringue **Add** the Whipped Cream	**50** min	● Method 1: lighten the cream with a little Italian meringue and then combine it with the rest of the meringue. ● Method 2: pour the warm cream into the meringue, carefully combining them with a whisk. ● Carefully fold in the whipped cream, using a whisk.
Smooth the Mousse	**1** hr	● Whip with a whisk, using a quick circular movement. ● This smooths the mixture without causing it to fall.
USING THE FINISHED MOUSSE		● Use immediately, before the mousse congeals.

STORING: ● Whole-egg mousses will keep for 48 hours in the refrigerator, 5°C (40°F); they also keep for several weeks in the freezer.

B - Milk- and Egg-yolk-based Mousses: Crème Anglaise Method

Equipment

Assemble the necessary equipment to prepare:

● crème anglaise (page 24)

● Italian meringue (volume 1, page 82)

● whipped cream (page 56)

Liquor-flavored Mousse

1 L milk (34 fl. oz.)
250 g sugar (9 oz.)
18 egg yolks
12 leaves (24 g) gelatin (1 oz.)
200 ml liquor or liqueur (6.5 fl. oz.)
8 egg whites
500 g sugar (17.5 oz.) plus 150 ml water (5 fl. oz.) plus 50 g glucose (1.5 oz.), cooked to 120°C (248°F)
1 L heavy cream (34 fl. oz.)

Coffee-flavored Mousse

1 L milk (34 fl. oz.)
300 g sugar (10.5 oz.)
16 egg yolks
50 ml coffee extract (1.5 fl. oz.)
12 leaves (24 g) gelatin (1 oz.)
100 ml rum (3.5 fl. oz.)
8 egg whites
500 g sugar (17.5 oz.) plus 150 ml water
    (5 fl. oz.) plus 50 g glucose, cooked
    to 120°C (248°F)
1 L heavy cream (34 fl. oz.), whipped

Procedure

Prepare the Crème Anglaise

See instructions for crème anglaise, pages 24 to 26:
• bring the sugar and milk to a boil
• prepare the sugar/egg yolk mixture
• thin the sugar/egg yolk mixture with the boiling milk
• cook the cream until it coats a spoon, to 85°C (185°F)

Add the Gelatin to the Crème Anglaise

Add the leaves of gelatin to the crème anglaise off the heat. Make sure that the gelatin leaves have first been soaked in cold water and excess water has been gently squeezed out. Stir the mixture with a whisk until the leaves dissolve.

Strain the Crème Anglaise

Straining eliminates egg shells, coagulated pieces of egg yolk, and pieces of incompletely dissolved gelatin.

Cool the Crème Anglaise

Stir the cream from time to time to

Milk- and egg-yolk-based Mousses: Crème Anglaise Method

PREPARATION	**0** min	
Assemble the Equipment **Prepare, Weigh, and Measure** the Raw Ingredients		• Assemble the equipment needed to prepare crème anglaise. • Assemble the equipment needed to prepare Italian meringue. • Assemble the equipment needed to prepare whipped cream. • Soak the gelatin leaves in cold water. • Keep the ingredients for each base mixture separate.
PROCEDURE	**20** min	
Prepare the Crème Anglaise		• Cook carefully until it naps a spoon.
Add the Gelatin to the Crème Anglaise **Strain** the Crème Anglaise **Cool** the Crème Anglaise/Gelatin Mixture	**30** min	• Add the soaked and drained gelatin leaves. • Stir with a whisk until dissolved. • Straining ensures that the crème anglaise is perfectly smooth. Stir from time to time to help the mixture cool evenly.
Prepare the Italian Meringue **Cool** the Italian Meringue	**35** min	• Take the usual precautions. • Beat at medium speed with an electric mixer until cool.
Flavor the Crème Anglaise	**45** min	• Add the desired flavoring. • Combine well with a whisk.
Combine the Meringue with the Crème Anglaise **Whip** the Heavy Cream **Combine** the Meringue/Cream Mixture with the Whipped Cream	**50** min	• Use the same technique as when using pastry cream method. • Whip by hand or use an electric mixer. • Take the usual precautions; do not overbeat. • Add the whipped cream to the meringue/crème anglaise mixture. • Combine carefully with a whisk.
Smooth the Mousse	**1** hr	• Whip with a whisk, using a quick, circular motion. • This smooths the mousse without causing it to fall.
USE		• Use immediately, before the mousse congeals.

STORAGE: • This mousse will keep for 48 hours in the refrigerator, 5°C (40°F); it will keep for several weeks in the freezer.

prevent a skin from forming on the surface and to help it cool evenly.

Prepare the Italian Meringue

See instructions in volume 1, page 82.

Flavor the Crème Anglaise

Add the flavoring, as well as food coloring if desired.

Combine the Crème Anglaise with the Italian Meringue

Use the same method as when working with pastry cream.

Prepare the Whipped Cream

Take the usual precautions when whipping the cream (see pages 56 to 57).

Add the Whipped Cream to the Crème Anglaise/Italian Meringue Mixture

Finish combining the whipped cream with the cream/meringue mixture, whisking with a quick circular motion. This combines the components without causing the mousse to fall.

C - Egg-yolk-based Mousses: Bombe Mixture Method

Equipment

Gather the necessary equipment for:
- preparing the cooked sugar and for cooking the base mixture (page 15)
- making Italian meringue (volume 1, page 82)
- making whipped cream (page 56)
- combining the base mixtures (large mixing bowl and whisk)

Chocolate Mousse Using Cooked Sugar

20 egg yolks

400 g sugar (14 oz.) plus 150 ml water (5 fl. oz.) plus 100 g glucose (3.5 oz.), cooked to 116°C (241°F)
400 g couverture chocolate (14 oz.), melted
200 g cocoa powder (7 oz.)
600 g butter (21 oz.)
50 ml rum (1.5 fl. oz.)
10 egg whites
500 g sugar (17.5 oz.) plus 150 ml water (5 fl. oz.), cooked to 120°C (248°F)
500 ml heavy cream (17 fl. oz.)

Fruit Mousse

500 ml fruit juice (17 fl. oz.) plus 500 g sugar (17.5 oz.); this constitutes the syrup
24 egg yolks, thickened in a bain-marie
10 leaves (20 g) gelatin (2/3 oz.)
12 egg whites
500 g sugar (17.5 oz.) plus 150 ml water (5 fl. oz.), cooked to 120°C (248°F)
1 L crème fraîche or heavy cream (34 fl. oz.)
food coloring, optional

Chocolate Mousse Using Sugar Syrup

20 egg yolks
500 ml sugar syrup (17.5 fl. oz.), at 1260 D
600 g semisweet chocolate (21 oz.), melted
400 g cocoa powder (14 oz.)
600 g butter (21 oz.)
200 ml Grand Marnier (6.5 fl. oz.)
16 egg whites plus 800 g sugar (28 oz.) plus 250 ml water (8.5 fl. oz.), cooked to 120°C (248°F)
1 L heavy cream (34 fl. oz.)

Procedure

Cooked-sugar Method

Cook the sugar, taking the usual pre-

cautions (see pages 14 to 17)

Add the cooked sugar to the egg yolks, stirring rapidly with a whisk.

Strain this mixture, which is a bombe mixture. Beat the bombe mixture in an electric mixer.

Prepare the chocolate/butter/rum mixture. Melt the couverture with the cocoa powder. Add the softened, drained gelatin (if used). Cream the butter with a mixer on medium speed or with a wooden spoon and add it to the melted chocolate mixture. Work the mixture until it is smooth and add the rum.

Prepare the Italian meringue (see volume 1, pages 82 to 83).

Whip the heavy cream or the crème fraîche.

Combine the bombe mixture with the chocolate/butter mixture, bit by bit, and work until smooth.

Place the Italian meringue in a large mixing bowl and gradually add the chocolate mixture. Combine carefully using a whisk.

Add the whipped cream. Finish smoothing the mixture with a whisk,

using a quick circular motion. This completely incorporates the cream without causing the mousse to lose volume.

Sugar-syrup Method

Prepare the syrup using water or fruit juice combined with sugar. Bring the syrup to a boil for 1 minute.

Add the boiling syrup to the yolks in a steady stream. Beat quickly, without stopping, with a whisk.

Strain this mixture, which is a bombe mixture.

Cook the bombe mixture over a bain-marie (water bath). Stir it from time to time to ensure that it cooks evenly.

Prepare the Italian meringue (see volume 1, pages 82 to 83).

Whip the heavy cream or the crème fraîche.

Check the cooking of the bombe mixture. It is ready when it has thickened and has a smooth, creamy consistency.

Add the gelatin to the bombe mixture if desired.

Beat the bombe mixture using a whisk or with an electric mixer until it has completely cooled

To combine the components of the mousse, follow the procedures used in the cooked-sugar method, above.

D - Fruit-based Mousses

Equipment

Mixing bowl
Whisk
Plastic pastry scraper
Equipment for preparing Italian meringue
Equipment for whipping cream
Large mixing bowl for final mixing
Whisk for final mixing

Recipes

Raspberry Mousse

1 kg raspberry puree (35 oz.)
250 g confectioners' sugar (9 oz.)
juice of one lemon
12 egg whites plus 600 g sugar (21 oz.) plus 180 ml water (6 fl. oz.), cooked to 120°C (248°F)
10 leaves (20 g) gelatin (2/3 oz.)
1 L heavy cream (34 fl. oz.)

Strawberry Mousse

1 kg strawberry puree (35 oz.)
200 g confectioners' sugar (7 oz.)
juice of two lemons
12 egg whites plus 500 g sugar (17.5 oz.) plus 150 ml water (5 fl. oz.), cooked to 120°C (248°F)
10 leaves (20 g) gelatin (2/3 oz.)
1500 ml heavy cream (50.5 fl. oz.)

Black Currant Mousse

1 kg black currant puree (35 oz.)
200 g confectioners' sugar (7 oz.)

juice of two lemons
14 egg whites plus 500 g sugar (17.5 oz.) plus 150 ml water (5 fl. oz.) plus 50 g glucose (1.5 oz.), cooked to 120°C (248°F)
10 leaves (20 g) gelatin (2/3 oz.)
1500 ml heavy cream (50.5 fl. oz.)

Passion Fruit Mousse

1 kg passion fruit puree (35 oz.)
200 g confectioners' sugar (7 oz.)
juice of one lemon
12 egg whites plus 500 g sugar (17.5 oz.) plus 150 ml water (5 fl. oz.) plus 50 g glucose (1.5 oz.), cooked to 120°C (248°F)
10 leaves (20 g) gelatin (2/3 oz.)
1 L heavy cream (34 fl. oz.)

Procedure

Preparing the Sweetened Fruit Puree

Place the fruit puree in a large mixing bowl. Add the confectioners' sugar and the lemon juice. Mix well with a whisk.

Preparing the Italian Meringue

See volume 1, pages 82 to 83.

Adding the Gelatin to the Fruit Puree

Dissolve the gelatin over warm water and add it to the sweetened fruit puree.

Adding the Fruit Puree/Gelatin Mixture to the Italian Meringue

While the Italian meringue is still warm, place it into a large mixing bowl and add the fruit puree in a steady stream, using a whisk.

Adding the Whipped Cream

Carefully fold in the whipped cream with a whisk.

Finish combining the mixture, whisking with a rapid circular motion. This combines the components thoroughly without causing the mousse to fall.

Using the Finished Mousses

Mousses should be used as soon as they are prepared. Otherwise, the gelatin will cause the mousse to congeal and it will then break apart when applied to a cake or other pastry.

Storage

Once the mousses have been added to a finished pastry, they may be frozen for several weeks. They can be stored in the refrigerator for up to 2 weeks.

Chapter 4 Basic confections

Not Just a Specialty, a Profession

The History of Confections

The early Egyptians, Arabs, and Chinese first made sweet preparations based on fruit sugars, and more commonly, honey. In Europe, sugar was not widely used until after the Crusades, in the thirteenth century.

In fifteenth-century France, candied fruits from Auvergne were well known, as were "dragées à l'ambre"—sugar-coated almonds flavored with ambergris—and "gigembrats"—candied ginger—from Montpellier.

In 1660, Jean-Baptiste Colbert, prime minister to France's King Louis XIV, enforced regulations for candies made in Verdun, which were thought to have medicinal properties.

In the first encyclopedia, written by Diderot, a great deal of space and many illustrations were devoted to the work of the candy maker. Confections became very popular in the nineteenth century, with the discovery of the sugar beet and the improvement of professional equipment.

A Broad Field

There are numerous recipes for even the most basic confections such as nougat and caramels. The various presentations of nougatine, candies made with assorted chocolate fillings, and complicated sugar work demonstrate the limitless possibilities of candy making, which requires great skill, experience, and artistic ability.

It is in the area of artistry that pastry chefs strive to perfect their abilities. This area of pastry making is admired by all. For this reason volumes 3 and 4 of this series are largely devoted to sugar work and decoration, writing and decorating with a paper cone, ice carving, modeling with marzipan, and other decoration techniques.

*The word **confection** is from the Latin "confectus," a form of the verb "conficere," meaning "to prepare."*

Confections are the sweetest creations in all pastry making. The diversity of the products made in this area of pastry make it more than just a specialty but a diverse and interesting profession unto itself.

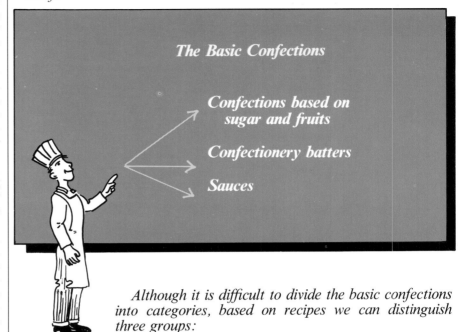

The Basic Confections

Confections based on sugar and fruits

Confectionery batters

Sauces

Although it is difficult to divide the basic confections into categories, based on recipes we can distinguish three groups:

1. Confections based on sugar and fruits:

- fondant
- jellies and fruit coulis
- crystallized candies
- jellied fruits

- water or rum glaze
- candied fruits
- preserves
- glazed chestnuts

2. Confectionery batters:

- almond paste
- Montélimar nougat
- marzipan (for modeling)
- marshmallow

- walnut paste
- nougatine
- caramel candies
- nut brittle

3. Sauces and the rest:

- praline paste
- gianduja
- fondant cream filling

- chocolate ganache fillings
- chocolate sauce
- sabayon sauce

Base of sugar and fruits	Le Fondant — Fondant	Le Sucre Candi — Crystallized Candy	Les Confitures — Preserves	Les Gelées et Coulis — Jellies, Coulis	Les Pâtes de Fruits — Jellied Fruits	Les Fruits Confits — Candied Fruits	Les Marrons Glacés — Glazed Chestnuts	La Glace à l'Eau ou au Rhum — Water or Rum Glaze
Sugar	1 kg (35 oz.)	2 kg (70 oz.)	1 kg (35 oz.)	750 g (26.5 oz.)	100 g plus 1 kg (3.5 oz. plus 35 oz.)	600 g (21 oz.)	800 g (28 oz.)	1 kg (35 oz.)
Glucose	200 g (7 oz.)	—	—	—	150 g (5 oz.)	—	50 g (1.5 oz.)	—
Water	300 ml (10 fl. oz.)	1 L (34 fl. oz.)	300 ml (10 fl. oz.)	—	—	1 L (34 fl. oz.)	1 L (34 fl. oz.)	250 ml (8.5 fl. oz.)
Fruit	—	—	1 kg (35 oz.)	1 L juice (34 fl. oz.)	1 kg apricot pulp (35 oz.)	1 kg (35 oz.)	1 kg (35 oz.)	—
Pectin	—	—	—	depends on fruit	10 g (1/2 oz.)	—	—	—
Acid Solution	—	—	—	—	20 g (2/3 oz.)	juice of 1 lemon	—	—
Flavoring	—	—	—	—	to taste	—	—	50 ml rum (1.5 fl. oz.)

Confectionery batters	La Pâte d'Amandes — Almond Paste	La Pâte d'Amandes Fondante — Marzipan, for Modeling	La Pâte aux Noix — Walnut Paste	La Pâte à Caramels — Caramels	La Pâte à Nougat de Montélimar — Montélimar Nougat	La Pâte à Guimauve — Marshmallow	La Nougatine — Nougatine	Le Craquelin — Almond Brittle	Les Amandes Craquelées — Almond Craquelées
Fruit and Nuts	1 kg almonds (35 oz.)	1 kg almonds (35 oz.)	500 g walnuts plus 300 g almonds (17.5 oz. plus 10.5 oz.)	—	500 g almonds plus 200 g hazelnuts plus 150 g pistachios (17.5 oz. plus 7 oz. plus 5 oz.)	—	600 g almonds (21 oz.)	1 kg almonds (35 oz.)	1 kg almonds (35 oz.)
Sugar	1 kg (35 oz.)	1.5 kg (53 oz.)	1 kg (35 oz.)	1 kg (35 oz.)	300 g (10.5 oz.)	1 kg (35 oz.)	1 kg (35 oz.)	1 kg (35 oz.)	500 g (17.5 oz.)
Glucose	—	500 g (17.5 oz.)	300 g (10.5 oz.)	300 g (10.5 oz.)	200 g (7 oz.)	100 g (3.5 oz.)	100 g (3.5 oz.)	—	—
Milk	—	—	—	1.5 L (50.5 fl. oz.)	—	—	—	—	—
Flavoring	—	—	—	2 vanilla beans	1 vanilla bean	orange flower water	—	—	orange flower water
Butter	—	—	—	150 g (5 oz.)	—	—	—	—	—
Honey	—	—	—	—	500 g (17.5 oz.)	—	—	—	—
Egg Whites	—	—	—	—	4	—	—	—	—
Water	—	—	—	—	100 ml (3.5 fl. oz.)	300 ml (10.5 fl. oz.)	—	—	—
Gelatin	—	—	—	—	—	40 g (1.5 oz.)	—	—	—

Sauces and the rest	Le Praline — Praline Paste	Le Gianduja — Gianduja	Les Crèmes Garniture — Fondant Cream Fillings	Les Ganaches Confiseur — Chocolate Ganache Fillings	La Sauce Chocolat — Chocolate Sauce	La Sauce Sabayon — Sabayon Sauce
Fruit and Nuts	1 kg almonds plus 1 kg hazelnuts (35 oz. plus 35 oz.)	500 g almonds plus 500 g hazelnuts (17.5 oz. plus 17.5 oz.)	—	—		—
Sugar	2 kg (70 oz.)	1 kg (35 oz.)	—	—	50 g, optional (1.5 oz.)	500 g (17.5 oz.)
Chocolate	—	1.5 kg (53 oz.)	—	1 kg (35 oz.)	300 g (10.5 oz.)	—
Butter	—	250 g (9 oz.)	1 kg (35 oz.)	500 g (17.5 oz.)	50 g (1.5 oz.)	—
Powdered Milk	—	250 g (9 oz.)	—	—	—	—
Fondant	—	—	1 kg (35 oz.)	—	—	—
Crème Fraîche or Heavy Cream	—	—	500 ml (17 fl. oz.)	500 ml (17 fl. oz.)	100 ml (3.5 fl. oz.)	—
Flavoring	—	—	200 ml liquor (6.5 fl. oz.)	250 ml liquor (8.5 fl. oz.)	—	500 ml wine or Champagne (17 fl. oz.)
Milk	—	—	—	—	300 ml (10 fl. oz.)	—
Egg Yolks	—	—	—	—	—	20

The Role of Confections in Pastry Making

Apart from the basic recipes, there are limitless possibilities for filling chocolates and candies. Most of the basic confectionery recipes are related to the recipes in pastry making with regard to flavoring (praline paste) or finishing various cakes (marzipan, glazing with ganache, preserves, or jellies). Sometimes certain techniques are so close to those used in pastry making that it is difficult to classify them as candy making or pastry making. Confections tend to be very sweet and therefore are only used in small individual pieces, never in large cakes.

Some of the following recipes are considered finished products, such as preserves, jellies, nougats, caramels, and almond paste, yet these can also be used to flavor, garnish, fill, or finish various preparations. For example, praline paste can be used to flavor creams and serve as the base for certain chocolate candies. Marzipan is used as a filling for almond candies and also attractively covers large and individual cakes. Marzipan can also be molded into flowers and other decorative shapes. Fondant can be used as a filling for bonbons and for glazing various pastries.

Establishments specializing in particular confections sometimes require special equipment to make them, as for candied fruits and dragées (candy-coated almonds).

Other preparations made by pastry chefs by hand require a great deal of time and skill, for example, caramels and white nougat from Montélimar; for this work, these chefs deserve recognition.

Le sucre candi (Crystallized candies)

History and Definition

The Arabs were the first to preserve various fruits by soaking them in heavily concentrated sugar syrups made with fruit juices.

The word candy is derived from the Italian *candi,* which in turn came from the Arabic *qand,* meaning "cane sugar."

Crystallized candy is a type of syrup saturated with sugar that crystallizes as it dries after cooling. It is hard to classify crystallized candy, as it is not a true syrup, but neither is it a cooked sugar, even though the same precautions for cooking sugar are followed in making it.

Uses

Candy is crystallized for two reasons:

1. Protection: the many sugar crystals that cover each piece prevent the candies from drying out.

2. Decoration: when sugar is crystallized, it is very brilliant because the tiny crystals shine.

Many confections can be crystallized;

- fruits confits (candied fruits) and dried fruits

- marzipan (all forms, which can be colored and flavored)

- jellied fruits

 All equipment used to make crystallized candy must be thoroughly clean throughout all stages.

The sugar should be completely dissolved before the syrup comes to a boil. Cool the syrup to 40° to 45°C (104° to 113°F) before pouring.

No special equipment is required. Allow 24 hours to prepare crystallized candies.

- bonbons filled with fondants

- fruits filled with almond paste

Equipment

Large saucepan with cover (a sheet pan
    or bowl can serve as a cover)
Pastry brush
Skimmer
Bowl
Damp towel
Funnel
High-sided sheet pan
Racks (2)
Parchment paper

Recipes

Professional Recipe

1 L water (34 fl. oz.)
2 kg sugar (72 oz.), granulated, crystal,
    or cubes

Alternative Recipe

1 L water (34 fl. oz.)
2.5 kg sugar (88 oz.), crystal, granulated,
    or cubes

To make enough crystallizing sugar
for one high-sided sheet pan (a génoise
pan can be substituted) measuring 40 ×
60 × 5 cm (16 × 24 × 2 in.), triple the
recipe.

Note: Acid, in the form of lemon juice
or cream of tartar, is never added to
crystallized candy, nor is inverted sugar
or any other ingredient that could prevent the sugar crystals from forming.

Preparation

At least 24 hours are needed to prepare the candies. Chilling the syrup requires 2 to 4 hours. Crystallization of
the syrup takes 10 to 24 hours. Drying
the syrup takes 2 to 6 hours.

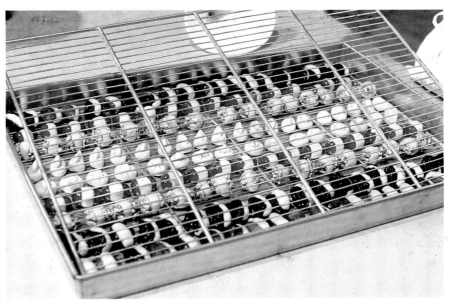

Make the crystallizing sugar first. The
candies to be crystallized can be made
while the syrup is cooling.

All equipment should be very clean.

Procedure

Making the Crystallizing Sugar

See Cooking Sugar, pages 14 to 17.

Place the sugar and the water in a
clean saucepan. The sugar can be gently
stirred with the skimmer to help it dissolve when placed on the heat.

While the sugar is dissolving, brush
the sides of the saucepan and skim the
mixture when necessary.

Bring to a boil for 1 minute. Remove
the saucepan from the heat and let cool
without stirring. Cover with a damp
towel and saucepan cover to prevent
crystals from forming too rapidly.

Setting Up the Pieces to be Crystallized

While the syrup is cooling, prepare the
items to be candied. The pieces should
be placed in a high-sided sheet pan that
can hold racks of the same size. The
racks must be able to fit perfectly inside
the sheet pans.

Place one rack on the bottom of the
sheet pan, and arrange the pieces so that
they are not touching. If they touch, they
cannot be completely covered with the
crystallizing sugar.

Invert a second rack over the pieces
to keep them in place as the crystallizing
sugar is poured over them.

It is best if the pieces are firm and at
room temperature, approximately 20°C
(68°F), before they are crystallized.

For firm jellied fruits, firm fondants,
and marzipan fruits, about 24 hours are
needed to form a light coating of crystals.

Pouring the Syrup

When the syrup has cooled to approxi-

mately 40° to 45°C (104° to 113°F), it can be poured through a funnel onto the pieces.

The funnel should rest firmly in place on the top rack so that it will not slip as the syrup is poured, and its tip should reach the lower rack.

This allows the syrup to cover all pieces evenly without having to move them, which could create lumps rather than delicate crystals

For this reason it is important not to shake or move the sheet pan.

Continue pouring the syrup until it reaches the top rack and covers the entire surface of the sheet pan. Each piece should be completely covered. Be careful to pour the syrup steadily so that it surrounds each piece evenly.

The racks will hold the pieces in place so they will not float around and will remain submerged in the syrup.

To prevent dust or other foreign particles from contaminating the candies, lay a sheet of parchment paper on top of the rack; perforations can be made in the paper to eliminate any buildup of condensation if the syrup is still warm.

Verifying the Crystallization

Allow the syrup to crystallize in a dry, temperate area without moving the pan. Depending on type of candy being crystallized and the sugar syrup, crystallization can take from 12 to 24 to up to 48 hours.

If the crystallization is taking too long, it can be speeded up after 24 hours by replacing the parchment paper with a heavier paper (such as butcher's paper) to absorb some of the humidity.

The crystals will form under the parchment paper, which adheres to the syrup as it drys. When the paper is lifted, the size of the crystals that will appear on the dried candies can be seen on the paper.

Drying the Candies

When crystallization is complete, remove the racks with the candies between them from the pan, remove the top rack, and let the candies drain above the sheet pan for one hour.

After draining, carefully turn the pieces over by hand.

Place the rack with the candies on a clean surface and allow to dry until they are no longer sticky.

Storage

The crystallized candies can be stored in airtight plastic containers, protected from heat, humidity, and dust.

They can be stored at room temperature for 10 to 15 days, and for 3 to 4 weeks in the refrigerator at 5°C (40°F).

Le Sucre Candi
(Crystallized Candies)

PREPARATION	**0** min	
Assemble the Equipment		• Verify the cleanliness of the equipment.
Prepare, Weigh, and Measure the Raw Ingredients		
PROCEDURE	**5** min	
Make the Syrup		• Follow all instructions given for cooking sugar syrup to the boiling point (pages 14 to 17), particularly the following: • When first heating, help the sugar melt by gently stirring with a skimmer. • Carefully skim the sugar throughout the cooking. • Rinse the sides of the saucepan with a pastry brush. • Allow the syrup to boil for 1 minute, then immediately remove from the heat.
Cool the Syrup	**15** min	• Cool the syrup off the heat, without stirring. • Cover with a damp towel and a saucepan cover.
Arrange the Pieces to be Candied	**20** min	• Arrange the pieces on a rack inside a sheet pan, so that they do not touch. • Place a second rack upside down on top of the pieces to keep them in place when the syrup is poured over them.
Pour the Crystallizing Sugar	**2** hrs	• Once the syrup has cooled to 40° to 45°C (104° to 113°F), pour it through a funnel into the sheet pan. • Totally cover the pieces with the syrup.
Cover the Sheet Pan	**2** hrs	• Cover the sheet pan with a sheet of parchment paper.
VERIFYING THE CRYSTALLIZATION	**18** hrs	• Crystals that form on the parchment paper will be indicative of the results to be expected once the candies dry.
DRYING THE PIECES	**24** hrs	• Once the candies have crystallized, remove the two racks with the candies, remove the top rack, and drain the candies above the sheet pan for approximately 1 hour. • Carefully turn the pieces over to dry on the bottom.
STORAGE:		• Crystallized candies can be stored for 10 to 15 days at room temperature in an airtight container, protected from heat and humidity. They can be stored for 3 to 4 weeks refrigerated at 5°C (40°F).

Les confitures (Preserves)

History

The word *confiture* can be traced to the thirteenth century. During the middle of the fourteenth century, preserves from the village Bar-le-Duc in the Lorrain region were already well known and appreciated throughout France. They were, however, found only on the tables of the rich; preserves were considered a luxury at the time.

Preserves from Metz and Verdun were equally well known and distributed throughout France under the reign of Louis XIV.

Eventually, every region, province, village, town, and family in France was able to enjoy wonderful preserves, usually made at home.

The Regulation of Preserves

In France, the appellation **"Confitures pur fruits/pur sucre"** (Preserves made with pure fruits/pure sugar) indicates preserves that are made with only granulated or refined sugar and fresh fruits, fresh fruit juices, or fruits preserved in any way other than drying.

Equipment

Copper, stainless steel, or aluminum bowl (a pressure cooker without a cover can be substituted)
Plastic pastry scraper
Wooden spatula
Skimmer

Bowls for the fruits
Plastic containers or preserve (Mason) jars

Recipe

To 1 kg (35 oz.) of cooked sugar, add 30 percent of its weight in water—300 ml (10 fl. oz.)—for every kg (35 oz.) of cleaned, pitted, and skinned fruit.

 Preserves are fairly easy to prepare. Observe the cooking of the sugar and preserves carefully. During cooking, avoid splattering.

No special equipment is required.

Preserves take 1 hour to prepare.

Preparation

Apricot preserves, for glazing

Preserves are made by cooking whole fruit or fruit cut into quarters in a **sugar**

syrup, also called **cooked sugar,** that is cooked between hard ball and soft crack stage. Apricot preserves are used in many pastry preparations, particularly in glazes, and so the procedure for making them is the one discussed here.

Use sugar cubes or granulated sugar (see Cooking Sugar, pages 14 to 17). Choose very ripe fruit. Wash the apricots, cut in half, and pit them, breaking a few pits and reserving them for later use. The almonds (blanched) inside the pits can be added to the preserves at the end of cooking.

Do not use rotten or bruised fruit, which could darken the color of the preserves.

Use a copper bowl capable of holding four times the volume of the sugar to be cooked. This will prevent burns from the sugar splattering and will help cook the sugar quickly.

Clean and sterilize (by boiling) the containers to be used for storing the preserves. Allow them to dry by turning them upside down and draining them on a clean towel or rack. Avoid wiping the containers, which could leave lint or bacteria. If necessary, they can be dried with a very clean towel.

Procedure

Place the sugar and water in the copper bowl or saucepan and carefully follow all instructions given in the discus-

sion or cooking sugar.

When the sugar has reached 140°C (284°F), slowly add the apricots to the bowl or pan of cooked sugar and gently stir with a skimmer or wooden spatula.

Cook the mixture over a high flame to maintain the maximum flavor of the fruit and quickly evaporate the water.

Stir occasionally, especially when the syrup starts to thicken, so the preserves do not stick to the sides of the saucepan or bowl. Skim occasionally, removing any impurities from the fruit that may rise to the top.

Verifying Doneness

It is not possible to give an exact cooking time. There are many variables, such as:

● the intensity of the heat source (never the same on any two stoves)

● the amount of water and sugar contained in the fruit.

The sugar content will vary among different fruits, depending on the variety of fruit, the season, and the climate.

Cooking time will also vary according to how the preserves will be used and the level of natural pectin in the fruit, which is discussed under pâte de fruits (jellied fruits), pages 86 to 89.

Doneness can be judged by:

● Touching the preserves, as for judging cooked sugar at the thread or soft ball stage (see Cooking Sugar, pages 14 to 17).

● Dipping a skimmer or wooden spatula in the mixture, lifting it, and holding it vertically. The droplets on the spatula should firm up after a few moments.

- Trickling a few drops of the mixture in a container of cold water. The preserves should rest on the bottom without dispersing or melting into the water.

- Placing a few drops of preserves on a cold plate and holding it vertically. The preserves should adhere to and not drip off the plate.

As a general guide, allow approximately 30 to 45 minutes of cooking time from the moment the fruit is added to the cooked sugar. If the almonds from the pits are to be used to improve flavor and texture, they should be blanched and added 3 to 5 minutes before the end of cooking.

Apricot preserves can be flavored with vanilla at the end of cooking.

Before removing the cooked preserves from the heat, bring them to a rolling boil and skim one more time.

Storage

Never cool the preserves in the same receptacle in which they were cooked, or they will not cool quickly enough.

After cooking, quickly pour the preserves into bowls, plastic containers,

preserve jars, or a high-sided sheet pan or cake pan, where they will cool rapidly.

Once completely cool, cover the preserves with either parchment paper soaked in a strong liquor or with a thin layer of melted wax. Adhesive plastic sheets that form an airtight seal can also be used.

Store the preserves in a cool area free from humidity and light. If properly made and sealed in perfectly clean jars, they will keep indefinitely.

Note

Strawberry and raspberry preserves can be made in the same way as apricot preserves, but the fruit will be more attractive and maintain its color and shape better if cooked as follows:

While the sugar is cooking, add the strawberries or raspberries. Allow them to cook for 10 minutes.

Remove the fruit with a skimmer and drain well. Then place it in appropriate containers or jars, filling only two-thirds full.

Continue to cook the sugar over a high heat to the soft crack stage and pour it over the fruit.

As for pâte de fruits (jellied fruits), adding natural pectin will help give certain preserves a thicker consistency.

If pectin is added, a shorter cooking time is required, which in turn helps maintain the flavor of the fruit. The amount of pectin used depends on the fruit.

Les Confitures (Preserves)		
PREPARATION **Assemble** the Equipment **Prepare, Weigh, and Measure** the Raw Ingredients	**0** min	• Verify the cleanliness of the equipment; clean the copper bowl with salt and vinegar. • Wash, cut, and pit the fruit.
PROCEDURE **Cook** the Sugar	**10** min	• Follow the instructions for cooking sugar and cook to 140° C (284° F).
Add the Apricots	**15** min	• Carefully add the fruit (in this case, apricots) to the cooked sugar. • Stir gently, with a skimmer or wooden spatula.
Cook the Preserves	**16** min	• Cook the mixture over a high heat to evaporate the water quickly and maintain the maximum flavor of the fruit. • Occasionally skim the preserves. • Stir and carefully observe the cooking, especially toward the end of the cooking time.
VERIFYING DONENESS	**55** min	• Verify that the preserves are cooked by touching, checking for the thread or soft ball stage, or by seeing if drops firm up when coating a skimmer, or by dropping a small amount of the preserves in water, or place a few drops of preserves on a cold plate.
TRANSFERRING	**60** min	• Immediately transfer the preserves to sterilized preserve jars. • Seal after completely cool.
STORAGE: • Store the preserves in airtight containers in a cool area, free from humidity and light.		

Les gelées et coulis de fruits

(Fruit jellies and coulis)

Jellies

Definition

Jellies are very similar to preserves. The major difference between the two is that jellies are made with fruit juice and not whole fruit as in preserves. Jellies also tend to be less sweet than preserves.

Before gelatins were used, it was necessary to choose fruits high in pectin such as blackberries, red currants, apples, and quince, to be sure the jellies would set.

Pectin in powdered form or gelatin can be added so that fruit juices low in pectin can be used without mixing with other juices high in the pectin required to set the jelly.

The amount of pectin added can be varied to control the consistency (firmness) of the jelly.

Jellies should be smooth and not too firm, less firm than pâte de fruits (jellied fruits).

Equipment

Drum sieve
China cap or strainer
Clean cloth or cheesecloth for straining the juice
Saucepan
Copper or stainless steel saucepan
Hydrometer
Jars with covers for storage

 Jellies and coulis are easy to prepare, as long as the instructions given are carefully followed.

Choose fruit that is ripe and free of bruises. Strain the juice after chopping the pulp.

Skim the jelly carefully toward the end of cooking to ensure a smooth texture. No special equipment is required.

Allow 20 to 25 minutes to make jelly and 15 to 20 minutes for the coulis.

Selecting the Fruit

Fruit from which the juice is extracted to make jelly should be ripe but not overripe. Avoid fruits with bruises or mold.

Prepare the Juice

There are two types of juice:
1. Juice obtained by simply squeezing such fruit as black currants, red currants, raspberries, and blueberries.
2. Juice from the pulp of fruit such as apples, peaches, and pears. These fruits must be peeled and turned into pulp before the juice can be extracted. An extra step, blanching, which is described below, is required to obtain the pulp.

Blanching the Fruit

Place the fruit in acidulated (with lemon juice) boiling water for a few seconds to prevent it from browning. Drain the fruit on a rack for approximately 10 minutes.

If using quinces, they should be very ripe; scrub the fruit well under water to remove the fuzz covering the skin. Then blanch as for apples and pears.

Cut the quinces in quarters after draining on a rack for 10 minutes.

Cooking the Fruit

Weigh the fruit after chopping (and blanching if necessary).

Place the chopped fruit in the heavy-bottomed saucepan and add 100 ml (3.5 fl. oz.) water for every kg (35 oz.) of fruit. Cook, covered, over low heat for 10 to 15 minutes, depending on the fruit.

Verify doneness with the tip of a knife. The knife should slide through the fruit easily, without resistance. Remove the fruit from the heat, and place on a drum sieve or in a strainer, over a container to catch the juice. Press the fruit into the sieve or strainer to extract the juice. Once the juice is extracted, the instructions for preparing jelly are the same, regardless of whether the juice is from pulp or from squeezed fresh fruit.

Recipe

1 L fruit juice (34 fl. oz.)
750 g sugar (26.5 oz.), plus pectin or gelatin if needed (depending on the fruit and desired results)

It is impossible to give the exact amount of pectin or gelatin needed because of the following variables:
- the amount of pectin in the fruit used
- the desired result—more or less firm
- the quality of the pectin
- the cooking time

Note: if powdered pectin or gelatin is used, it should be mixed with the dry sugar before cooking.

Procedure

Strain the fruit juice through a very clean cloth. Measure the quantity of juice obtained. Mix the juice with the sugar.

(If powdered gelatin or pectin is to be used, add it to the sugar first).

Pour the mixture into a copper sugar pan or stainless steel saucepan, place over

high heat, and cook, following the same precautions as for cooking sugar (see pages 14 to 17). Skim and brush the sides of the saucepan when necessary.

To determine if the jelly is ready, test for the coating stage (see Cooking Sugar) or use a hydrometer: the jelly should measure 1295 D.

Transfer the jelly to containers or jars already sterilized for this purpose. If using glass containers, wait a few minutes, until the jelly has cooled somewhat, before adding it to the container, to avoid breakage.

Storage

Jellies can be stored in airtight containers for several months in a dry, cool area.

Les Gelées de Fruits		
(Fruit Jellies)		
PREPARATION **Assemble** the Equipment **Prepare, Measure, and Weigh** the Raw Ingredients	**0** min	• Verify the cleanliness of the equipment. • Prepare the fruit juice. • Strain the fruit juice through a clean cloth.
PROCEDURE **Make** the Jelly	**10** min	• Follow the same precautions as for cooking sugar and making a syrup. • Bring the mixture of sugar, pectin (if used), and juice to a boil. • Skim and brush the sides of the saucepan regularly.
VERIFYING DONENESS OR DENSITY	**20** min	• Cook the jelly to the coating stage, to 1295 D. • Transfer the jelly to sterilized containers immediately.

STORAGE: • Jellies can be stored in airtight containers for several months in a cool, dry area.

Les coulis (Coulis)

Definition

Coulis fall between preserves and jellies in texture. They are made with either fruit pulp or juice.

The major difference between coulis and preserves or jellies is that coulis are not cooked, which limits their storage time. On the other hand, they freeze very well.

Uses

Coulis are used as a sauce to accompany various desserts, such as ice creams and mousses.

Equipment

Drum sieve or china cap
Electric mixer (optional)
Bowl for the fruit
Pastry scraper
Saucepan
Skimmer
Container with cover, for storage
Bowl to soften the gelatin, if used

Professional Recipe

1 L fruit pulp (34 fl. oz.)
600 g sugar (21 oz.)
50 ml fruit brandy (1.5 fl. oz.), plus fruit extract plus several drops of coloring, optional

Alternative Recipe A

1 L sugar syrup (34 fl. oz.), at 1260 D
300 g glucose (10.5 oz.)
1 L fruit pulp (34 fl. oz.)
50 ml fruit brandy or liqueur (1.5 fl. oz.)
4 leaves (8 to 10 g) gelatin (1/4 to 1/3 oz.)

Alternative Recipe B

1 L fruit juice (34 fl. oz.)
750 g sugar (26.5 oz.)
250 g glucose (9 oz.)
50 ml fruit brandy (1.5 fl. oz.) plus fruit extract to taste
4 leaves (8 to 10 g) gelatin (1/4 to 1/3 oz.)
coloring, optional

Black Currant Coulis

500 ml (17 fl. oz.) coulis serves twelve

1 kg black currant jelly (35 oz.)
500 ml water (17 fl. oz.)
100 ml black currant brandy (3.5 fl. oz.)
500 ml crème de cassis—black currant
    liqueur (17 fl. oz.)

Red Currant or Raspberry Coulis

1 kg red currant or raspberry jelly
    (35 oz.)
150 ml Kirsch (5 fl. oz.)
several drops of red coloring

Preparation

Preparing the Fruit Pulp

Choose ripe, fresh fruit.
Mash the pulp in a mixer. Strain it through a china cap or strainer.
Make a sugar syrup of 1260 D (see Cooking Sugar, pages 14 to 17).
If gelatin is to be used, soften it in cold water.

Procedure

Coulis is made like sugar syrup. It is a very simple procedure.
Place the fruit pulp or fruit juice, sugar or syrup, glucose (if used), softened gelatin, and coloring in a saucepan. Bring the mixture to a boil and let boil for 1 minute, as for sugar syrup. Skim well if necessary.

Remove from heat and strain before adding liquor. Cover with a clean towel as it cools to prevent a skin from forming.

Coulis are often used while still warm to coat a dessert, or they are used cold as a sauce.

Storage

Transfer to a container and cover.

Coulis can be stored in a refrigerator at 5°C (40°F) for up to 1 week, or they can be frozen for several months. Before freezing, divide the coulis into small quantities so only the quantity needed can be thawed.

Les Coulis de Fruits
(Fruit Coulis)

PREPARATION **Assemble** the Equipment **Prepare, Weigh, and Measure** the Raw Ingredients	**0** min	● Verify the cleanliness of the equipment. ● Prepare the fruit pulp or juice. ● Make a sugar syrup of 1260 D, if used.
PROCEDURE **Make** the Coulis	**5** min	● Follow the procedures for sugar syrup or cooking sugar. ● Bring all ingredients to a boil for 1 minute. ● Skim and brush the sides with water if necessary. ● Strain the mixture. ● Off the heat, add liquor if desired.
COOLING	**15** min	● Cover with a clean towel.
USES		● Warm, to nap or glaze desserts. ● Serve cold as a sauce to accompany desserts.

STORAGE: ● Coulis can be stored for approximately 1 week at 5°C (40°F) in an airtight container. Coulis freeze well.

La glace à l'eau ou au rhum (Water or rum glaze)

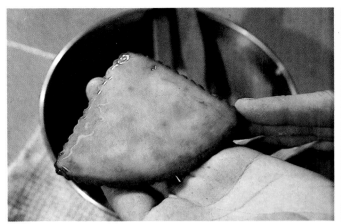

Definition

Glace à l'eau is a semiliquid water-sugar glaze made from a base of confectioners' sugar or fondant to which warm water is added to achieve the desired consistency.

This water-sugar glaze can be flavored with any liquor or liqueur, most often rum, in which case the glaze is called **glace au rum** (rum glaze).

Uses

This type of glaze is used to cover almond croissants, petits fours secs, and various types of sablés (shortbread cookies).

Equipment

Recipe Based on Confectioners' Sugar

Saucepan
Measuring cup
Drum sieve with fine mesh and paper (for sifting)
Pastry scraper
Wooden spatula

Recipe Based on Fondant

Saucepan
Measuring cup
Plastic scraper
Wooden spatula

Professional Recipe

Based on Confectioners' Sugar

1 kg confectioners' sugar (35 oz.)
250 ml hot water (8.5 fl. oz.)
50 ml rum (1.5 fl. oz.)

Based on Fondant

1 kg fondant (35 oz.)
350 g glucose (12.5 oz.)
300 ml syrup (10 fl. oz.), at 1260 D
150 ml rum (5 fl. oz.)

Recipe for a Small Quantity

250 g confectioners' sugar (9 oz.)
60 ml water (2 fl. oz.)
10 ml rum (1/2 fl. oz.)

Preparation

Assemble the equipment.
Prepare, weigh, and measure the raw ingredients.
Sift the confectioners' sugar.
Soften the fondant by working it between the hands.

Procedure

Based on Confectioners' Sugar

Sift the confectioners' sugar and place it in a saucepan. Slowly add hot water, mixing well with a whisk. Flavor with rum or other liquor.

Heat the glaze over a low flame, stirring constantly, until it reaches 45° to 50°C (113° to 122°F).

Based on Fondant

Place the softened fondant in a saucepan with the glucose and mix with a wooden spatula.

Soften the mixture with warm sugar

syrup (1260 D). Then add the flavoring.

Heat the mixture over a low flame to approximately 37°C (98°F).

Storage

Once the glaze is ready, it must be used immediately and cannot be stored.

		La Glace à l'Eau ou au Rhum *(Water or Rum Glaze)*	
PREPARATION	**0** min		
Assemble the Equipment **Prepare, Weigh, and Measure** the Raw Ingredients		• Verify the cleanliness of the equipment. • Sift the confectioners' sugar. • Soften the fondant by working it between the hands.	
PROCEDURE			
Based on Confectioners' Sugar	**5** min		
Mix the Confectioners' Sugar with Water		• Slowly add the water. • Smooth the mixture with a whisk.	
Add Flavoring	**7** min	• Flavor the glaze with rum.	
Heat the Glaze	**10** min	• Heat over a low flame, stirring constantly, until it reaches 45° to 50° C (113° to 122° F).	
Based on Fondant	**5** min		
Mix the Fondant		• Mix the fondant with the glucose using a wooden spatula.	
Soften the Fondant/Glucose Mixture	**8** min	• With warm, not hot, sugar syrup (1260 D), soften the mixture.	
Add Flavoring		• Flavor the glaze with rum or other liquor.	
Heat the Glaze	**10** min	• Heat over a low flame, stirring constantly, until the glaze reaches 37° C (98° F).	
STORAGE: • These glazes must be used immediately after they are made and cannot be stored.			

La sauce sabayon (Sabayon sauce)

History

Sabayon sauce originated in Italy. The word *sabayon* is derived from the Italian name for the same sauce, *zabaglione,* also called *zabajone.*

Sabayon is a particluraly airy and creamy preparation made from a mixture of fresh egg yolks, sugar, wine, and flavoring, thickened by whisking while cooking.

Zabaglione always uses Marsala wine. Sabayon, however, can be flavored with various white wines, such as Muscat, Tokay, Riesling, and Gewurtztraminer; with aromatic cooking wines such as Frontignan, sherry, Madeira, port, and Malaga; with Champagnes; with liquors such as rum, Kirsch, and Cognac; or with liqueurs including Grand Marnier, Cointreau, and Curaçao. Sabayon can also be flavored with the zests of lemons and oranges.

Uses

Sabayon is used as a sauce to accompany various desserts, such as puddings and fresh fruit.

It can also be served in a glass, warm, as is popular in Italian cuisine, or cold, with petits fours secs or ladyfingers. It is also the base for sabayon glacé, a frozen dessert.

Equipment

Electric mixer, bowl and whisk attachment

Bowls - Measuring cup
Pastry scraper - Whisk

Professional Recipe

20 egg yolks
500 g sugar (17.5 oz.)
500 ml wine or Champagne (17 fl. oz.)

Alternative Recipe

16 to 20 egg yolks
400 to 600 g sugar (14 to 21 oz.)
400 to 600 ml wine or Champagne (13.5 to 21 fl. oz.)

Recipe for a Small Quantity

10 egg yolks
250 g sugar (9 oz.)
250 ml wine or Champagne (8.5 fl. oz.)

Preparation

Assemble all the equipment.
Prepare, weigh, and measure the raw ingredients.
Very carefully separate the eggs. The success of this sauce depends on how the eggs are separated and cooked.

Procedure

Mixing the Yolks and Sugar

Vigorously mix the egg yolks and sugar, with a whisk, in the mixing bowl (for the mixer) or in a stainless steel bowl.

Warming the Yolks and Sugar

Whisk the egg yolks and sugar, following the same procedure as for génoise batter (see volume 1, pages 72 to 75): vigorously beat the yolks and sugar over

a warm water bath (bain-marie) or directly over a low flame until the mixture reaches 45°C (113°F).

Beating the Mixture (by hand or electric mixer)

Take the mixture off the heat and continue to beat it with a whisk. If using a mixer, turn the machine to high speed and beat with the whisk attachment.

While whisking, slowly add the wine or Champagne.

Finish beating on medium speed until the sauce has a light, creamy consistency.

Verifying Doneness

The sabayon is done and beating can be stopped when the mixture forms a ribbon (when it can be folded over itself) and does not flow off the whisk when raised above the mixture. The sauce should be light, airy, and creamy.

Storage

This sauce is best when used immediately, while it is still warm.

Sabayon sauce can be kept warm in a bowl covered with a clean towel set over a warm water bath at 60°C (140°F). It can be held in this way for up to 1 hour.

La Sauce Sabayon (Sabayon Sauce)		
PREPARATION **Assemble** the Equipment **Prepare, Weigh, and Measure** the Raw Ingredients	**0** min	● Verify the cleanliness of the equipment. ● Separate the eggs.
PROCEDURE Mix the Yolks and the Sugar	**5** min	● Combine the yolks and sugar with a whisk in the bowl of an electric mixer or in a stainless steel bowl.
Warm the Yolk/Sugar Mixture	**↑5** min	● Over a warm water bath or low flame, warm the mixture until it reaches 45°C (113°F). ● Beat constantly, without stopping.
Increase the Volume	**20** min	● Beat either by hand using a whisk or in the mixer with the whisk attachment, off the heat. ● Slowly add the wine or Champagne while whisking.
VERIFYING DONENESS		● The sabayon is done when it can fold over itself, forming a ribbon.

STORAGE: ● Sabayon should be used immediately and is best served warm.

La sauce chocolat (Chocolate sauce)

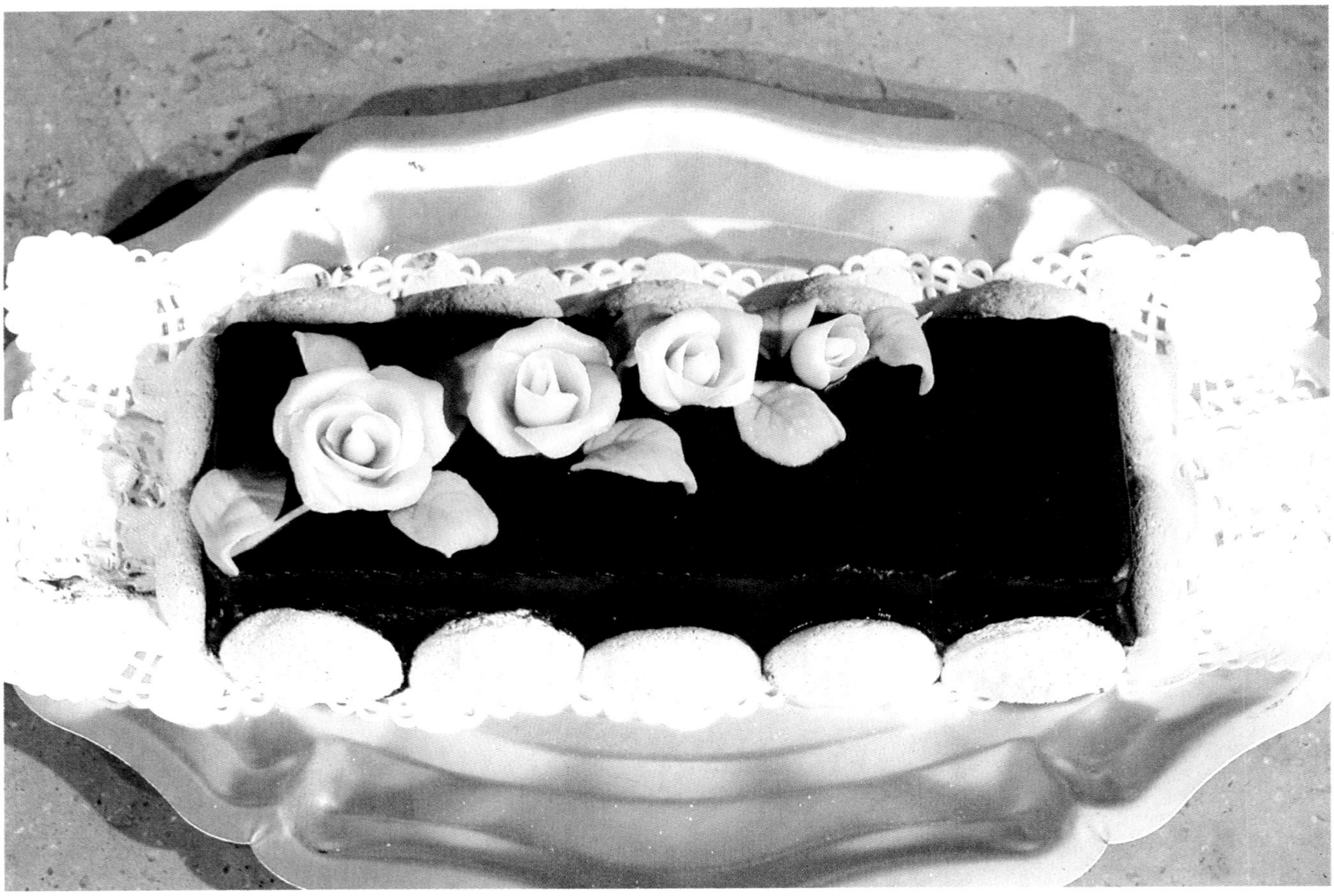

Definition

Chocolate sauce is a smooth, creamy, flavorful sauce.

It is made from a mixture of milk, chocolate, cream, butter, and sometimes sugar syrup and egg yolks.

Uses

Chocolate sauce can accompany various desserts and ice creams. It is also used to glaze various desserts and frozen desserts.

Equipment

Saucepans (2)
Bowls (2)
Whisk

Measuring cup
Pastry scraper
China cap or strainer

Professional Recipe

300 ml milk (10 fl. oz.), brought to a boil

300 g semisweet chocolate (10.5 oz.)
100 ml crème fraîche or heavy cream (3.5 fl. oz.)
50 g butter (1.5 oz.)
50 g sugar (1.5 oz.), optional

Alternative Recipe A

500 ml milk (17 fl. oz.), brought to a boil
350 g semisweet chocolate (12.5 oz.)
400 g coating chocolate (14 oz.)
125 ml heavy cream (4 fl. oz.)

Alternative Recipe B

250 ml milk (8.5 fl. oz.) plus 250 ml heavy cream (8.5 fl. oz.), boiled together
300 g semisweet chocolate (10.5 oz.)

Chocolate sauce is easy to prepare and poses no major difficulties.
Watch the sauce carefully during poaching.
Chocolate sauce is often made just before serving.
Allow approximately 15 minutes for its preparation.
Chocolate sauce is the basis for "sauce profiteroles" and "chocolate coulis."

Alternative Recipe C

400 ml milk (14 fl. oz.), brought to a boil
300 g semisweet chocolate (10.5 oz.)
50 g butter (1.5 oz.)

Alternative Recipe D

500 g coating chocolate (17.5 oz.) plus 200 g couverture chocolate (7 oz.), melted over warm water
70 ml oil (2.5 fl. oz.)

Alternative Recipe E

250 ml butter (9 oz.) plus 350 g unsweetened chocolate (12.5 oz.), melted over warm water
1 L hot sugar syrup (34 fl. oz.), at 1260 D

Alternative Recipe F

300 g couverture chocolate (10.5 oz.) plus 200 g unsweetened chocolate (7 oz.), melted over warm water
250 ml sugar syrup (8.5 fl. oz.), at 1260 D
250 ml milk (8.5 fl. oz.), hot
250 ml crème fraîche or heavy cream (8.5 fl. oz.)

Alternative Recipe G

250 g chocolate (9 oz.) plus 50 g butter (1.5 oz.), melted over warm water
8 egg yolks
500 ml milk (17 fl. oz.), brought to a boil

Preparation

Soften the butter.
Chop the chocolate.
Make the sugar syrup (1260 D), if needed. See Cooking Sugar, pages 14 to 17.

Procedure

Bring the milk to a boil.
Add the chopped chocolate.

Stir the mixture well over low heat, with a whisk.
Add the cream and the butter.
Blend the mixture well with the whisk until the sauce is homogeneous.
Strain the sauce.
Keep the sauce warm until it is used.
Chocolate sauce can be replaced with

ganache (see ganache, pages 46 to 47), softened and thinned with milk. Ganache is easier to use for glazing cakes and frozen desserts, providing a neater appearance than chocolate sauce because of its more fluid consistency. The taste and texture are not the same as chocolate sauce.

Almonds, hazelnuts, or walnuts, lightly roasted and chopped, can be added to the sauce to vary the appearance for frozen-dessert glazes.

Sauce Profiteroles

1 L milk (17 fl. oz.)
1 kg semisweet chocolate (17.5 oz.)
125 g butter (4.5 oz.)
500 ml crème fraîche or heavy cream (17 fl. oz.)

Allow four cream puffs for one serving and 500 ml (17 fl. oz.) of chocolate sauce for six servings (twenty-four cream puffs altogether).

Chocolate Coulis

1 L boiling water (34 fl. oz.) plus 650 g semisweet chocolate (23 oz.) plus 300 g unsweetened chocolate, heated together
125 g butter (4.5 oz.); add to the heated chocolate
500 ml crème fraîche or heavy cream (17 fl. oz.); add off the heat

La Sauce Chocolat (Chocolate Sauce)		
PREPARATION Assemble the Equipment Prepare, Weigh, and Measure the Raw Ingredients	**0** min	● Verify the cleanliness of the equipment. ● Chop the chocolate. ● Soften the butter.
PROCEDURE Boil the Milk	**5** min	● Use a large saucepan.
Add the Chocolate	**8** min	● Add the chopped chocolate to the boiling milk. ● Mix well over low heat.
Add the Cream	**10** min	
Add the Butter	**12** min	● Blend the mixture well with a whisk.
Strain the Sauce	**14** min	● Strain into an inert container.
HOLDING THE SAUCE	**15** min	● Keep warm until needed.

STORAGE: ● Chocolate sauce is best when made just before it is served. Depending on its application, it can be held at 5°C (40°F) for up to 24 hours.

Les pâtes de fruits (Jellied fruits)

History

Sweets based on fruit, sugar, and honey can be traced to the early Egyptians, Chinese, and Arabs.

During the Middle Ages, these sweets were transported to Europe during the Crusades. It was also at this time that sugar, though not readily available, became better known. Jellied fruits very quickly became popular.

A version of jellied fruits based on dried preserves and candied fruits was being made in the region of Auvergne in France, considered to have the best confections and preserves.

As the refinement of sugar made from sugar beets (first introduced by Napoleon) became industrialized, sugar became readily available, and candies such as jellied fruits became more common and popular.

Jellied fruits are fairly easy to prepare. They offer the taste of natural fruit and cost little to make.

Definition

Jellied fruits are made from fruit pulp, sometimes with fruit juice or extract and coloring added, that is cooked with gelatin and sugar (granulated sugar and glucose). Sometimes acid, in the form of lemon juice or cream of tartar, is added. The acid serves three purposes:

1. to help the pectin coagulate
2. to prolong the storage of jellied fruits
3. to prevent the formation of sugar crystals

Categories

Depending of the fruit used, jellied fruits are divided into three categories:

1. **golden fruit:** apricots, oranges, tangerines, quinces, mirabelles (a European golden plum), peaches, and various types of yellow plums, to name a few.

2. **red fruit:** black currants, strawberries, raspberries, red currants, blueberries, cherries, and blackberries

3. **starchy fruit:** such as chestnuts and bananas

Many other fruits are rich in starch, such as almonds, hazelnuts, and walnuts (nuts are fruits, although they are sometimes considered separately). Not used for jellied fruits, these are worked differently and used for almond paste, praline paste, hazelnut paste, and other similar pastes.

If jellied fruits are made with only one type of fruit or a minimum of 75 percent of that fruit, they can be called by the name of that fruit. For example, jellied apricot is made with only apricot.

Jellied fruits should contain a minimum of 75 percent fruit.

Uses

Individual pieces of jellied fruits can be cut into various forms. Larger pieces can also be cut into various shapes.

   Jellied fruits require constant attention from start to finish.

Carefully watch when reducing the fruit pulp and cooking the sugar and then the mixture.

Pour the mixture immediately after cooking.

No special equipment is required.

Allow approximately 1 hour and 45 minutes to prepare jellied fruits.

Equipment

Saucepan, drum sieve, pastry scraper, copper sugar pan, wooden spatula, thermometer, chef's knife, metal rulers or a high-sided sheet pan (or hotel pan) for starch and molds for making imprints

Professional Recipe

1 kg apricot pulp (17.5 oz.)
100 g sugar (3.5 oz.) plus 10 g pectin (2 tsp.)
1 kg sugar (35 oz.)
150 g glucose or trimoline (5 oz.)
20 ml citric acid or lemon juice (1.5 Tbsp.)
flavoring, as needed

Alternative Recipes

Banana

1 kg banana pulp (35 oz.)
250 g apricot pulp (9 oz.)
100 g sugar (3.5 oz.) plus 10 g pectin (2 tsp.)
1 kg sugar (35 oz.)
150 g glucose (5 oz.)
20 ml citric acid (1.5 Tbsp.)
40 ml banana extract (1.5 fl. oz.)

Black Currant

1 kg black currant pulp (35 oz.)
250 g apricot pulp (9 oz.)
100 g sugar (3.5 oz.) plus 10 g pectin (2 tsp.)
1 kg sugar (35 oz.)
150 g glucose (5 oz.)
20 ml citric acid (1.5 Tbsp.)
35 ml black currant extract (1 fl. oz.)

Raspberry

500 g raspberry pulp (17.5 oz.)
750 g apricot pulp (26.5 oz.)
100 g sugar (3.5 oz.) plus 10 g pectin (2 tsp.)
1 kg sugar (35 oz.)
150 g glucose (5 oz.)
20 ml g citric acid (1.5 Tbsp.)
35 ml raspberry extract (1 fl. oz.)

Mandarin

1,250 g apricot pulp (44 oz.)
100 g sugar (3.5 oz.) plus 10 g pectin (2 tsp.)
1 kg sugar (35 oz.)
150 g glucose (5 oz.)
20 ml citric acid (1.5 Tbsp.)
35 ml mandarin extract (1 fl. oz.)

Orange

1 kg orange pulp (35 oz.)
250 g apricot pulp (9 oz.)
100 g sugar (3.5 oz.) plus 10 g pectin (2 tsp.)
1 kg sugar (35 oz.)
150 g glucose (5 oz.)
20 ml citric acid (1.5 Tbsp.)
15 ml orange extract (1 Tbsp.)

Plum

1,250 g apricot pulp (44 oz.)
100 g sugar (3.5 oz.) plus 10 g pectin (2 tsp.)
1 kg sugar (35 oz.)
150 g glucose (5 oz.)
20 ml citric acid (1.5 Tbsp.)
40 ml plum extract (1.5 fl. oz.), plus coloring (optional)

Preparation

Preparing the Fruit Pulp

For Golden Fruit

Peel, pit, and slice or quarter the fruit so it will cook evenly and quickly.

Poach the fruit by placing it into a saucepan of simmering water and simmering for 5 minutes. (Note that soft

golden fruit, such as peaches, plums, and oranges, need not be poached. For soft golden fruit, follow the instructions for red fruit.)

The fruit is finished poaching when it is soft in the center. Check the softness by inserting the tip of a knife into the fruit; it should slide through the fruit easily.

Drain the fruit well in a strainer, colander, or drum sieve to eliminate as much water as possible, to help shorten the time required to reduce it.

Crush the poached fruit to extract the pulp. Use a drum sieve with a pastry scraper over a bowl or saucepan. A food mill can also be used.

Note

It is important to choose fruit that is very ripe and without blemishes or bruises to obtain the best final results possible.

If the fruit is low in pectin, half of it can be replaced with apple or quince without altering the flavor. Apples and quince are rich in pectin and serve as a natural liaison.

The flavor of the fruit can be strengthened by adding a natural extract of the same fruit. The color can also be reinforced by adding natural food colorings.

To reduce the pulp, after sieving the fruit, place it in a heavy-bottomed saucepan over low heat. Stirring constantly, reduce by half.

This is an important step. If heated too quickly, the pulp can burn, imparting a bitter taste and dark color to the final product.

Thick fruit pulps can splatter if they are not stirred quickly enough.

To avoid burns caused by splattering, place the hand used for stirring in a pastry bag and hold the handle of the wooden spatula through the bag.

The pulp can also be reduced over a hot water bath, which would eliminate the problems of burning and splattering. Unfortunately, this technique is more time consuming, although it does not require constant stirring.

Evaporating the water through reduction creates a pulp high in pectin, which is the thickening agent necessary for making jellied fruits.

For Red Fruit

Red fruit to be used for jellied fruits should also be as ripe as possible, without bruises or blemishes.

Crush the fruit through a drum sieve; it need not be softened by poaching. After crushing the pulp, strain it to eliminate excess moisture and reduce it, as for golden fruit.

Because these fruits do not require poaching, the juice from straining can be used for other preparations.

Once the pulp has been reduced, all procedures to prepare jellied fruits are the same, regardless of the fruit used.

Frozen fruit pulp, ready to use, can replace the fresh pulp.

Preparing the Acid Solution

The acid should always be diluted with an equal quantity of hot water. This solution can be stored in an airtight container. Acid solutions can consist of 100 g (3.5 oz.) cream of tartar plus 100 ml (3.5 fl. oz.) hot water, or 100 g (3.5 oz.) citric acid plus 100 ml (3.5 fl. oz.) hot water, for example.

For fruit low in pectin, such as plums, rhubarb, pears, cherries, peaches, strawberries, and melons, it is often necessary to add pectin that can be bought commercially in a powdered form. It is important to read the ingredients listed for the pectin: it should be a base of natural pectin with no artificial ingredients added. This will maintain the high quality of the final product, so that it can be considered a "natural product."

The amount of pectin used depends on the type of fruit and the quality of fruit and pectin used. It is best to refer to the indications supplied by the manufacturer. The pectin can be added at the beginning of cooking the sugar, or if mixed with an equal quantity of sugar, it can be added at the same time as the fruit pulp.

Procedure

Cook the sugar following the usual precautions (see Cooking Sugar, pages 14 to 17), in a saucepan large enough to hold all the fruit pulp to be added.

Skim the sugar and, with a pastry brush, brush the sides of the saucepan if crystals form. Add the glucose. Check the cooking, which should almost always reach the soft crack stage, between 130° and 135°C (266° and 275°F).

While the sugar is cooking, add the pectin mixed with an equal amount of sugar to the warm fruit pulp and mix well with a whisk.

Once the sugar has reached the proper temperature, add the pulp, mixing gently over low heat with a wooden spatula to obtain a homogeneous mixture.

Continue to cook the mixture for approximately 5 minutes, until it is shiny and translucent.

Verify doneness with a thermometer —the mixture should be 106° to 109°C (223° to 228°F)—or with a refractometer, which should indicate 72 to 75 percent.

Finally, add the acid, which will speed up the coagulation of the pectin.

It is important to be able to transfer the mixture as soon as it is ready. Transfer the mixture by pouring it between metal rulers already set up on a marble that has been lightly covered with cornstarch (to prevent the mixture from sticking to the marble). Level the mixture with a metal spatula and sprinkle lightly with granulated sugar to prevent a crust from forming.

The mixture can also be poured into sheet pans lined with aluminum foil that has been liberally sprinkled with cornstarch or into imprints that have been made in cornstarch in a sheet cake pan or high-sided sheet pan. Use a funnel, previously warmed under hot water, to fill the molds.

The mixture should be transferred as quickly as possible. Let it set for approximately 2 hours. Then remove the metal rulers, if used. Brush off the cornstarch. If too much starch remains, the jellied fruits can be rinsed under cold running water.

Dry the jellied fruits for 24 to 48 hours, depending on the fruit used, in a dry warm area, 40°C (104°F).

Cut the jellied fruits into various shapes and sizes with a chef's knife or cutters of various sizes. Warm the knife or cutters under hot running water to make clean cuts.

Softening and Coating the Fruit

Place the jellied fruits in a drum sieve over a container filled with boiling water for just a few seconds to allow the exte-

rior to soften slightly. This will help the sugar adhere to the pieces.

Roll the jellied fruits in crystal or granulated sugar. Use:

- a container with sugar inside

- a drum sieve with sugar

- a sheet of paper covered with a layer of sugar

The jellied fruits can also be candied (see crystallized candies, pages 72 to 74).

To Use Fruit High in Starch

Bananas: peel and mash through a drum sieve or strainer.

Chestnuts: plunge into boiling water for several minutes, then shell, being careful to remove the fibrous membrane covering them. Finish as for golden fruit.

Storage

Jellied fruits can be stored for 3 to 4 weeks in airtight containers in a cool area.

			Les Pâtes de Fruits (Jellied Fruits)
PREPARATION **Assemble** the Equipment **Prepare, Weigh, and Measure** the Raw Ingredients	**0** min		• Make imprints in a layer of cornstarch, or set metal rulers in place on a marble, sprinkling the marble with cornstarch. • Prepare the acid solution. • Prepare the fruit pulp, according to the fruit used.
PROCEDURE Heat the Pulp Add the Pectin	**15** min		• Depending on the type of fruit, reduce over a warm water bath or directly over heat. • Mix the pectin with an equal quantity of sugar. • Add the pectin to the fruit pulp with a whisk.
Cook the Sugar	**1 hr 15**		• Cook the sugar and glucose, following the usual procedure. • Skim and brush the sides of the saucepan to prevent crystals from forming. • Cook the sugar to 130° to 135°C (266° to 275°F), the soft crack stage.
Cook the Mixture	**1 hr 30**		• Add the warm fruit pulp to the cooked sugar. • Stir constantly with a wooden spatula.
Verify Doneness	**1 hr 40**		• Check the cooking with a thermometer, which should read 109°C (228°F), or a refractometer, which should read 75 percent.
Add the Acid Solution			• Add the acid just before transferring or molding the mixture.
TRANSFERRING Finish	**1 hr 45**		• Pour the fruit into the imprints made in cornstarch or onto marble between rulers before it cools. • Cut after completely cool. • Roll in crystal or granulated sugar or crystallize the fruits.
STORAGE: • Jellied fruits can be stored for 3 to 4 weeks in airtight containers in a cool, dry area.			

Les fruits confits (Candied fruits)

History

Fruit, plants, and grains covered with honey can be traced to ancient Rome, Greece, Egypt, the Middle East, and China.

During the Middle Ages, fruit was candied in honey to preserve it and maintain its nutrients, so that it could be used as medication.

In the middle of the fourteenth century, after the Crusades, the first candied fruits were made with cane sugar. In Apt, a city in France, the technique of using cane sugar (to replace honey) for preserving fruits was developed by a supplier to King Clément VI.

Today, the industry making candied fruits in France is known throughout the world, as approximately half of their production is exported.

Candied fruits are rarely made by hand, as their preparation is very time consuming.

Definition

Candied fruits are made from whole fresh fruit that is repeatedly saturated in a sugar syrup. The goal is to replace the water of the fruit with a highly concentrated sugar solution that preserves the fruit while maintaining its original form.

Uses

Candied fruits can be macerated in Kirsch, Grand Marnier, Cognac, and other liquors and liqueurs; whole fruits can be crystallized with sugar syrup (see crystallized candies, pages 72 to 74).

Candied fruits can also be macerated to garnish and flavor ice cream (as for Plombière), can be added to various desserts, Swiss brioches, and pound cake (see volume 1, pound cake with candied fruit, pages 54 to 57) and can be used to fill chocolates.

They can also be used to decorate desserts, honey spice cakes, ice creams, savarins, fruit desserts, frozen deserts, and petits fours.

Equipment

Bowl
Drum sieve or colander
Vegetable peeler
Saucepan with cover

Paring knife
Pastry brush
Towel
Skimmer
Hydrometer

Candied fruits are demanding preparations.

All equipment must be carefully cleaned.

The progressively concentrated syrups must be prepared exactly.

Candied fruits can take from several days to several months when made by hand.

Professional Recipe

To prepare enough syrup (at 1160 D) for 1 kg (35 oz.) of fruit:

1 L water (34 fl. oz.)
600 g sugar (21 oz.)
juice of one lemon

Preparation

Choosing the proper fruit to be candied is very important. It is best to use fruit that is slightly unripe. The fruit should be unblemished and without bruises.

Whole fruit should be no more than 5 cm (2 in.), so it can be evenly candied. Large fruit such as melons and watermelons can be cut into quarters or cubes.

Procedure

Sort the Fruit

Choose fruits of the same size. Eliminate any rotten or overripe fruit. Wash and prepare the same type of fruit at a time; for example, remove the stems of all strawberries, peel all the pears, then pit the cherries.

Wash the Fruit

Remove any trace of dust, insects, or dirt.

Blanch the Fruit

Properly blanching the fruit will affect the final result to a large extent.

Blanch the fruit by placing it in boiling water. This helps the syrup penetrate more easily and softens the flesh of the fruit.

The length of time for blanching depends on the fruit. The fruit should be tender but not mushy.

Plunge the fruit under cold water until cool to stop the cooking. Drain the fruit.

Tender fruits, such as strawberries, apricots, and plums, are not blanched.

Placing in Syrup: Candying

Once drained, arrange the fruit on a colander or round rack (a cooling rack can be used) that can fit inside a saucepan.

Make a sugar syrup that is 1160 D, following the usual precautions (see Cooking Sugar, pages 14 to 17). Boil the water and sugar for 1 minute. Remove from the heat and place the fruit in the boiling hot syrup.

Place a second rack on top of the fruit to submerge it totally in the syrup.

Cover the saucepan with a clean towel and a saucepan lid. Allow the fruit to macerate for a minimum of 24 hours.

After 24 hours, remove and drain the fruit, reserving the syrup. Bring the syrup back to a boil for 3 minutes to thicken it.

Return the fruit to the saucepan, submerging it in the syrup, and cover as before, with a towel and lid, for 24 hours.

This procedure can be repeated for 5 days to 3 months, depending on the type, size, and ripeness of the fruit used. Once the syrup reaches a density of 1200 D, it will be necessary to add a small amount of glucose to prevent crystals from forming in the syrup as it cools.

Avoid boiling the syrup for too long at a time to raise the density. It is preferable to add powdered sugar to increase the density.

After the last boiling and resting, drain the fruit for 48 hours before storing in inert containers.

The density of the syrup at each stage

Stage	Density of the Syrup	Resting Time
First	1160 D	24 hrs
Second	1180 D	24 hrs
Third	1200 D	24 hrs
Fourth	1200 D (add glucose)	24 hrs
Fifth	1240 D (add glucose)	24 hrs
Sixth	1260 D (add glucose)	24 hrs
Seventh	1280 D (add glucose)	24 hrs
Eighth	1300 D (add glucose)	24 hrs
Ninth	1330 D (add glucose)	24 hrs
Tenth	1340 D (add glucose)	24 hrs

Storage

Candied fruits can be stored for several months refrigerated, at 5°C (40°F), in airtight, inert containers.

Candied fruits sold commercially are packaged after draining or are packaged in the same syrup in which they were cooked. They can be purchased as whole fruits, in quarters, slices, thin strips, or cubes of various sizes, depending on their use.

Fruits that can be candied include apricots, bananas, cherries, figs, strawberries, mandarins, chestnuts, melons, oranges, watermelons, peaches, pears, and various plums. Angelica, which is an herb, is also often candied.

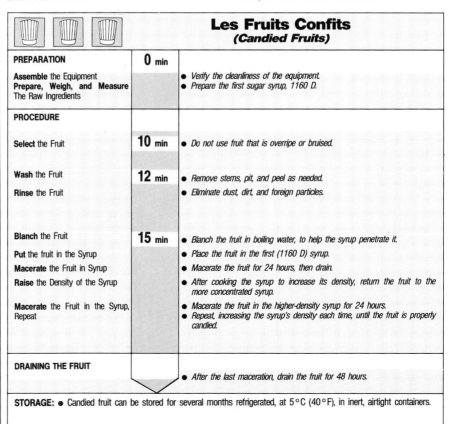

	Les Fruits Confits (Candied Fruits)	
PREPARATION	**0** min	
Assemble the Equipment Prepare, Weigh, and Measure The Raw Ingredients		● Verify the cleanliness of the equipment. ● Prepare the first sugar syrup, 1160 D.
PROCEDURE		
Select the Fruit	**10** min	● Do not use fruit that is overripe or bruised.
Wash the Fruit	**12** min	● Remove stems, pit, and peel as needed.
Rinse the Fruit		● Eliminate dust, dirt, and foreign particles.
Blanch the Fruit	**15** min	● Blanch the fruit in boiling water, to help the syrup penetrate it.
Put the fruit in the Syrup		● Place the fruit in the first (1160 D) syrup.
Macerate the Fruit in Syrup		● Macerate the fruit for 24 hours, then drain.
Raise the Density of the Syrup		● After cooking the syrup to increase its density, return the fruit to the more concentrated syrup.
Macerate the Fruit in the Syrup, Repeat		● Macerate the fruit in the higher-density syrup for 24 hours. ● Repeat, increasing the syrup's density each time, until the fruit is properly candied.
DRAINING THE FRUIT		● After the last maceration, drain the fruit for 48 hours.
STORAGE: ● Candied fruit can be stored for several months refrigerated, at 5°C (40°F), in inert, airtight containers.		

Les marrons glacés (Glazed chestnuts)

Making glazed chestnuts is similar to making candied fruits, as the chestnuts are candied or partially candied before being glazed.

The preparation differs from candied fruits in that the chestnuts are precooked to remove their shells.

In France, chestnuts favored for this preparation come from the Lyons and Ardèche regions. In Italy they are from Turin. Chestnuts are widely grown in the United States.

Equipment

Same as for candied fruits (see pages 90 to 91).

Professional Recipe

To prepare enough syrup (at 1220 D) for 1 kg (35 oz.) of chestnuts:

1 L water (34 fl. oz.)
800 g sugar (28 oz.)
50 g glucose (1.5 oz.)

Preparation for Glazing

First Step

Choose the best chestnuts possible. Make a small incision in the bottoms of the shells, being careful not to cut through them. This will speed the pre-cooking, as the water can pass through these incisions, and it facilitates removing the shell afterward.

Certain chestnuts are very difficult to peel and break easily, making it important to choose the highest-quality chestnuts possible.

Precooking the Chestnuts

Place the chestnuts in boiling water and cook for approximately 30 minutes, or just until the shell can be removed. It is very important not to overcook the chestnuts.

Checking Doneness

Try to shell a chestnut carefully, with a paring knife. If the shell comes off easily, stop the cooking.

Second Step

Shelling the Chestnuts

With a paring knife, remove the shells

A delicate preparation, glazed chestnuts require experience with cooking syrups of different densities.

Shell the chestnuts with care.

Do not overcook the chestnuts.

Allow 48 hours to prepare glazed chestnuts.

carefully without cutting the chestnut meat. Any cuts in the chestnuts will brown when they are cooked later.

Peeling the Chestnuts

The fuzzy brown skin of the chestnut is removed by following a procedure similar to that used for peeling almonds. Blanch the chestnuts in boiling water for 4 to 5 minutes.

Put them in a towel and gently roll and rub them around inside until their skins come off. Check each one for any bits of remaining peel.

Cooking the Chestnuts

Once the chestnuts are completely shelled and peeled, double-check that no skin remains in the grooves of the chestnuts. Place the chestnuts inside a colander or on a towel or cheesecloth. Tie the cloth, allowing enough extra space for the chestnuts to expand as they cook. Place a round rack on the bottom of the saucepan and set the chestnuts on top. Add cold water and bring to a simmer; continue to simmer for approximately 30 to 45 minutes. Be careful: do not let the water come to a boil.

Verifying Doneness

Check if the chestnuts are cooked by piercing several of them with a pin. The pin should slide through without meeting resistance. Avoid overcooking the chestnuts.

Rinsing the Chestnuts

Remove the chestnuts from the saucepan and rinse them with warm water. This step is optional. Remove them from the towel or cloth if used.

Draining the Chestnuts

Drain the chestnuts on a rack for 10 to 15 minutes before glazing them.

Candying the Chestnuts

The chestnuts are placed in the first syrup with glucose (1220 D). They are finished in a syrup of 1280 D.

Allow the syrup to evaporate and slowly become concentrated over low heat. If the syrup becomes too thick too

quickly, a small amount of syrup with glucose (1220 D) can be added.

The chestnuts can also be candied in the same way as candied fruits (see candied fruits, pages 90 to 91).

Glazing the Chestnuts

Draining the Chestnuts

Drain the chestnuts for a minimum of 48 hours after they are candied or semicandied.

Preparing a Water Glaze

Make a water glaze by blending confectioners' sugar with water flavored lightly with vanilla extract. The consistency should be similar to that of a fondant for glazing desserts, fluid, with a temperature of approximately 45°C (113°F). See water or rum glaze, page 81.

Glazing

With a fork, dip the chestnuts into the water glaze. Remove and immediately place on a rack placed over a sheet pan.

Setting the Glaze

Put the glazed chestnuts in a hot oven for a few seconds to set the glaze and make it shiny.

Any chestnuts that have been broken or cut in any of the steps will taste as good as the perfect ones, although they will be less attractive. They can be chopped for making chestnut paste or used as a garnish in cakes made with chestnut cream.

Storage

Same as for candied fruits.

				Les Marrons Glacés *(Glazed Chestnuts)*
PROCEDURE	**0** min			
Assemble the Equipment **Prepare, Weigh, and Measure** the Raw Ingredients				● *Verify the cleanliness of the equipment.* ● *Select the best possible chestnuts.*
PROCEDURE	**5** min			
Prepare the Chestnuts				● *Shell and peel the chestnuts.*
Cook the Chestnuts	**30** min			● *Cook for 60 to 90 minutes.*
Verify Doneness	**1** hr **45**			● *A pin should slide easily through the chestnuts; avoid overcooking.*
Rinse the Chestnuts				● *The chestnuts can be rinsed with hot water (optional).*
Drain the Chestnuts	**2** hrs			● *Drain on a rack.* ● *Place the chestnuts in a syrup of 1220 D.*
Candy the Chestnuts				*Cook over a low heat, gradually increasing the density of the syrup to 1280 D; allow 48 hours to drain the chestnuts.*
GLAZING THE CHESTNUTS				
Use a Vanilla Water Glaze				● *Dip the chestnuts in the glaze, then place them on a rack set over a sheet pan.*
Set the Glaze				● *Set the glaze in a hot oven for a few seconds.*
STORAGE: ● *Glazed chestnuts can be stored for several months refrigerated, at 5°C (40°F), in inert, airtight containers.*				

La pâte d'amandes crue (Almond paste)

History

Almond paste dates back to ancient Rome, where desserts were made with ground almonds, known as Greek almonds.

During the Middle Ages, ground almonds were jellied, colored red, green, and yellow, and used as a garnish. These almond jellies were the origin of the almond paste used today.

Definition

Almond paste is based on equal quantities of peeled almonds and sugar ground together to create a preparation known as "tant pour tant," meaning "as much as." Moist almonds are used for making almond paste.

The moisture from the almonds melts the sugar and forms a pastelike mixture. Dry almonds and equal quantities of sugar are used to make almond powder. Both types of almond/sugar mixtures are called tant pour tant almond (see volume 1, page 89).

Uses

Almond paste is not often used. It is usually replaced by the tant pour tant almond powder, which can be stored for a longer time.

Recipes that use almond paste include: pains de Gênes (almond cake), tea biscuits, and other cookies.

Almond paste is also used for decorating certain cakes and other desserts.

Equipment

Strainer, bowl, pastry scraper, towel, airtight inert container, grinder for nuts or other uses

Professional Recipe

1 kg blanched, peeled almonds (35 oz.)
1 kg sugar (35 oz.), half granulated sugar, half confectioners' sugar
syrup at 1260 D, as needed, or raw egg white

Alternative Recipe

1 kg blanched, peeled almonds (35 oz.)
950 to 1,150 g sugar (33.5 to 40.5 oz.)
100 g invert sugar (3.5 oz.)
syrup at 1260 D, as needed, or raw egg white

 Almond paste is a fairly easy preparation. Always use freshly peeled almonds.

Carefully observe the procedure for grinding the almonds so that the paste does not become oily.

A special grinder must be used to grind the almonds.

Allow 20 to 25 minutes to make almond paste.

Preparation

Use large almonds if possible.

Note: Use the same amount of almonds, whether blanched and peeled or unpeeled. When the unpeeled almonds are blanched for peeling, the moisture absorbed by the almonds will equal the weight of the removed peel.

If using unpeeled almonds, rinse in cold water to clean off any dust or impurities.

Then place them in boiling water, using approximately 750 ml (25 fl. oz.) of water per kg (35 oz.) of almonds.

Stir the almonds gently with a skimmer so they blanch evenly. Test for doneness by pinching an almond between two fingers. When the peel pops off easily, remove them from the water. Drain the almonds in a strainer or colander over a sink.

Do not leave the almonds in the boiling water longer than necessary, or they will lose their oil and diminish in flavor. Run cold water over the almonds as soon as they are drained to cool them quickly.

On a clean work surface, pinch the almonds between the thumb and index finger against the work surface to remove the peels. The peel will remain between the fingers (and not become mixed with the peeled almonds); this will also prevent the almonds from sliding off the work surface.

Use both hands to speed up the process, which can be long and tedious. There are also machines commercially used to peel almonds.

Check that all almonds have been peeled, and discard any that are rotten or bruised. Rinse again in cold water to remove any traces of peel. Drain the almonds and dry them off.

Procedure
Method A: Grinder

Mixing the Peeled Almonds with the Sugar

Mix the sugar with the almonds, which should still be moist after peeling, or with dry almonds that have been moistened by rinsing in cold water.

Grinding the Mixture

Place the sugar and almonds in the grinder. Begin grinding with the wheels apart to crush the almonds lightly.

Run the almonds through the grinder again, tightening the wheels. Repeat this process, continuing to tighten the wheels each time the almonds and sugar are passed through, until a smooth paste is obtained. Avoid overtightening the wheels, which would squeeze the oil from the almonds, causing the powder to be oily and limiting its use and storage.

Transfering the Paste

Always transfer this paste in an airtight plastic container for storage, as it easily forms a skin.

Storage

Almond paste can be refrigerated for 4 to 6 weeks at 5°C (40°F). For longer storage, it can be wrapped in parchment paper that has been moistened with a strong liquor. This will prevent mold from growing.

Method B: Multiple-use Grinder (food processor)

Mix the half-dry peeled almonds with the granulated sugar.

Grinding the Mixture

Place the mixture in the bowl of a food processor.

With the metal blade attachment, grind the mixture on medium speed, being careful to stop the machine before lumps form.

Add the confectioners' sugar and again grind at medium speed. Stop grinding before the oil separates from the almonds.

Verifying Doneness

If a moister paste is necessary for final use, add liquid at this point. Use egg whites or syrup at 1260 D (with glucose) or trimoline (invert sugar). Finish mixing on slow speed, being careful not to heat the paste.

Transfer and store the almond paste as indicated in method A.

		La Pâte d'Amandes Crue (Almond Paste)
PREPARATION	**0** min	
Assemble the Equipment. Prepare, Weigh, and Measure the Raw Ingredients		● Verify the cleanliness of the equipment. ● Peel the almonds. ● Examine the almonds carefully, removing any that are rotten.
PROCEDURE	**15** min	
Method A: Grinder		
Mix the Almonds and Sugar **Grind** the Mixture		● Mix the almonds and sugar in a bowl with a wooden spatula. ● Progressively tighten the wheels each time the mixture is run through the machine.
Check the Grinding **Achieve** Proper Consistency	**25** min	● The paste should be smooth but not oily. ● Add liquid (egg white or syrup) at this point if needed
Method B: Food Processor	**15** min	
Mix the Peeled Almonds and Granulated Sugar.		● Mix the sugar and almonds in the bowl of the processor.
Grind the Mixture	**16** min	● Grind the sugar and almonds on medium speed; stop before lumps form.
Add Confectioners' Sugar	**18** min	● Add confectioners' sugar and grind again at medium speed; avoid overgrinding, which would make the mixture oily.
Achieve Proper Consistency	**19** min	● Add any liquid (syrup or egg white) if needed.
Finish Grinding	**20** min	● Grind on first speed until the paste is smooth but not oily.
STORAGE: Almond paste can be stored for 4 to 6 weeks refrigerated, at 5°C (40°F), in inert, airtight containers.		

La pâte d'amandes fondante ou confiseur (Marzipan or almond modeling paste)

Definition

Marzipan, a derivative of almond paste (see pages 94 to 95), is used in many diverse preparations, as well as to create various decorative figures.

With the help of modern machinery, it is fairly easy to obtain a high-quality marzipan. The consistency of marzipan can vary, but it should always remain malleable for modeling.

As indicated by its French name, pâte d'amandes confiseur (literally confectionery almond paste), marzipan is made with almonds and used specifically in confectionery.

Marzipan is made by mixing almonds with cooked sugar and glucose.

Depending on the percentage of almonds used, in France different types of marzipan are categorized as follows:

Marzipan *supérieure*	**66%**
Marzipan *extra*	**50%**
Marzipan *fondante or confiseur*	**33%**
Marzipan *d'office*	**25%**

Uses

Marzipan is widely used by chefs making confections. It can be flavored, colored, and shaped into various forms, to be presented alone or combined with other candies.

In pastry making, marzipan is used primarily as decoration (to cover cakes, make flowers, leaves, ribbons, braids, and various other figures).

Note: Depending on how it is used, marzipan can be made more or less malleable:

- relatively **soft** when it is flavored with liquor and used to garnish chocolates and other candies

- **medium** consistency, for decorations, covering cakes, and modeling

- **firm** when cut and shaped into various forms and soaked in liquor.

The consistency of marzipan can be altered by varying the amount of time the sugar is cooked and by varying the dryness of the almonds. The longer the sugar is cooked and the dryer the almonds, the more firm the marzipan will be.

When using the more modern method with the food processor, the almonds should always be fairly moist. This moisture is necessary to compensate for the

 Marzipan is a delicate preparation that requires a great deal of precision.

Follow all key points and precautions given.

Carefully watch the sugar as it cooks.

Either a grinder or food processor is necessary for its preparation.

Allow approximately 35 minutes to make marzipan with a food processor; 90 minutes with a grinder.

heat of the machine when run on high speed, which causes the moisture in the almonds to evaporate.

Note

Certain food processors will heat and grind and chop more or less finely than others. For this reason the amount of time for grinding, the temperature for cooking the sugar, and the moisture of the almonds are given as suggestions, to be adjusted according to the machine used.

Equipment

Method A: Grinder

Copper sugar pan plus candy thermometer
Large bowl, wooden spatula
Plastic cutting board, plastic wrap
Pastry scraper
Container with cover

Method B: Food Processor

Copper sugar pan plus candy thermometer
Plastic cutting board, plastic wrap
Container with cover
Pastry scraper

Professional Recipe A

1 kg peeled almonds (35 oz.)
1,500 g sugar (53 oz.) plus 500 g glucose (17.5 oz.), cooked to 115° to 123°C (239° to 253°F)

Professional Recipe B

1 kg peeled almonds (35 oz.)
500 g confectioners' sugar (17.5 oz.)
1 kg sugar (35 oz.) plus 450 g glucose (16 oz.), cooked to 114° to 117°C (237° to 242°F)

Alternative Recipe

1 kg almonds (35 oz.)
1 to 2 kg sugar with glucose (35 to 70.5 oz.)
a drop of blue food coloring (optional)

Preparation

As for almond paste, there are two ways to make marzipan, with the grinder or with the food processor.

As in making almond paste, it is important when making marzipan to choose high-quality almonds with skins, rather than purchasing almonds that are already peeled. Peeled almonds do not store as well and therefore tend not to be as fresh.

Depending on the method followed, the almonds will be dried or partially dried.

Marzipan should be made at least one day before it is to be used. It will be hot after it is made and should be slowly cooled to room temperature, approximately 20°C (68°F).

If it is cooled too quickly, the exterior will become firm while the interior stays soft, making it difficult to work with.

The glucose plays an important role in the recipe, as it helps make the marzipan malleable and prevents it from drying out.

Procedure

Method A: Grinder

Cooking the Sugar and Glucose

Cook the sugar and glucose, following the usual precautions (see Cooking Sugar, pages 14 to 17).

With this method (using the grinder and dry almonds), depending on the desired consistency and how the marzipan will be used, cook the sugar to between 115° and 123°C (239° and 253°F).

Pouring the Cooked Sugar over the Almonds

Once the sugar is cooked to the proper temperature, pour it over the almonds in a large bowl and stir with a wooden spatula. This can be done in two ways:

a. If possible, have a second person help with this step. Have one person slowly pour a fine stream of cooked sugar over the almonds while the other stirs constantly with a wooden spatula until all the almonds are completely coated with sugar. The almonds will have a slightly dull finish.
b. If working alone, pour the cooked sugar over the almonds all at once, trying to cover as many of the almonds as possible. Stir immediately and vigorously with the wooden spatula until all the almonds are completely coated with sugar and have a slightly dull finish.

Transfer the mixture to an oiled board or oiled marble. Allow the mixture to cool completely before grinding.

Grinding the Mixture

Verify the cleanliness of the grinder. With the wheels spread to 1 cm (1/2 in.), pass the mixture through.

This first grinding should simply break up the almonds into evenly sized pieces. Continue to grind the almonds at a slow speed, progressively tightening the wheels 1 to 2 mm (1/16 to 1/8 in.) each time the almonds are passed through.

Continue to grind the almonds in this way until they become a paste.

Be careful not to overgrind the paste, or the oil will separate from the almonds, rise to the surface of the paste, and give a sticky, flaccid quality to the marzipan.

This would make it difficult to work with and limit its storage, as once the oil rises to the surface, the paste will quickly become rancid.

Once the powder is very fine, working it with the hands will help it turn into a paste.

Transfer the paste to a board and cover it with plastic wrap or place it in an airtight container.

Method B: Food Processor

Cooking the Sugar and Glucose

Cook the sugar and glucose, following the usual precautions (see Cooking Sugar, pages 14 to 17).

Grinding the Almonds with the Confectioners' Sugar

After checking the food processor for cleanliness, use it to grind the peeled almonds with the confectioners' sugar, on medium speed, until a fine powder is formed.

This should take 1 to 2 minutes. Do not overgrind, or the powder might become warm, causing the oil to rise to the surface.

Verifying the Cooking of the Sugar

The temperature of the sugar will vary, depending on the desired consistency of the paste and the moisture in the almonds. For a medium consistency (to decorate and cover cakes), the sugar can be cooked to 114°C (237°F) if the almonds are almost dry; if the almonds are moist, for a paste of the same consistency, cook the sugar to 117°C (242°F).

The temperature range for cooking the sugar lies between 110° and 123°C (230° to 253°F).

Stopping the Sugar from Cooking

Stop the sugar from cooking once it has reached the proper temperature by placing the bottom of the saucepan in cold water for a few seconds.

Adding the Cooked Sugar to the Almond Powder

Pour the sugar either:

• Directly over the powder of almond and confectioners' sugar with the food processor turned off. Once the sugar has been added, with the feed tube closed, run the machine at medium speed for 3 minutes.

This time, grind the powder much finer. Because of the heat of the sugar syrup, the almond paste will be partially pasteurized.

• Or, slowly in a fine stream, over the powder through the feed tube, with the machine on slow speed.

Stop the machine, and scrape down the sides of the bowl and the cover if necessary. Run the machine at medium speed for 1 to 2 minutes, with the feed tube open to allow the steam to escape.

La Pâte d'Amandes Fondante ou Confiseur
(Marzipan)

PREPARATION	**0** min	
Assemble the Equipment **Prepare, Weigh, and Measure** the Raw Ingredients		• *Verify the cleanliness of the equipment.* • *Peel the almonds.* • *Examine the almonds after peeling and discard any that are rotten.*
PROCEDURE	**15** min	
Method A: Grinder **Cook** the Sugar and Glucose		• *Follow all precautions for cooking sugar. Plunge the pan into cold water to stop the sugar from cooking when it reaches the correct temperature.*
Pour the Cooked Sugar over the Almonds	**25** min	• *When the sugar has reached the desired temperature, pour it over the almonds and stir with a wooden spatula; allow the mixture to cool.*
Break Up the Mixture	**1** hr **15**	• *Use the grinder with the wheels open 1 cm (1/2 in.) wide.*
Grind the Mixture into a Fine Powder	**1** hr **20**	• *Progressively tighten the wheels by 1 to 2 mm (1/16 to 1/8 in.) each time the mixture is passed through.*
Grind into a Paste	**1** hr **25**	• *The wheels should be almost completely closed.* • *Be careful not to overheat the mixture, which would cause the oil to rise to the surface of the mixture.*
Transfer	**1** hr **30**	• *Transfer the paste to a sheet pan and cover with plastic wrap, or place in an airtight container.*
Method B: Food Processor	**15** min	
Cook the Sugar and Glucose		• *Follow all precautions for cooking sugar. Plunge the saucepan in cool water to stop the sugar from cooking when it reaches the correct temperature.*
Grind the Mixture	**20** min	• *Grind the mixture to a fine powder.*
Add the Cooked Sugar and Glucose	**25** min	• *Pour the cooked sugar over the almond/confectioners' sugar mixture.*
Grind the Mixture to a Paste		• *Close the food processor and grind for 3 minutes. Scrape the sides of the bowl if necessary.*
VERIFYING THE QUALITY OF THE PASTE	**30** min	• *Smooth a piece of warm paste on the work surface with a metal spatula.*
TRANSFERING	**35** min	• *Transfer the paste to a sheet pan and cover with plastic wrap, or place in an airtight container.*

STORAGE: • Marzipan can be stored for several weeks wrapped airtight in a cool, dry area at 15° to 20°C (60° to 68°F). It can be stored for several months in the refrigerator if wrapped airtight.

Verifying the Quality of the Paste

Check the quality of the paste by spreading a small amount of hot paste on a marble or work surface with a metal spatula or triangle. It should be smooth and homogeneous.

Do not grind longer than necessary or the oil in the almonds will rise to the surface, presenting the same problems mentioned in method A. Transfer and store as indicated in method A.

Note: This second method, using a food processor, is faster and produces a better result.

Storage

Marzipan **fondant** or **confiseur**—33 percent almond—keeps well in a dry, cool area at 15° to 20°C (60° to 68°F) for several weeks. If stored at or below 10°C (50°F) in an airtight container, it will keep for several months. Marzipan **extra**—50 percent almond—or **supérieure**—66 percent almond—has a more limited storage time, as the higher percentage of almond can more easily become rancid. It is best to store these types of marzipan in the refrigerator at 5°C (40°F).

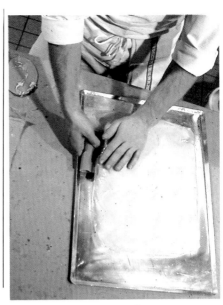

La pâte aux noix (Walnut paste)

Walnut paste is a derivative of almond paste. The proportions and procedures are very similar.

Walnut paste is used to flavor certain doughs, as well as to fill confections.

Equipment

Grinder or food processor
Measuring cup, plastic scraper, inert, airtight container

Professional Recipe

500 g walnuts (17.5 oz.)
300 g almonds (10.5 oz.)
300 g glucose or trimoline (10.5 oz.)
1 kg confectioners' sugar (35 oz.) plus syrup at 1260 D if necessary

Alternative Recipe

500 g almonds (17.5 oz.)
500 g walnuts (17.5 oz.)
1 kg confectioners' sugar (35 oz.)
egg whites (as needed)
flavoring to taste (Kirsch, rum, or Grand Marnier)

Procedure

Same as for almond paste (see pages 94 to 95).

Walnut Fondante (Marzipan)

Walnut marzipan is a derivative of almond marzipan. The proportions and procedures are very similar.

Walnut marzipan can be flavored to taste. It is used to fill candies and for modeling.

Equipment

Food processor or grinder
Copper sugar pan plus candy thermometer
Skimmer, pastry scraper, bowl, pastry brush
Inert, airtight container

Professional Recipe

1 kg walnuts (35 oz.)
600 g almonds (21 oz.)
500 g confectioners' sugar (17.5 oz.)
400 g trimoline (14 oz.)
1,800 g confectioners' sugar (63.5 oz.) plus 200 g glucose (7 oz.) plus 60 ml water (2 fl. oz.), cooked to 120°C (248°F)

Alternative Recipe

500 g almonds (17.5 oz.)
500 g walnuts (17.5 oz.)
500 g confectioners' sugar (17.5 oz.)
1 kg sugar (35 oz.) plus 250 g glucose (9 oz.), cooked to 114° to 118°C (237° to 244°F)

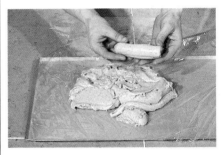

Same as for almond marzipan (see pages 96 to 99).

La pâte à fondant (Fondant)

Definition

Fondant is made from cooked sugar worked by hand or machine until it becomes white, to varying degrees of firmness depending on how it is to be used.

Fondant can be classified as a paste of cooked sugar (it must pass from a liquid state to a paste).

Uses

Fondant is commonly used in pastry making, confectionery, and chocolate work. It can be **flavored** with any flavoring and **colored** with any food coloring.

In pastry making: it is used to glaze pâte à choux (cream puff pastry), desserts, small cakes, barquettes, mille-feuilles (napoleons), and other cakes.

In confectionery: it is used to cover cherries soaked in eau-de-vie, liquor candies, and marzipan, as well as for soft interiors in candies and chocolates.

Equipment

By Hand
Copper sugar pan and equipment for cooking sugar
Metal spatula
Pastry cutter or triangle
Inert container
Metal fondant rulers

By Machine
Same as for hand method, plus:

Mixing bowl with paddle or hook attachment

Recipe

1 kg sugar (35 oz.), cubes, granulated, or crystal, cooked to the firm ball stage, 120°C (248°F)
water equal to 30 percent of the sugar's weight, 300 ml (10 fl. oz.)
200 g glucose (7 oz.)

The **temperature** to which the sugar should be cooked can vary, depending on the consistency desired. The sugar is cooked to achieve:

● a higher temperature for firmer fondant

● a lower temperature for softer fondant

The fondants are cooked to from 115° to 125°C (239° to 257°F).

Fondant requires experience with cooking sugar.

Carefully follow all precautions for cooking sugar.

No special equipment is required.

Fondant is often made in a mixer with the hook attachment.

Allow approximately 40 minutes to make fondant.

Preparation

Clean the copper sugar pan with coarse salt and vinegar (see Cooking Sugar, pages 14 to 17). While the sugar is cooking, carefully clean the marble.

Lightly moisten the marble, rulers, and all tools to be used with the fondant. This will prevent the fondant from sticking to the equipment and work surface, and make it easier to handle.

The metal rulers will prevent the fondant from running off the marble. If rulers are not available, the cooked sugar can be poured onto a plastic cutting board or on the center of the marble so it will not run over the sides.

Procedure

Cooking the Sugar

Cook the sugar, following the instructions for cooking sugar on pages 14 to 17, until the temperature reaches 115° to 125°C (239° to 257°F).

Cooling the Cooked Sugar

Pour the cooked sugar onto the marble between the metal rulers.

Before working the fondant, allow it to cool to about 50°C (122°F), until it can be touched with the fingers.

Once the sugar is cool, remove the rulers and start to work the sugar with a pastry cutter or a metal triangle by scraping it in from the edges to the center, working to and fro in this way very quickly.

Continue to work the sugar until it begins to whiten and thicken.

As soon as the sugar takes on a sandy texture, scrape it with the pastry cutter or with the palm of the hand until it is smooth and very white.

If the fondant is worked when it is **too hot,** it will become grainy and too firm.

If the fondant is worked when it is **too cold,** it will be necessary to work the sugar for a much longer time to achieve the proper consistency.

Using the Mixer

Making fondant with the mixer takes less time. Cook the sugar as for the hand method, and pour it onto the marble to cool. Once cool, place it in the bowl of the mixer.

Turn the machine to slow speed and mix with the hook attachment until it becomes white and smooth.

Note: If the sugar takes a long time to firm up, add a small amount of fondant (previously made) to help bring the cooked sugar to the proper consistency.

Storage

Immediately place the fondant in a plastic airtight container to prevent a crust from forming. Fondant can be stored in a cool, dry area for several months if it is carefully made under clean conditions.

	La Pâte à Fondant *(Fondant)*	
PROCEDURE Assemble the Equipment. **Prepare, Weigh, and Measure** the Raw Ingredients.	**0** min	● *Verify the cleanliness of the equipment.* ● *Use a high-quality sugar.*
PROCEDURE **Cook** the Sugar	**10** min	● *Cook to the correct temperature.*
Verify Doneness	**20** min	● *When the mixture has reached the correct stage, stop the cooking by plunging the pan in cool water.*
Cool the Cooked Sugar.		● *Pour the cooked sugar between the metal rulers on the marble.*
Work the Cooked Sugar	**30** min	● *Once the sugar cools to 50° C (122° F), begin to work it either on the marble or in the mixer with the hook attachment.*
VERIFYING DONENESS	**40** min	● *Work the fondant until it is white, smooth, and malleable.*
STORAGE: Fondant can be stored in a cool, dry place for several months in an airtight plastic container.		

La pâte à caramels (Caramel)

History

The word *caramel* first appeared in 1680 in the French dictionary by Fichelet. It stems from the Spanish *caramelo* a derivation from the Latin *calamellus* from the Greek *kalamos,* meaning *reed* and referring to sugar cane.

Defnition

Caramel is made by cooking together cream or milk, sugar (with glucose or inverted sugar), sometimes butter, and flavoring.

The texture of caramel is determined by the temperature to which the sugar is cooked. The mixture for a *caramel fondant* (soft caramel for fillings) is cooked less than that for a *caramel dur* (hard caramel for candies).

Uses

Basic caramel can be made in a variety of consistencies and shapes.

Caramel fondant: cooked to the thread, 110°C (230°F), or soft ball, 115°C (239°F) stage. Use half the amount of glucose for this preparation. Flavoring can be infused with the milk or cream or added at the end.

The caramel mixture is poured onto a lightly oiled marble and worked in the same way as a fondant until it is almost cold.

After being worked, a small amount of confectioners' sugar or cornstarch is added. The caramels are then rolled out and cut to shape.

Application: caramel fondant can be used as a filling for bonbons and chocolates, or it can be added to other preparations such as nougats and hard or soft caramel candies.

Soft caramel: cooked to soft ball, 117°C (243°F), or firm ball, 122°C (252°F) stage.

Application: soft caramel can contain various flavorings, such as coffee, chocolate, honey, hazelnut, pistachio, and walnut, and can be used as a filling.

Hard caramel: cooked from the hard ball 125°C (257°F) to soft crack 135°C (275°F) stage.

Application: hard caramel can be flavored like soft caramel, can be added to other preparations, and can be used to coat other confections such as soft and fondant caramels and nougat.

Caramels are somewhat difficult to prepare. Experience in cooking sugar is essential, and careful attention must be paid to this step.
No special equipment is required.
Allow approximately 25 minutes to prepare caramel.

Equipment

Copper sugar pan
Wooden spatula
Saucepan
Bowl
Pastry scraper
Metal rulers
Molds and cutters (optional)

Professional Recipe

1 kg sugar (35 oz.) plus 300 g glucose
  (10 oz.) plus 1.5 L milk (50.5 fl. oz.),
  cooked to 120°C (248°F)
two vanilla beans
150 g butter (5 oz.), optional

Alternative Recipe A

1 kg sugar (35 oz.) plus 150 g invert
  sugar (trimoline) (5 oz.) or 300 g glucose (10.5 oz.) plus 1 L crème fraîche
  or heavy cream (34 fl. oz.) or 1 L milk
  (34 fl. oz.), cooked to 120°C (248°F)
two vanilla beans
50 g butter (1.5 oz.), optional

Alternative Recipe B

500 g sugar (17.5 oz.)
500 g honey (17.5 oz.)
200 g glucose (7 oz.) or 100 g invert
  sugar (3.5 oz.)
1 L milk or cream (34 fl. oz.)
two vanilla beans
100 g butter (3.5 oz.), optional

Adding butter is optional. It makes
the texture more creamy and smooth but
shortens storage time.

Although various recipes are given, in
general the basic rule to follow for
making caramels is to *use equal amounts
of sugar and cream or milk.*
Coffee caramels: add 60 to 80 ml (2 to
3 fl. oz.) of coffee extract or instant
coffee dissolved in a small amount of
water.
Orange caramels: add the zest of three
oranges, finely chopped.
Chocolate caramels: add 200 to 300 g (7
to 10.5 oz.) of unsweetened chocolate.

Honey caramels: use alternative recipe B
and add several drops of vanilla extract
to bring out the honey flavor.

Hazelnut caramels: add 100 to 200 g (3.5
to 7 oz.) praline paste (optional) and 100
to 200 g (3.5 to 7 oz.) coarsely chopped,
lightly roasted, peeled hazelnuts.

Walnut caramels: add 100 to 200 g (3.5
to 7 oz.) coarsely ground walnuts.

Fruit caramels: add 400 g (14 oz.) fruit
puree.

Recipe for a Small Quantity

350 g sugar (12.5 oz.)
350 ml cream or milk (12 fl. oz.)
50 g butter (1.5 oz.)
180 to 200 g semisweet chocolate (6 to
  7 oz.) *or* 200 ml strong coffee (6.5 fl.
  oz.) *or* 5 to 10 ml coffee extract (1 to
  2 tsp.) *or* 1 to 2 tsp. instant coffee

Preparation

Weigh and measure all ingredients. If
cream is used, it is not necessary to add
butter. If milk is used, however, butter
is recommended, to provide a creamier
texture.

The amount of glucose or invert sugar
can be cut in half for caramel fondant
and caramels with fresh fruits.

The purpose of adding glucose or
invert sugar is to give a smooth texture
and minimize the risk of crystallization
during cooking.

Prepare the work surface by lightly
oiling the marble or moistening it with
water. The metal rulers or molds should
be oiled, if used.

Clean the copper bowl or copper sugar
pan with water, salt, and vinegar.

Procedure (for soft caramels)

Cooking the Mixture

Bring the cream or milk to a boil in
the copper bowl.

Add the sugar and glucose (or invert
sugar) along with the vanilla (split the
bean lengthwise) or other flavoring such

as chocolate or coffee. Stir the mixture
with a wooden spatula to help dissolve
the sugar and keep it from sticking to
the bottom of the bowl.

Continue to stir the mixture gently
over moderate heat with the wooden
spatula.

Wash down the sides of the bowl often
with a moistened pastry brush, being
careful not to add water to the mixture.

When the mixture has reached the
thread stage, add the butter if used.

Cook the mixture to between 117°
and 120°C (242° and 248°F) for soft
caramel. Verify doneness with the fingers
or by dropping a small amount of caramel in cold water, as indicated in the
discussion of cooking sugar (see pages
14 to 17).

For those experienced in cooking sugar, it is best to test the doneness with the fingers, as this gives the best indication of the consistency of the caramels.

Many factors can alter the temperature to which the caramels should be cooked, such as the quantity of glucose or sugar used and the acidity of the milk or fruit.

For this reason the temperatures given are approximate.

It is more accurate to determine the consistency of the mixture by feeling the caramel with the fingers.

Once the mixture has reached the proper consistency, remove the bowl from the heat and stir the mixture for 5 seconds.

It is important that the mixture has cooked evenly to prevent the caramel from sticking to the bowl.

At this point, chopped or diced hazelnuts, pistachios, walnuts, or almonds can be added. Stir the nuts thoroughly into the caramel before pouring.

Pouring the Caramel

Immediately pour the soft caramel between the metal bars on the oiled marble or into oiled caramel molds. If molds are used, simply unmold when cool.

Scrape out any remaining caramel adhering to the bowl with a flexible metal scraper and set it aside to be heated later; it could crystallize the mixture.

Allow the mixture to cool:

a. the caramel can be left whole and its surface can be smoothed with the palm of the hand, lightly oiled

b. or a grooved rolling pin can be rolled over both sides of the caramel

Shaping the Caramels

The caramel can be shaped in two ways:

- make an imprint to indicate the shape to be cut, then cut with a knife

- simply cut strips of caramel with a knife, and then cut the strips into squares, rectangles, diamonds, or other shapes

After cutting, wrap the pieces in cellophane.

Storage

The caramels should be stored in airtight containers at room temperature, free from humidity. Storage time:

- approximately 15 days for caramels made with butter

- approximately 1 month for caramels with milk or cream but no butter

La Pâte à Caramels
(Caramel)

PREPARATION	0 min	
Assemble the Equipment **Prepare, Weigh, and Measure** the Raw Ingredients		• Verify the cleanliness of the equipment. • Prepare the work surface.
PREPARATION	**5** min	
Cook the Mixture		• Bring the cream or milk to a boil. • Add the sugar, glucose, and flavoring; stir the mixture well. • Continue to stir the mixture gently and evenly as it cooks, until the desired temperature is reached.
Verify Doneness	**20** min	• Once the mixture has reached the correct stage, remove the bowl from the heat and continue to stir for several seconds.
Pour the Caramel	**25** min	• Immediately pour the caramel between the metal rulers or into appropriate caramel molds.
Cool the Mixture.		• As the caramel cools, smooth the mixture either with the palm of the hand or with a grooved rolling pin.
CUTTING THE CARAMELS	**1** hr **30**	• Caramels can be cut into various shapes and sizes, such as squares, diamonds, and rectangles.
STORAGE:		Caramels can be stored for 15 days (with butter) to 1 month (without butter), wrapped airtight in cellophane, at room temperature in a dry area.

La pâte à nougat de Montélimar

(Montélimar nougat)

History

The word *nougat* first appeared in the sixteenth century. It is a derivation of the southern French word *nogat,* from the Latin *nux,* meaning *nut.*

It originated from a cake based on honey and candied walnuts.

In Provence, a region in the south of France, nougat was given its traditional shape and present-day composition. In the sixteenth century, pastry chefs replaced the walnuts with almonds.

In the nineteenth century, part of the honey was replaced with sugar. In the twentieth century, glucose was added to the sugar.

Although nougat was first made in Marseille, it traveled to Montélimar, where it quickly became popular. A friend of the duke of Sully, who lived near Montélimar and was an advisor to King Henry IV, brought the first almond trees to France from Asia and Greece.

Pastry chefs made nougat twice a year, to celebrate Easter and Christmas.

In 1701 nougat from Montélimar became well known when the grandchildren of King Louis XIV, stopped in Montélimar after seeing their brother crowned king of Spain.

They were given 100 kg (243 lbs.) of nougat from Montélimar as a gift.

Legend has it that Montélimar nougat was created by a pastry apprentice who was in love with a beautiful princess.

As he dreamed of her one day, he made a mixture in his copper sugar pot of honey, to represent her shining hair, almonds, which reminded him of her eyes, and sugar, which recalled her sweet smile.

There are two varieties of nougat: **black** and **white.** Many different types of white nougat can be made.

 Montélimar nougat is a fairly difficult preparation.

Follow all instructions given, especially those for cooking the sugar.

Allow approximately 45 minutes to prepare Montélimar nougat.

Types

Basic nougat batter can be used to create various white and colored nougats:

● **nougat fondant:** this type of nougat is cooked to the firm to hard ball stage, between 120° and 130°C (248° and 266°F); it is used to fill interiors of candies

● **soft nougat:** this type of nougat is cooked to the soft to hard crack stage, between 140° and 150°C (284° and 302°F)

● **hard nougat:** this type of nougat is cooked to the pale to golden caramel

stage, between 155° and 165°C (311° and 329°F)

● **black nougat:** this type of nougat is made with unpeeled almonds and cooked to the caramel stage, between 165° and 170°C (329° and 338°F)

Equipment

Copper sugar pans (2), for sugar and honey
Bowl and whisk for beating egg whites

Mixing bowl and paddle or hook attachment *or*
Bowl and wooden spatula
Candy thermometer
Plastic scraper
Metal rulers (optional)

Professional Recipe

500 g honey (17.5 oz.), cooked to 115°C (239°F)
300 g sugar cubes (10.5 oz.) plus 200 g glucose (7 oz.), cooked with 100 ml water (3.5 fl. oz.) to 155°C (310°F)
4 egg whites
500 g almonds (17.5 oz.)
200 g hazelnuts (7 oz.)
150 g roasted pistachios (5 oz.), preferably peeled
one vanilla bean

Alternative Recipe A

300 g honey (10.5 oz.), cooked to 115°C (239°F)
600 g sugar (21 oz.) plus 300 g glucose (10.5 oz.), cooked to 155°C (311°F)
4 egg whites
1 kg roasted and peeled almonds and hazelnuts (35 oz.)
200 g candied cherries (7 oz.), coarsely chopped

Alternative Recipe B

500 g honey (17.5 oz.), cooked to 115°C (239°F)
1,250 g sugar (44 oz.) plus 600 g glucose (21 oz.), cooked to 155°C (311°F)
6 egg whites
400 g almonds (14 oz.) plus 400 g hazelnuts (14 oz.) plus 250 g pistachios (9 oz.), roasted, peeled, and ground
200 g candied fruits (7 oz.)

Other Variations

Use pistachios, walnuts, pignolis, and candied fruits.

Preparation

Measure the raw ingredients. Chop the candied fruits if used.

Peel the almonds, pistachios, and hazelnuts, and roast lightly. Grind the almonds, hazelnuts, pistachios, and walnuts to desired size. Keep warm.

Clean the work surface. Use either the metal rulers or a cutting board generously powdered with cornstarch.

Procedure

Two methods can be used.

Method A

Cooking the Sugar and Honey

Cook the sugar to hard crack stage, 145° to 150°C (293° to 302°F), following the usual precautions (see Cooking Sugar, pages 14 to 17). This is for a semisoft nougat. Cook the sugar more if a firmer nougat is desired.

Cook the honey to soft ball stage, 115°C (239°F). Carefully watch the honey once it comes to a boil—it can easily boil over the sides of the saucepan.

Beating the Egg Whites

Start beating the egg whites by hand or with a mixer once the honey comes to a boil. The egg whites should almost reach firm peaks (see volume 1, Italian meringue).

Adding the Cooked Honey and Sugar

Slowly, in a fine stream, pour the cooked honey over the beaten egg whites while the mixer is running on high speed. Continue to beat for 4 to 5 minutes. (If

beating by hand, use a whisk and follow the same basic procedure.) Once the sugar is cooked, add it in the same way as the honey to the beaten egg whites. After adding all the sugar, remove the whisk attachment and replace it with the paddle. Scrape the sides of the mixing bowl if necessary. Turn the mixer to medium speed.

Drying Out the Meringue

The machine should be on medium speed with either a hot water bath or a

flame (made by placing denatured alcohol in bowl and lighting it) underneath the mixing bowl.

Verify doneness in the same way as for sugar by placing a small piece of meringue in cold water. Once the meringue is cold, take it out of the water;

if ready, it will not stick to the fingers.

Adding the Fruit

Add the fruit:

● by hand, with a wooden spatula
● by machine, with the hook or paddle attachment

If using the mixer, set it at slow speed. Add the warm almonds and hazelnuts (as well as the pistachios, candied cherries, or other nuts or candied fruit if used). A quick blending is sufficient. If overworked, the nuts and fruits become too finely ground.

Shaping

Transfer the mixture onto a marble between metal rulers if available, or onto a cutting board generously dusted with cornstarch.

Dust the mixture with cornstarch before rolling it out. With a rolling pin, quickly roll out the mixture to be

approximately 1 cm (1/2 in.) thick, between the metal rulers.

Again cover the nougat with a layer of cornstarch.

Let cool, either on the marble or in the refrigerator, and cut into the desired shapes with a chef's knife or bread knife. If using a bread knife, cut with a sawing motion.

Dipping the Nougat

Once the nougat is cut to size, it can be dipped in tempered chocolate (see volume 3, Tempering Chocolate, pages 40 to 42).

Method B

Cook the sugar to 155°C (310°F) for a semisoft nougat.

Heat the honey until it comes to a boil as in method A.

Beat the egg whites to almost firm peaks, and add the heated honey.

Slowly add the cooked sugar over the mixture of beaten egg white and honey.

Continue to cook the mixture by heating the bottom of the mixing bowl (with a hot water bath underneath) until the mixture reaches the desired texture.

Test for doneness by placing a small piece of meringue in cold water, as in method A.

Storage

Nougat can be stored for 1 month in covered containers after being wrapped in aluminum foil or plastic.

Nougat "Tonio"

500 g honey (17.5 oz.) cooked to between the thread and soft ball stage, plus 6 firmly beaten egg whites (beaten for 4 to 5 minutes on high speed)

1 kg sugar (35 oz.) plus 500 g glucose (17.5 oz.), cooked to the soft crack stage

600 g peeled almonds (21 oz.) plus 600 g peeled hazelnuts (21 oz.), lightly toasted and ground to a powder

Follow the same procedure as for Montélimar nougat.

			La Pâte à Nougat de Montélimar
			(Montélimar Nougat)

PREPARATION	**0** min	
Assemble the Equipment. **Prepare, Weigh, and Measure** the Raw Ingredients.		• *Check the cleanliness of the equipment.* • *Peel the almonds, hazelnuts, and any other nuts used.* • *Roast the nuts lightly and grind them to the desired texture.*
PROCEDURE	**10** min	
Cook the Sugar.		• *Following the usual precautions, cook the sugar to 145° to 150° C (293° to 302° F).*
Cook the Honey.		• *Following the same precautions as for cooking sugar, cook the honey to 115° C (239° F). Be careful the honey does not boil over.*
Beat the Egg Whites	**22** min	• *Begin to beat the egg whites once the honey reaches 105° to 110° C (221° to 230° F). Beat until the whites have soft peaks.*
Add the Honey	**25** min	• *Pour the honey in a fine stream over the beaten egg whites, with the mixer on high speed. Beat at high speed for approximately 5 minutes.*
Add the Sugar	**30** min	• *Pour the cooked sugar in a fine stream over the egg white and honey mixture. Scrape the mixing bowl if needed. Remove the whisk attachment and replace it with the paddle.*
Dry Out the Mixture	**32** min	• *Dry the mixture by beating at medium speed, placing a heat source under the mixing bowl.*
TESTING DONENESS	**40** min	• *Test the meringue mixture as for sugar, by dipping a piece in cold water and seeing if it is sticky.*
ADDING THE NUTS	**43** min	• *Add the nuts and fruit by hand with a wooden spatula, or in the mixer, at slow speed, with the paddle or hook attachment.*
TRANSFERRING	**45** min	• *Transfer to a cutting board or onto a marble between metal rulers.*
ROLLING AND CUTTING		• *Roll the nougat to be approximately 1 cm (1/2 in.) thick.* • *After cooling, cut to size.*

STORAGE: Nougat can be stored for approximately 1 month wrapped in plastic, in airtight containers.

La nougatine (Nougatine)

History

Nougatine was invented by Louis-Jules Bourumeau à Nevers during the nineteenth century.

After seeing the work of Bourumeau, Empress Eugénie de Montijo, wife of Napoleon III, so enjoyed the nougatine that she helped popularize it. Nougatine became very popular for making elaborate, tall pieces called "pièces montées," used to hold fruit, as pedestals for various cakes, or alone, shaped into historical monuments. Nougatine thus replaced products made by Antonin Carême, who used a type of nougat that was very hard and less easy to shape and work with.

Nougatine became very popular because it can not only serve as the foundation of an elaborate dessert, but it can also be eaten.

Today, nougatine has unlimited uses and can be shaped and decorated in ways limited only by the imagination of the pastry chef.

Uses

In Pastry Making:

Nougatine is used to form supports or pedestals for elaborate pieces.

Various molds can be used to create nougatine decorations such as baskets.

It can also be used to create bases of various shapes for individual desserts, such as cones, cups, timbales, and baskets.

It can decorate various desserts by covering them (as in the shape of a book), or as a separate decoration, such as a braid.

It can also be used to prepare various petits fours frais.

In Confectionery:

Nougatine is used to fill candies.

In Frozen Desserts:

Nougatine can decorate or be mixed with ice cream.

  Nougatine is a difficult preparation that requires a great deal of precision, and experience in pastry making.

Cutting and shaping nougatine requires artistic sense and judgment.

No special equipment is necessary, except as needed to mold or cut certain shapes. Allow 25 minutes to make nougatine.

Equipment

Dry Method

Sheet pan plus parchment paper
Bowl or copper bowl plus wooden
   spatula
Chef's knife
Paring knife
Pastry cutter or metal triangle

Lightly oil all the equipment the cooked nougat will touch.

Cooked Sugar Method

Use the same equipment as above, plus a copper sugar pan, thermometer, a bowl with water, and a pastry brush and skimmer for the sugar.

If the nougatine is to be used immediately after it is made, all equipment must be ready before proceeding.

Professional Recipe

1 kg granulated sugar (35 oz.) for dry
   method or 1 kg cubed or crystal
   sugar (35 oz.) for cooked sugar
   method
100 g glucose (3.5 oz.)
600 g chopped or sliced almonds (21 oz.)
150 g butter (5 oz.), optional

Alternative Recipe

1 kg granulated or cubed sugar (35 oz.)
100 to 400 g glucose (3.5 to 14 oz.)
500 to 1,000 g chopped or sliced almonds
   or sliced hazelnuts (17.5 to 35 oz.)
150 g butter (5 oz.), optional

Recipe for a Small Quantity

250 g granulated sugar (9 oz.)
25 g glucose (1 oz.) or several drops of
   lemon juice or vinegar
150 g chopped or sliced almonds (5 oz.)

Note: The intended use of the nougatine —how solid or soft it should be—determines the proportions of the recipe. The amount of almonds (either chopped or

sliced) can be doubled, as indicated in the alternative recipe.

Today a portion of the almonds are sometimes replaced with sliced hazelnuts, which give a different taste, preferred by some.

Preparation

Raw Ingredients

Make sure the sugar is clean, and set it aside in a bowl.

Sift through the almonds to remove any foreign particles, and place them on a sheet of paper on a clean sheet pan. Heat the almonds in an oven or in a hot proof box.

The almonds are heated to eliminate the possibility of chilling the cooked sugar too quickly, which would cause it to crystallize.

Weigh the glucose directly into the copper sugar pan or copper bowl or on top of the sugar. This will prevent the glucose from sticking to the scale.

Prepare the lemon juice if it is to be used, or measure the vinegar.

Equipment

Clean the copper sugar pan or the copper bowl with coarse salt and vinegar; rinse well with cold water. Clean and dry the wooden spatula.

Lightly oil the work surface as well as the utensils to be used for cutting and shaping the nougatine: molds, pastry cutter, knives, cutters, triangles, and rolling pin.

If possible, use a metal rolling pin; otherwise use a wooden rolling pin reserved for nougatine.

Lightly oil one or several sheet pans (depending on the quantity being made) that will hold the nougatine waiting to be cut.

Procedure : Dry Method

Over a flame, gently melt the glucose in the copper bowl or sugar pan.

Add the sugar in small amounts at a time, either by stirring in circles or in figure eights with the wooden spatula.

To obtain a golden color, the first addition of sugar should be melted into the glucose before adding the next quantity.

Be sure to mix in the sugar that sticks to the sides of the bowl or the spatula to ensure that all the sugar has melted.

Checking the Color

To prevent the nougatine from becoming too dark, lower the heat after adding all the sugar.

All the sugar should be melted at this point. Any crystals of sugar that remain unmelted (by adhering to the side of the bowl) can dull the nougatine and cause it to coagulate, making it difficult to work with because it will break easily.

Once the sugar has become golden, it should be shiny and coat the spatula when lifted.

When no crystals of sugar are found, the sugar will be between pale and medium caramel.

Adding the Hot Almonds

Once the sugar has reached the proper golden color, lower the heat and add the almonds all at once.

Immediately raise the heat to facilitate mixing. Mix vigorously with a wooden spatula to ensure even cooking.

This step, mixing the almonds into the cooked sugar, should take approximately 1 minute. If heated too long or at too high a temperature, the nougatine will become overly dark and taste bitter.

Cooling the Nougatine

Once the nougatine has been properly blended, turn it out onto either:

• a sheet pan, 40 × 60 cm (16 × 24 in.)

In either case, flatten the nougatine with a lightly oiled metal spatula to approximately 1 cm (1/2 in.). Turn the nougatine over several times so it can cool quickly and evenly and to prevent it from continuing to brown.

Generally:

• the nougatine is placed onto sheet pans if it is to be used immediately

• it is placed on the marble if it is for later use

Immediate Use

Place the sheet pan with nougatine in front of an open oven heated to 180° to 190°C (355° to 375°F).

When the nougatine is to be rolled out, use a lightly oiled rolling pin (preferably a metal one), and work with the nougatine while it is very hot.

The warmer the work area, the easier it will be to shape and cut the nougatine.

Later Use

Once the nougatine is cut to size, allow it to cool completely. It can be left in a dry, cool area in a covered container for later use.

The nougatine is placed on sheet pans and heated in the oven when needed.

Procedure : Cooked Sugar Method

Cooking the Sugar

Cook the sugar with 30 percent of its weight in water and 20 percent of its weight in glucose until it reaches the pale caramel stage. Follow all precautions necessary (see Cooking Sugar, pages 14 to 17).

After the sugar reaches the hard crack stage, lower the heat to complete cooking and ensure an even color.

In no case should the sugar be cooked beyond the pale caramel stage or begin to smoke. This would result in an overly dark and bitter-tasting nougatine.

Adding the Hot Almonds

Off the heat, add the hot almonds (previously sifted to eliminate any small broken pieces or almond powder, which

could cause the sugar to coagulate). From this point on, follow the same procedure as for the first method.

Note: This method is best when the nougatine is to be used immediately. Because water is used in this method, the nougatine cannot be stored for as long, and it will sweat and lose its shape faster than that made with the dry method, which has a lower moisture content.

Tips for Working with Nougatine

Most utensils used for cutting and shaping nougatine should be lightly oiled, as should the work surface.

The work surface should be as close as possible to the oven used for keeping the nougatine hot.

It is best to work with the nougatine hot, because it can crack and break as it cools. While working on certain pieces, leave the remainder of the nougatine in the oven so it will stay malleable.

Work with only the amount of nougatine needed at a time. The two reasons for this are:

1. most often the nougatine is rolled out very thinly, causing it to cool quickly (except when it is used for pedestals and bases for mounted pieces)

2. it is easier to cut, shape, and mold smaller amounts quickly; speed is important for working with nougatine

After cutting the nougatine, place any trimmings or scraps onto a hot sheet pan to melt them down while working on the original piece.

Be careful not to allow the trimmings to brown as they melt, or the final presentation piece will not have a consistent color. As the trimmings melt, add small quantities to the larger pieces until the work is finished.

Add small amounts of fresh nougatine to the pieces being worked, to maintain an even color.

A metal rolling pin is recommended because it is often necessary to cut the nougatine by tapping the cutters with the rolling pin, and a wooden pin might crack.

A metal rolling pin also tends to stick less to the nougatine. And, a metal rolling pin conducts heat better than a wooden rolling pin, making it easier to work with the nougatine.

If a wooden rolling pin is used, it is best to reserve one for nougatine only, so it remains perfectly clean; any foreign substance, such as flour, will cause it to stick to the nougatine.

As previously mentioned, it is best to work with the nougatine in front of the oven door. If this is not possible, use a cast-iron (or blue-steel) sheet pan, reserved for working with nougatine. Also try to stay as close to a heat source or oven as possible.

It is best to work with the nougatine:
- on a work surface that holds heat well
- on a nonrefrigerated marble
- on a warming tray or table

It is also possible to place hot sheet pans on the work surface for several minutes before beginning the first pieces. This will help provide a hot surface on which the nougatine can be cut and shaped.

La Nougatine
(Nougatine)

PREPARATION	0 min	
Assemble the Equipment Prepare, Weigh, and Measure the Raw Ingredients		• Verify the cleanliness of the equipment. • Lightly oil the equipment and work surface. • Hold the sugar in a bowl. • Weigh the glucose directly in the copper bowl or sugar pan.
PROCEDURE		
A. *Dry Method*		
Melt the Glucose	10 min	• Melt the glucose over medium heat.
Add the Sugar		• Gradually add the sugar in small quantities, while constantly stirring with a wooden spatula. • Wait until the first amount of sugar has partially melted before adding more.
Verify Doneness	20 min	• Reduce the heat after all the sugar has melted. • The cooked sugar should be shiny, between pale and medium caramel.
Add the Hot Almonds	22 min	• Add the hot almonds all at once, vigorously stirring until the mixture is well blended.
Cool Quickly	24 min	• Pour the mixture onto a sheet pan, marble, or stainless steel surface.
Use	25 min	• The nougatine can be used immediately or later.
B. *Cooked Sugar Method*		
Cook the Sugar	10 min	• Cook the sugar with 30 percent of its weight in water and 20 percent in glucose. Follow all precautions for cooking sugar.
Verify Cooking Sugar	18 min	• Cook the sugar to a light caramel.
Add the Hot Almonds	20 min	• Off the heat, add the hot almonds in the same way as for the dry method. • Finish the nougatine as for the dry method.
STORAGE:		*Dry method:* nougatine can be stored for several weeks if protected from moisture in a dry, well-ventilated area. *Cooked sugar method:* it is best to use this nougatine as quickly as possible as it will sweat and lose its shape more quickly because of the water in the recipe.

Le craquelin (Almond brittle)

Definition

Craquelin is a derivative of nougatine. Trimmings of nougatine are often broken up or ground and used as a garnish or decoration for certain desserts in place of craquelin.

When craquelin is used for frozen desserts, ice creams, decoration of bavarians and mousses the following proportions are used:

- 50 percent sugar
- 50 percent chopped almonds

Professional Recipe

Praline Method

1 kg almonds or hazelnuts (35 oz.), peeled and lightly roasted, plus 1 kg sugar (35 oz.), cooked to a light or medium caramel *or*
1 kg sugar (35 oz.), melted dry, plus 1 kg almonds or hazelnuts (35 oz.), lightly roasted

Nougatine Method

1 kg granulated sugar (35 oz.), cooked dry
1 kg almonds (35 oz.), warm and chopped

Procedure

To use the praline method, see praline paste, pages 114 to 117. To use the nougatine method, refer to nougatine, pages 108 to 111.

 Craquelin is not difficult to make, although care must be taken when working with hot cooked sugar.

Allow 25 minutes for its preparation.

Grinding the Mixture

The mixture of nuts and sugar can be chopped or ground to size, depending on use. It can be ground by:

- tapping with a rolling pin

- running through a grinder

- running through the food processor

The craquelin can be sifted through a drum sieve with different-size meshes to obtain various textures.

Storage

Craquelin can be stored in sheets like nougatine and kept in a dry area. If ground, craquelin can be stored in airtight containers or in a dry proof box for 8 to 10 days.

Because nuts contain a high percentage of oil, they become rancid quickly. Moreover, the craquelin sweats and releases moisture easily, thus limiting its storage.

Uses for Almonds

Roasted, sliced, or chopped almonds can be used in various desserts in pastry making as well as in confectionery and for frozen desserts.

Roasting Sliced and Chopped Almonds

Place the almonds on a heavy sheet pan, preferably blue steel, and sprinkle lightly with sugar.

Mix well, and roast in a moderate oven at 200°C (400°F). Occasionally stir the almonds with a pastry cutter while roasting to ensure an even color. Roast the almonds until they become golden.

Remove the almonds from the oven and cool them on parchment paper.

They can be stored in airtight plastic containers in a cool, dry area to prevent them from becoming rancid.

Almond Craquelées (Sweet, Crumbled Almonds)

Almonds can be roasted with the technique given above after being moistened and mixed with granulated or confectioners' sugar. To every kg (35 oz.) of almonds, add 400 to 500 g (14 to 17.5 oz.) of sugar.

In a bowl, place the chopped or sliced almonds (hazelnuts can be prepared in the same way), and moisten them with a few drops of orange flower water or Kirsch and mix with the hands.

Once moistened, add the sugar and blend the mixture well.

Place one layer of the almond/sugar

mixture on a sheet pan (preferably blue steel), and roast them in the oven, as described for roasting almonds.

Check the almonds often as they roast, and stir them around so they roast evenly.

They will roast quickly because only a thin layer is placed on the sheet pans.

Coloring Almonds

To color almonds, use green and yellow liquor colorings, which will give the almonds a deep green color similar to pistachios.

In a bowl, moisten chopped almonds with Kirsch and mix with very small amounts of coloring.

Once the almonds are colored, place them on a sheet pan and allow them to dry in a proof box or on top of a warm oven.

 Roasting almonds is a very easy procedure.

No special equipment is required.

Allow approximately 15 minutes to prepare almond craquelées.

Le praliné ou pralin

(Praline paste)

History

Praline paste is a derivative of praline, almonds that are coated in cooked sugar, often caramelized. Praline was invented by Praslin, the chef for Maréchal Duc de Choiseul, in the seventeenth century. Originally named after the chef and called praslines, the name of this confection was eventually changed to praline.

In the eighteenth century, praline was very popular in the court of France.

By the end of the eighteenth century, praline was ground into a paste.

Definition

Praline paste is creamy, smooth, and flavorful. The strength of flavor and firmness of texture can vary, depending on its intended use.

It is made with an equal quantity of almonds and sugar. Often some of the almonds are replaced with hazelnuts.

Uses

In pastry making praline paste is used as a flavoring for creams, butter cream, Paris-Brest, hazelnut brioches, and frozen desserts.

In confectionery, praline paste is most commonly used to fill candies and garnish various petits fours.

Equipment

Making praline paste is a fairly difficult procedure that requires experience in cooking sugar.

Carefully follow all precautions given for cooking sugar.

The only special equipment required is a grinder or food processor.

Allow approximately 25 minutes to make praline paste with a food processor, 1 hour and 45 minutes with a grinder.

Method A: Grinder

Copper bowl
Wooden and metal spatulas
Lightly oiled sheet pan
Grinder
Plastic container with covers for storage

Method B: Food Processor

Sheet pans (2) plus parchment paper
Bowl
Food processor
Plastic scraper
Large-mesh drum sieve
Plastic container with covers for storage

Professional Recipe

Method A

1 kg almonds (35 oz.)
1 kg hazelnuts (35 oz.)
2 kg granulated sugar (70 oz.), cooked dry, *or* 2 kg crystal sugar or sugar cubes (70 oz.), cooked to soft crack stage

Method B

1 kg hazelnuts (35 oz.), darkly roasted
1 kg almonds (35 oz.), darkly roasted
2 kg confectioners' sugar (70 oz.)

Alternative Recipe

2.5 kg *tant pour tant (88 oz.)*: almonds plus hazelnuts to taste or all almonds or all hazelnuts
2.5 kg sugar (88 oz.)
One-quarter of the nuts can be replaced with walnuts.

Preparation

It is necessary to use either a grinder or food processor to make praline paste, making this a procedure limited to those who own the appropriate equipment.

Regardless of the machine used, the results are the same.

Regardless of the method chosen, the nuts should be roasted. Place the nuts on a sheet pan. To ensure even roasting, place only one layer of nuts on a sheet pan at a time.

Roasting can be controlled by checking both the exterior and the interior color of the nuts. Cut several nuts in half with a knife to see if they have sufficiently colored.

The hazelnuts can be peeled by rubbing them in a drum sieve with a mesh large enough for the peel, but not the nut, to fall through.

The almonds can also be peeled before roasting by blanching them (see almond paste, pages 94 to 95).

With a grinder, when using the dry method, granulated sugar is used; when using moistened cooked sugar, crystal sugar or sugar cubes are used. With a food processor, it is best to use confectioners' sugar.

Praline paste can be stored for several months, so it is important to verify the cleanliness of all the equipment.

Procedure

Method A: Grinder

Two procedures can be used with the grinder.

1. *Procedure with Dry Cooked Sugar*

Cooking the Sugar

Place the sugar in a copper bowl previously cleaned with salt and vinegar and well rinsed with cold water. Cook the sugar, without adding water, until it is a caramel color, as for nougatine.

Adding the Hot Roasted Nuts

Once all the sugar is completely melted and caramel colored, add the hot roasted nuts all at once, stirring constantly.

When this method is used, the nuts should be lightly roasted and golden inside.

Continue to stir the mixture with a wooden spatula until the nuts are completely coated with the caramel.

Cooling the Mixture

Turn the mixture of nuts and sugar onto a lightly oiled sheet pan.

2. *Procedure with Moistened Cooked Sugar*

Cooking the Sugar

Cook the sugar with water to the soft ball stage, following the usual precautions (see Cooking Sugar, pages 14 to 17).

Adding the Hot Roasted Nuts

Add the hot, lightly roasted nuts all at once, as for the preceding method. Stir the mixture with a wooden spatula until the sugar takes on a sandy texture.

Crystallizing the Sugar

As the sugar is stirred, it will crystallize. It is necessary to continue to stir the mixture over moderate heat with the wooden spatula until the sugar slowly melts again and caramelizes.

through until a fine powder is obtained. At this point, check that no praline has stuck to the wheels.

Now tighten the wheels completely and pass the powder through the grinder to bring the oil out of the nuts.

Sometimes it is difficult to bring the oil to the surface of the nuts to create a paste. If so, add a few drops of corn oil or other vegetable oil to the mixture the last few times it is run through the grinder.

Transfer the mixture to an airtight, inert container (a plastic container with a cover).

Storage

Praline paste can be stored for 2 to 3 months refrigerated, at 5°C (40°F), in an inert, airtight container.

Note: A vanilla bean can be added to the praline paste to bring out its flavor. Infuse the bean with the nuts as they cook in the sugar.

It is now popular to add leftover pieces or trimmings of nougatine to the pralines before grinding into a paste. Be careful that the trimmings are still fresh; if they are not, they can give an off (rancid) taste to the product and limit its storage.

Method B: Food Processor

Roast the nuts on a sheet pan, as for the grinder method. This time the nuts should be roasted for a longer time so they become quite dark.

The color of the nuts will determine the color and flavor of the praline paste.

Grinding the Mixture

Place the cooled, roasted nuts and sugar in the food processor with the metal blade attachment.

With the feed tube closed, turn the machine on (medium speed if the machine has speed controls) for 7 to 10 minutes.

Check the sugar on the bottom of the bowl to make sure the caramel is not becoming too dark.

Verifying Doneness

For both methods, check to see if the praline is done by looking at both the exterior and interior of the nuts.

The praline can be cooked until it is more or less dark, depending on its intended use. The coloration is obtained by both the roasting the nuts and cooking the sugar.

The nuts are usually golden inside after cooking in the caramel, which gives the praline paste its appealing light brown color.

If the caramel is cooked too long and becomes too dark, the praline paste will have a bitter taste.

Preventing Burns

Burns can be avoided by carefully holding the bowl with a thick, dry towel while stirring the mixture gently.

Cooling the Mixture

Once the mixture of sugar and nuts is the correct color, transfer it to a lightly oiled sheet pan. Spread the mixture evenly with a wooden spatula or triangle to facilitate cooling.

Work carefully, and do not forget that the mixture is very hot, approximately 160°C (320°F).

Grinding the Mixture

After the mixture has completely cooled, break it up by tapping it with a rolling pin or chopping it up with a knife. This will make it easier to pass it through the grinder.

Check the grinder for cleanliness, then open the wheels for the first grinding.

Progressively tighten the wheels of the grinder each time the mixture is passed

Bringing the Oil out of the Nuts

After between 7 and 10 minutes of processing, the oil in the nuts will separate and come to the surface, creating a pastelike texture. Turn off the machine and scrape down the sides of the work bowl. Cover, turn the machine to medium speed, and process for 3 minutes more with the feed tube closed.

Check the smoothness of the paste and process the mixture longer if necessary.

Transfer the praline paste to an airtight inert container (plastic, with a cover).

To Avoid Burns

As the food processor runs, it will heat the nuts and sugar (especially when a commercial food processor is used). This heat will caramelize the sugar and partially pasteurize the product. Be careful when handling the paste and the machine to prevent burns.

Storage

Because the praline paste has been partially pasteurized, this method offers a slightly longer storage time. It is best not to store the paste for more than 3 months. It can be stored in the same way as for praline paste made with the grinder.

Le Praliné ou Pralin
(Praline Paste)

PREPARATION	**0** min	
Assemble the Equipment **Prepare, Weigh, and Measure** the Raw Ingredients		• *Verify the cleanliness of the equipment.* • *Roast the nuts (almonds and hazelnuts) and peel (optional).*
PROCEDURE	**10** min	
Method A: Grinder		
1. Procedure with Dry Cooked Sugar		
Cook the Sugar without Water		• *Proceed as for nougatine.*
Verify the Color of the Sugar	**25** min	• *The sugar should be melted, with no traces of crystals.* • *The sugar should have a golden caramel color and be shiny.*
Add the Hot, Roasted Nuts	**27** min	• *Add all the nuts at once, continuing to stir the mixture with a wooden spatula until they are covered with caramel.*
Cool the Mixture	**30** min	• *Place the mixture on a lightly oiled sheet pan.*
2. Procedure with Moistened Sugar		
Cook the Sugar and Water	**10** min	• *Moisten the sugar with 30 percent of its weight in water and, following the usual precautions, cook to the soft crack stage.*
Add the Hot, Roasted Nuts	**20** min	• *Add the nuts all at once, continuing to stir with a wooden spoon until the sugar crystallizes.*
Crystallize the Sugar	**25** min	• *Continue to stir the mixture over medium heat until the sugar melts again and caramelizes, covering the nuts.*
Cool the Mixture	**30** min	• *Transfer the mixture to a lightly oiled sheet pan to cool.*
Grind the Cool Mixture	**1** hr **30**	
Break Up the Mixture		• *With a rolling pin or a knife, break the mixture into coarse pieces to facilitate running it through the grinder.*
Grind to a Fine Powder		• *Progressively tighten the wheels of the grinder each time the nuts are passed through until a fine powder is obtained.*
Make a Paste	**1** hr **45**	• *Completely tighten the wheels of the grinder.* • *Pass the fine powder through the grinder until it turns into a paste.*
Method B: Food Processor	**10** min	
Grind the Roasted Nuts and Confectioners' Sugar		• *Grind the cool, roasted nuts and the confectioners' sugar on medium speed (if available) for 7 to 10 minutes, with the feed tube closed. Stop grinding when the nuts become oily.*
Control the Texture	**17** min	• *Scrape down the bowl so the nuts grind evenly.*
Make a Paste	**20** min	• *Turn the food processor to medium speed and process, with the feed tube closed, for 2 minutes. Check to be sure the paste is smooth.*
TRANSFERRING	**25** min	• *Place the praline paste in an airtight, inert container.*

STORAGE: • Praline paste can be stored for 2 to 3 months in the refrigerator at 5°C (40°F) in an inert, airtight container.

Le gianduja (Gianduja)

Definition

Gianduja is a flavorful, creamy mixture made from ground, roasted nuts, couverture chocolate, confectioners' sugar, cocoa butter, and flavoring such as vanilla or coffee.

The nuts most commonly used are almonds and hazelnuts.

Uses

In Pastry Making:

- to garnish and decorate individual cakes and desserts
- to flavor fillings for certain cakes and desserts
- to mix with creams, such as whipped cream
- To sandwich certain petits fours together

In Candy Making:

- to fill candies
- to fill paper candy cups
- to make rochers (petits fours and individual-sized candies)
- to make bûchettes
- to decorate other candies, with the pastry bag

In Frozen Desserts:

- to flavor frozen desserts, bombes, ice creams
- to decorate praline ice cream; the gianduja is used either when it is cold to make decorative ribbons and curls, or when it is warmer and softer, piped out with a pastry bag

Professional Recipes

Recipes for gianduja vary depending on:
- the mixture and type of nuts used and the degree to which they are roasted
- the type and quality of chocolate used: baking chocolate, milk chocolate, white chocolate, or other flavor
- the amount of sugar used
Gianduja can be made sweet or slightly bitter, depending on taste.

Professional Recipe

500 g hazelnuts (17.5 oz.), roasted
500 g almonds (17.5 oz.), roasted
1 kg confectioners' sugar (35 oz.)
1.5 kg couverture chocolate (53 oz.)
250 g butter (9 oz.)
250 g powdered whole milk (9 oz.)

Alternative Recipe A

200 g walnuts (7 oz.), lightly roasted
400 g almonds (14 oz.), roasted
400 g hazelnuts (14 oz.), lightly roasted
850 g confectioners' sugar (30 oz.)
50 g instant coffee granules (1.5 oz.)
1 kg coffee-flavored chocolate (35 oz.)

Alternative Recipe B

500 g hazelnuts (17.5 oz.), roasted
500 g confectioners' sugar (17.5 oz.)
100 g cocoa butter (3.5 oz.)
400 g milk chocolate (14 oz.)

Preparation

Verify the cleanliness of all equipment.
Prepare and weigh the nuts, then roast and peel them.
Melt the chocolate and warm the butter.

Procedure

Roasting the Nuts

Mix the nuts together and place them on a sheet pan. They can be placed inside tart circles to prevent them from rolling off the sheet pan in the oven. Roast the nuts in a moderate oven at 220°C (425°F).

Roast the nuts according to taste. The degree to which the nuts are roasted will help determine the final result of the gianduja.

Gianduja is a simple preparation as long as all instructions are followed.
Carefully observe the grinding of the nuts.
Allow 40 minutes to make gianduja.

Peeling the Nuts

Rub the roasted nuts in a large-mesh drum sieve to remove the skins.

Grinding the Nuts with Confectioners' Sugar

Mix the confectioners' sugar with the nuts and grind together either in a grinder or food processor. Continue to grind the mixture until the oil separates from the nuts and a paste is formed. It should be similar to, though thicker than, praline paste (see praline paste, pages 114 to 117).

Adding the Chocolate

Put the paste on a marble and pour the melted chocolate on top of it. The amount of chocolate used depends on the texture desired and quality of the chocolate.

It is possible to add cocoa butter or shortening **that does not contain water** at this point (do not use butter because its water content adversely affects the mixture).

Mix the ingredients together with a pastry cutter until they are well blended and smooth.

Uses

Gianduja is often used while it is still a soft paste or slightly firm, piped out of a pastry bag or rolled into balls by hand.

The texture can be altered by the temperature at which it is worked and the amount of chocolate added. More chocolate yields a firmer gianduja.

Gianduja can be tempered like couverture chocolate (see volume 3, Tempering Chocolate, page 40). The temperatures, however, are less exact. It is sufficient to melt the gianduja, then temper it by spreading it out on a marble to cool before using.

If gianduja is used when it is too cool, it will have a marbled or streaky appearance. If it is used when it is too hot, it will never become completely firm and will tend to be sticky.

Storage

Gianduja can be stored for 2 months refrigerated, at 5°C (40°F), in an inert, airtight container.

		Le Gianduja *(Gianduja)*
PREPARATION	**0** min	
Assemble the Equipment **Prepare, Weigh, and Measure** the Raw Ingredients.		• Verify the cleanliness of the equipment. • Melt the chocolate. • Soften the butter.
PROCEDURE	**5** min	
Roast the Nuts		• Place the nuts on a sheet pan and roast in a 220°C (425°F) oven.
Peel the Nuts	**15** min	• Rub the nuts in a sieve with a large mesh.
Grind the Nuts	**20** min	• Grind the nuts together with the confectioners' sugar, either in a grinder or food processor. • Grind until the nuts start to turn into a thick paste.
Add the Chocolate	**30** min	• On the marble, mix the nut paste and melted chocolate, then add the shortening if used.
Blend the Mixture Well	**35** min	• Continue mixing until the gianduja is homogeneous.
USES	**40** min	• Gianduja can be used immediately if tempered on a marble first. • If it is to be used at a later time, melt and temper the gianduja when needed.
STORAGE:		Gianduja can be stored for 2 months at 5°C (40°F) in an inert, airtight container.

La crème garniture confiseur
(Fondant cream filling)

Definition

Fondant cream is similar to butter cream but is made with fondant. It is used as a filling for molded chocolates and is very popular in northern European countries, particularly Belgium and Holland, where these candies originated.

In the countries where creams are popular, fondant cream (in large pieces) is coated in chocolate and eaten as an individual desert.

Equipment

Electric mixer with bowl and whisk attachment - Pastry scraper
Saucepan - Pastry bag and tip

Professional Recipe

1 kg butter (35 oz.)
1 kg fondant (35 oz.)
500 ml crème fraîche or heavy cream (17 fl. oz.)
200 ml liquor flavoring (6.5 fl. oz.)
4 g potassium sorbate (1 tsp.), as a preservative

Alternative Recipes

Oyster Shaped

250 g butter (9 oz.)
500 g fondant (17.5 oz.)
1 L crème fraîche or heavy cream (34 fl. oz.)
one vanilla bean
4 g potassium sorbate (1 tsp.)

Praline Paste with Crème Fraîche
500 g butter (17.5 oz.)
250 g fondant (9 oz.) plus 300 g praline paste (10.5 oz.)
1 L crème fraîche or heavy cream (34 fl. oz.)
one vanilla bean
500 g couverture chocolate (17.5 oz.)

Smoked Oysters
250 g butter (9 oz.)
250 g fondant (9 oz.)
1 L crème fraîche or heavy cream (34 fl. oz.)
300 g golden caramel (10.5 oz.)
250 g chopped walnuts (9 oz.)

Preparation

Fondant cream is used as a filling for chocolates. It is therefore necessary to prepare the molds by lining them with tempered chocolate (see volume 3, page 53).

Fondant cream is totally covered with chocolate, making it interesting to have a different shape for each flavor. For example, the cream can be molded in the shape of an oyster for crème fraîche filling and in the form of a snail for praline filling.

Making fondant cream filling is a fairly difficult procedure.
It is important to follow the temperatures given for working with the cream. No special equipment is required.
The cream can be molded into various shapes.
Allow 90 minutes to make the fondant cream filling, ready for molding.

In certain recipes the flavoring can be infused in the crème fraîche or heavy cream when it is heated. Place the crème fraîche or heavy cream in a saucepan with the flavoring to be infused, such as a vanilla bean cut lengthwise, mint leaves, or coarsely broken coffee beans. Bring the cream to a boil and allow it to cool with the flavoring to bring out the maximum flavor. Once cool, strain the cream.

Procedure

Softening the Fondant

Work the fondant by hand to soften and smooth it. Continue to work the fondant until it is very malleable and has a consistency similar to softened butter.

Softening the Butter

If the butter is hard and cold, allow it to come to room temperature, until it is the same consistency as the fondant. The butter can also be softened by working

it by hand on a clean marble. In either case it is important that the fondant and butter are the same consistency.

Mixing the Fondant and Butter

With a pastry scraper, mix the butter and fondant on the marble until the mixture is malleable and well blended.

Heating the Crème Fraîche

If the cream has not been boiled with a flavoring, place it in a saucepan and heat it to approximately 60°C (140°F).

Whipping the Cream

Place the mixture of fondant and butter in the mixing bowl of the electric mixer with the whisk attachment and turn the machine to medium speed. Slowly pour in the warm crème fraîche or heavy cream in small amounts. When all the cream has been added, turn the machine to high speed.

Verifying Doneness

The cream mixture should be beaten until smooth and fluffy.

Flavoring and Coloring the Cream

If the flavoring has not already been infused in the cream, it is added at this point. If coloring is used, it is also added at this time.

Piping Out the Cream

Place the cream into a bowl and fill the chocolate-lined molds by piping out the cream with a pastry bag and tip.

Sometimes it is necessary to reheat the filling to keep it creamy and soft enough to pipe out.

Note: While the cream is still warm, 30 to 50 g (1 to 1.5 oz.) of cocoa butter can be added. The cocoa butter will give a firmer consistency to the cream when it cools and will act as a natural preservative.

La Crème Garniture Confiseur
(Fondant Cream Filling)

PREPARATION	**0** min	
Assemble the Equipment **Prepare, Weigh, and Measure** the Raw Ingredients.		• Verify the cleanliness of the equipment. • Prepare the molds by lining them with tempered chocolate.
PROCEDURE	**5** min	
Soften the Fondant		• Work the fondant by hand until it is malleable.
Soften the Butter		• The butter should be the same consistency as the fondant.
Blend the Mixture	**15** min	• Mix the fondant and butter until they are homogeneous and malleable.
Heat the Crème Fraîche		• Heat the crème fraîche or heavy cream to 60° C (140° F).
Whip the Mixture		• In the electric mixer with the whisk attachment, whip the mixture while slowly pouring in the heated cream.
Verify Doneness	**25** min	• The cream should be smooth and fluffy.
Flavor and Color the Cream		• The cream can be flavored or colored at this point.
MOLDING	**30** min	• Immediately fill the molds with a pastry bag and tip.
FINISHING/UNMOLDING		• See volume 3 for unmolding and coating the candies.
STORAGE: Fondant cream filling can be stored for 8 to 10 days in the refrigerator at 5°C (40°F).		

La pâte à guimauve (Marshmallow)

Definition

Marshmallow is a light, soft, and somewhat chewy confection.

It is made from a mixture based on cooked sugar and gelatin folded into beaten egg whites.

Marshmallow batter is used to make candies of the same name.

Equipment

Bowl - Copper sugar pan or stainless steel saucepan

Skimmer, pastry brush, and bowl of

water for cooking the sugar

Candy thermometer

Copper or stainless steel bowl, whisk, measuring cup, and pastry scraper for beating egg whites

Cake sheet pan or metal rulers

Professional Recipe

1 kg sugar (35 oz.) plus 300 ml water (10 fl. oz.) plus 100 g glucose (3.5 oz.), cooked to 125° to 130°C (257° to 266°F)

20 leaves (40 g) gelatin (1.5 oz.)

8 egg whites

flavoring: several drops orange flower water

Alternative Recipe

1 kg sugar (35 oz.) plus 300 ml water (10 fl. oz.) plus 80 to 120 g glucose (3 to 4 oz.)

18 to 25 leaves (35 to 50 g) gelatin (1 to 1.5 oz.)

8 to 12 firm egg whites

flavoring: orange flower water, rose water, or strawberry, vanilla, raspberry, lemon, or coffee extract

Recipe for a Small Quantity

500 g sugar (17.5 oz.) plus 150 ml water (5 fl oz.) plus 50 g glucose (1.5 oz.)

10 leaves (20 g) gelatin (3/4 oz.)

4 egg whites

flavoring to taste

Preparation

Assemble the equipment.

Assemble, weigh, and measure the raw ingredients.

Soften the gelatin leaves by placing them in a bowl and covering them with cold water.

Prepare a mixture of equal amounts of cornstarch and confectioners' sugar to cover the batter.

If molds are used, they should be oiled and lined with parchment paper (or tempered chocolate, see volume 3, page 53, Lining Molds).

Procedure

Cooking the Sugar

Cook the sugar with 30 percent of its weight in water and glucose to 125° to 130°C (257° to 266°F)

Adding the Softened Gelatin

Squeeze any excess water from the gelatin and melt it over a hot water bath or double boiler (do not let it get too hot). Add the melted gelatin to the cooked sugar off the heat.

Beating the Egg Whites

Begin beating the egg whites once the sugar has reached 115°C (239°F), so that they will have almost firm peaks when the sugar reaches the correct temperature (see volume 1, Italian meringue, pages 82 to 83).

Adding the Cooked Sugar/Gelatin to the Egg Whites

Slowly, in a fine stream, pour the cooked sugar/gelatin mixture into the beaten egg whites while continuing to beat the mixture.

 Marshmallow batter is an easy preparation when all instructions are followed and the sugar is cooked correctly.

Marshmallow batter requires no special equipment.

Allow 3 hours for the its preparation.

Flavor the mixture and scrape down the sides of the mixing bowl if necessary.

Verifying Doneness

The mixture should be beaten until it is smooth, light, fluffy, and makes a ribbon when folded over itself.

Molding the Mixture

Place the metal rulers on the work surface, over a sheet of parchment paper sprinkled with the confectioners' sugar/cornstarch mixture; or use paper-lined génoise pans sprinkled with the mixture. Pour the batter inside the metal rulers or into the cake sheet pan. Smooth and even out the top of the batter with a

metal spatula, then sprinkle it with the confectioners' sugar/cornstarch mixture.

Allow the batter to set, which takes at least 2 hours.

The batter can also be poured into lightly oiled molds.

Cutting the Marshmallow to Size

Once firm, cut the marshmallow into strips 2 to 2.5 cm (3/4 to 1 inch) wide, with a chef's knife. The knife can be lightly oiled to prevent the marshmallow from sticking to it. The strips can also be cut with scissors. Cut the strips into square cubes.

Roll the marshmallows in the confectioners' sugar/cornstarch mixture, covering them well.

They can be placed in a drum sieve to shake off excess powder gently if necessary.

Storage

Marshmallows can be stored for 10 to 15 days stacked in between parchment paper, in airtight containers.

La Pâte à Guimauve
(Marshmallow)

PREPARATION	**0** min	
Assemble the Equipment **Prepare, Weigh, and Measure** the Raw Ingredients		• Verify the cleanliness of the equipment. • If molds are to be used, oil and line them with parchment paper or tempered chocolate. • Soften the gelatin leaves in cold water. • Combine equal amounts of confectioners' sugar and cornstarch.
PROCEDURE	**5** min	
Cook the Sugar and Glucose		• Following the usual precautions, cook the sugar and glucose to 125° to 130° C (257° to 266° F).
Add the Melted Gelatin	**15** min	• After the sugar is cooked, add the gelatin to it, off the heat.
Beat the Egg Whites		• Begin beating the egg whites once the sugar has reached 115° to 117° C (239° to 242° F).
Add the Cooked Sugar/Glucose/Gelatin to the Whites	**18** min	• In a fine stream, pour the cooked sugar/glucose/gelatin into the firmly beaten egg whites, continuing to beat the mixture.
Verify Doneness	**25** min	• The mixture should be smooth, light, and fluffy, and it should make a ribbon.
Mold the Mixture	**30** min	• Pour the mixture between the metal rulers, onto the génoise sheet pan, or into molds.
Allow the Mixture to Set		• Allow 2 hours minimum to set.
Cut the Marshmallows.	**3** hr	• The marshmallow can be cut into cubes with a knife or scissors. Roll them in the confectioners' sugar/cornstarch mixture.

STORAGE: Marshmallows can be stored for 10 to 15 days in airtight containers.

Les ganaches confiseur (Ganache fillings)

Ganaches are classified as cream mixtures (see ganaches montées, pages 46 to 47). In this section, several recipes are given as examples of how ganache can be used to fill candies and pastries.

Definition

Ganache is a mixture based on chocolate used to glaze, fill, or frost (when whipped) various preparations. Ganache can be made with crème fraîche, heavy cream, fresh whole milk, or evaporated unsweetened milk, combined with butter, chocolate, and flavoring.

There are many different qualities and types of chocolate. In France the best chocolate to use for ganache is called couverture (covering chocolate), which should not be confused with cake-coating chocolate, a lesser-quality chocolate. Couverture chocolate is recommended, although other semisweet or baking chocolates can be used (according to the quality desired) for the recipes in these volumes.

Macerated, chopped, or plain dried fruits and nuts can be added to the recipes that follow, for example, raisins, currants, chopped chestnuts, hazelnuts, walnuts, almonds, and pignolis.

Uses

Ganache can be used to fill or glaze desserts, individual cakes, and petits fours, as well as to fill bonbons, truffles, and other chocolate confections.

Recipes for Ganaches

Ganache Fondant

1 L crème fraîche or heavy cream (34 fl. oz.)
2 kg semisweet chocolate (70.5 oz)
45 ml vanilla extract (3 Tbsp.)

Lemon Ganache

500 ml crème fraîche or heavy cream (17 fl. oz.)
250 g butter (9 oz.)
1 kg milk chocolate (35 oz.)
500 g semisweet chocolate (17.5 oz.)
500 g candied lemon rind (17.5 oz.), ground
150 ml Kirsch (5 fl. oz.)

Pistachio Ganache

1 kg white chocolate (35 oz.)
500 ml condensed milk (17 fl. oz.)
250 g butter (9 oz.)
200 g pistachio paste (7 oz.)

Rum Ganache

1 L crème fraîche or heavy cream (34 fl. oz.)
1.5 kg semisweet chocolate (53 oz.)
500 g milk chocolate (17.5 oz.)
250 g butter (9 oz.)
30 ml vanilla extract (2 Tbsp.)
250 ml dark rum (8.5 fl. oz.)
250 to 500 g dried currants (9 to 17.5 oz.), macerated in rum, optional

Grand Marnier Ganache

1 L crème fraîche or heavy cream (34 fl. oz.)
1 kg semisweet chocolate (35 oz.)
1 kg milk chocolate (35 oz.)
400 g butter (14 oz.)
400 ml orange extract (13.5 fl. oz.) or 250 ml orange extract (8.5 fl. oz.) plus 200 ml Grand Marnier (6.5 fl. oz.)
400 to 500 g orange rind (14 to 17.5 oz.), macerated in Grand Marnier and finely ground, optional

Liquor Ganache

500 ml crème fraîche or heavy cream (17 fl. oz.)

Ganaches can be prepared without difficulty.

It is important that the raw ingredients are very fresh.

No special equipment is required. Allow 1 hour for preparation.

In general, the storage of ganache is very limited.

500 g butter (17.5 oz.)
250 ml liquor (8.5 fl. oz.)
750 g semisweet chocolate (26.5 oz.)
250 g milk chocolate (9 oz.)

Note: This ganache can be used to cover fruits macerated in the same liquor.

Praline Ganache

1 kg semisweet chocolate (35 oz.)
500 ml crème fraîche or heavy cream (17 fl. oz.)
500 g butter (17.5 oz.)
250 g praline (9 oz.)
75 ml Maraschino or other liqueur (2.5 fl. oz.)

Coffee Ganache

1 L crème fraîche or heavy cream (34 fl. oz.)
50 g coffee beans (1.5 oz.), coarsely ground and infused in the crème fraîche
150 g trimoline (5 oz.)
1.5 kg milk chocolate (53 oz.)
500 g semisweet chocolate (17.5 oz.)
10 g instant coffee (2 tsp.), dissolved in 50 ml rum (1.5 fl. oz.)

Tea Ganache

1 L crème fraîche or heavy cream (34 fl. oz.)
50 ml tea (1.5 fl. oz.) infused in the crème fraîche
1 kg semisweet chocolate (35 oz.)
500 g white chocolate (17.5 oz.)
several drops vanilla extract

Mint Ganache

1 L crème fraîche or heavy cream (34 fl. oz.)
50 g mint leaves (1.5 oz.) infused in the crème fraîche
250 ml evaporated milk (8.5 fl. oz.)
1.5 kg white chocolate (53 oz.)
150 g trimoline (1.5 oz.)

Vanilla Ganache

1 L crème fraîche or heavy cream (34 fl. oz.)
two vanilla beans infused in the crème fraîche
250 ml evaporated milk (8.5 fl. oz.)
1 kg milk chocolate (35 oz.)
250 g semisweet chocolate (9 oz.)

Hazelnut Ganache

500 g butter (17.5 oz.), lightly browned (beurre noisette)
500 ml crème fraîche or heavy cream (17 fl. oz.)
1 kg milk chocolate (35 oz.)
500 g semisweet chocolate (17.5 oz.)

Honey Ganache

1 kg milk chocolate (35 oz.)
750 g semisweet chocolate (26.5 oz.)
250 g baking chocolate (9 oz.)
1 L crème fraîche or heavy cream (34 fl. oz.)
750 g to 1 kg honey (26.5 to 35 oz.)
several drops vanilla extract

Caramel Ganache

500 g sugar (17.5 oz.), cooked to caramel stage with 500 ml milk (17 fl. oz.)
500 ml crème fraîche or heavy cream (17 fl. oz.)
500 g semisweet chocolate (17.5 oz.)
750 g milk chocolate (26.5 oz.)
100 g butter (3.5 oz.)

Anise Ganache

1 L crème fraîche or heavy cream (34 fl. oz.)
500 ml milk (17 fl. oz.)
150 ml anise-flavored liqueur (1.5 fl oz), such as Pernod, Ricard, Marie-Brizard
2 kg milk chocolate (70.5 oz.)
500 g semisweet chocolate (17.5 oz.)

White Ganache

1 kg white chocolate (35 oz.)
250 ml crème fraîche or heavy cream (8.5 fl. oz.)
250 ml milk (8.5 fl. oz.)
100 g trimoline (3.5 oz.)
150 g butter (5 oz.)

Chapter 5 Finished products based on pâte à choux (cream puff pastry)

Basic Techniques

Characteristics

The preparation of pâte à choux–based cakes and pastries is difficult, not only because the batter requires careful preparation but because assembly can be demanding as well.

Using the Pastry Bag

Using the pastry bag to pipe out dough and batters requires a certain level of expertise and experience. The final shape of the pastries depends solely on the pastry chef's understanding and skill. When using a pastry bag, it is not possible to rely on molds or cutouts to give the final shape to the pastries (see volume 1, Using the Pastry Bag, pages 34 to 35).

Preparing the Pâte à Choux for Baking

Once the pâte à choux has been piped out into the desired shapes with a pastry bag, it should be brushed with egg wash and gently pressed with a moistened fork. Usually, however, the egg wash is of little importance because the pastries will be coated with fondant or other glazes after they are baked.

Moisten the piped-out pâte à choux with a finger or the back of a spoon before baking and lightly press it down. This helps prevent the formation of a crust during baking and prevents cracking in the oven.

Baking

The temperature of the oven should be closely regulated. To avoid the accumulation of moisture in the oven, the vents (if available) should be left open. The door to the oven may also be left ajar.

It is best not to increase the oven temperature while the pastries are in the oven but to lower it during baking.

Checking the Doneness

The pastries should be light brown on top and slightly lighter on the sides. It is important that they be dry on the inside, or they will fall once out of the oven.

Let them cool on cake racks as soon as they are done baking. This prevents them from getting soggy.

Filling the Pastries

Pâte à choux pastries should be filled only after they have completely cooled. The filling is piped into the pastries through a hole pierced in the bottom.

Filling the pastries is a straightforward procedure, but it is important to make sure that the filling is evenly distributed: individual pieces require between 70 and 80 g (2.5 to 3 oz.) of filling. Petits fours (miniature pastries) should be filled completely.

Glazing

The application of a particular glaze is extremely important for the final appearance of the pastries and must be carried out very carefully (see fondant, pages 100 to 101, and Glazing Pâte à Choux, pages 128 to 131).

Varieties

The classic shapes and uses of pâte à choux are presented in this chapter. It is of course possible to shape pâte à choux in innumerable ways—into mice, rabbits, little nests, butterflies, and many other shapes.

Individual Pâte à Choux–based Pastries

Shape	Piping Method (Number of Pieces)	Filling	Glaze or Topping	Serving Temperature (Storage)
Choux (cream puffs) 6 cm (2.5 in.) diam., round	Plain tip no. 10/12 (4 × 5 = 20) (4 × 6 = 24)	Pastry cream, mousseline cream, any flavor, Chantilly cream	Fondant, cooked sugar, confectioners' sugar	Room temperature (24 hours, 10°C/50°F)
Choux praliné (praline-filled cream puffs) rounds 6 cm (2.5 in.) diam.; oval, 4 × 8 cm (1.5 × 3 in.)	Plain tip no. 10/12 (4 × 5 = 20) (4 × 6 = 24)	Pastry cream, mousseline cream, praline	Coffee/chocolate fondant, butter cream	Room temperature (24 hours, 10°C/50°F)
Croquembouches 3 to 4 cm (1 to 1.5 in.), round	Plain tip no. 7 (6 × 10 = 60) (5 × 9 = 45)	Pastry cream with liquor	Cooked sugar (pale yellow)	Room temperature (24 hours, 10°C/50°F)
Cygnes (swans) cone or pear shape, heads in S or ? shape	Plain tip no. 10/12 (4 × 6 = 24) Plain tip no.5 or paper cone	Chantilly cream, mousseline cream	Confectioners' sugar	10°C (50°F) (12 hours, 10°C/50°F)
Paniers (baskets) round, 6 cm (2.5 in.) diam.; oval, 4 × 8 cm (1.5 to 3 in.); handles: horseshoe shaped	Plain tip no. 10/12 (4 × 6 = 24) Plain tip no. 5 or paper cone	Chantilly cream, mousseline cream	Confectioners' sugar	10°C (50°F) (12 hours, 10°C/50°F)
Eclairs 10 to 12 × 2 cm (4 to 4.5 × 3/4 in.)	Plain tip no. 10/12 (3 × 8 = 24) (2 × 7) + (1 × 6) = 20	Pastry cream, mousseline cream, with coffee, chocolate, or vanilla flavoring	Coffee fondant, white chocolate	Room temperature (24 hours, 10°C/50°F)
Bananes (bananas) long and curved	Plain tip no. 10/12 (3 × 8 = 24) (2 × 7) + (1 × 6) = 20	Pastry cream, mousseline cream, with banana or vanilla flavoring	Yellow fondant, chocolate accents	Room temperature (24 hours, 10°C/50°F)
Glands (acorns) cone or pear shape	Plain tip no. 10/12 (4 × 6 = 24)	Pastry cream, mousseline cream with liquor (Kirsch)	Green fondant, yellow fondant, chocolate sprinkles	Room temperature (24 hours, 10°C/50°F)
Paris-Brest round, long, or in S shape	Plain tip no. 8 or medium star tip (round: 4 × 4 = 16) (long: 4 × 6 = 24)	Pastry cream, praline-flavored mousseline	Confectioners' sugar	Room temperature (24 hours, 10°C/50°F)
Religieuses (double cream puffs) round, 5 cm (2 in.); heads: 2 cm (3/4 in.) rounds	Plain tip no. 10/12 (5 × 6 = 30) Plain tip no. 7 (6 × 10 = 60)	Pastry cream, chocolate or coffee mousseline cream	Coffee or chocolate fondant, butter cream for accents	Room temperature (24 hours, 10°C/50°F)
Salambos oval, 4 × 8 cm (1.5 × 3 in.)	Plain tip no. 10/12 (4 × 6 = 24)	Pastry cream, coffee or chocolate mousseline cream	Cooked sugar (pale yellow), assorted fondants	Room temperature (24 hours, 10°C/50°F)

Note: Each of the above pastries may be prepared as petits fours. When preparing petits fours, 1 L (34 fl. oz.) of pâte à choux will be enough for 350 to 400 pieces. Allow 3 L (101 fl. oz.) of pastry cream to fill the petits fours.

Filling and glazing pâte à choux–based pastries

(Basic Techniques)

Individual-size Pâte à Choux Pastries

One L (34 fl. oz.) of pâte à choux will make from 80 to 100 individual-size pastries.

Pastries made from 1 L (34 fl. oz.) of pâte à choux require 3 L (101 fl. oz.) of pastry cream or other filling, so that 1 L (34 fl. oz.) of filling fills about thirty individual pastries.

Occasionally pâte à choux–based pastries are filled with mousseline. In this case, 1 L (34 fl. oz.) of mousseline will fill seventy to eighty individual-size pastries.

About 1 kg (35 oz.) of fondant is required to glaze this number of individual pastries.

Petits Fours Made with Pâte à Choux

Petits fours are miniature versions of individual-size pastries. They are eaten in one bite.

One L (34 fl. oz.) of pâte à choux will make 350 to 450 pâte à choux–based petits fours. Allow either 3 L (101 fl. oz.) of pastry cream or 2 L (67.5 fl. oz.) of mousseline to fill them. For glazing, plan to use 1 L (34 fl. oz.) of fondant.

Filling the Pastries

Never fill pâte à choux pastries until they have completely cooled.

Pâte à choux pastries are usually filled by first piercing a hole in the bottom or sides with a pastry tip set aside for this purpose. For example:

- three holes are made for eclairs (in the bottom or sides)
- two holes are made for salambos or acorns (in the bottom or sides)
- one hole is made for large choux (cream puffs) or religieuses (in the bottom)

Petits fours usually require one or two holes, depending on their shape and size.

Eclairs are occasionally cut down the middle, with the filling simply piped into the bottom half. We advise against this method, not only because this makes the eclairs more difficult to glaze, but it also makes the cream filling more susceptible to contamination.

Pâte à choux–based pastries are usually filled using a plain no. 5 pastry tip.

Individual-size pastries usually weigh from 80 to 100 g (2.5 to 3.5 oz.) when completed.

When filling these pastries, hold them firmly in the palm of the hand. Hold the pastry bag in the other hand and pipe in the filling until the pastry begins to press back slightly.

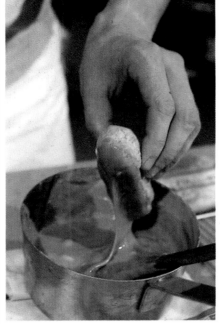

It is also possible to tell if these pastries have been correctly filled by feeling their weight in the hand. This method, however, requires considerable experience.

To make sure that the cream is well distributed on the insides of the eclairs, it is best to start by filling the two holes at each end of the pastries, filling the center hole last.

Once the eclairs are filled, they should be turned upside down on a cake rack. This will prevent the filling from draining out of the holes in the bottom, and it will give the cream filling time to set. It also saves time when glazing the eclairs because they are facing in the right direction.

Glazing

There are two possible methods:

A. Dipping the eclairs or other pastries directly in the saucepan containing the fondant

B. Spreading the fondant over the surface of the pastries with a metal spatula

Method A

Use a saucepan that will facilitate the dipping of the pastries.

Place the saucepan on a support instead of directly on the pastry marble to prevent it from cooling too rapidly.

Dip the surface of the pastry in the fondant. Make sure that it is well coated; hold it long enough in the fondant to ensure that the fondant adheres to the surface.

Lift the pastries vertically so that the fondant does not drip over the sides.

Remove the excess fondant from the edges of the pastries using a finger. Make sure that the fondant is spread evenly over the surface of the pastry.

Using the same finger, distribute the excess of fondant from the edges over the rest of the pastry. This helps prevent the excess fondant from running over the sides and improves the final presentation. This method is used regardless of the shape of the pastry.

The amount of surface that should be glazed depends on the size of the pastries. If the piece is small, it is best to cover the entire available surface with the fondant. On the other hand, if the pieces are relatively large, leave an area unglazed.

Method B

Hold the piece directly over the saucepan containing the fondant. It should face you and be almost completely vertical.

Pick up a quantity of fondant with a spatula and carefully let it drip over the top surface of the pastry.

Apply the fondant to the pastry by moving the spatula both up and down.

With experience, this can be accomplished in one swift movement. Once the desired amount of fondant has been applied to the pastry, distribute it evenly over the surface with a finger.

Using Fondant to Glaze Pastries

Flavoring and Coloring the Fondant

Fondant may be colored or flavored with any authorized food coloring or natural extract.

In France, food coloring is available in both liquid and paste forms. In America, the liquid form is usually used.

When coloring fondant be careful to avoid bright colors. Soft, pastel hues are always more appetizing than garish colors. The only exception to this rule is when chocolate or coffee is used; these should not be pale but dark and rich looking. They serve to both color and flavor the fondant.

When using chocolate to color and flavor fondant, it is best to use melted baking chocolate rather than cocoa powder. A few drops of red food coloring will help give the fondant a warmer hue.

Coffee extract should be used in sufficient quantity to ensure that the fondant is well flavored. A few drops of red food coloring will reinforce the color.

Choosing the Color for the Fondant Based on the Pastry to be Glazed

For example, use:

- white fondant for the following filling flavors: Kirsch, rum, cherry, Triple Sec, Curaçao, Cointreau

- pink fondant for Grand Marnier, black currant, Curaçao,

- green fondant for Kirsch, chestnut, Maraschino

- coffee fondant for coffee, praline, walnut, chestnut

- chocolate fondant for chocolate, ganache, chestnut, walnut

The ability to choose and create appropriate colors and flavors for pastries is an essential step in the development of a professional pastry chef. It is in these areas that good taste and sophistication are most required. A cake or pastry covered with garish colored creams and decorations is not appealing to the customer. Nor is a perfectly decorated cake with warm harmonious coloring but carelessly flavored creams and fillings.

Saucepans for Fondant

Many pastry shops keep several small saucepans that are used only for fondant. This proves convenient in situations where many different colored fondants are used in the course of a day.

When preparing fondant, heat only the amount necessary for a particular project. This ensures that the fondant will keep its characteristic sheen and will help avoid the formation of lumps. Fondant that is continually reheated will lose its sheen.

When preparing a series of colored fondants, always start with plain white fondant and end with chocolate. The fondant remaining from one color can then be added to the newly prepared color, for example, white may be added to pink, pink to chocolate. This not only saves fondant but limits the number of dirty pans.

Fondant should be taken from the tub with wet hands and worked between the hands to soften it before finally working it with a wooden spatula.

Adjusting the Temperature, Color, and Consistency of Fondant

Put the fondant, which has already been softened between the palms of the hands, in a saucepan over a very low flame.

Work the mass of fondant over a flame or in a bain-marie while continuously checking its temperature with the back of the finger. There should be no sensation of heat.

Remove the saucepan from the heat

as soon as the fondant moves from the semisolid stage to the semiliquid stage.

Continue stirring the fondant off the heat. Warm it slightly from time to time if necessary.

Checking the Temperature of Fondant

Fondant should never be overheated:
- 36° to 37°C (97° to 99°F) under normal conditions
- 37° to 38°C (99° to 100°F) under humid conditions

There are two methods for checking the temperature:

1. Touch the surface of the fondant with the back of the index finger. The fondant should feel neither hot nor cold.

2. Using a spatula, touch some of the fondant to the lower lip. Again the fondant should feel neither hot nor cold.

Checking the Consistency of Fondant

Once the temperature, color, and flavor of the fondant have been adjusted, the consistency should be adjusted with sugar syrup at 1260 D.

The desired final consistency depends on two factors:

- the type of cake or pastry to be glazed
- the humidity of the work area

In general the consistency of the fondant should be:

- somewhat liquid for cakes (when the fondant is lifted over the saucepan with a spatula, its traces on the surface quickly disappear)

- thicker for pastries made from pâte à choux (fondant dripped over the surface with a spatula remains on the surface for several seconds)

Storage

When finished using the fondant, immediately scrape the inside walls of the saucepan. If necessary, clean the inside walls of the saucepans with a clean, damp dish rag.

It is extremely important to prevent the formation of a crust on the surface of the fondant. This would interfere with its use in the next project.

Clean the outside of the saucepan before placing it in the refrigerator.

Reusing Fondant

Remove the saucepan containing the fondant from the refrigerator several hours before making the final adjustments to temperature and consistency.

Removing Crust from the Surface

Pour a small amount of warm water on

the surface of the fondant and leave it for several minutes to soften the crust.

Adding Fresh Fondant

Pour off the warm water and add the fresh fondant. From this point, the procedure is the same as above:

- dissolve the fresh fondant
- heat to the correct temperature
- adjust the color, flavor, and consistency

Eclairs, religieuses (double cream puffs), choux (cream puffs), glands (acorn, pear, and cone shapes), salambos, choux praliné (praline cream puffs)

Eclairs

Composition

Pâte à choux, pastry cream or mousseline, fondant

One L (34 fl. oz.) of pâte à choux will make 80 to 100 individual pastries.

One L (34 fl. oz.) of pastry cream is needed to fill thirty to thirty-five individual pastries.

One L (34 fl. oz.) of mousseline is needed to fill seventy to eighty individual pastries.

Piping

Pipe the pâte à choux in 10- to 12-cm (4.5- to 5.5-in.) lengths onto buttered sheet pans using a pastry bag with a no. 10 or no. 12 plain tip.

Each 40 × 60 cm (16 × 24 in.) sheet pan can hold the following arrangements:

- (2 × 7) + (1 × 6) = 20
- 3 × 8 = 24

Brush each strip with egg wash and gently press down with the back of a fork.

Baking

Bake in a 210° to 230°C (400° to 450°F) oven with vents open (if available) and door ajar.

Filling

Fill the baked eclairs with either pastry cream or mousseline cream, flavored with coffee, chocolate, or vanilla.

Use a plain no. 5 tip.

Cut three small holes in the pastries with a pastry tip reserved for this purpose or cut lengthwise through the pastries with a bread knife.

Glazing

Glaze with fondant (see Glazing and Using Fondant to Glaze Pastries, pages 129 to 131).

Storage

These pastries should be made fresh daily. They can be stored for a maximum of 24 hours in the refrigerator.

They should be served at room temperature, 20°C (68°F).

Religieuses (Double Cream Puffs)

Composition

Pâte à choux, pastry cream, or mousseline (filling), fondant (glaze), butter cream (decoration), coffee, chocolate, and sometimes vanilla flavoring

Piping

Both large and small rounds of pâte à choux should be piped out for religieuses:

- 1 large round for each bottom cream puff
- 1 small round for each top cream puff (the top should be about the size of a walnut, one-quarter the size of the bottom)
- 24 bottoms per sheet pan (6 × 4 = 24)
- 60 tops per sheet pan (10 × 6 = 60)

Filling

To fill the pastries, pierce a small hole in the underside of the top section and in the top of the bottom section. When the small cream puff is placed atop the larger one, the holes will not show.

The small cream puff is placed over the larger bottom one after each is glazed.

A small ring of butter cream can be placed around the base of the top section of the religieuse. A little rose-shaped swirl of butter cream on the top is also an attractive touch.

The proportions, glazes, flavors, and storage times are the same as for eclairs.

Choux (Cream Puffs)

Composition

Pâte à choux; pastry cream or mousseline (filling); coffee, chocolate, praline, vanilla, Grand Marnier, Cointreau, Kirsch, or rum flavoring; sometimes butter cream for decoration

Piping

Use a pastry bag with a no. 10 or no. 12 plain tip. There should be 24 pastries on a 40 × 60 cm (16 × 24 in.) sheet pan. These can be arranged in rows, 4 × 6 = 24

The proportions of the various components for filling, glazing, and decoration are the same as for eclairs. The cooking and storage times are also the same.

Salambos

Composition

Pâte à choux, pastry cream or mousseline (filling), rum, cooked sugar, preserved fruit (optional decoration)

Piping

Pipe the pâte à choux into oval shapes, thicker and shorter than for eclairs. Use a pastry bag with a no. 10 or no. 12 plain tip. Arrange the pastry in rows: $4 \times 6 = 24$ for a 40×60 cm $(16 \times 24$ in.) sheet pan.

The quantities of the different components and the baking time are the same as for eclairs.

Glazing

Salambos are often glazed with cooked sugar, cooked to the pale yellow stage (petit jaune). The top of the pastry is dipped into the sugar and placed face down on the marble. This method requires a certain amount of attention and skill—the sugar must be cooked to just the right degree, $155\,^{\circ}$C ($280\,^{\circ}$F). It is also easy to burn the fingers. The presentation of salambos is the same as for eclairs.

Glands (Acorn, Pear, and Cone Shapes)

Composition

Pâte à choux, pastry cream or mousseline (filling), flavoring (often Kirsch), glaze (often green), chocolate sprinkles (decoration)

Piping

Pipe the pâte à choux with a pastry bag using a no. 10 or no. 12 plain tip into the shape of a cone or pear. Arrange in rows: $4 \times 6 = 24$ for each 40×60 cm (16×24 in.) sheet pan.

Glazing

Cover with fondant.

The thick end of the pastry may be dipped in chocolate sprinkles to imitate the base of an acorn.

The quantity of each component, the fillings, baking time, and presentation are the same as for eclairs.

Choux Praliné (Praline Cream Puffs)

Composition

Pâte à choux, praline-flavored pastry cream, coffee or chocolate fondant, plain butter cream (decoration)

Piping

The pastry shells are made in the same shape as salambos.

Fill with praline-flavored pastry cream. Glaze with both chocolate and coffee fondant, glazing half at a time lengthwise, sideways, or diagonally.

The butter cream should be piped from a pastry bag with a star tip to decorate the pastries. The storage and baking times and serving methods are the same as for eclairs.

Pâte à choux–based Petits Fours

Petits fours (miniature pastries) are composed of the same elements as individual pastries but are smaller and can be eaten in one bite.

They are often combined and served as assortments.

The photo below shows an assortment of petits fours, all based on pâte à choux.

Profiteroles, chouquettes, Paris-Brest

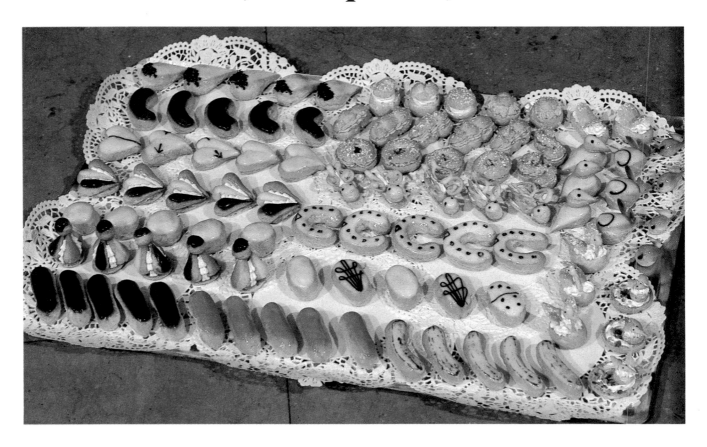

Profiteroles

Composition

Pâte à choux, pastry cream or vanilla ice cream (filling), chocolate sauce, crème anglaise, or sabayon

Piping

See Building Croquembouches, pages 139 to 140.

Filling

Hot profiteroles are most often filled with pastry cream. Vanilla ice cream is most often used for cold profiteroles.

Profiteroles are usually served with chocolate sauce or crème anglaise (sometimes both) served on the side.

Presentation

Stack the profiteroles in a pile on a plate or platter. Cover them with the chocolate sauce or crème anglaise at the table or serve the sauce on the side.

Note: When serving frozen profiteroles, the sauce should be added at the last minute, just before serving.

Variation

Profiteroles may be filled with other creams. For example, 3 parts crème Chantilly and 1 part raspberry jam or preserves can be carefully folded together with a spatula. In this case the profiteroles should be cut open and the cream spooned in.

Sabayon sauce is a nice alternative to the usual chocolate sauce or crème anglaise.

Slivered and toasted almonds and raspberries may be sprinkled over the entire presentation.

Serve cold, 5°C (40°F).

Other fruits, such as strawberries, currants, blueberries, and blackberries, may also be used in place of the raspberries.

Chouquettes et Couronnes (Miniature Cream Puffs and Crowns)

Composition

Classic pâte à choux or milk-based pâte à choux, plus an additional 25 g (1 oz.) of sugar per L (34 fl. oz.) of batter, a few drops of orange flower water, egg wash, crystallized sugar for decoration

Piping

Chouquettes

Pipe out the pâte à choux into walnut-sized rounds on a buttered sheet pan. One L (34 fl. oz.) of batter should yield about 250 pastries.

Glaze lightly with egg wash.

Sprinkle liberally with the crystallized sugar before the egg wash has a chance to dry.

Shake off the excess sugar.

Bake in a hot oven, 230° to 240°C (450° to 475°F) with the vents open (if available) and the door ajar.

Note: It is often necessary to double the sheet pans under the pastries either at the beginning or during the baking to prevent the bottoms of the pastries from getting too dark. The pastries should be baked until they are pale brown.

Couronnes (Crowns)

The method for preparing crowns is the same as for chouquettes except that each individual piece is piped in a circle to obtain a crown shape. Use a plain no. 8, no. 9, or no. 10 pastry tip, depending on the desired size. Crowns are sometimes piped out using a fluted tip.

These same techniques can be used to make other shapes such as squares, hearts, or clovers.

Paris-Brest

Composition

Pâte à choux, slivered or chopped almonds, sometimes slivered or chopped hazelnuts, Paris-Brest cream, confectioners' sugar for decoration

Piping

Pâte à choux for Paris-Brest can be piped out:

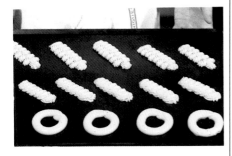

- in long strips or in spiral shapes, like eclairs (20 to 24 per sheet pan)
- in crowns (rows of 4 × 4 = 16)
- in strips extending the whole length of the sheet pan, using a no. 8 plain pastry tip (3 strips per sheet pan) or in spiral shapes using a fluted tip

Brush with egg wash and sprinkle with slivered or chopped almonds.

Turn the sheet pan on its side to shake off excess almonds.

When preparing Paris-Brest in strips, an extra narrower and shorter strip can be inserted between layers of cream. This not only makes it possible to use less cream, but also gives support to the finished Paris-Brest. Large, crown-shaped Paris-Brests are prepared in this way by piping the pâte à choux over a marked sheet pan.

Make two sets of markings on the sheet pan, one for the base and another for the center piece.

Baking

For individual-sized pastries, the baking times and technique are the same as for eclairs (page 132). Larger pastries should be baked at a lower temperature, 180° to 200°C (350° to 375°F), with the oven vents open (if available) and the door ajar.

Filling

Use Paris-Brest cream (see pages 44 to 45) or praline mousse (see pages 63 to 69).

Note: Large strips of Paris-Brest can be filled with strips of génoise or ladyfingers that have been soaked in a rum-flavored simple syrup.

Paris-Brest should be served chilled, 10°C (50°F).

Storage

Paris-Brest will keep for 24 hours at 10°C (50°F).

Paniers, cygnes, choux Chantilly (Baskets, swans, Chantilly cream filled puffs)

Paniers (Baskets)

Composition

Pâte à choux, Chantilly cream or mousseline, flavoring (vanilla, Grand Marnier, Cointreau, or Kirsch), confectioners' sugar (decoration)

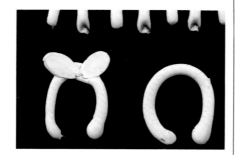

Piping

Pipe out like salambos (see page 133).

The handles to the baskets are piped out in a horseshoe shape with a no. 5 pastry tip or a plastic cone.

Quantities and Baking:

See eclairs (page 132).

Filling

Carefully cut into the pastries and fill them with a fluted pastry tip.

Decoration

Cut the top part of the pastries in two and sprinkle with confectioners' sugar. Put the handles on last.

Storage

Paniers will keep for 24 hours in a cool place, 10°C (50°F).

Cygnes (Swans)

Composition

Pâte à choux, Chantilly cream or mousseline, flavoring (vanilla, Grand Marnier, Cointreau, or Kirsch), confectioners' sugar (decoration)

Piping

The bases are formed in the same way as glands (acorns; see page 133). Pipe out the heads using a no. 5 plain tip or a paper cone.

Quantities and Baking:

See eclairs (page 132).

Filling

Carefully cut the tops off the pastries and fill them with a fluted pastry tip.

Decoration

Cut the top part of the pastries in half lengthwise to make the wings. Sprinkle with confectioners' sugar and place the wings and head in the cream.

Storage

Swans will keep for 14 hours in a cool place, 10°C (50°F).

136

Choux Chantilly (Chantilly cream–filled Puffs)

Composition

Pâte à choux, Chantilly cream, flavoring (vanilla, Grand Marnier, Cointreau, or Kirsch), confectioners' sugar (decoration)

Piping

Use a no. 10 or no. 12 plain tip. Pipe out rounds on a 40 × 60 cm (16 × 24 in.) sheet pan in rows: 5 × 4 = 20 or 6 × 4 = 24.

Quantity and Baking

Same as eclairs (page 132).

Filling

Cut off the tops of the pastries with a knife, and trim these lids into even rounds using a plain, circular cookie cutter. Fill the pastries using a fluted pastry tip. Sprinkle the lids with confectioners' sugar and place atop the cream.

Storage

Choux Chantilly will keep for 24 hours in a cool place, 10°C (50°F).

Marguerite Tart Bases

Pâte à choux is sometimes used to decorate the bases of Saint-Honoré tarts and special tarts such as the one shown here.

These bases are prepared in a variety of forms and are made with feuilletée (puff pastry) trimmings, pâte à foncer (basic tart and pie dough) or pâte sucrée (sweetened tart and pie dough).

After rolling the dough for the base into the desired shape and size, be sure to let it rest for at least an hour before baking.

Moisten the base dough where the pâte à choux is to be attached or brush the entire surface with egg wash.

Brushing egg wash over the entire surface of the tart base will help protect it from the moisture in the cream and pre-

vent it from becoming soggy after it is baked. Pâte à choux is usually applied to tart bases using a plain no. 5 or no. 6 pastry tip. Occasionally a no. 7 tip is used for the base of a gâteau Saint-Honoré or the bottom of a large religieuse. The pâte à choux should be piped about 5 mm (1/4 in.) away from the edge of the dough to allow for shrinkage of the pastry base.

Sometimes pâte à choux is piped into the center of a tart base. This serves several purposes:
- to separate the different sections (as in a marguerite tart)
- to reinforce the tart base (as in a flat religieuse)
- to save cream filling (as for a base for a Saint-Honoré)

Saint-Honoré

Composition

Base

Pâte à foncer (basic tart and pie dough) or feuilletée (puff pastry) trimmings (see volume 1, pages 112 to 117, 128 to 133), egg wash, pâte à choux, sugar cooked to the pale yellow stage (petit jaune)

Filling

Saint-Honoré cream or Chantilly cream (advised) or mousseline

Procedure

Preparing the Tart Bases

Roll out the pastry dough to about 2 mm (1/8 in.) thick. Poke holes in it with a fork or roller docker. Cut out pieces in the desired size and shape:

- large rounds, size depending on the number of people to be served

- small individual-sized pastries, using a 4-inch cookie cutter.

After the dough has been cut to the appropriate size, place it on a moistened sheet pan. Lightly brush the bases with egg wash.

Pipe a ring of pâte à choux around the edges of the rings of pastry dough, slightly in from the edge. Use a pastry bag with a no. 7 or no. 8 plain tip.

Pipe a small piece of pâte à choux in the center of individual-size bases.

For large Saint-Honoré bases, pipe the pâte à choux in a spiral pattern, starting in about 1 cm (3/8 in.) away from the rim. This helps reinforce the base and prevents it from warping or becoming misshapen during baking.

Prepare the individual cream puffs to be used for decoration on a separate sheet pan and bake in the usual way (see page 132).

Baking the Saint-Honoré Bases

Brush the bases with egg wash and bake in a 200° to 210°C (400°F) oven.

Garnishing the Tart Base

Once the individual pâte à choux puffs have completely cooled, dip them one by one into the hot cooked sugar (pale yellow stage). Let them cool on sheet pans. Trim if necessary.

Dip the bases of the individual puffs into the hot sugar again and place them immediately on the ring of pâte à choux attached to the tart base.

They may be placed next to one another or at regular intervals. Use three to five cream puffs for individual-size Saint-Honorés.

Filling

Large Saint-Honorés: Place a layer of cream in the pastry base using a metal spatula or a plastic pastry scraper. Make sure that this layer is even and smooth. To finish the decoration, pipe over a final layer of cream using the Saint-Honoré pastry tip designed especially for this purpose.

Small Saint-Honorés: Use a regular fluted pastry tip to pipe the cream directly into the bases

Storage

Storage time in the refrigerator depends on the type of cream used:

● Saint-Honoré cream: 4 to 6 hours

● Chantilly cream: 24 hours maximum

● mousseline cream: 24 to 48 hours maximum

Building croquembouches (Cream puff pyramids)

Composition

Pâte à choux, egg wash, pastry cream, cooked sugar (pale yellow stage)

Depending on the particular style, allow from three to five individual cream puffs per person.

Components of a Croquembouche

A croquembouche is a kind of "pièce montée" that is constructed by layering individual cream puffs in a pyramid shape.

For a croquembouche serving fifty people, the following components are needed:

● 1 L pâte à choux (34 fl. oz.)

● 3 L pastry cream (101 fl. oz.)

● 1 kg cooked sugar containing 20% glucose (35 oz.)

Piping the Individual Puffs

Pipe the cream puffs onto lightly buttered sheet pans, using a no.7, no.8, or no.9 pastry tip. Brush with egg wash and gently press the surfaces with the back of a fork.

Baking

Leave the vents open (if available) and the door ajar to avoid the accumulation of moisture in the oven. Bake at 210°C (400°F); avoid using too hot an oven, or the individual cream puffs will become too dark before drying properly.

When baked, they should be pale brown in color. It is best to bake the individual cream puffs for a croquembouche the day before it is to be assembled.

This gives them time to dry out and remain firm.

Filling the Cream Puffs

The cream puffs should always be filled at the last minute with pastry cream flavored as desired.

Glazing the Cream Puffs

The individual cream puffs should be glazed generously with sugar cooked to the pale yellow stage after being filled, before constructing the croquembouche.

Trim away any excess sugar before the final construction of the pyramid.

Constructing the Croquembouche

To construct the pyramid, the individual cream puffs should be stuck together in groups of from three to five. These sections constitute individual serving sizes.

The pyramids are constructed by attaching the cream puffs with cooked sugar.

This may be done using an oiled paper cone to apply the cooked sugar to the puffs or by dipping the puffs directly in the sugar.

The dipping method requires a bit of experience but allows the pastry chef more flexibility when shaping the pyramid.

Note: It is easier to construct a croquembouche using large cream puffs, but a croquembouche made with small puffs is usually more attractive and impressive.

Pedestals

The croquembouche can be mounted on a nougatine pedestal shaped in various ways:

● plain

● shaped, with scallop-shaped cutouts

● round or oval, with scallop-shaped cutouts.

Decoration

Use royal icing (see volume 4, pages 18 to 19), pulled-sugar roses, candy-coated almonds (dragées), or other appropriate decorations.

Constructing large religieuses

Large Constructed Religieuses

Composition

Large religieuse-type pâte à choux pastries are usually constructed on a base of pâte sucrée (sweetened tart and pie dough) that has been baked in a génoise pan:
- use a 12-cm (4.5-in.) pan for the base, to serve twelve people
- prepare eight triangular eclairs, 20 cm (8 in.) long with 4-cm (1.5-in-) bases
- pipe out three pâte à choux rings with no. 10 pastry tip:
—1 ring 10 cm (4 in.) in diameter
—1 ring 8 cm (3 in.) in diameter
—1 ring 6 cm (2.5 in.) in diameter
—1 medium-sized cream puff

Filling the Eclairs

Use coffee- and chocolate-flavored pastry cream, to fill four chocolate eclairs and four coffee eclairs.

Glazing the Eclairs

Glaze with coffee or chocolate fondant.

Cream Coating for the Base

Use a light-textured cream, flavored with vanilla, chocolate, or coffee.

Decorating:
Decorate as desired with butter cream.

Procedure

Shape and bake the tart base the day before assembling the religieuse. When placing the eclairs around the outer edges of the base, it is a good idea to place a bottle or cup in the middle of the tart, to act as a guide.

Constructing the Religieuses

Attach the glazed eclairs to the rim of the pâte sucrée base. Adjust the sizes of the eclairs by trimming if necessary. They should fit closely and neatly so that none of the cream on the base can seep out.

Remove the bottle or cup placed in the middle of the religieuse once the eclairs have been arranged evenly around the center.

Even the surfaces of the eclairs and make sure they are centered before putting on the first ring of pâte à choux.

Decorate the rim of the pâte sucrée base with butter cream. Patch any holes using pâte à choux trimmings.

Filling the Rings

Stack the rings on top of one another, in the center of the religieuse, atop the eclairs. Fill the rings with flavored light-textured cream.

The cream should be slightly warm when it is piped into the religieuse so that it does not set prematurely. If it is too hot, it will stay warm and may go sour.

Place the filled cream puff on the top.

Decorate the finished religieuse with butter cream.

Storage

Large religieuses will keep for 12 hours maximum in the refrigerator, 5°C (40°F). The religieuse should be served at 10°C (50°F).

Note: These large-style religieuses can be made with a single cream and fondant flavoring, either coffee or chocolate, rather than both.

Flat, Large Religieuses

The recipe is the same as for the tower-style religieuses described above except that the base is larger and the rings and cream puff are not used. A large Saint-Honoré base, 24 cm (9.5 in.), is used to serve twelve people.

The eclairs are shaped in triangles again but are only 12 cm (4.5 in.) long.

Procedure

Fill the Saint-Honoré base with cream piped out into the shape of a dome. Place the eclairs on the cream with the triangular tip of each at the center. Adjust their lengths if necessary.

Decorate the top of the religieuse using butter cream piped out with a pastry bag. Use either a plain tip or a Saint-Honoré tip.

Storing and Serving

These religieuses are stored and served in the same way as the tower-style religieuse.

Chapter 6 Assembling cakes

Assembling cakes with a metal spatula

History

In French, a cake is often referred to as an *entremet*. In modern French usage, entremet always signifies a sweet dessert, but originally, the word, which literally means "between courses," was used to designate a dish that was used to break up the succession of courses served in a meal. These dishes were often prepared with vegetables but frequently contained meats or fish. The very earliest use of the word was during the Middle Ages when a theatrical diversion was presented around giant centerpieces to diners between courses.

Nowadays, entremets are cakes based on génoise or sponge cake, and various creams.

Assembling a Génoise-based Cake

Trim the génoise with a serrated knife. Place the génoise on a round section of cardboard. The cardboard should have a glossy finish so it does not get soggy. It should be about 4 mm (1/8 in.) larger in diameter than the cake, so that it extends 2 mm (1/16 in.) beyond the perimeter of the cake all the way around. This rim of cardboard acts as a guide for the spatula

when cream is being applied to the sides.

Place a dollop of butter cream on the cardboard base to help anchor the cake during the assembly.

Cut the génoise into two or three layers using a serrated bread knife.

Each layer of génoise will be brushed with liquor- or liqueur-flavored sugar syrup using a pastry brush.

Check the quantity of syrup absorbed by each layer by gently pressing with the tip of the finger; liquid should ooze from the cake.

If cutting the génoise into two layers, brush both the top of the bottom layer and the underside of the top layer with the flavored syrup.

It is advisable, however, to cut the génoise into three layers, so that more layers of filling can be used. This also allows for a better distribution of the garnishing components.

Brush the base of the génoise with the flavored syrup. Spread an even layer of butter cream over the bottom layer using a metal spatula.

Sprinkle the layer of butter cream with the chosen garniture, such as preserved fruits or nut brittle.

Place the second layer of génoise atop the first.

It is best not to brush the second layer of cake with the syrup until it has been placed on the first layer; otherwise it tends to be too fragile and tear.

Once the second layer is in place, brush its top liberally with the sugar syrup.

Also brush the underside of the third, top layer.

Let the syrup soak into the top layer while spreading the butter cream on the middle layer.

Flip the top layer over onto the second layer. Adjust it so that it fits evenly over the bottom two sections.

Check the surface to make sure that it is well soaked with syrup. If not, brush it again to make sure that it is completely moist.

Press the surface of the cake with a cake pan or tart ring gently to even out the surface and ensure that the cake is

completely flat before the final application of butter cream.

Brush the surface of the cake to eliminate crumbs that might interfere with butter cream coating.

The butter cream for the final coating should be smooth and lightly flavored with liquor, liqueur, or other flavorings. Too much alcoholic flavoring will cause the cream to break apart.

Also avoid using a butter cream that is overwhipped and frothy. Such a cream forms a porous rather than a perfectly smooth surface.

Coating the Cake

If the cake is small enough, place the base atop the tips of the fingers of the left hand (if right-handed).

Be careful to keep the fingers spread apart. Hold the cake at eye level while coating it with the cream. (If the cake is too large to hold in one hand, bend over it so that the cake is at eye level.)

Using a large metal spatula, coat the sides of the cake with the butter cream. Scrape off any excess butter cream that accumulates near the edge of the cardboard.

Once the edges have been well coated, place the génoise back on the work surface and cover the top with a relatively

thick layer of butter cream, 5 mm (1/4 in.). Spread the cream over the surface using a long metal spatula (its length should exceed the diameter of the cake).

Move the spatula back and forth until the surface is smooth and the butter cream layer perfectly even.

This technique requires considerable experience, especially when working with round cakes, which often have uneven surfaces.

Once the top layer of cream has been applied and is smooth and even, bring the génoise back up to eye level.

Still using the long metal spatula, remove the excess cream that has accumulated on the top edge of the cake when the top layer was smoothed over.

Spread this excess over the sides of the cake. Always keep the spatula at an angle facing downward toward the bottom of the cake so that the cream is not forced back up over the rim of the cake, spoiling its surface.

Once the cake has been completely coated with cream, place it in the refrigerator, 5°C (40°F), for at least an hour.

Give the cake a second coating of cream if necessary.

Once the cake has been coated with butter cream, there are numerous decorating possibilities. It can be finished with slivered and grilled almonds or hazelnuts or nut brittle, covered with a layer of almond paste, and then decorated using a paper cone.

It can be decorated using a pastry bag with a fluted tip.

The surface can be covered with different shaped ornaments, such as cigarettes, flowers, mushrooms, glazed chestnuts, fondant coating, or butter cream decorations.

There are so many possibilities for the final decoration of the génoise that it is impractical to try to list all possibilities.

The opportunities for improvisation are almost limitless.

Using sponge cake

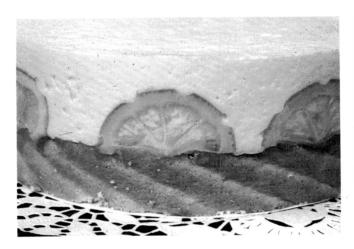

Circular cakes are sometimes molded in metal rings that have been lined with a layer of pâte à biscuit (sponge cake).

The sponge cake can be used to line the top half of the cake and may even

rise over the top of the ring so that thicker cakes may be prepared. The sponge-cake-lined metal cake rings may then be filled with layers of cream, génoise, sponge cake, meringue, garniture, or other desired fillings. Layers of meringue may also be used.

Different sponge cake recipes, such as plain, almond, or hazelnut, can be used. (See volume 1, pages 68 to 71; also Russian-style and Dijon-style meringues, page 91).

The sponge cake batter can be piped out in various styles and shapes.

Examples:

1. *Sponge cake batter spread onto a sheet pan, 40 × 60 cm (16 × 24 in.)*

Sponge cake prepared in this way forms a single thin layer, which can be cut into rounds or other desired shapes and placed in the metal cake ring, forming layers of the cake. It can also be cut into strips to line the sides of the ring.

Place a buttered sheet of parchment paper over a sheet pan and spread the sponge cake batter over it using a metal spatula (use the procedure for spreading génoise batter; see volume 1, page 74).

Various flavorings such as powdered or slivered almonds, coconut, or colored or chocolate sprinkles may be sprinkled over the layer of sponge cake batter.

2. *Sponge cake batter piped onto a sheet pan*

With this method, sponge cake is piped into strips that resemble ladyfingers. The strips should just touch one another. When baked, they will form a sheet that can then be cut to size or used as is to line the sides of the metal cake ring. Hereafter, the strips produced using this method will be referred to as ladyfingers or strips of ladyfinger.

Use a plain no. 6 to no. 8 pastry tip. Pipe parallel lines of batter over buttered paper on a sheet pan or pipe a diagonal line down the center of the sheet pan and continue piping diagonally toward each corner.

The sponge cake batter can be decorated with names and motifs before baking using a paper cone. Decorate as soon as the batter has been piped out onto the sheet pan. Use one of the following recipes.

Recipes for Decoration

Chocolate

200 g butter (7 oz.)
250 g confectioners' sugar (9 oz.)
250 g flour (9 oz.)
7 egg whites
50 g cocoa powder (1.5 oz.)

Coffee

200 g butter (7 oz.)

250 g confectioners' sugar (9 oz.)
250 g flour (9 oz.)
6 egg whites
40 ml coffee extract (1.5 fl. oz.)

The preparation of these mixtures is the same as for copeaux (corkscrew cookies; see volume 3, page 21).

Gently heat the mixture if necessary before applying it to the sponge cake batter. It should be thin and fluid enough to use a paper cone with a very fine tip for delicate writing and designs.

To help write on the batter, mark the outlines of the letters with a paring knife. A ruler with two straight (clean) nails

stuck in each end can also be used to make guidelines (the distance between the two nails should correspond to the height of the letters or design).

The sponge cake should be baked in the normal way as soon as decoration is completed.

3. *Jelly-coated sponge cake*

After baking, cut the sheets of sponge cake into strips about 5 to 6 cm (2 to 2.5 in.) wide. Spread them with jelly and stack them.

Slice the stacks to the desired height and place the slices around the insides of cake rings (see pages 148 to 149 in this volume).

Instead of stacking and slicing, single sheets can be spread with jelly and rolled. The rolls are then sliced like the stacks and used to line the metal cake rings.

Rings of meringue or progrès/succès can also be used as layers in cakes.

(See recipes in volume 1.)

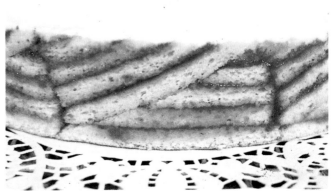

Constructing cakes in rings

This method is now used more frequently in modern pastry kitchens because it is easier and gives more consistent results than assembling cakes with a metal spatula does.

Preparing cakes in rings is also faster than the metal spatula method and offers certain other advantages:

- Constructed cakes can be frozen and then finished as needed. Left in the rings, they are easier to store than cakes constructed with a spatula.

- Glazing is much easier when using the ring because it prevents glaze (fondant glaze, chocolate glaze, jellies, fruit coulis) from dripping over the sides.

- With rings, garniture can be placed on the bottom of the cake; then, when the cake is flipped over, the garniture is already set into the cream: pineapples, candied oranges, angelica, melons are possible garnitures.

This method is frequently used for ice cream cakes, bavarians, mousses, and cakes dressed with Chantilly cream.

Assembling a Cake in a Cake Ring

Preparation

Choose a ring that corresponds to the diameter and height of the cake to be prepared.

Prepare all the necessary components to be used in the cake, such as rings or strips of baked sponge cake, flavored simple syrup, cream filling, fruit.

Assembly

Two methods can be used to assemble the cakes.

Method A: for glazed or frosted cakes decorated with a pastry bag and coated with almonds or chocolate shavings

Place the metal cake ring on top of a round of cardboard. The glazed side of the cardboard should face up.

Brush a round of sponge cake or génoise with the flavored sugar syrup and place it on the cardboard ring, inside the cake ring.

Fill the metal cake ring with cream to the desired height, using a metal spatula or a pastry bag.

Be sure that the cake round at the bottom is well covered with the cream and that the cream reaches all the edges.

Spread the garniture of candied fruit or preserves over the layer of cream filling.

Brush the second layer of cake with flavored syrup and place it over the first layer covered with cream filling and garniture. Brush the second layer with sugar syrup again, using a pastry brush.

Spread the second layer of cake with the cream and smooth over the surface with a metal spatula, sliding it along the rim of the metal ring.

Chill the cake before removing the cake ring. It is imperative that the cake be chilled completely before unmolding. The time needed for complete chilling depends on the type of cream filling being used:

- 1 hour for cakes filled with butter cream

- 6 hours for cakes filled with Chantilly cream or pastry cream

- 12 hours for frozen cream cakes

Remove the circle by first rubbing the outside with warm hands (warmed under hot water).

If necessary, trim the edges of the cardboard base with scissors.

The final decoration of these cakes is the same as cakes constructed using a metal spatula.

Method B: for upside-down cakes

With this method, the cake is prepared upside down, so that the garniture to appear on top of the cake (usually marzipan or preserved fruit) is placed in the ring first, followed by the cake and cream, with the cardboard on top. The cake is flipped over after the cream has set and then decorated conventionally.

Place the metal cake ring on a sheet pan covered with parchment paper. Line the edge of the ring with strips of ladyfinger if desired.

The bottom of the cake ring may be covered with a layer of marzipan (this will be the top), which may later be decorated using a paper cone. The marzipan can cover the entire base of the ring or can be cut into decorative sections. If a whole layer is to be used, cut it out with a paring knife by following the inner rim of the metal cake ring.

Decorative shapes may be cut out of marzipan by using a plastic or cardboard template and following its edges with a paring knife.

Instead of covering the base with marzipan, garniture such as preserved fruit can be placed decoratively on it.

Once the marzipan or fruit is in place, spread a thin layer of the cream filling over it. Make sure that the cream covers the entire base, extending to the entire perimeter of the ring.

Place the first layer of cake, which should first be soaked with the flavored sugar syrup, over the layer of cream filling. Brush it once more with the flavored syrup to make sure that none of it is left dry. Add a layer of cream or garniture and continue assembling the cake, upside down, in the standard manner.

When the cake is completely assembled, place a cardboard ring (shiny side facing down) on the top of the cake (remember when the cake is turned out, this will form the base). The cardboard should fit snugly inside the cake ring. Chill the cake until the filling sets.

After the filling has set completely, flip the cake over and remove the cake ring in the same way as described for method A.

Note: When using layers of sponge cake or génoise, they should have a diameter 5 mm (1/4 in.) less than the inside diameter of the metal cake rings.

The decoration of the cakes may be completed by turning them onto a sheet

of parchment paper or aluminum foil and decorating the top in the normal way. The sides of the cake may also be decorated in this way.

To reinforce the perimeter of the cake, pieces of génoise can be inserted around its edges during assembly.

Assembling miniature and individual cakes with metal cake rings

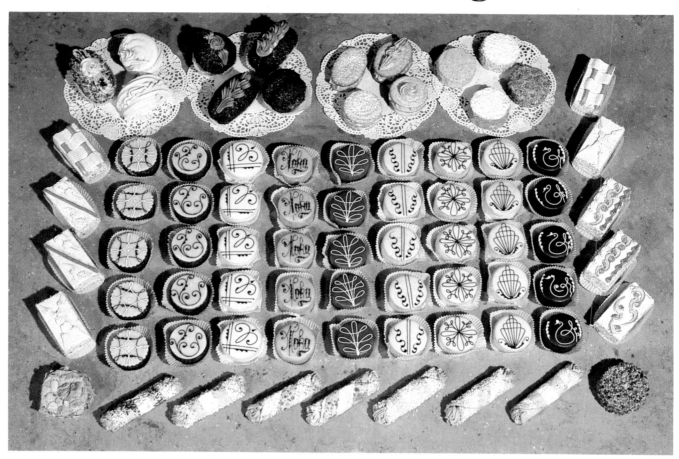

Miniature, butter-cream-filled cakes can be made in a variety of shapes and sizes. They are assembled using the same components as regular-sized cakes.

There are three different shapes:

Miniature square and rectangular cakes: These cakes are cut from a long rectangular cake prepared in the usual way. Many shapes and sizes are possible, including squares, rectangles, and lozenge shapes.

Individually constructed miniature cakes: These cakes are also derived from larger cakes that are cut to the required size. They differ in that they are constructed individually and may be made of several types of cakes and fillings.

Circular miniature cakes: These cakes are constructed either from small rings that have been piped out to the appropriate size, or from rings cut from a sheet of cake with a cookie cutter. The cakes are then constructed using small circular cake molds.

Individual-size circular cakes can be assembled using one of two methods:

First method: Each cake is molded in an individual-sized circular cake ring. They are then chilled, and the rings are removed. The disadvantage to this method is that it requires a metal ring for each cake.

Second method: Each cake is molded in a cake ring but is then immediately removed from the ring and refrigerated. This method has the advantage of not requiring so many rings, but producing neat, attractive cakes is more difficult than with the first method.

Assembling the Cakes

1. **Using Rings for Each Cake**

Moisten the individual circles of cake with the flavored sugar syrup by dipping the top surfaces of the circles directly in the syrup.

Place the syrup-soaked cake circles on a clean sheet pan. Place the metal cake rings over them.

Make sure that the cream filling is not too stiff, so that it can fill the cake rings evenly.

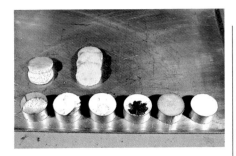

Fill each of the rings with the cream filling. Use a small metal spatula to distribute the cream by working from the center of the cake circles toward the walls. Make sure that the cream extends

all the way up the sides of the metal ring, but leave a hollow well in the middle for the garniture. Add the garniture.

Place the second cake circles on the cakes; these will form the tops. Press the tops firmly with the palm of the hand

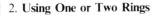

to make sure they are in place and do not extend over the edge of the metal rings.

Spread the top surface of the cake with a cream filling.

Chill the cakes in the refrigerator to firm them.

Remove the individual metal cake rings either by rubbing the outside wall with warm hands (as for large cakes) or by pushing the cakes out with a baba mold, as shown above.

2. Using One or Two Rings

Warm the cake ring by dipping it in hot water between uses. Make sure that the cream filling is cold and firm.

Work quickly so the cream does not melt.

Fill the cakes as for the first method, but remove the metal cake rings as soon as the cakes are molded by pushing the cakes out with a baba mold.

Specially Shaped Cakes

These cakes are constructed from layers of pâte sucrée (sweetened tart dough), on layers of pâte à succès/progrés (almond/hazelnut meringue), or on layers of plain or almond meringue (see volume 1, pages 116 to 118, 88 to 90, 81 to 87).

These layers are prepared in advance to the desired sizes and shapes.

For example, *round layers* are prepared in the usual way and then cut into various shapes, such as squirrels, frogs, or little chickens. *Oval layers* are also prepared in the usual way and are used for chestnut cream barquettes, and for bases for special shapes such as mice, rabbits, and ducks.

These special shapes require experience in working with cakes and especially in glazing and decorating.

Finishing Individual and Miniature Cakes

Innumerable methods can be used to decorate and shape individual and miniature cakes. They may be decorated with a pastry bag or a paper cone. Glazes may include fondant or chocolate. The cakes may also be covered with marzipan.

Finishing miniature cakes with a pastry bag or metal spatula

Miniature cakes can be finished using either a pastry bag or a metal spatula. Both methods offer a wide variety of possibilities.

Using a Metal Spatula

This method may be used for filling tartlet or barquette (boat-shaped) bases made from pâte sucrée (sweetened tart dough) filled with, for example, almond cream, chestnut cream, or meringue before baking. The baked bases are then covered with another cream.

The most commonly used creams for the final topping are butter cream and chestnut cream. Any natural flavoring can be used. The miniature cakes may also be garnished with dried fruits, preserved fruits, or other garniture.

Method

Line lightly buttered barquette or tartlet molds with pâte sucrée. Gently press the dough into the molds.

Let the lined molds rest in the refrigerator for 12 to 24 hours to prevent shrinking during the baking.

The tartlet or barquette shells are then filled with almond cream using a pastry bag with a no. 7 tip or a plastic pastry scraper. Do not overfill them.

Bake the filled tartlet or barquette bases in a 200°C (400°F) oven until they are lightly browned on both top and bottom.

Let the baked bases cool completely before finishing them with more cream.

Finishing the Miniature Cakes

Score or poke the surfaces of the bases with the tip of a sharp knife to help the sugar syrup penetrate.

Lightly brush the surfaces of the tartlets or barquettes with flavored sugar syrup, using a clean pastry brush.

Spread a thin layer of flavored cream over the pastries using a metal spatula or a pastry bag.

Apply the garniture at this point if it is being used.

Finish the tartlets or barquettes with a soft, malleable cream. Hold the base of the pastry with the tips of the fingers of the left hand. Add a large dollop of

cream using the end of the metal spatula. Spread the cream evenly over the surface of the pastry, using the whole length of the spatula.

Shape the surface of the cream by pulling the spatula down along the sides while giving quarter turns to the pastry with the left hand. Continue with this method until the cream is even and smooth and forms a sharp, even crest centered on the pastry.

The most difficult finish to achieve is an even peak on a cone-shaped tartlet.

Using a Pastry Bag

The composition of the tartlets or barquettes finished with a pastry bag is the same as that for those finished with a metal spatula.

The main difference is that a greater variety of shapes can be obtained with the pastry bag. The final shaping and success of the finished product depend entirely on the skill and dexterity of the pastry chef.

Chestnut Barquettes

Composition

Pâte sucrée barquette shells, base filling of almond or frangipane cream, rum, sections of génoise or sponge cake, chestnut cream, fondant glaze.

Procedure

Line the barquette molds with the pâte sucrée and fill with almond or frangipane cream. Leave a slight dip in the middle of the cream so the top of the barquette is even after baking.

Bake the barquettes in a medium oven, 180° to 200°C (350° to 400°F) for about 20 minutes.

Assembling the Barquettes

Brush the sections of génoise or sponge cake with rum-flavored syrup and place them atop the centers of the barquettes.

With a small metal spatula, spread chestnut cream over the barquette. Shape the cream so that it forms a sharp, even crest on the top of the barquette.

Refrigerate the barquettes before the final glazing with fondant.

Glazing

Two methods can be used to glaze the barquettes. One way is to dip the tops of the barquettes in a pot of melted fondant so that their surfaces are entirely glazed with a single color, such as choco-

late or coffee. The other method is to spread the fondant on the sides of the barquettes with a metal spatula. With this method, each side can be glazed with a different flavor of fondant.

Decoration

The surfaces of the barquettes may be decorated with different colors of fondant, white butter cream (using a pastry bag with a fluted tip), royal icing, or cocoa powder.

Storage

Chestnut barquettes can be kept for 4 to 5 days in the refrigerator, 5°C (40°F), before glazing. Once glazed, the barquettes should not be stored for longer than 24 hours.

Variations

Pineapple Barquettes

Use well-drained, chopped, candied pineapple. Combine it with Kirsch-flavored butter cream. Construct the barquettes like chestnut barquettes. The barquette bases as well as the sponge cake or génoise sections should be brushed with Kirsch-flavored syrup.

Coat with the butter cream and let set in the refrigerator before coating with yellow fondant.

Decorate on one side with *pineapple* written in royal icing colored with cocoa powder or draw arabesque patterns over the entire surface.

Candied Fruit Barquettes

Chop the candied fruits and macerate them in Kirsch, Grand Marnier, Cointreau, or cherry liqueur.

Combine the chopped candied fruits with butter cream, which should be flavored with the same liqueur used to macerate the fruits. Construct the barquettes as described above and let set in the refrigerator. Glaze with white, orange, or pink fondant. Decorate using a paper cone or with pieces of preserved fruits.

These techniques and components can be used to prepare a variety of special shapes:

- round tartlet bases for frogs, squirrels, baby chicks
- barquette bases for cats, rabbits, ducks and mice

Glazing full-sized and miniature cakes

Glazing Cakes

The final glazing of cakes is one of the most difficult skills to master in pastry making. It requires considerable professional experience, careful organization of the work area, and extreme attention to cleanliness. The success of the final glazing and decoration depends on perfect execution of the techniques involved.

Different Types of Glazes

Cakes can be glazed in a variety of ways:
- with fondant
- with butter cream
- with coulis, fruit preserves and jellies, crème anglaise, diplomat cream, bavarian cream, sabayon sauce, chocolate sauce, or ganache

Glazing Cakes with Fondant

Preparation

Assemble the equipment for the preparation of the fondant and glazing (fondant saucepan, wooden spatula, clean sheet pan, cake rack, molds to support cake rack, large metal spatula).

If working with leftover fondant, remove the crust and add additional fondant as necessary. Warm the fondant to the correct temperature (see Glazing, pages 129 to 131). The temperature of the fondant should be one degree Celsius less than fondant used on pâte à choux–based pastries; that is, the temperature here should be 35° to 36°C (95° to 97°F). If the fondant is too warm, the cream will melt, making the final glazing impossible.

Adjusting the Consistency of the Fondant

Lift the spatula and let the fondant drip back down into the saucepan. Streaks that quickly disappear should form on the surface of the fondant.

Glazing

Set the cake rack on inverted molds over a sheet pan or clean marble.

Cover the entire surface of the cake

with fondant. Remove the excess fondant using a metal spatula or work in the same way as when preparing a butter-cream-covered cake (see pages 143 to 145).

Tap the cake rack a few times with

the spatula to help distribute the fondant over the surface and sides of the cake.

Let the fondant set for a few minutes and then remove any excess that has accumulated on the rim of the cardboard base.

The cakes should be decorated with a paper cone. Marzipan or pulled-sugar roses can also be added.

Glazing Cakes with Butter Cream

Preparation

Assemble the equipment for preparing butter cream (mixing bowl, whisks, cake rack, and molds to support the cake rack).

Adjust the temperature and consistency of the butter cream by heating it over a low flame until it has the consistency of thick cream.

Glaze the cake using the same method as for glazing with fondant.

The same methods should be used for glazing with other mixtures, such as fruit preserves and jellies, crème anglaise, or other glazes.

Glazing Miniature Cakes

Glazing Miniature Cakes with Fondant

The consistency and temperature of the fondant should be adjusted just as for full-sized cakes.

Three different methods can be used to glaze miniature cakes:
- on cake racks
- by dipping
- in circular cake rings

Glazing on Cake Racks

Place the miniature cakes on cake racks and cover them entirely with the fondant.

Tap the rack so that the fondant coats the cakes evenly and is not too thick.

Let the fondant set for a few minutes; then lift the cakes off the cake rack with a metal spatula. The cakes can be decorated with a paper cone.

Glazing by Dipping

Insert the tip of a paring knife in the bottom of the cake. Using the knife as a dipping stick, submerge the cake face down in the fondant. Lift it out slowly,

with an up-and-down motion, so that it is covered with a thin layer of the fondant.

When the cake is out of the fondant, hold it above the saucepan for a few seconds so the excess can drip off. Rotate for the last few seconds to help distribute the fondant.

Turn the cakes out into cardboard boxes or serving trays. Decorate with a paper cone.

Glazing in Metal Cake Rings

Press the metal cake ring up around the sides of the cake so that it forms a rim above the top of the cake about 1 millimeter (about 1/16 in.) high.

Fill the metal cake ring to the top with fondant. Smooth the surface with a metal spatula.

Let the fondant harden for a few minutes; then carefully remove the cake rings, leaving smooth, even layers of fondant on the tops of the cakes.

Decorate the cakes with a paper cone.

155

Les roulés et les bûches
(Rolled cakes and Yule logs)

Rolled cakes and logs form the foundation for several well-known cakes, the most famous of which is the bûche de Noël (Yule log).

They can also be sliced and used to decorate other molded cakes.

Rolled Cakes

Turn a sheet of génoise onto a sheet of clean plastic wrap.

Remove the parchment paper from the back of the génoise.

Brush the entire surface of the génoise with flavored sugar syrup using a large brush or pastry brush.

Place another sheet of plastic wrap over the back of the génoise. Slide a cake

rack between the génoise and the marble and place a second cake rack atop the génoise.

Flip the cake over, with the two grills held with both hands.

Remove the grill that is now on the top, remove the plastic wrap, and brush this side of the cake with flavored sugar syrup as well. Make sure that the cake is evenly soaked with the syrup.

Use a large metal spatula to spread the surface of the cake with cream. Sprinkle the surface with macerated candied

fruits, macerated raisins, chopped walnuts, or other garniture.

Roll the cake, using the layer of plastic wrap to keep it tight over its entire length.

Coat the ends of the rolled cake with cream.

Wrap the rolled cake tightly in plastic wrap and place it in the refrigerator, 5°C (40°F).

Yule Logs

Cut a rolled cake into the desired lengths. Cut the ends of the logs at a slight angle. The resulting wedges will be used to form the knots on the sides of the logs.

Place a section of rolled cake on a gilded cardboard base. Place a dollop of the cream filling on the base to help anchor it in place.

Attach the knot or knots to the top side of the log with a little of the cream filling.

Use a pastry bag to pipe a decorative, circular pattern on the end of each log. Different colored creams can be used for this.

Cover the entire surface of the log using a special flat, fluted pastry tip called a "chemin de fer."

Stroke the surface of the log with a serrated pastry comb or a fork to imitate the tree bark.

Check to make sure the surface of the log is completely covered with cream. Remove excess cream if necessary.

Place the coated logs in the refrigerator, 5°C (40°F), for at least an hour.

Decorating the Logs

Form the bark on the sides of the knots by incising with a paring knife dipped in boiling water.

The log can be then decorated with meringue mushrooms, ivy leaves, or made from marzipan holly berries and leaves and other appropriate additions.

Covering cakes with marzipan

Preparing a sheet of marzipan to cover the surface of a cake requires considerable dexterity and experience with the rolling pin.

Each stage of the rolling must be carried out very carefully.

Procedure

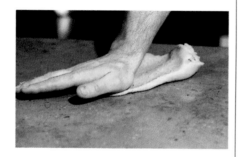

Work the marzipan on the pastry marble with the palm of the hand until it is smooth and malleable.

Form it into a ball and roll it into a thin sheet (see volume 1, Using the Rolling Pin, page 36).

Roll the sheet of marzipan onto the rolling pin. Hold the rolling pin over the cake and carefully unroll the sheet of marzipan.

Gently smooth the marzipan over the surface of the cake with the hand held flat. Be sure that there are no air pockets trapped between the cake and the marzipan.

Gently press the marzipan onto the sides of the cake. Use both hands and make sure that the marzipan fits tightly

and evenly around the sides. Be sure that no wrinkles or fingerprints are left on the surface of the marzipan. The sides should be perfectly smooth.

Cut off the excess marzipan on the sides of the cake with a chef's knife. Keep the side of the knife against the cake and cut with a vertical movement.

This method helps avoid tearing the marzipan.

The cake may be decorated with a paper cone and marzipan or pulled-sugar flowers.

Chapter 7 Finished cakes

Examples of different cakes

Poire (Pear)

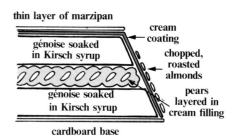

Abricotine (Apricot)

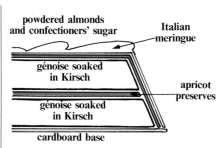

Alcazar

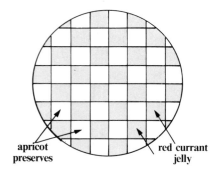

apricot preserves

red currant jelly

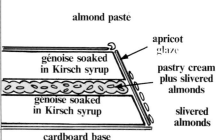

Poire (Pear)

thin layer of marzipan
cream coating
génoise soaked in Kirsch syrup
chopped, roasted almonds
pears layered in cream filling
génoise soaked in Kirsch syrup
cardboard base

Recipe (serves 8)

1 génoise, 19 to 20 cm (7.5 to 8 in.)
150 ml sugar syrup (5 fl. oz.), at 1260 D, plus 50 ml Kirsch (1.5 fl. oz.)
200 g cream filling (7 oz.): 100 g pastry cream (3.5 oz.) plus 100 g whipped cream (3.5 oz.), flavored with 50 ml Kirsch (1.5 fl. oz.)
200 g poached or canned pears (7 oz.)
50 g marzipan (1.5 oz.)
pale yellow fondant
30 g chopped, roasted almonds (1 oz.)
chocolate or royal icing for decoration

Procedure

Trim the cake if necessary

Cut the génoise into two layers and anchor the bottom layer to the cardboard base with a bit of cream. Brush the layers with the Kirsch-flavored sugar syrup. Coat the bottom layer with about 150 g (5 oz.) of the cream filling.

Slice the pears and place them in a 1-cm-thick (3/8 in.) layer over the cream.

Place the second layer of cake over the pears.

Coat the surface of the cake with the remaining cream filling and chill in the refrigerator, 5°C (40°F), for at least an hour.

Cover the surface of the cake with a sheet of marzipan rolled out to a thickness of 1.5 mm (1/16 in.). Cut the marzipan into a circle that fits over the top of the cake, using a large template.

Decorate the surface of the cake with chocolate or royal icing using a paper cone. Serve cool, 10°C (50°F).

This cake may be stored for up to 24 hours at a temperature no higher than 10°C (50°F).

Abricotine (Apricot)

powdered almonds and confectioners' sugar
Italian meringue
génoise soaked in Kirsch
apricot preserves
génoise soaked in Kirsch
cardboard base

Recipe (serves 8)

1 génoise, 19 to 20 cm (7.5 to 8 in.)
150 ml sugar syrup (5 fl. oz.), at 1260 D, plus 50 ml Kirsch (1.5 fl. oz.)
300 g apricot preserves (10.5 oz.)
200 g Italian meringue (7 oz.)
50 g powdered almonds (1.5 oz.)
25 g confectioners' sugar (1 oz.)

Procedure

Trim the cake if necessary

Cut the cake into two layers, anchor the bottom layer to the cardboard base with a bit of the apricot preserves, and brush both layers with the Kirsch-flavored sugar syrup. Spread each half with a layer of the apricot preserves. The preserves can be thinned and flavored with a little Kirsch if too stiff.

Turn the second layer of cake, apricot side down, onto the first. Brush the top surface with the sugar syrup.

Coat the cake with the Italian meringue.

Decorate the cake by piping on additional Italian meringue, using a medium-sized fluted tip.

Sprinkle the surface with the powdered almonds and then with the confectioners' sugar.

Place the finished cake in a hot oven, 260°C (500°F), long enough to lightly color it.

Serve at room temperature, 20°C (68°F).

This cake may be kept for 4 to 5 days in a cool place or in the refrigerator, 5° to 10°C (40° to 50°F).

Alcazar

almond paste
apricot glaze
génoise soaked in Kirsch syrup
pastry cream plus slivered almonds
génoise soaked in Kirsch syrup
slivered almonds
cardboard base

Recipe (serves 8)

1 génoise, 19 to 20 cm (7.5 to 8 in.)
150 ml sugar syrup (5 fl. oz.), at 1260 D, plus 50 ml Kirsch (1.5 fl. oz.)
250 g pastry cream (9 oz.)
75 g slivered almonds (2.5 oz.)
150 g almond paste (5 oz.), softened with egg whites
125 g apricot preserves (4 oz.)
125 g red currant, raspberry, black currant, or other jelly (4 oz.)

Procedure

Trim the génoise if necessary. Cut the cake into two layers. Anchor the bottom layer of the génoise to the cardboard ring with a bit of the apricot preserves. Brush the layers with the Kirch-flavored sugar syrup. Coat the bottom layer with the pastry cream and sprinkle with the slivered almonds.

Cover the bottom, cream-coated layer, with the top layer of génoise. Brush the surface of the cake to remove crumbs. Spread on a layer of almond paste, softened with egg white. Make a checkerboard pattern with a knife.

Decorate the edges of the almond paste using a pastry bag with a small fluted tip.

Place the cake, on doubled sheet pans, into a hot oven until the surface has colored. Using a spoon, fill the empty squares on the surface of the cake with the preserves and jelly. Alternate the colors.

Brush the sides of the cake with apricot glaze, made by diluting apricot preserves with an equal volume of water, using a pastry brush; then coat halfway up with slivered almonds. Serve at room temperature, 20°C (68°F).

This cake may be stored for up to 24 hours in a cool place, 5°C (40°F). It may also be prepared in a square shape and presented as a chessboard topped with chess pieces made of marzipan.

Ananas (Pineapple)

Slices of candied pineapple are layered over the surface of the cake to form scales.
The decoration is finished with chocolate applied with a pastry brush. Pieces of angelica can be used decoratively.
Further decoration is completed with dark chocolate butter cream applied with a plain no. 5 pastry tip.

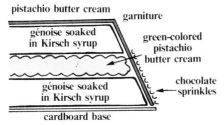

Recipe (serves 8)

1 oval génoise, 24 × 14 cm (9.5 × 5.5 in.)
150 ml sugar syrup (5 fl. oz.), at 1260 D, plus 50 ml Kirsch (1.5 fl. oz.)
250 g butter cream (9 oz.) plus 20 g pistachio paste (1 oz.)
3 slices candied pineapple
50 g chocolate sprinkles (1.5 oz.)
50 g dark chocolate butter cream (1.5 oz.)

Procedure

Cut the génoise into two layers. Anchor the bottom layer to the cardboard base with a bit of butter cream. Brush the cake layers with sugar syrup. Coat the bottom layer with the pistachio butter cream. Cover with the top layer and coat the cake with the pistachio butter cream.

Chill the cake in the refrigerator for at least an hour. To decorate:

● Write on the surface of the cake with the chocolate butter cream using a plain no. 5 pastry tip.
● Cut the pieces of candied pineapple and position them on the cake, with the angelica.
● Finish decorating the cake by brushing the edges of the pineapple sections with cocoa powder, using a pastry brush.

Coat the sides of the cake with the chocolate sprinkles, using a metal spatula. Serve cool, 10°C (50°F). This cake may be stored for 4 to 5 days in the refrigerator.

Noisette (Hazelnut)

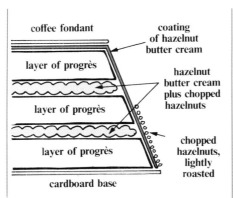

Recipe (serves 8)

3 progrès/succès layers, each 20 cm (8 in.) in diameter
filling: 300 g butter cream (10.5 oz.) plus 50 g hazelnut paste (1.5 oz.)
100 g finely chopped, blanched hazelnuts (3.5 oz.)
50 g coffee fondant (1.5 oz.)
cocoa, several hazelnuts, marzipan, fondant, for decoration.

Procedure

Trim the progrès/succès layers together so they are exactly the same size. Attach one of them to a cardboard cake base with a bit of butter cream. Spread the surface of the first layer with the hazelnut butter cream and sprinkle with an even layer of chopped hazelnuts.

Cover the base progrès/succès layer with the second layer and coat it with a layer of the filling and the chopped hazelnuts as above.

Place the third layer on top, smooth side facing up. Coat the entire cake with the hazelnut butter cream.

Chill the cake for 1 hour in the refrigerator, 5°C (40°F).

Glaze the top of the cake with the coffee fondant. Coat the sides with the remaining chopped hazelnuts, using a metal spatula.

Decorate the cake with a paper cone using chocolate or royal icing. Hazelnuts made of green marzipan are attractive additions.

Serve at room temperature, 20°C (68°F).

This cake may be stored for up to 6 days in a cool place, 10°C (50°F).

Noix (Walnut)

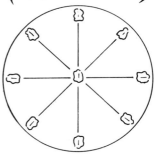

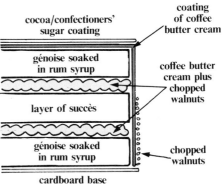

Recipe (serves 8)

1 génoise, 16 cm (6 in.) in diameter
1 succès layer, 12 cm (5 in.) in diameter
150 ml sugar syrup (5 fl. oz.) at 1260 D, plus 50 ml rum (1.5 fl. oz.)
300 g lightly flavored coffee butter cream (10.5 oz.)
100 g walnut halves (3.5 oz.)
10 g cocoa powder (1 Tbsp.) combined with 10 g confectioners' sugar (1 Tbsp.)
small quantity of pale butter cream for decoration

Procedure

Trim the génoise if necessary. Cut the génoise into two layers, and anchor the bottom layer to the cardboard base with a bit of the butter cream.

Brush the two génoise halves with rum-flavored sugar syrup. Spread the coffee butter cream over the bottom layer. Sprinkle the bottom layer with chopped walnuts.

Place the succès layer over the bottom layer of génoise and spread it with another layer of the coffee butter cream. Sprinkle again with chopped walnuts. Add the second layer of génoise. Brush the top of the cake with the sugar syrup, and gently press the cake to even it.

Cover the entire surface of the cake with the coffee butter cream.

Sprinkle the top of the cake with the mixture of cocoa powder and confectioners' sugar. Cover the sides of the cake with chopped walnuts. Finish decorating the cake with a paper cone, using additional butter cream. Make small butter cream swirls around the edges of the cake and gently place a walnut half on each swirl. Serve the cake at room temperature, 20°C (68°F).

The cake will keep for 5 to 6 days in a cool place, 10°C (50°F). The same method may be used for a hazelnut cake, which would be called *noisetier*.

4/21

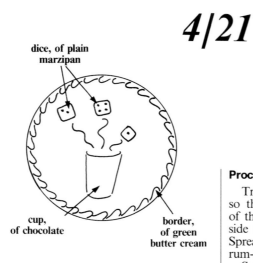

dice, of plain
marzipan

cup,
of chocolate

border,
of green
butter cream

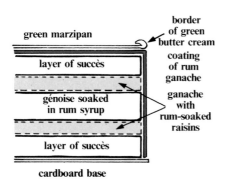

green marzipan

border
of green
butter cream

layer of succès

coating
of rum
ganache

génoise soaked
in rum syrup

ganache
with
rum-soaked
raisins

layer of succès

cardboard base

Recipe (serves 8)

2 succès layers, 20 cm. (8 in.) in diameter
1/2 génoise, 19 cm (7.5 in.) in diameter
50 ml sugar syrup (1.5 fl. oz.), at 1260 D, flavored with rum
300 g rum-flavored ganache (10.5 oz.)
100 g rum-soaked raisins (3.5 oz.)
50 g green marzipan (1.5 oz.)
15 g plain marzipan (1/2 oz.)
500 g green butter cream (17.5 oz.)
25 g chocolate sprinkles (1 oz.)

Procedure

Trim the edges of the two succès layers so they are the same size. Anchor one of the layers to the cardboard base, flat side down, with a bit of butter cream. Spread this first layer with a layer of the rum-flavored ganache.

Sprinkle half the rum-soaked raisins over the ganache.

Place the génoise half on the first layer, cut side facing up, and brush it with the rum syrup.

Spread the génoise layer with ganache and sprinkle over the rest of the raisins.

Cover with the second succès layer. Keep the smooth side of the succès facing up.

Cover the entire cake with the ganache.

Coat the sides of the cake with the chocolate sprinkles, using a metal spatula.

Cover the top of the cake with a thin sheet of green marzipan, which should be cut to the correct size with a large template.

Decorate the rim of the cake with flame-shaped or rose-shaped decorations using the green butter cream. Use a plain no. 5 pastry tip. The edge of the cake may also be decorated with marzipan formed into a braid or rope, decorated with pastry pinchers. Make sure it is securely attached to the edges of the cake.

Finish the decorating with a paper cone.

The cake should be served at room temperature, 20°C (68°F).

It may be stored for 5 to 6 days in a cool place, 10°C (50°F).

Le sega malaga (Rum coconut)

Recipe (serves 8 to 10)

1 chocolate génoise, 20 to 22 cm (8 to 9 in.) in diameter
300 to 400 g rum-flavored mousseline cream (10.5 to 14 oz.)
100 g candied pineapple (3.5 oz.), diced and macerated in rum
200 to 250 ml rum syrup (6.5 to 8.5 fl. oz.)
120 to 150 g grated coconut (4 to 5 oz.)

Procedure

Cut the génoise into three layers, and anchor the bottom layer to the cardboard base with a bit of mousseline cream.

Brush the bottom layer with the rum syrup and coat it with mousseline cream. Sprinkle the surface with half the macerated pineapple cubes.

Add the second layer of génoise and coat it with the rum syrup. Spread the second layer with the mousseline cream. Sprinkle the second layer with the remaining macerated pineapple cubes.

Cover with the last layer of génoise. Brush the top of the cake with the rum syrup and make sure the cake is even.

Coat the entire cake with the mousseline cream and refrigerate until firm.

Coat the entire surface of the cake with the grated coconut.

Royal

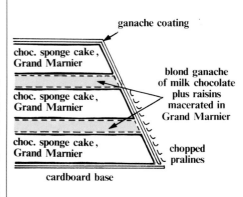

ganache coating

choc. sponge cake,
Grand Marnier

choc. sponge cake,
Grand Marnier

choc. sponge cake,
Grand Marnier

blond ganache
of milk chocolate
plus raisins
macerated in
Grand Marnier

chopped
pralines

cardboard base

Recipe (serves 8)

3 rings of chocolate sponge cake, with the following diameters:
16 cm (6.5 in.)
12 cm (4.5 in.)
8 cm (3 in.)
125 ml sugar syrup (4 fl. oz.), at 1260 D, flavored with 25 ml Grand Marnier (1 fl. oz.)
300 g Grand Marnier–flavored blond (milk chocolate) ganache (10.5 oz.)
50 g macerated raisins (1.5 oz.)
50 g chopped pralines (1.5 oz.)
1 attractive marzipan rose with three leaves

Procedure

Anchor the largest layer of sponge cake to the cardboard base with a bit of ganache, and brush it lightly with the Grand Marnier syrup. Coat the surface with the Grand Marnier blond ganache.

Sprinkle the surface with half the macerated raisins.

Add the second layer of sponge cake and brush it with the Grand Marnier syrup.

Coat once again with the Grand Marnier blond ganache and sprinkle with the remaining macerated raisins.

Add the small layer of sponge cake and brush it lightly with the syrup.

Coat the entire cake with the Grand Marnier blond ganache.

Sprinkle the surface of the cake with the chopped pralines.

Finish the decoration by attaching the marzipan rose.

This cake should be served at room temperature, 20°C (68°F).

It will keep for 5 to 6 days in a cool place, 10°C (50°F).

Marrons (Chestnut)

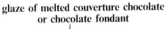

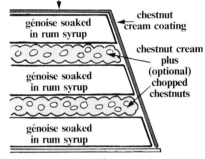

glaze of melted couverture chocolate
or chocolate fondant

génoise soaked in rum syrup — chestnut cream coating

génoise soaked in rum syrup — chestnut cream plus (optional) chopped chestnuts

génoise soaked in rum syrup

cardboard base

Recipe (serves 8)

1 génoise, round, 19 cm (7.5 in.) in diameter, or oval, 24 × 16 cm (9.5 × 6.5 in.)
150 ml sugar syrup (5 fl. oz.), at 1260 D, plus 50 ml rum (1.5 fl. oz.)
300 g chestnut cream (10.5 oz.)
50 g chopped chestnuts (1.5 oz.), optional
150 g melted couverture chocolate (5 oz.) or 150 g chocolate fondant (5 oz.)
15 g marzipan (1/2 oz.), for decoration

Procedure

Trim the génoise if necessary. Cut it into three layers, and anchor the bottom layer to the cardboard base with a bit of chestnut cream.

Brush the bottom layer with the rum-flavored syrup and coat it with a layer of the chestnut cream. Sprinkle the surface with half the chestnut pieces if they are being used.

Add the second génoise layer, brush it with the sugar syrup, and coat it in the same way as the first layer.

Add the third layer, smooth side up, and brush it with sugar syrup.

Coat the entire cake with the chestnut cream and refrigerate for 1 hour, 5°C (40°F).

The top or entire surface of the cake is then glazed with either melted couverture chocolate or chocolate fondant.

If only the top is being glazed, coat the sides with chocolate sprinkles.

Additional decoration can include marzipan chestnuts and royal icing.

Serve the cake at room temperature, 20°C (68°F).

The cake will keep for 4 to 5 days in a cool place, 10°C (50°F).

Flamboyant

Recipe (serves 8)

1 chocolate génoise, 20 to 22 cm (8 to 9 in.) in diameter
300 to 400 g rum-flavored chocolate ganache (10.5 to 14 oz.)
200 to 250 ml rum-flavored sugar syrup (6.5 to 8.5 fl. oz.), at 1260 D
100 g raisins (3.5 oz.), macerated in rum
150 g rum-flavored ganache (5 oz.)

Procedure

Trim the génoise if necessary. Cut the génoise into three layers, and anchor the bottom layer to the cardboard base with a bit of ganache. Brush the bottom layer with the rum-flavored sugar syrup. Coat with the rum-flavored chocolate ganache.

Sprinkle with half the raisins.

Add the second layer of génoise, brush it with the rum syrup, and add another layer of the rum-flavored chocolate ganache. Sprinkle with the remaining raisins.

Brush the underside of the final génoise layer with rum syrup and attach it to the top of the cake. Brush the top surface with syrup and adjust the sides of the cake so it is even.

Cover the cake with a thin layer of the rum-flavored ganache and refrigerate for 1 hour, 5°C (40°F).

Give the cake a final glaze with the rum-flavored ganache.

Decoration should include a marzipan rose with three leaves and writing with royal icing.

Succès

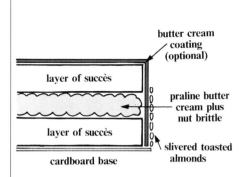

butter cream coating (optional)

layer of succès

praline butter cream plus nut brittle

layer of succès

slivered toasted almonds

cardboard base

Recipe (serves 8)

2 thick layers of succès, 18 cm (7 in.) in diameter
200 g praline butter cream (7 oz.)
50 g ground or finely chopped nut brittle or nougatine (1.5 oz.)
75 g slivered toasted almonds (3 oz.)
10 g confectioners' sugar (1/3 oz.)

Procedure

Trim the two succès layers together to the exact same size.

Anchor the smooth side of one of the layers to the cardboard base with a bit of butter cream. Coat it with a layer of the praline butter cream. Sprinkle the surface with the chopped nut brittle or nougatine.

Add the second succès layer. Coat the entire cake with the butter cream.

Cover the surface of the cake with the slivered almonds.

Lightly sprinkle the surface with the confectioners' sugar.

This cake should be served at room temperature, 20°C (68°F).

It will keep for up to 6 days in a cool place, 10°C (50°F).

Variations

See volume 1, pages 88 to 90.

Marquise

(chocolate/coffee)

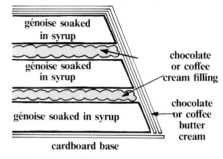

decoration of royal icing
or butter cream
chocolate, coffee, or vanilla fondant

génoise soaked
in syrup

génoise soaked
in syrup

génoise soaked in syrup

chocolate
or coffee
cream filling

chocolate
or coffee
butter
cream

cardboard base

Recipe (serves 8)

1 génoise, 19 to 20 cm (7.5 to 8 in.) in diameter

150 ml sugar syrup (5 fl. oz.) at 1260 D, plus 50 ml rum, Grand Marnier, or Cointreau (1.5 fl. oz.)

300 g pastry cream (10.5 oz.), or other cream filling, such as 200 g flavored mousseline cream (7 oz.) or 150 g mousseline cream (5 oz.) and 50 g flavored whipped cream or butter cream (1.5 oz.)

100 g chocolate, coffee, or vanilla butter cream (3.5 oz.)

150 g chocolate, coffee, or white fondant royal icing for decoration

Procedure

Trim the génoise if necessary. Cut it into three layers, and anchor the bottom layer to the cardboard base with a bit of butter cream.

Brush the bottom layer with the flavored sugar syrup and then coat it with the cream filling.

Place the second layer over the first, brush it with flavored sugar syrup, and coat it with the cream filling.

Cover with the third layer of génoise, uncut side up, and brush it with flavored sugar syrup. Press gently on the cake to make it even and level.

Coat the cake with the butter cream and put it in the refrigerator, 5°C (40°F), for 1 hour to firm. Give the cake a final glazing with fondant.

Decoration

Place the cake on a paper doily and decorate it with royal icing, using a paper cone.

Serve at room temperature, 20°C (68°F).

This cake can be stored in a cool place, 10°C (50°F), for 48 hours.

Pouf

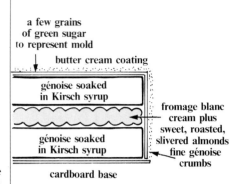

chocolate shavings

sponge cake soaked
in rum syrup

cream
filling

sponge cake soaked
in rum syrup

sponge cake soaked
in rum syrup

chocolate
sprinkles

cardboard base

Recipe (serves 8)

3 layers of sponge cake, 16 cm (6.5 in.) in diameter, piped in a spiral shape with a pastry bag using a no. 10 plain tip

150 ml sugar syrup (5 fl. oz.), at 1260 D, plus 50 ml rum (1.5 fl. oz.)

450 g cream filling (16 oz.): 300 g highly flavored chocolate butter cream (10.5 oz.) plus 150 g Italian meringue (5 oz.)

50 g chocolate sprinkles (1.5 oz.)

100 g chocolate shavings (3.5 oz.)

10 g confectioners' sugar (1/3 oz.)

Procedure

Trim the three sponge cake layers to be exactly the same size.

Anchor the smooth side of one of the layers to the shiny surface of the cardboard base with a bit of cream filling. Brush with the rum-flavored sugar syrup. Coat with 125 g (4.5 oz.) of cream filling.

Place the second sponge cake layer over the first and brush it with the rum-flavored sugar syrup. Coat with 125 g (4.5 oz.) of the cream filling.

Place the third layer of sponge cake on top and brush it with the rum-flavored sugar syrup. Use the remaining cream to coat the top and sides.

Put the chocolate sprinkles on the sides of the cake with a metal spatula.

Decoration

Decorate the top surface of the cake with the chocolate shavings, which can be arranged in flower patterns.

Sprinkle very lightly with the confectioners' sugar.

The cake should be served at room temperature, 20°C (68°F).

It will keep from 5 to 6 days in a cool place, 15°C (59°F).

Brie

a few grains
of green sugar
to represent mold

butter cream coating

génoise soaked
in Kirsch syrup

fromage blanc
cream plus
sweet, roasted,
slivered almonds

génoise soaked
in Kirsch syrup

fine génoise
crumbs

cardboard base

Recipe (serves 8)

1 génoise, 20 cm (8 in.) in diameter

150 ml sugar syrup (5 fl. oz.), at 1260 D, plus 50 ml Kirsch (1.5 fl. oz.)

250 g fromage blanc cream (9 oz.)

100 g Kirsch-flavored butter cream (3.5 oz.)

25 g sweet, roasted, slivered almonds (1 oz.)

30 g génoise crumbs (1 oz.)

5 g green sugar (1 tsp.) plus 5 g confectioners' sugar (1 tsp.)

marzipan, for decoration

Procedure

Trim the génoise if necessary. Cut it in two, and anchor the bottom layer to the cardboard base with a bit of butter cream.

Brush the bottom layer with the Kirsch syrup and coat it with the cream filling. Sprinkle the surface of the cream with the roasted almonds.

Place the second layer of génoise over the first. Brush it with sugar syrup. Press the cake gently to even the layers.

Coat the entire cake with the Kirsch-flavored butter cream and then with the génoise crumbs, which should be spread with a metal spatula. Sprinkle the green-colored sugar here and there to imitate the mold.

Decoration

Lightly sprinkle the surface of the cake with confectioners' sugar. A marzipan mouse is also a clever touch.

This cake should be served cool, 10°C (50°F).

It will keep for up to 48 hours if stored at 10°C (50°F).

Delice fraise ou fraisier (Strawberry delight)

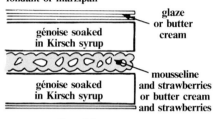

fondant or marzipan

génoise soaked in Kirsch syrup — glaze or butter cream

génoise soaked in Kirsch syrup — mousseline and strawberries or butter cream and strawberries

cardboard base

Recipe (serves 8)

1 square génoise, 16 × 16 cm (6.5 × 6.5 in.)
150 ml sugar syrup (5 fl. oz.), at 1260 D, plus 50 ml Kirsch (1.5 fl. oz.)
250 g mousseline cream (9 oz.), lightly flavored with Kirsch *or* Kirsch-flavored butter cream (9 oz.)
250 g medium-size strawberries (9 oz.), *or* 50 g apricot glaze (1.5 oz.) plus 75 g white or pink fondant (2.5 oz.), *or* 50 g butter cream (1.5 oz.) plus 50 g yellow or pink marzipan (1.5 oz.)
chocolate or royal icing, for decoration

Procedure

Trim the génoise as needed. Cut it into two layers and anchor the bottom layer to the cardboard base with the apricot glaze.

Brush the bottom layer with the Kirsch-flavored sugar syrup. Spread the Kirsch-flavored cream filling over it.

Wash the strawberries and remove their stems. Place them, points upward, in the cream filling.

Cover the strawberries with cream filling and then with the second layer of the génoise. Brush the second layer with the sugar syrup. Press gently to even out the cake's surface.

Coat the surface of the cake with either apricot glaze or butter cream.

Chill the cake in the refrigerator for about 2 hours. Coat the top with the yellow or pink fondant or cover with a thin layer of pink or yellow marzipan.

Return the cake to the refrigerator if necessary to stiffen the cream filling. Trim the edges of the cake with a serrated knife. The edges should be even, and the strawberries should be visible.

Decoration

Using a paper cone, decorate the surface of the cake with chocolate or royal icing.

A few small strawberries and marzipan leaves are also appealing decorations.

The cake should be served cool, 10°C (50°F). It will keep for up to 24 hours in a cool place, 10°C (50°F). The same techniques may be applied to round cakes made with other berries, such as raspberries and blueberries.

Outremer (Overseas)

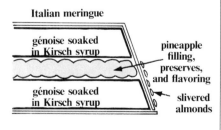

Italian meringue

génoise soaked in Kirsch syrup — pineapple filling, preserves, and flavoring

génoise soaked in Kirsch syrup — slivered almonds

cardboard base

Recipe (serves 8)

1 square génoise, 16 to 17 × 16 to 17 cm (6.5 to 7 × 6.5 to 7 in.)
150 ml sugar syrup (5 oz.), at 1260 D, plus 50 ml Kirsch (1.5 fl. oz.)
300 g pineapple compote (10.5 oz.), cooked with 100 g apricot preserves (3.5 oz.) and Kirsch to flavor
250 g Italian meringue (9 oz.)
50 g slivered almonds (1.5 oz.)
20 g confectioners' sugar (2/3 oz.)

Procedure

Trim the génoise if necessary. Slice it into two layers, and anchor the bottom layer to the cardboard base with a bit of the preserves. Brush the bottom layer with the Kirsch-flavored sugar syrup and then coat it with the Kirsch-flavored compote mixture.

Cover with the top layer of génoise, and brush with syrup. Brush off any crumbs, and adjust the sides of the cake so they are even. Coat the entire surface of the cake with two-thirds of the Italian meringue. Attach the slivered almonds to the sides, using a metal spatula.

Decoration

Decorate the surface of the cake with the rest of the Italian meringue, using a medium-sized fluted pastry tip. Sprinkle the surface with confectioners' sugar.

Place the cake in a very hot oven, 260°C (500°F), to color it lightly.

This cake should be served cool or at room temperature, 10° to 20°C (50° to 68°F). It will keep for 3 to 4 days at room temperature, 20°C (68°F).

Pêche lègére (Peach)

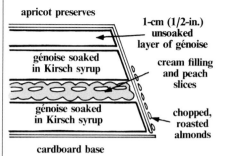

apricot preserves

1-cm (1/2-in.) unsoaked layer of génoise

génoise soaked in Kirsch syrup — cream filling and peach slices

génoise soaked in Kirsch syrup — chopped, roasted almonds

cardboard base

Recipe (serves 8)

génoise, 16 cm (6.5 in.) in diameter
100 ml sugar syrup (3.5 fl. oz.), at 1260 D, plus 30 ml Kirsch (1 fl. oz.)
150 g cream filling (5 oz.): 100 g pastry cream (3.5 oz.) plus 50 g whipped cream (1.5 oz.) plus 30 ml Kirsch (1 fl. oz.)
150 g poached or canned peaches (5 oz.)
200 g Chantilly cream (7 oz.) or 150 g other light-textured cream (5 oz.)
30 g chopped, roasted almonds (1 oz.)
50 g apricot preserves (1.5 oz.)

Procedure

Trim the génoise if necessary. Cut the génoise into three layers, with the top layer 1 cm (1/2 in.) thick. Anchor the bottom layer to the cardboard base with a bit of preserves.

Brush the bottom layer with the Kirsch-flavored sugar syrup and spread it with the cream filling. Place the peach slices over the filling. Put the second layer of génoise in place and brush it with the Kirsch-flavored sugar syrup. Place the third layer in position, but do not brush it with sugar syrup.

Cut the top layer into eight equal sections using a bread knife. Coat each of the sections with the apricot preserves, and coat the sides of the cake as well.

Cover the sides two-thirds of the way up with the chopped almonds, using a metal spatula.

Decoration

Decorate with the Chantilly cream or other light-textured cream piped out with a pastry bag using a medium fluted tip. The cream may be piped out in a spiral pattern under the edges of each section.

This cake should be served cool, 10°C (50°F).

It will keep for only 24 hours, in a cool place, 10°C (50°F).

Délice du père Labat

La belle Créole

L'ile Bourbon

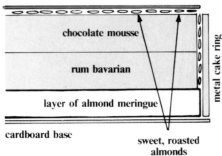

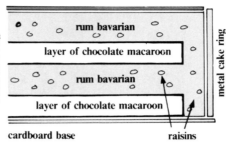

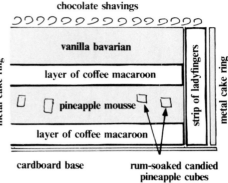

(Father Labat's delight)

Recipe (serves 8 to 10)

1 almond meringue ring, 20 cm (8 in.) in diameter
400 g rum bavarian (14 oz.)
300 g sweet, roasted almonds (10.5 oz.)
400 g chocolate mousse (14 oz.)
toasted almonds, to decorate
milk-chocolate coating

Procedure

Use a metal cake ring with a height of about 4 cm (1.5 in.) and a diameter of 20 cm (8 in.). Brush the inside of the ring with butter and sprinkle some of the almonds over the inside walls.

Place the metal cake layer over a cardboard cake base of the same diameter. Fit the almond meringue layer into the metal cake ring, over the cardboard base.

Fill the ring halfway up with the rum bavarian, and put it in the refrigerator to set.

Once the bavarian cream has set, fill the ring to the top with the chocolate mousse. Smooth off the surface, and place in the freezer, −15° to −20°C (5° to −5°F) to firm.

Decoration

Coat the surface of the cake with the toasted almonds.

Cover the surface with the milk-based glaze.

To remove the metal ring, warm it by quickly waving a propane torch over its outside surface.

(Créole belle)

Recipe (serves 8 to 10)

2 chocolate macaroon rings, 20 cm (8 in.) in diameter
800 g rum bavarian (28 oz.)
rum-soaked raisins
200 ml rum-flavored sugar syrup (6.5 fl. oz.), at 1260 D
150 ml chocolate sauce (5 fl. oz.)

Procedure

Use a metal cake ring with a height of about 4 cm (1.5 in.) and a diameter of 20 cm (8 in.).

Coat the inside of the cake ring with a thick layer of the bavarian cream, to ensure that the sides of the cake are perfectly smooth once it is unmolded.

Place the metal cake ring over a cardboard base and then insert one of the chocolate macaroon layers, fitting it snugly.

Brush the macaroon base with the rum syrup and fill the ring halfway up with bavarian cream.

Place the second macaroon layer over the layer of cream and brush it with the rum syrup. Finish filling the ring to the top with bavarian cream.

Smooth the top of the cake and place in the freezer, −15° to −20°C (5° to −5°F) to firm.

Decoration

Coat the surface of the cake with the chocolate sauce.

Remove any excess chocolate that has dripped over the sides of the ring.

Loosen the cake ring by waving a propane torch quickly around the sides of the ring.

Decorate the cake with a marzipan rose with chocolate leaves. Marzipan or pulled-sugar leaves may also be used.

(Bourbon island)

Recipe (serves 8 to 10)

2 coffee macaroon rings, 20 cm (8 in.) in diameter
strip of ladyfingers to line the metal ring
400 g pineapple mousse (14 oz.)
rum-macerated cubes of candied pineapple
400 g vanilla bavarian (14 oz.)
rum-macerated raisins, optional
300 ml rum-flavored sugar syrup (10 fl. oz.), at 1260 D
chocolate shavings

Procedure

Use a metal cake ring with a height of about 4 cm (1.5 in.) and a diameter of 20 cm (8 in.).

Cut the strip of ladyfingers in half.

Line the inside of the cake ring with the strip of ladyfingers, smooth side facing in toward the cake. Fit the ring over a cardboard base.

Trim the coffee macaroon layers so that they fit snugly inside the ladyfinger-lined metal cake ring. Place one macaroon layer inside the bottom of the metal layer.

Brush the ladyfingers and the macaroon base with the rum syrup.

Fill the ring halfway up with the pineapple mousse and the cubed candied pineapple.

Brush the second macaroon layer with rum syrup and place it over the layer of pineapple mousse. Fill the cake ring to the top with the vanilla bavarian and the rum-macerated raisins (optional).

Smooth the top of the cake and place in the freezer, −15° to −20°C (5° to −5°F), to firm.

Decoration

Remove the cake from the ring and cover the surface with chocolate shavings.

168

Le Cilaos   Délice au café Le Stanislas
(Coffee delight)

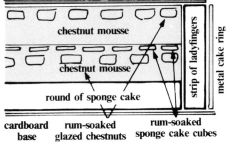

glaze of chocolate sauce

chestnut mousse

chestnut mousse

round of sponge cake

strip of ladyfingers

metal cake ring

cardboard base

rum-soaked glazed chestnuts

rum-soaked sponge cake cubes

caramel glaze

coffee bavarian cream

coffee génoise or sponge cake

coffee bavarian cream

coffee génoise or sponge cake

metal cake ring

cardboard base

Italian meringue or Chantilly cream to decorate

vanilla bavarian cream plus rum-soaked raisins

layer of rum-soaked baba

vanilla bavarian cream plus rum-soaked raisins

layer of progrès/succès

strip of ladyfingers

metal cake ring

cardboard base

Recipe (serves 8 to 10)

round of sponge cake, 20 cm (8 in.) in diameter
strip of ladyfingers to line the metal ring
700 g chestnut mousse (24.5 oz.)
glazed chestnuts macerated in rum
250 ml rum-flavored sugar syrup (8.5 fl. oz.), at 1260 D
chocolate sauce for glaze

Procedure

Use a metal cake ring with a height of about 4 cm (1.5 in.) and a diameter of 20 cm (8 in.). Place it over a cardboard base and fit the sponge cake round snugly over the bottom of the ring.
Cut the strip of ladyfingers in half.
Line the inside of the cake ring with the ladyfingers, smooth side facing in toward the cake. Trim if necessary.
Brush the ladyfingers with the rum syrup. Fill the cake ring halfway up with the chestnut mousse, and sprinkle the surface with pieces of rum-soaked glazed chestnuts. The surface may also be sprinkled with cubes of rum-soaked sponge cake, but this is optional.
Finish filling the cake ring with the chestnut mousse. Smooth the surface of the cake. Sprinkle with the rum-soaked glazed chestnuts.
Put the cake in the freezer to firm.

Decoration

Glaze the surface of the cake with the chocolate sauce. Wipe off any excess sauce that may have dripped over the sides of the cake ring.
Remove the cake ring.
Decorate the surface of the cake with glazed chestnuts and marzipan decorations.

Recipe (serves 8 to 10)

2 layers coffee-flavored génoise or sponge cake, 20 cm (8 in.) in diameter
250 ml rum- or Grand Marnier–flavored syrup (8.5 fl. oz.)
800 g coffee bavarian (28 oz.) cream
caramel for glaze

Procedure

Use a metal cake ring with a height of about 4 cm (1.5 in.) and a diameter of 20 cm (8 in.).
Line the inside of the cake ring with the coffee bavarian cream.
Trim the layers of génoise or sponge cake to fit snugly inside the metal cake ring. Place the cream-lined metal cake ring over a cardboard base and carefully insert one layer of génoise or sponge cake. Brush with the rum- or Grand Marnier–flavored syrup.
Fill the cake ring halfway with the coffee bavarian cream and sprinkle with a few granules of ground coffee.
Place the second layer of génoise or sponge cake over the layer of cream and brush it with the syrup. Fill the metal cake ring to the top with the remaining coffee bavarian cream and smooth over the surface.
Place the cake in the freezer to firm.

Decoration

Glaze the surface of the cake with the caramel while it is still in the cake ring. Coffee fondant may also be used. Be sure to wipe off any excess glaze that may have dripped over the sides of the cake ring.
Remove the cake from the cake ring by waving a propane torch around the outer sides.
Chocolate shavings may be sprinkled on the sides of the cake if desired.

Recipe (serves 8 to 10)

1 layer of progrès/succès, 20 cm (8 in.) in diameter
1 layer of baba, 20 cm (8 in.) in diameter
strip of ladyfingers to line the metal cake ring
800 g vanilla bavarian cream (28 oz.)
rum-soaked raisins
350 ml rum-flavored sugar syrup (12 fl. oz.), at 1260 D
Italian meringue or Chantilly cream for decoration

Procedure

Fit a 4-cm-high (1.5-in.), 20-cm-diameter (8-in.) metal cake ring over a cardboard base.
Cut the strip of ladyfingers in half and line the inside of the metal cake ring with them, smooth sides facing the inside of the mold. Brush them with rum syrup.
Trim the layer of progrès/succès, brush it with the rum syrup, and fit it into the base of the cake ring.
Fill the cake ring one-third of the way up with the vanilla bavarian cream; sprinkle with rum-soaked raisins.
Soak the layer of baba/savarin in the rum syrup and place it on top of the bavarian cream. Fill the metal cake ring all the way up with the vanilla bavarian cream. Smooth off the surface. Sprinkle with rum-soaked raisins.
Freeze the cake, −20°C (5°F) to firm.

Decoration

Coat the cake with Italian meringue. Form waves in the surface of the meringue with a metal spatula.
The surface of the meringue should then be lightly caramelized using a propane torch. The cake may also be coated with Chantilly cream.
The sides and center of the cake should be decorated with miniature savarins.
Make a spiral with Chantilly cream in the center of each miniature savarin and place a rum-soaked raisin in the center of each.

Les fonds et coques en meringue (Individual meringues and meringue cake bases)

Make an outline of the desired shape and size on a floured sheet pan, using an appropriately sized mold or cookie cutter.

Use a plain pastry tip with a no. 7 to no. 12 tip, depending on the desired thickness of the meringue. Hold the pastry bag vertically above the sheet pan. Start from the center of the outline and dress the meringue in a spiral until the outline is filled.

The process is the same for preparing miniature cake bases.

Individual Meringues

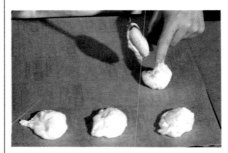

These may be dressed using a plain or fluted tip. They can also be spooned out or placed on the sheet pans with a plastic pastry scraper.

Composition

French or Swiss meringue

Cake bases are used to construct cakes, as well as in special ice-cream preparations

Individual meringues are shaped in a variety of ways and eaten alone.

Equipment

All types of meringue are baked on buttered and floured sheet pans or sheet pans covered with buttered parchment paper.

Baking

Principles

Meringues should always be baked in a low oven, 100° to 120°C (210° to 250°F), with the vents open (if available) and the door left ajar. Double or triple sheet pans are recommended.

Meringues do not actually cook in the oven; rather, they dry. Depending on the thickness of the meringues, allow from 1 to 3 hours to dry them out completely.

Meringue Cake Bases

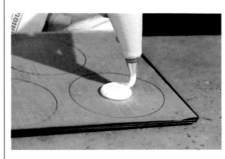

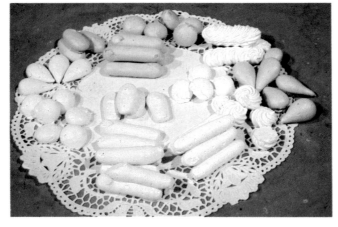

Examples of Different-shaped Individual Meringues

Batons

Pipe a spiral of meringue on a salambo-shaped base of meringue (see page 133), using a no. 5 fluted tip.

Birds

Pipe a tear-dropped base of meringue onto a buttered sheet pan. Pipe a small flame-shaped piece of meringue on each side of the base to form the wings. The head is then added by piping on a circle of meringue and pulling rapidly to the side to form the beak.

The birds may be colored after baking by brushing with food coloring.

The birds can be served with other shapes as petits fours.

Mushrooms

There are several methods for preparing mushroom-shaped meringues.

Prepare the mushroom stems by dressing cones onto the sheet pan and pulling upward with a rapid vertical movement. The caps of the mushrooms are piped out separately in smooth round shapes. The caps should be colored before baking.

Food coloring should be sprinkled over the mushroom caps with a stiff brush or a small knife. The caps can also be sprinkled with cocoa powder, using a sugar shaker.

Attaching the Caps to the Stems

After the caps and stems have been baked separately, hollow out the bases of the caps with the tip of a paring knife and fill the holes with a little raw meringue. Place the caps on the cone-shaped stems and let the assembled mushrooms dry in a very low oven or proof box, 70°C (160°F) for several hours.

Another method involves delicately attaching the caps to the stems before they are completely dried out and then finishing the drying of the assembled mushrooms in a low oven or proof box, 100°C (210°F) for 2 hours.

Vacherins

A vacherin consists of a meringue shell and alternating layers of ice cream and Chantilly cream.

Vacherins are constructed in a variety of shapes.

Examples

Rings of cooked meringue are built onto a meringue disk to form a large shell. They are attached with Swiss meringue. The whole shell is then dried out in an oven or proof box.

Pipe out a disk of meringue to the desired size, as well as four or five rings of the same diameter.

Constructing the Vacherin Shell

Stack the meringue rings on the disk. Attach each ring with Swiss meringue and decorate the outside of the shell with additional Swiss meringue. Dry the entire shell in a low oven or proof box.

Chapter 8 Finished products based on pâte brisée (tart dough)

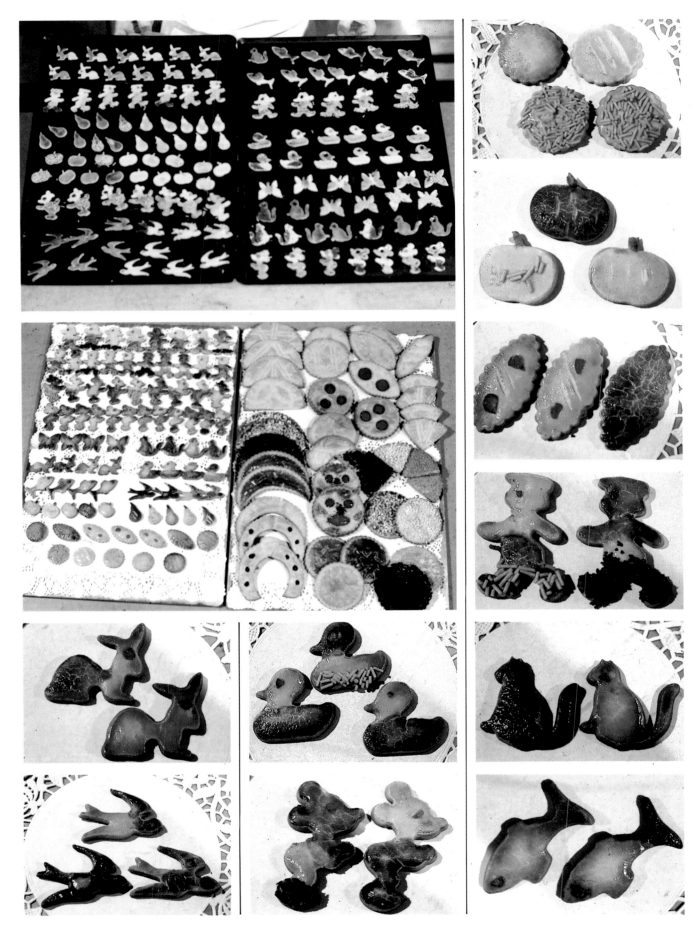

Examples of sablés (shortbread cookies)

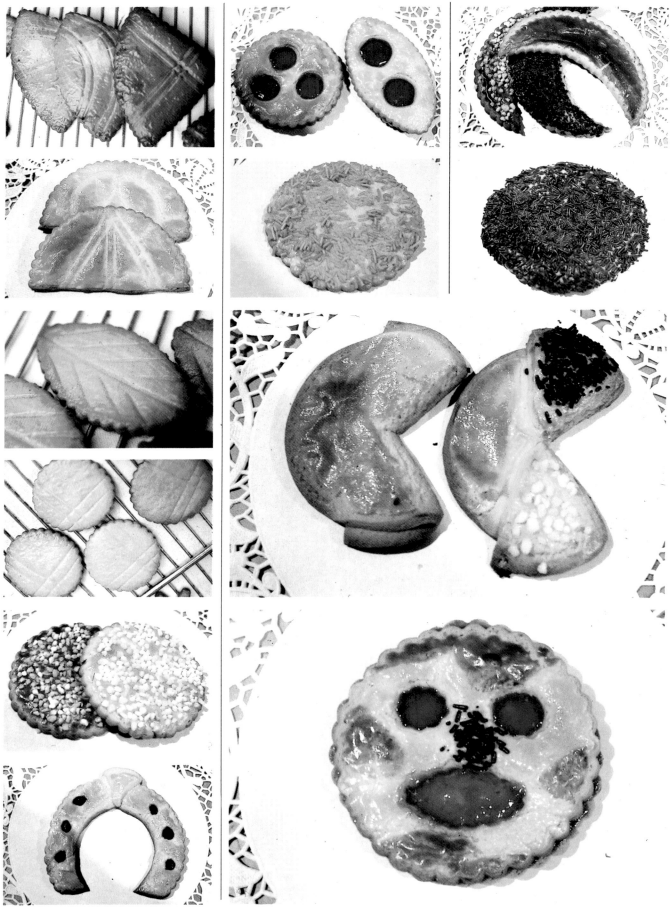

Tarts made with half-baked shells

Tarte alsacienne (Alsatian tart)

Composition

Basic tart dough (pâte à foncer), apples for garnish, Alsatian tart batter
The batter can be replaced with apple compote mixed with frangipane cream.

Batter

3 tarts, 22 cm (8.5 in.) in diameter, serving 6:

3 eggs
500 ml créme fraîche or heavy cream (17 fl. oz.)
200 g granulated sugar (7 oz.)
50 g cornstarch (1.5 oz.)
vanilla extract and Grand Marnier, to taste

or

3 eggs
250 ml milk (8.5 fl. oz.)
250 ml crème fraîche or heavy cream (8.5 fl. oz.)
200 g granulated sugar (7 oz.)
50 g cornstarch (1.5 oz.)
50 g butter (1.5 oz.), melted
vanilla extract and Grand Marnier, to taste

Procedure

Line the dough in tart rings and place them in the refrigerator to rest for 8 to 10 minutes. Half-blind-bake the tart shells at 200° to 220°C (375° to 425°F). The tart shells can be prepared up to this point several hours in advance, or even a day ahead, in which case they should be stored in the freezer overnight.

Lightly beat the eggs in a bowl, then add the crème fraîche or heavy cream and mix together.

In a second bowl, combine the cornstarch and the sugar and slowly add the cream/egg mixture, being careful to keep the batter smooth.

Flavor the batter with vanilla and Grand Marnier to taste.

Place the half-baked tart shells on a round sheet pan.

Peel the apples and cut them in half. Remove the core with the tip of the peeler or with an apple corer and cut each half in half again.

Arrange the apple quarters inside the tart shell in a rosette; the apples should barely touch. Place a few apple quarters in the center of the rosette.

Pour the batter into the tart shell with a ladle. Pour the batter in at the border of the tart to prevent the apples from moving out of place.

Wait a few moments before adding all the batter; let it spread evenly throughout the tart. Then add as much batter as necessary to reach to about 2 mm (1/16 in.) below the crests (top edges) of the apple slices.

Baking

Being careful not to spill any of the batter, place the tart in a moderate oven, 180° to 200°C (350° to 375°F) for 30 to 35 minutes.
Alsatian tarts are best served warm.

Variations

Before placing the apple quarters inside the tart shell, spread a thin layer of apple compote, frangipane, or a mixture of the two on the bottom of the tart shell. Then proceed following the above method.

Tarte normande (Normandy tart)

This recipe makes 1 tart, 22 cm (8.5 in.) in diameter, serving 6.

Peel, core, and quarter 3 apples. Sprinkle the quarters with confectioners' sugar, and allow the sugar to melt into the apples for 30 minutes. Then toss the apples in a sauté pan with 30 g (1 oz.) of butter and a pinch of cinnamon.

Sauté the apples until they are light golden in color, then flambé the slices with Calvados.

Place the apples in a half-baked tart shell and add 300 to 400 ml (10 to 13.5 fl. oz.) of Alsatian tart batter (see the note below).

Note: When making the batter for the Normandy tart, follow the recipe for the Alsatian tart batter but replace the liquid with an equal measure of crème fraîche or heavy cream.

Bake as for the Alsatian tart.

Tarts made with prebaked shells

A wide variety of tarts can be made with prebaked tart shells. These types of tarts usually have the following characteristics:

Plain tart shells using: basic tart dough (pâte à foncer), sweetened tart dough (pâte sucrée), or puff pastry trimmings (rognures de feuilletage)

The shape of the tart shell can be: round, bordered, marguerites (tarts with sections), or formed in various ways, such as four-leaf clovers or horseshoes.

Fillings are: pastry cream, mousseline cream, Chantilly cream.

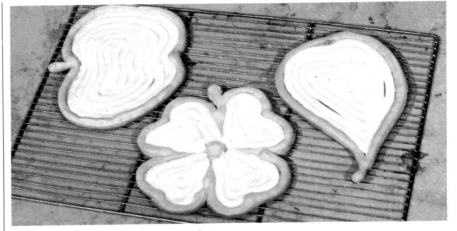

The fruit can include:

- fresh fruit (raw, poached, or in syrup): apricots, bananas, pineapples, cherries, prunes, peaches, pears

- fresh red fruit: strawberries, raspberries, red currants. blueberries, blackberries, black currants, wild strawberries

- frozen fruit

Decoration

For light-colored fruits, a light fruit glaze is used to give sheen as well as keep the fruits fresh longer, as it acts as a protective covering. Apricot glaze is most commonly used for light-colored fruits.

Red glaze is used to glaze all red fruits.

Examples of tarts made

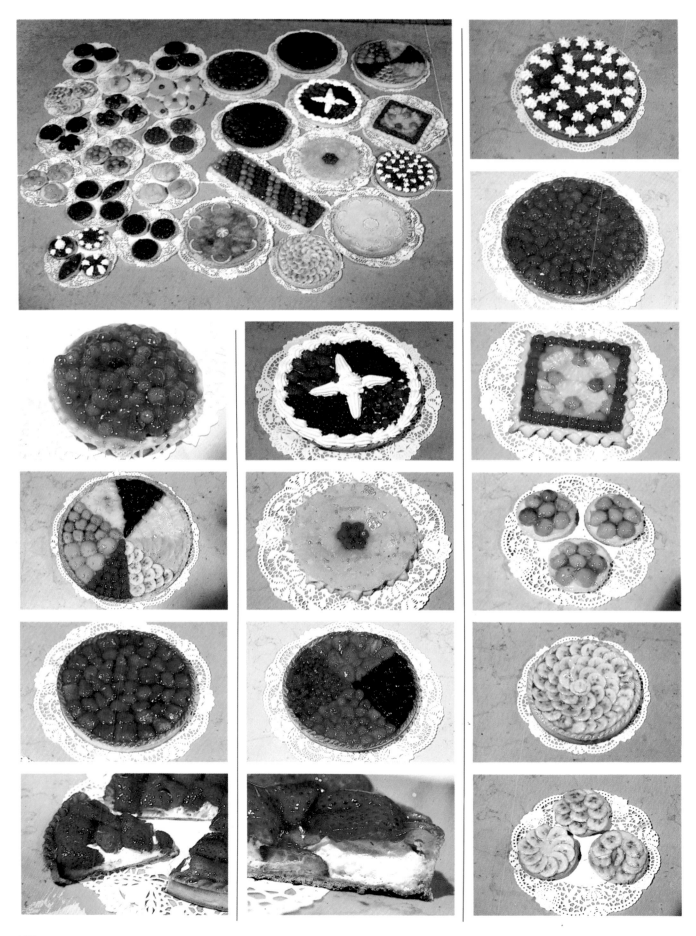

with prebaked shells

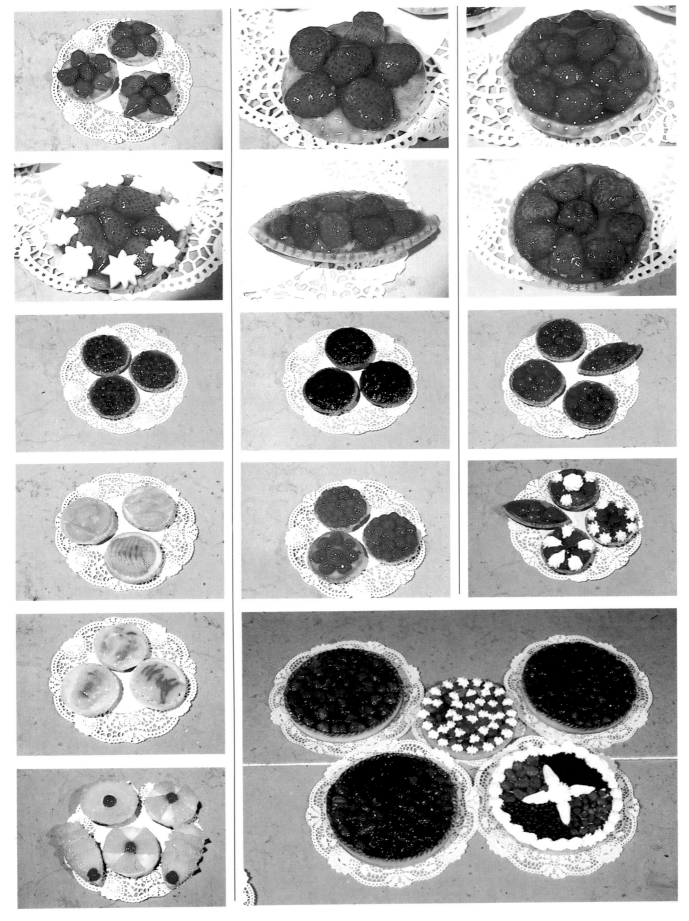

Tarte Tatin (Tatin tart)

History

This is one of the most popular French tarts. It was first made in Sologne à Lamotte-Beuvron by the Tatin sisters; hence, its name.

Composition

To fill 1 génoise mold, 22 cm (8.5 in.) in diameter, serving 8 to 10

1 kg apples (35 oz.)
80 g butter (3 oz.)
80 to 100 g sugar (3 to 3.5 oz.)
200 to 250 g basic or sweetened tart dough or puff pastry trimmings (7 to 9 oz.)

Equipment

Génoise mold (originally a copper génoise mold was used; it is still best to use when available)
Vegetable peeler
Paring knife
Rolling pin, flour brush, roller docker

Procedure

Preparing the Mold

Butter the mold well, around the sides and on the bottom. Cover the bottom of the mold with approximately 3 mm (1/8 in.) of sugar.

Preparing the Apples

Choose the best apples available, of equal size. Peel and halve the apples and

remove the cores with the tip of the peeler. They can be left in halves or cut in quarters.

Filling the Mold

Pack the apple halves or quarters, standing on end, tightly into the mold.

Sprinkle the top of the apples with granulated sugar and several chunks of butter.

Caramelizing the Sugar and Cooking the Apples

Place the molds over low heat. Be careful: if the heat is too high, the sugar will caramelize before the apples are cooked, and may even burn.

During cooking, turn the mold so the sugar caramelizes evenly over the heat.

Allow 50 to 60 minutes to cook the apples. Never cook them over a high flame; be sure to keep the flame low.

This tart is special because, as the apples cook, the sugar is caramelizing on their bottoms (which will eventually be the top of the tart).

Verifying Doneness

With the point of a paring knife, pierce the apples; if the knife slides through the apples easily, they are done.

Placing the Apples in the Dough

Roll out a circle of dough to the diameter of the mold. Cover the apples with the dough, tucking the border inside the mold.

Baking the Tart

Place the tart in a moderate oven, approximately 220°C (425°F). Remove

the tart when the dough is baked to a light golden brown.

Unmolding the Tart

The tart can be unmolded in two ways:
1. Unmold as soon as the tart comes out of the oven by turning it over onto a stainless steel platter.

2. Once the tart is baked, stop the apples from cooking immediately after removing from the oven by placing the bottom of the mold in cold water. Allow the tart to cool for approximately 30 minutes so the caramel can set. Then heat the bottom of the mold to warm the caramel so it will release easily from the mold. Turn the tart over as in the first method. This method makes it easier to produce a shiny, neatly caramelized surface.

Variation

Butter the mold, and pour a layer of caramelized sugar on the bottom and sides.

Prepare the apples as in the first procedure. Sauté the apples in a sauté pan with butter, being careful not to break or crush the apples. Place the sautéed apples in the caramel-lined mold, as in the first procedure.

Cover the apples with a circle of dough and bake, as for the first procedure. The tart can be unmolded by using either method 1 or 2.

Although this technique for making the Tatin tart is faster, the final results and taste do not compare to a genuine Tatin tart. Only proper heating over a low flame, cooking the apples and caramelizing the sugar at the same time, produces the distinctive flavor of a true Tatin tart.

Tarte bourdaloue aux poires (Frangipane pear tart)

This tart is made with a sweetened tart dough (pâte sucrée), filled with frangipane cream and garnished with finely sliced pears. See the photo, top right, on page 178.

Composition
(serves 6 to 8)

sweetened tart dough to fill a 22-cm (8.5-in.) tart ring
250 g frangipane cream (9 oz.)
6 to 8 pear halves
vanilla extract
apricot glaze

Equipment
Rolling pin, flour brush, tart ring, pastry crimpers, roller docker, metal spatula, plastic pastry scraper, pastry brush

Procedure
Line the tart ring with sweetened tart dough following the usual procedure (see volume 1, Lining Tart Rings, pages 37 and 38).

Place the lined tart ring on a round sheet pan.

Using a metal spatula, or pastry bag and tip, spread an even layer of frangipane on the bottom of the tart dough.

Slice each pear in half lengthwise, then thinly slice crosswise, keeping each pear half together after slicing. Flatten the halves slightly. With a metal spatula, place each sliced pear half in the filled tart, maintaining its shape. This not only gives an attractive appearance but allows each serving to contain a complete pear half.

Bake the tart in a moderate oven, approximately 220°C (425°F).

Immediately place the tart on a cooling rack after removing it from the oven.

Once cool, lightly brush the top of the tart with apricot glaze.

Amandine — Puits d'amour ou polka

(Almond tarts — Wishing wells or polkas)

Almond Tarts

Composition
Sweetened tart dough (pâte sucrée), almond cream, frangipane cream; plus apricot slices, apricot preserves, or apple compote if desired (filling)

For 500 to 560 g (17.5 to 19.5 oz.) of sweetened tart dough, allow 900 g (31.5 oz.) of filling, for 25 individual molds or tart rings.

Procedure

Lining the Molds
Line individual tart molds or rings with the sweetened tart dough (see volume 1, Lining Tart Rings, pages 37 and 38).

Filling the Molds
Fill the molds three-quarters full, using a pastry bag and tip, pastry scraper, or metal spatula.

If the apricot slices, preserves, or apple compote are used, place them in the bottom of the mold before adding the cream.

Sprinkle the surface of the filling with slivered almonds.

Baking
Bake the almond tarts in a moderate oven at 200°C (375°F) for 25 minutes.

Unmold the tarts immediately after removing them from the oven, and place them upside down onto the same sheet pan for several minutes before placing them on cooling racks.

Finishing
After the tarts are completely cool, lightly glaze (with apricot glaze) their surfaces with a pastry brush.

Candied cherries can be placed in the centers of the tarts for decoration.

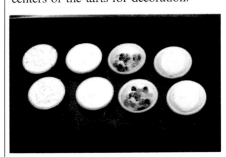

Puits d'Amour ou Polka (Wishing Wells or Polkas)
Composition
Basic tart dough or puff pastry trimmings or pâte à choux, pastry cream (filling)

Procedure
Roll out a sheet of basic tart dough 2 to 3 mm (1/16 to 1/8 in.) thick. Prick the sheet of dough with a roller docker, and cut out small circles with an 8-cm (4-in.) cookie cutter.

Place them upside down on a sheet pan lightly moistened with water. Brush the circles with a thin layer of egg wash.

On the borders of the circles of dough, place a thin ring of pâte à choux (cream puff pastry), using a pastry bag and no. 5 tip. The pâte à choux can be replaced with a ring of puff pastry. Brush the ring of dough with egg wash.

Place the pieces in the refrigerator to rest for several minutes. Bake in a moderate oven at 210°C (400°F). After baking, place the pieces on a cooling rack.

After they are completely cool, fill the shells with vanilla-flavored pastry cream.

Sprinkle the top of the cream with granulated sugar and caramelize the sugar with a hot metal rod.

Storage
Wishing wells (or polkas) can be stored for up to 24 hours in the refrigerator.

Tartes et tartelettes à l'orange
(Orange tarts and tartlets)

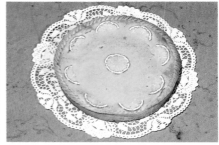

Composition

Sweetened tart dough, orange batter (filling), orange slices, Italian meringue, confectioners' sugar (decoration)

Recipe for the Batter

10 oranges, zested and juiced
600 g confectioners' sugar (21 oz.), sifted
    125 g cornstarch (4.5 oz.) plus 50 g flan powder (1.5 oz.)
15 eggs
250 g butter (9 oz.), melted
or
10 oranges, zested
500 ml orange juice (17 fl. oz.), from the 10 oranges
600 g tant pour tant* (21 oz.), plus 60 g cornstarch (2 oz.)
10 eggs

125 g butter (4.5 oz.), melted
*Tant pour tant is a mixture of equal amounts of unpeeled almonds and sugar, ground into a powder (see volume 1, pâte à succès/progrès, pages 88 to 90).

Procedure

Line the tart rings and rest the dough in the refrigerator while the batter is being made.

Making the Batter

Zest the oranges, grate the zest, squeeze the juice, and combine the juice and zest.

Mix the confectioners' sugar, cornstarch, and flan powder. Add this mixture to the orange juice and zest, and mix well until smooth.

Beat the eggs in a separate bowl, then add them to the orange mixture.

Finally, add the cooled, melted butter to finish the batter.

Filling, Baking, Decorating, and Storage

Follow the procedure for tarts au citron (lemon tarts), below.

Variation

By substituting lemons for the oranges, this batter can be easily adapted for lemon tarts. If necessary, add 150 g (5 oz.) confectioners' sugar to the recipe.

Tartes et tartelettes au citron
(Lemon tarts and tartlets)

Composition

Sweetened tart dough, lemon batter (filling), lemon slices, Italian meringue, confectioners' sugar (decoration)

Recipe for the Batter

To fill 12 tartlets

125 g butter (4.5 oz.), melted
200 g confectioners' sugar (7 oz.), sifted
8 eggs
2 lemons, zested and juiced
vanilla extract, to taste, optional

Procedure

Line twelve small tartlet molds or one tart ring for six to eight servings.

Rest the lined tart shells in the refrigerator while the batter is being prepared.

Making the Batter

Melt the butter over low heat.

Add the sifted confectioners' sugar, stirring constantly, but gently, with a whisk.

Beat the eggs separately, then add them to the butter/sugar mixture, whisking constantly over low heat. Once the mixture is well blended, replace the whisk with a wooden spoon.

Add the lemon zest and juice and a few drops of vanilla extract. If necessary, the lemon flavor can be strengthened with a little lemon extract.

Poach the mixture over low heat, stirring constantly as for crème anglaise (see pages 24 to 26 in this volume). Be careful not to let the mixture come to a boil. When the mixture coats the back of the wooden spatula, immediately transfer it to a bowl. Continue to stir until it cools slightly.

Filling the Tarts

Once the batter has cooled slightly fill the molds three-quarters full with a small ladle.

Baking

Bake the tarts in a moderate oven, 180° to 200°C (350° to 375°F).

Decoration

Before baking, thin fluted slices of lemon halves or quarters can be placed on top. Or, after baking halfway, Italian meringue can be decoratively piped on the tart using a pastry bag and fluted tip.

After baking, place the tart on a cooling rack. Once cool, the tart can also be decorated with lightly candied fluted lemon slices, left whole, cut in half, or quartered.

With any of these decorating methods, confectioners' sugar can be sprinkled either along the border or over the entire tart.

Storage

Lemon tarts can be stored in the refrigerator, at 5°C (40°F), for up to 24 hours.

Far breton (Brittany tart)

The procedure for making a Brittany tart is very similar to that for making a flan (see flan cream, pages 30 to 31 in this volume) or clafoutis.

Prunes are almost always added to the filling.

Use a tart ring or génoise mold, and line it with either basic or sweetened tart dough.

Composition

For 1 tart, serving 6 to 8

Recipe for the Batter

1 L milk (34 fl. oz.)
4 eggs
200 g sugar (7 oz.)
200 g flour (7 oz.) plus 20 g baking powder (1 Tbsp.)
200 g butter (7 oz.)
vanilla extract and rum to taste

Garniture

Pitted prunes are usually used; blanched raisins can also be added but are optional.

Procedure and Baking

Same as for flan or clafoutis.

Cerisier alsacien (Alsatian cherry tart)

Composition

Tart rings lined with sweetened tart dough, tart batter with pitted cherries (filling)

For 2 tarts serving 6 each, use 1 L (34 fl. oz.) of cherries added to batter made from the following recipe:
6 egg whites, beaten to firm peaks and stiffened with 50 g sugar (1.5 oz.)
150 g tant pour tant brut* (5 oz.) plus 30 g flour (1 oz.), sifted together
vanilla extract and Kirsch to taste
*Tant pour tant brut is a mixture of equal amounts of sugar and unpeeled almonds, ground into powder (see volume 1, pâte à succès/progrès, pages 88 to 90).

Procedure

Delicately fold the mixture of tant pour tant and sifted flour into the beaten egg whites with a rubber spatula or skimmer. Flavor to taste.

Place the cherries on the bottom of the tart shell.

Fill the tart shell with the batter, 1 to 2 cm (3/8 to 3/4 in.) from the top.

Bake in a moderate oven at 180° to 200°C (350° to 375°F).

Sprinkle the tart with confectioners' sugar after it has cooled.

Clafoutis

(Cherries, apricots, apples)

Composition

Serves 6 to 8

4 eggs plus 250 g sugar (9 oz.)
200 g cake flour (7 oz.) plus 1 L milk (34 fl. oz.)
vanilla extract and Grand Marnier to taste
or
4 eggs plus 4 egg yolks plus 250 g sugar (9 oz.)
100 g cake flour (3.5 oz.) plus 25 g flan powder (2 Tbsp.)
1 L milk (34 fl. oz.)
vanilla extract plus Grand Marnier to taste

Procedure

Beat the eggs and sugar together with a whisk until they lighten in color and form a ribbon.

Add a small amount of milk, about 100 ml (3.5 fl. oz.) to the egg/sugar mixture, to lighten it. Add the flavoring.

Add the sifted flour (sifted with the flan powder, if used) and add the remaining milk.

Filling the Tart

For 6 servings, allow 300 g (10.5 oz.) of cherries or other fruit.

Place the cherries or other fruit on the bottom of a tart ring lined with either basic or sweetened tart dough or with puff pastry trimmings.

Pour the batter over the fruit.

Baking

Bake in a moderate oven, approximately 200°C (375°F).

Finishing

Sprinkle the tart with confectioners' sugar after it has completely cooled.

Tartes et tartelettes aux fruits cuits (Tarts and tartlets baked with fruit)

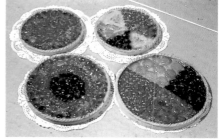

Both large and individual tarts baked with fruit can be made in various styles with a variety of fruits.

These types of fruit tarts are usually lined with basic tart dough, puff pastry trimmings, or less often, sweetened tart dough (see Lining Tart Rings, volume 1, pages 37 to 38).

The filling is usually a cream, such as almond cream, frangipane cream, pastry cream, or apple compote, which is used for the well-known French apple tart.

The fruit used is either seasonal fresh fruit or fruit stored in syrup. The fruit, whether it be one type or several in the same tart, is attractively placed over the filling in the tart shell.

The tarts are baked in a moderate oven at 220°C (425°F), with the vents half open (if available). Place the tart on a cooling rack immediately after removing it from the oven.

After they are cool, the tarts are glazed with apricot or other jelly used for glazing.

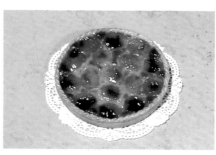

amounts of pâte à choux (cream puff pastry) and pastry cream, *or* two-thirds pâte à choux, one-third pastry cream, plus orange flower water to flavor (filling)

Procedure

In advance, line individual tartlet molds with basic tart dough or puff pastry trimmings.

Fill the tartlet shells three-quarters full with the mixture of pâte à choux and pastry cream flavored with orange flower water.

Place strips of basic tart dough or puff pastry on top of the filling, dividing the tartlets into quarters (see the photo at the bottom of the page).

Bake the tartlets in a moderate oven, 220°C (425°F).

Place the tartlets on a cooling rack immediately after removing them from the oven.

With a small pastry brush, glaze the strips with white fondant.

Glaze the top of the filling, inside the strips, with strawberry or raspberry jelly alternated with confectioners' sugar.

Storage

Pont neuf tarts can be stored for up to 24 hours in the refrigerator, 5°C (40°F).

Pont neuf

Composition

Tartlet rings lined with basic tart dough or puff pastry trimmings, equal

Galettes bretonnes (Brittany shortbread cookies)

Recipe

500 g flour (17.5 oz.) plus 10 g baking powder (2 tsp.), sifted together
125 g butter (4.5 oz.)
250 g confectioners' sugar (9 oz.)
100 g almonds (3.5 oz.), ground to a powder
2 eggs plus 3 egg yolks
100 g chopped candied fruits (3.5 oz.)
60 g hazelnuts (2 oz.), ground to a powder
hazelnut or vanilla extract

Procedure

Prepare the dough using the same procedure as for sweetened tart dough (see volume 1, pages 116 to 118).

Shaping and Baking

Follow the procedure for shortbread (see volume 1, pages 119 to 121).

Decorating

Glaze the cookies with jelly immediately after removing them from the oven; then glaze with a water or rum glaze.

They can also be served plain, without any glaze.

Storage

Plain, unglazed Brittany shortbread cookies can be stored for several weeks in airtight containers.

Glazed cookies can be stored in the same way for up to 48 hours.

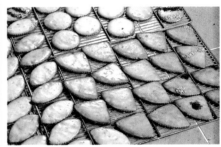

Sablés nantais (Nantais shortbread cookies)

Recipe

Yields 45 cookies

1 kg flour (35 oz.)
500 g sugar (17.5 oz.)
400 g butter (14 oz.)
4 eggs
35 ml milk (1 fl. oz.)

Procedure

To prepare the dough, follow the procedure for either sweetened tart dough or basic tart dough (see volume 1, pages 112 to 118).

Cutting and Shaping

Roll out a sheet of the dough 5 mm (1/4 in.) thick. Cut out the cookies with a 10-cm (4-in.) fluted cutter.

Place the shortbread cookies on a lightly buttered sheet pan.

Glaze with egg wash. Rest the pieces for 1/2 to 1 hour in the refrigerator.

Decorating and Baking

Brush on a second layer of egg wash, and score the pieces with the tongs of a fork (bend the two outer tongs up) or with a cutter. Bake the sablés in a moderate oven, 180°C (350°F).

Chapter 9 Finished products based on puff pastry

Le feuilletage nature (Plain puff pastry)

Vol-au-Vent

Composition

Puff pastry with five or six turns, egg wash

From a pâton (envelope) of puff pastry weighing 1.5 kg (53 oz.), 2 large vol-au-vents serving 8 to 10 each can be made. Allow 100 g (3.5 oz.) of puff pastry per serving.

Procedure

Method A: Two Layers

After weighing the puff pastry, cut the dough into two equal squares. Cut off the corners of the squares and place the trimmings in the center of the squares.

Roll out two circles to the size needed.

Shake the dough after rolling it out to relax it. With a paring knife, cut two even circles using a Pithiviers form (or cardboard circle) as a guide, 20 cm (8 in.) in diameter for 8 to 10 servings.

Place the first circle on a round sheet pan lightly moistened with water. Press lightly on the dough so it will adhere to the sheet pan. Brush off any excess flour from the dough.

Cutting the Ring

Choose a cutter smaller than the circle to create a border. For a 20-cm (8-in.) circle, leave a 2.5-cm (1-in.) border.

Carefully center the cutter on the second circle and cut out the center to obtain a ring of dough.

Brush off any excess flour.

Lightly brush egg wash on the ring and place it on top of the circle, centering it carefully.

To seal the two pieces together, place a round sheet pan or other flat, round object on top of the dough and apply even pressure.

Flute all around the top edge with the back of a paring knife held vertically. This helps the two pieces to rise uniformly and also gives an attractive presentation. (See *chiqueter* in the Glossary).

Glaze the entire piece with egg wash.

Method B: Three Layers

Place a circle of dough on a round sheet pan moistened with water, as for method A.

Brush the border of the circle with egg wash and place a ring of puff pastry over the circle, as for method A.

Roll out the dough cut from the center of the ring to the same size as the other circles. Shake it out to relax it.

Then cut out a circle the same size as the first. Brush egg wash on the ring, and place the third layer of dough on top of the ring. Press down gently on the three layers to seal them together as in method A.

Flute as in method A.

Glaze with an egg wash.

To prevent the third layer of dough (the cover) from sticking to the base, lightly sprinkle flour on the first layer after adding the ring but before placing the third layer on top.

For Both Methods

Resting

Allow the pieces to rest for 40 to 60 minutes in the refrigerator.

Baking

Glaze with egg wash for a second time before baking.

The pieces can be decorated by making incisions with a paring knife in the dough. Do not cut deeper than 1 mm (1/16 in.) into the dough. This step is optional but recommended, as it enhances appearance.

Prick the vol-au-vent at 12, 3, 6, and 9 o'clock with a toothpick or the point of a knife so that it rises evenly.

Begin baking the vol-au-vent in an oven preheated to 240° to 250°C (450° to 475°F), for several minutes. Once the puff pastry begins to rise, lower the oven to 180° to 220°C (350° to 425°F).

Vol-au-vents take 20 to 30 minutes to bake and require constant attention throughout baking.

Finishing

If method B was used, after baking, cut the middle of the top of the vol-au-vent off with a paring knife. This will be the cover of the vol-au-vent.

After removing the cover, remove any uncooked dough from the middle, inside the vol-au-vent.

While the dough is still hot, the butter that has come to the surface will still be liquid. The top of the vol-au-vent can be given a sheen by brushing this butter around the piece.

Bouchées à la Reine Rondes (Round Bouchées)

Composition

Puff pastry with five or six turns, egg wash

1.5 kg (53 oz.) of puff pastry yields 21 bouchées, 3 mm (1/8 in.) thick, made with a 9-cm (4.5-in.) fluted cutter and plain 5-cm (2-in.) cutter.

Procedure

Roll out a square of puff pastry 3 mm (1/8 in.) thick. Use the fluted cutter to cut out circles. Brush off any excess flour.

Place half of the circles, which are to be the bases, upside down in staggered rows on a sheet pan lightly moistened with water.

Glaze the surface of the dough with egg wash, and decorate the center of the pieces by scoring them with a paring knife.

With the plain smaller cutter, remove the centers of the remaining circles. Brush off any excess flour.

Make light incisions in the centers of the dough circles with the plain cutter. Cut no more than halfway into the dough; be careful not to cut too deeply. Although this step is optional, it will facilitate removing the centers, which will be used as covers after baking.

Place the rings upside down on top of the circles of dough on the sheet pan. Press lightly on the pieces to seal them together.

Glaze with egg wash.

Resting

Allow the pieces to rest for 20 to 30 minutes in the refrigerator.

Baking

Glaze the pieces a second time with egg wash, and prick them as for vol-au-vents. The borders can be decorated like vol-au-vents.

Begin baking the bouchées in a hot preheated oven at 240° to 250°C (450° to 475°F). Once they begin to color, lower the oven to 210° to 220°C (400° to 425°F) and continue baking for about 20 minutes.

After baking, remove the middle section from the bases for covers. Brush the butter that has risen to the surface of the pastry to create a sheen, as for vol-au-vents.

Collapsing Bouchées

To prevent bouchées from falling or collapsing, be sure to allow the dough to rest in the refrigerator before baking, and do not forget to prick the dough four times before baking.

Two methods will help the bouchées rise evenly:

- Place a rack 7.5 cm (3 in.) above the bouchées, holding it in place with four baba or brioche molds at each corner of the sheet pan. This will prevent the bouchées from rising above the rack. The rack can be removed once the bouchées have risen fully and formed a crust.
- Once the egg wash is dry, place sheets of parchment paper over the bouchées.

Square Bouchées

Composition

Puff pastry with four or five turns, egg wash

Procedure

Roll out the puff pastry 3 to 4 mm (about 1/8 in.) thick.

Cut the dough into 10-cm (4-in.) squares. Fold each square on the diagonal to form a triangle. Cut a border 1 cm (3/8 in.) thick from the edge of the triangle, but leave 2 cm (3/4 in.) of space uncut at the tip of the triangle. Be careful not to cut off the border completely.

Unfold the triangle, brush off any excess flour, and brush egg wash on the square.

Cross the borders over to the opposite corners of the square.

Resting

Allow the bouchées to rest for 20 to 30 minutes in the refrigerator.

Baking

Glaze a second time with egg wash. Score the centers. Begin baking the bouchées in a hot preheated oven, 240° to 250°C (450° to 475°F), lowering the temperature to 210° to 220°C (400° to 425°F) as the pieces rise and form a crust.

Square Tartlets

Composition

Puff pastry with six turns, egg wash, pastry cream (filling), and fruit (garniture)

Procedure

Roll the puff pastry dough to a thickness of 2 to 3 mm (1/16 to 1/8 in.). Prick the dough with a roller docker.

Cut the dough into 10-cm (4-in.) squares. Make borders and brush with egg wash as for square bouchées.

Finishing

Rest the dough for 30 minutes before garnishing with pastry cream and fruit; or bake blind and then garnish. Baking procedure is the same as for bouchées.

Fruit Strips

Composition

Puff pastry with fixe or six turns, pastry cream, almond cream, or frangipane cream (when almond or frangipane creams are used, they must be cooked with the pastry), fresh fruit, sugar syrup or egg wash for glazing

1.5 kg (53 oz.) of puff pastry yields 3 strips for a total of 30 servings.

Procedure

For one strip, use 500 g (17.5 oz.) puff pastry dough

Roll out the dough 3 mm (1/8 in.) thick, 60 cm (24 in.) long (to the length of a blue steel sheet pan) or cut the strip to the length of the sheet pan used. Fold the dough in half lengthwise. Cut two thin strips 1.5 cm (5/8 in.) wide from the sides of the dough.

Again roll out the strip so it is 12 cm (4.5 in.) wide (width of a pastry cutter), 2.5 mm (1 in.) thick, and 60 cm (24 in.) long.

Prick the dough with a roller docker (do not prick the thin strips) and fold it in half crosswise.

Unfold the dough onto a sheet pan lightly moistened with water. Brush egg wash on the borders of the dough sheet, and place the thin strips on top of the egg-washed borders. Avoid stretching the strips as they are placed in position.

Seal the thin strips onto the base by pressing them gently with the fingers.

With a chefs' knife, trim the ends of the strips if necessary. Flute the sides of the strips with a paring knife. Brush egg wash on the border strips and score them decoratively.

Resting

Rest for 20 to 30 minutes before baking.

Filling and Garniture

The filling and garniture should be related:

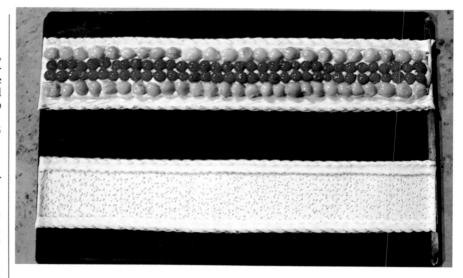

- with flavored pastry cream, use fruits such as cherries, apricots, and plums

- with apple compote, use apples.

Place the filling in the center of the strip, using a spoon, pastry scraper, or pastry bag and tip. Avoid getting any on the borders. Smooth the cream with a metal spatula if necessary.

Place the fruit on the cream.

Baking

The strips can be baked blind in a moderate oven at 210°C (400°F). In this case the strip is weighed down and

brushed with egg wash. After cooling, garnish with pastry cream and fruit, such as cherries, plums, pears, peaches, apricots, strawberries, raspberries, or blueberries. The strip can also be filled with Chantilly cream and garnished with strawberries, raspberries, or blueberries.

Finishing

Once the tart is baked, place it on a cooling rack.

All the strips should be glazed, using a pastry brush, with:

- apricot jelly for light-colored fruits

- red currant jelly (or other red jelly) for red fruits

- jelly of the fruit used in the tart

Cut the strip with a chef's knife dipped in hot water and wiped dry. Warming the knife will prevent the jelly from sticking to it.

Storage

Fruit strips can be stored in the refrigerator for 24 hours.

Large Square Tarts

Composition

Puff pastry with six turns, egg wash, pastry or almond cream and desired fruits (filling)

This tart can be made with the trimmings of puff pastry, as it does not need to rise very high. Allow 375 g (13.5 oz.) of dough for 1 tart serving 8.

Procedure   *Method A*

Roll out a square of dough 2 to 3 mm (1/16 to 1/8 in.) thick.

Prick it with a roller docker and cut into equal squares of the desired size. Place each square on a sheet pan moistened with water.

Cut four strips to make a border for the tart (use fresh puff pastry, not trimmings). Each strip should be 1.5 to 2 cm (5/8 to 3/4 in.) wide and slightly longer than the length of the tart.

Brush egg wash or water on the edges of the tart. Place the border strips on top. Overlap the ends of the strips at the corners.

Press gently to seal; flute the sides with a paring knife and glaze the strips with egg wash.

Method B

Roll out the dough as for method A to 2 to 3 mm (1/16 to 1/8 in.) thick. Place a cardboard or wooden template cut to the size and shape desired over the dough.

Cut around the template, leaving an additional 1.5-cm (5/8-in.) border of dough. Cut each corner off with a chef's knife.

Cut off the four border strips. Prick the square of puff pastry dough with the roller docker. Moisten the edges of the square with egg wash or water and place the four strips upside down on the borders. Press down on strips to seal them to the dough. Flute the sides of the tart.

Method C

Roll out a square 3 to 4 cm (about 1/8 in.) thick, as for method A. Using the template mentioned in method B, cut a square, leaving an extra 1.5 cm (5/8 in.) border around the tart.

Incise a frame, 1.5 to 2 cm (5/8 to 3/4 in.) wide, around the square, but do not cut too deeply or cut off the frame completely. Prick the center of the square with the docker; do not prick the frame.

Flute the border and glaze with egg wash.

Square Tart, Method A
press on the border

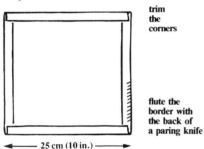

trim
the
corners

flute the
border with
the back of
a paring knife

◄─── 25 cm (10 in.) ───►

Square Tart, Method B

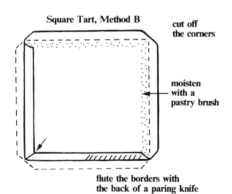

cut off
the corners

moisten
with a
pastry brush

flute the borders with
the back of a paring knife

Square Tart, Method C

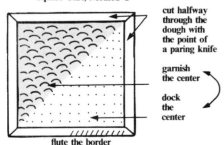

cut halfway
through the
dough with
the point of
a paring knife

garnish
the center

dock
the
center

flute the border

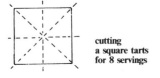

cutting
a square tarts
for 8 servings

Round Tarts with Borders

These round tarts have the same composition as the large square tarts.

Procedure

Cut a square of puff pastry as needed; for example, 375 g (13.5 oz.) of dough will serve 8.

Cut off the corners of the square and place them in the center of the puff pastry.

Roll the dough into a circle slightly larger than needed. Relax the dough by shaking it out.

Using a template, either a Pithiviers form or tart ring, cut an even circle with a paring knife.

Cut a circle with a second template about 3 cm (1 1/8 in.) smaller in diameter than the first. Remove the center, leaving a ring about 1.5 cm (5/8 in.) wide.

Roll out the center again until it is the size it was before cutting the ring; use the first template to trim it evenly.

Prick the circle with a roller docker, turn it upside down, and place it on a moistened sheet pan.

Moisten the ring with water or egg wash and place it on top of the dough circle. Seal the two together by pressing gently with the fingers. Flute the border.

Resting

Allow the dough to rest for 20 to 30 minutes in the refrigerator. If trimmings were used to make the base, rest the dough for a longer time, according to how elastic it became.

Baking

Glaze the border for a second time with egg wash, and score it decoratively. Bake the tart, then garnish as desired; or bake with a cream filling and fruit.

Galettes des Rois en Pâte Feuilletée (Twelfth Night Cake)

Composition

Puff pastry with four or five turns, 1 fava bean, sugar syrup at 1260 D, egg wash

A pâton of puff pastry weighing 1.5 kg (53 oz.) will make
- 6 galettes, 4 servings each: 250 g (9 oz.)
- 4 galettes, 6 servings each: 375 g (13.5 oz.)
- 3 galettes, 8 servings each: 500 g (17.5 oz.)

Procedure

Cut squares to make the number of galettes needed. Roll them out to even the dough if necessary.

Fold the four corners in toward the middle of the piece.

Turn the dough over, and form a ball carefully, without breaking the structure of the puff pastry dough (see Lining Tart Rings, volume 1, pages 37 and 38).

Gently flatten the dough slightly with the palm of the hand.

Resting

The dough should rest for 5 to 10 minutes.

Shaping the Galette

Turn the dough upside down. Roll out each round of dough as for lining a tart ring, 1/2 cm (1/4 in.) thick (the thickness can vary depending on the size of the galette made).

Placing the Fava Bean

In France this tart is made during Epiphany and is sold with a golden paper crown (as a symbol of the three kings). The literal translation of *galette des rois* is "galette of the kings." It is a tradition to hide a dry bean inside the tart; the child who finds the bean wins the crown.

With a paring knife, make a 1- to 2-cm (3/8- to 3/4-in.) incision in the dough, and place the bean in the direction of the cut. This way the bean will not be seen easily when the tart is cut. Moisten the area of dough over the bean to seal it.

Flute the border and place the galette on a lightly moistened sheet pan.

Note: To flute galettes, hold a paring knife or metal spatula at a 45-degree angle to the dough, and make the indentations very close together. If necessary, brush off any excess flour before brushing on the first egg wash.

Resting

Allow the galettes to rest for 20 to 30 minutes, depending on the elasticity of the dough.

Decoration

Glaze with egg wash a second time, and score the galettes with the tip of a paring knife. Various designs can be made: chevrons, rosettes, stars, crisscross patterns, diamonds, or evergreen branches. Special designs can also be created, including cartoon animals, palm trees, even the three wise men.

Baking

Place the galettes in a hot oven preheated to 250°C (475°F) and bake until the dough begins to become golden. Lower the heat to 210°C (400°F) to finish baking. At the end of baking, glaze with sugar syrup, as for Pithiviers (see page 196).

Le feuilletage sucré (Sweet puff pastry)

Palmiers (Palm Leaves)

1 pâton of puff pastry weighing 1.5 kg (53 oz.) yields 30 palmiers.

Procedure

Roll out a sheet of sweet puff pastry (see feuilletage fantaisie, page 189), 80 to 85 cm (31.5 to 33.5 in.) long and 4 to 5 mm (1/8 to 1/4 in.) thick. The length depends on how much dough is used.

Fold each end twice around itself, lengthwise. After folding, the two ends should meet in the center of the sheet of

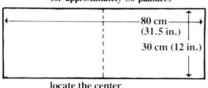

for a pâton of 1.5 kg (53 oz.),
for approximately 30 palmiers

—80 cm— (31.5 in.)

30 cm (12 in.)

locate the center
by folding the dough in half

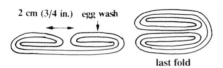

2 cm (3/4 in.)   egg wash

last fold

dough with about 2 cm (3/4 in.) of space between. Even the dough with the rolling pin if necessary. Lightly brush on egg wash, and fold the two halves together. Even the dough out again with the rolling pin.

Cut slices approximately 1 cm (3/8 in.) thick with a chef's knife.

Place the slices in staggered rows on a clean, well-buttered sheet pan. Space them out well, so they will have room to expand without touching while baking.

Resting

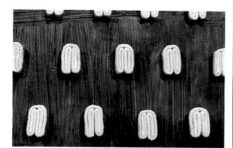

The palmiers should rest in the refrigerator for a minimum of 20 to 30 minutes.

Baking

Bake the palmiers in a moderate oven, at 210° to 220°C (400° to 425°F). Halfway through the baking, when they are golden on the bottom, turn the palmiers over and bake until they are lightly caramelized and golden on both sides.

Storage

Palmiers can be stored for 24 hours if well protected from moisture.

Eventails (Fans)

Procedure

Roll out a sheet of sweet puff pastry (see feuilletage fantaisie, page 189) 3 mm (1/8 in.) thick and 90 cm (35.5 in.) wide. The length depends on the quantity of dough used.

Divide the sheet into three strips: two strips 36 cm (14 in.) wide and one 18 cm (7 in.) wide. Fold the two ends of the wide strips to meet in the middle. Flatten the strips with the rolling pin. Place one strip on top of the other. Fold the narrow strip in half and place it on top of the top wide strip, with the folded end up and the open end facing the two

Fans

wide strips; all cut edges should be in the center. Glaze with egg wash to attach the pieces together.

Fold up all three strips to form a fan. Flatten the dough lightly with a rolling pin to even and seal the dough together. Cut slices of 1 cm (3/8 in.) thick.

Resting

Allow the fans to rest in the refrigerator for 20 to 30 minutes.

Baking and Storing

Same as for palmiers.

Pailles d'Or à la Framboise (Golden Straws with Raspberry)

Procedure

To prepare the dough, give puff pastry a third turn with sugar.

Roll out a sheet of dough 1.5 cm (5/8 in.) thick. Trim the edges if necessary.

Divide the dough in strips 10 to 12 cm (4 to 4.75 in.) wide, and cut each strip in slices 1 cm (3/8 in.) thick. Place the strips on a sheet pan with the cut side down.

Resting

Rest the dough for approximately 20 minutes in the refrigerator.

Baking

Same as for palmiers.

Garnishing

After the strips cool, with the caramelized sides facing out, make sandwiches with two strips filled with raspberry or other preserves, flavored to taste with Cointreau, Grand Marnier, Kirsch, or rum.

Storage

Same as for palmiers.

Papillons (Butterflies)

Procedure

Use puff pastry with six turns, the last two turns with sugar. Roll out a sheet of dough approximately 2.5 cm (1 in.) thick.

Trim the ends to even them out. Divide the sheet of puff pastry dough into

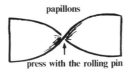

papillons

press with the rolling pin

strips 12 to 14 cm (4.5 to 5.5 in.) thick. Mark the middle of each strip with an indentation by pressing with the rolling pin lengthwise.

Cut slices 1 to 1.5 cm (3/8 to 5/8 in.) wide and give a half twist in the middle (where the indent was made) to each slice before placing it on a buttered sheet pan.

Resting, Baking, and Storing

Same as for palmiers

Feuilletage Fantaisie (Sweet Puff Pastry)

Composition

Puff pastry with five or six turns, granulated or confectioners' sugar.

Procedure

To make sweet puff pastry, the last two simple turns (folding in thirds) of the puff pastry are made by dusting the marble or work surface with sugar. In place of flour, generously sprinkle the puff pastry dough with sugar when giving the dough the fifth and sixth turns. (Use a small amount of flour to prevent the dough from sticking to the work surface.)

Petits Fours Feuilletés Sucrés (Petits Fours of Sweet Puff Pastry)

Miniature Palmiers

Composition

The composition of miniature palmiers is the same as for larger ones, except that it is best to use confectioners' sugar to replace the granulated sugar.

Procedure

Roll out a sheet of dough 3 mm (1/8 in.) thick. Cut strips 10 to 12 cm (4 to 4.5 in.) wide.

Proceed as for the larger palmiers, folding both ends of each strip over toward the middle of the strip. Fold a second time until the two rolls almost join at the middle.

Brush egg wash on the two halves and fold them together.

Even out the strip by rolling it with the rolling pin, or pressing gently with the blade of a chef's knife.

Cut slices approximately 1/2 cm (1/4 in.) thick. Place the slices on a buttered sheet pan as for the larger palmiers.

Resting

Rest the dough for approximately 20 to 30 minutes.

Baking

Miniature palmiers are baked in the same way as the larger pieces. Place the palmiers in the oven at 230°C (450°F). When they are caramelized on the bottom, turn the pieces over and sprinkle them with confectioners' sugar. Then place the palmiers back in the oven at 250°C (475°F) to caramelize the other side.

Miniature Papillons

Procedure

Roll out a sheet of sweet puff pastry dough 1 cm (3/8 in.) thick. Trim the sheet if necessary. Cut strips 4 to 5 cm (1.5 to 2 in.) thick. With the rolling pin, press in the middle to make indentations lengthwise.

Cut slices 1.5 cm (5/8 in.) thick. Finish as for the larger papillons.

Baking

Same as for miniature palmiers.

Miniature Pailles d'Or

Procedure

When making puff pastry, the last three turns are with sugar to replace the flour. Roll out a sheet 7 to 8 mm (about 1/4 in.) thick. Cut strips 4 to 5 cm (1.5 to 2 in.) wide.

Cut the strips into slices 1/2 cm (1/4 in.) thick. Place the slices on a sheet pan, cut side down.

Resting

Rest the slices in the refrigerator for 10 to 20 minutes.

Baking

Same as for miniature palmiers.

Garnish

Same as for the larger pailles d'or.

Fantaisies (Fantasies)

Composition

Puff pastry with five turns, egg whites, almond paste, flavoring: Grand Marnier, Cointreau, Kirsch, or vanilla

Procedure

Roll out a sheet of regular (nonsweetened) puff pastry dough, 2 to 3 mm (1/16 to 1/8 in.) thick.

Brush off any excess flour, and cut strips 12 to 14 cm (4.5 to 5.5 in.) thick.

Soften flavored almond paste by mixing it with egg white (pink coloring can be added but is optional). Spread a thin layer of the softened almond paste on the sheet of dough, using a metal spatula. Roll the sheet of dough up, lengthwise, to form a sausage. Place the roll of puff pastry dough on a sheet pan and chill it in the refrigerator until firm, for a minimum of 30 minutes.

Make an incision halfway through the dough lengthwise. Cut slices 1.5 cm (5/8 in.) thick. Place the slices on a sheet pan.

Baking

Bake the pieces in a moderate oven preheated to 200° to 210°C (400°F) until golden brown and cooked through.

Sacristains (Corkscrews)

Composition

Puff pastry with five turns, chopped almonds, granulated sugar, egg wash for glazing

Procedure

Roll out a sheet of sweet puff pastry 3 to 4 mm (about 1/8 in.) thick.

Brush off any excess flour from the dough and work surface. Glaze the surface of the dough with egg wash. Sprinkle equal amounts of chopped almonds and granulated sugar over the dough.

Roll the rolling pin over the dough to help the mixture adhere to it. Turn the sheet of dough over, and brush off any excess flour if necessary. Repeat the procedure for applying the almonds and sugar.

Cut the sheet in strips 6 cm (2.5 in.) wide, then into 1/2-cm (1/4-in.) slices. Twist the strips two times around, one by one, and place them on a lightly buttered sheet pan. Press on the two ends

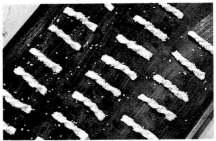

so they will stay twisted during baking.

Resting

Rest the strips for 20 to 30 minutes in the refrigerator.

Baking

Bake in an oven preheated to 200° to 210°C (400°F) until golden brown and cooked through. Double the sheet pan if necessary.

Le feuilletage salé (Savory puff pastry)

Allumettes au Fromage (Cheese Straws)

Composition

Puff pastry with three turns, egg wash, Gruyère cheese, salt, pepper

One pâton of puff pastry weighing 1.5 kg (53 oz.) yields 1.2 kg (42.5 oz.) of cheese straws, to be baked on two sheet pans, 40 × 60 cm (16 × 24 in.).

Procedure

While rolling out the last two turns for the puff pastry dough, sprinkle grated Gruyère cheese over the dough before folding (in thirds).

Roll out a sheet of dough 3 mm (1/8 in.) thick. Brush off any excess flour, and lightly prick the dough with a roller docker.

Place the rolled-out dough on a sheet pan lightly moistened with water. Trim the edges if necessary.

Glaze the dough with egg wash and sprinkle generously with grated Gruyère cheese, salt, and pepper.

Roll over the dough gently with the rolling pin to help the cheese stick to the dough.

Place the dough in the refrigerator for 30 to 40 minutes.

Using a ruler as a guide, with a paring knife, cut strips lengthwise, 1 to 1.5 cm (3/8 to 5/8 in.) wide.

Cut the strips across to obtain small rectangles 6 to 10 cm (2.5 to 4 in.) long to form the straws.

Baking

Bake the cheese straws in a moderate oven preheated to 210° to 220°C (400° to 425°F) until golden brown and cooked through.

After baking, the cheese straws can be easily pulled apart from each other. It is best if they are pulled apart while they are still warm.

Galettes Fromage (Cheese Galettes)

Composition

Puff pastry with five turns, egg wash, Gruyère cheese, Mornay sauce (to garnish)

A pâton of puff pastry dough weighing 1.5 kg (53 oz.) yields 2 kg (70 oz.) of galettes.

Procedure

Roll out a sheet of puff pastry dough 3 mm (1/8 in.) thick. Prick the sheet lightly with the roller docker. Brush off any excess flour if necessary.

With round plain cutters, approximately 5 cm (2 in.) in diameter, cut circles from the sheet of dough.

Place the circles of dough close together on a sheet pan lightly moistened with water.

Glaze the circles with egg wash and sprinkle with grated Gruyère cheese.

Rest the dough in the refrigerator for 30 to 40 minutes.

Baking

Bake the galettes in a hot oven preheated to 230° to 240°C (450° to 475°F) until golden brown and cooked through.

Garniture

After baking, slice the top off each galette, fill with Mornay sauce, and put the top back in place.

Storage

Cheese galettes can be stored for approximately 24 hours.

Croissants au Jambon (Miniature Ham Croissants)

Composition

Puff pastry with five or six turns, ham

Procedure

Roll out a sheet of puff pastry dough 2 mm (1/16 in.) thick. Cut it into bands 4 to 6 cm (1.5 to 2.5 in.) wide, and cut each band into triangles with a base of 4 to 6 cm (1.5 to 2.5 in.).

Place a small piece of ham on each triangle and roll each croissant with two hands. Proceed as for rolling croissants (see volume 1, Cutting and Baking Croissants, pages 182 to 185).

Glaze with egg wash.

Place the croissants in the refrigerator to rest for 1 hour.

Baking

Glaze the croissants with egg wash a second time and bake in a moderate oven at 220°C (425°F) until golden brown.

Variations

Croissants with anchovies

Croissants with Parmesan cheese

Bouchées Croûtes Fours (Pastry Shells)

Composition

Same as for the round bouchées (see pages 184 to 185 of this volume).

Procedure

The procedure is the same as for round bouchées.

Roll out a sheet of puff pastry dough 2 mm (1/16 in.) thick. Cut out the bottom circles, then the rings, seal together with egg wash, and finish as for round bouchées.

The bouchées can also be made using one piece of dough. Roll out a sheet of dough approximately 3 mm (1/8 in.) thick, and cut circles with a cutter.

To form a cover, mark the circles of dough by cutting only partially through them with a second plain cutter smaller than the first (allowing enough of space to form a border for the top). Dip the cutter in hot water to make cutting easier.

Place the pieces in the refrigerator to rest for approximately 30 to 40 minutes.

Baking

Glaze with egg wash and bake in a hot preheated oven, 230° to 240°C (450° to 475°F) until golden brown; when lifted, they should feel very light, almost empty inside.

Open the pieces after baking by carefully removing the top middle section, to be used as the lid. Remove the dough inside and discard.

Garnishing

Garnish the pieces as desired and cover them with the lid.

Les fruits secs salés (Salted nuts)

Pour the hot nuts all at once into the mixture of egg white and salt. Mix vigorously with a wooden spatula.

Place the nuts on a stainless steel sheet pan to cool.

Salted nuts are easy to prepare. Use nuts that are very dry and skinless, such as almonds, hazelnuts, peanuts, pistachios, pignolis, and cashews.

Recipe

1 kg dry, shelled nuts (35 oz.)
1 egg white
5 to 8 g salt (1 to 1.5 tsp.)

Equipment

Bowl, whisk, measuring cup, wooden spatula, stainless steel sheet pan

Procedure

Roast the nuts in a moderate oven, 180° to 200°C (350° to 375°F).
Blend the egg white and salt with a whisk.

Storage

Salted nuts can be stored for several weeks in airtight containers in a cool, dry place.

Le feuilletage fourré (Filled puff pastry)

Chaussons aux Pommes (Apple Turnovers)

Composition

Puff pastry with six turns, apple compote, egg wash for glazing

1 pâton of puff pastry weighing 1.5 kg (53 oz.) yields approximately 20 turnovers.

Procedure

Roll out a sheet of puff pastry 3 mm (1/8 in.) thick. Cut out circles of puff pastry dough with a plain or fluted cutter 12 cm (4.5 in.) in diameter. With the rolling pin, roll over the circles of dough until they form ovals. Roll them so that they are thinner in the center, leaving the edges slightly thicker. Brush egg wash or water on the borders of the ovals.

With a spoon or pastry bag, place a dollop of apple compote flavored with vanilla in the centers of the puff pastry ovals.

Fold the ovals in half so that the ends meet, and press gently on the ends to seal them together (see pictures on bottom of page 192). Turn the pieces over and place them on a sheet pan lightly moistened with water.

Glaze with egg wash.

Allow the turnovers to rest for 30 minutes in the refrigerator at 5°C (40°F). Then glaze them a second time with egg wash and score them decoratively with a sharp paring knife.

Baking

Bake the turnovers at 220° to 240°C (425° to 475°F) until golden brown and fully risen. Just before the turnovers are finished baking, sprinkle confectioners' sugar on them and return them to the oven. Or, with a pastry brush, brush sugar syrup at 1260 D on them as they are taken out of the oven.

Variations

The apple compote can be replaced with pastry cream or preserves or marmalade from various fruits.

Storage

Once the turnovers are baked, they can be stored for 24 hours.

They freeze well:
- unbaked, for several weeks
- baked, for several days

Chaussons Italiens ou Napolitains
(Italian Cream-filled Turnovers)

Composition

Puff pastry with six turns, softened butter, filling: two parts pâte à choux (cream puff pastry), one part pastry cream, plus orange flower water and raisins or candied fruits macerated in rum.

A pâton of puff pastry weighing 1.5 kg (53 oz.) yields 35 turnovers.

Making the Batter

In a bowl, with a wooden spoon, mix 250 g (9 oz.) pâte à choux flavored with 1 Tbsp. orange flower water, 125 g (4.5 oz.) pastry cream flavored with rum, and 100 g (3.5 oz.) raisins blanched and macerated in rum.

This batter can be stored in the refrigerator for 24 hours.

Making the Turnovers

Roll out a sheet of puff pastry 2 to 3 mm (1/16 to 1/8 in.) thick, 70 cm (27.5 in.) long, and 40 cm (15.5 in.) wide.

With a pastry brush or metal spatula, smooth a thin layer of softened butter over the sheet of dough.

Roll up the sheet of dough to form a large sausage approximately 8 to 10 cm (3 to 4 in.) in diameter. Chill the dough in the refrigerator for several hours. It is best to prepare the dough up to this step a day ahead of time, so it can rest.

After resting, cut slices 1 cm (3/8 in.) thick. Place the slices on a well-floured work surface and roll them out with a rolling pin to form ovals (as for apple turnovers).

Place the filling (about the size of an egg) in the center of the turnover.

Fold one side of the dough over as for apple turnovers, but do not moisten or press down the edges to seal.

Allow the pieces to rest for 20 to 30 minutes in the refrigerator.

Baking

Bake the turnovers in a moderate oven, at 220° to 230°C (425° to 450°F), without glazing, until golden brown.

After baking, sprinkle with confectioners' sugar.

Storage

Unbaked, the turnovers can be frozen for approximately 1 week. Baked, they can be stored for 24 hours in the refrigerator.

Italian turnovers are best eaten while still warm after baking.

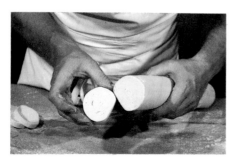

Pithiviers

History

In the sixteenth century, King Charles IX, returning from visiting his mistress Marie Touchet, was captured in the Orléans forest, near a village called Pithiviers, by a band of Huguenots. Realizing they had captured the king, the outlaws offered him the best food of the village in order to be forgiven for their mistake.

One of the dishes consisted of a pâté enclosed in puff pastry decorated with scoring to represent the wheels of the king's coach.

Once home, the king honored the pastry chef of Pithiviers, Provenchère, for his pâté with the royal certificate for pastry making.

During the reign of King Louis-Philippe in the nineteenth century, the pâté was replace with a cream filling.

Composition

Puff pastry with five turns, almond cream, egg wash

From a pâton weighing 1.5 kg (53 oz.), the following can be made:

- 6 Pithiviers serving 4 each, filled with 160 to 200 g (5.5 to 7 oz.) of almond or frangipane cream

- 4 Pithiviers serving 6 each, filled with 240 to 300 g (8.5 to 10.5 oz.) of almond or frangipane cream

- 3 Pithiviers serving 8 each, filled with 320 to 400 g (11 to 14 oz.) of almond or frangipane cream

Procedure

Cut two squares of puff pastry (the sizes of which are determined by the sizes of the final pastries desired). Cut off the four corners and place these trimmings in the center of the dough. Roll out the two pieces of puff pastry dough to form two circles approximately 3 mm (1/8 in.) thick.

Place one of the circles of dough on a round, preferably blue steel, sheet pan lightly moistened with water, or on a marble, smooth side down. Moisten approximately 4 cm (1.5 in.) of the border of this circle with water or egg wash. Fill the circle with almond or frangipane cream with a pastry bag or a metal spatula, shaping a dome with the cream. Be sure to leave a generous border.

Cover by placing the second sheet of puff pastry dough over the first. Seal the borders well by pressing gently and carefully all around, so the cream will not seep out during baking.

Place a large cutter or tart circle on the dough. Its diameter should be several centimeters (about 2 inches) smaller than the Pithiviers, to leave room for a border.

With a small paring knife held vertically, using the cutter as a guide, cut a scalloped edge. The size of the scalloping can be large or very small. Remove the trimmings.

If the dough was cut on the marble, turn the Pithiviers over onto a lightly moistened round sheet pan. Regardless of where it was prepared, glaze the Pithiviers with egg wash.

Rest the Pithiviers in the refrigerator for 20 minutes.

Baking

Glaze a second time with egg wash, and score a pinwheel into the top with a small paring knife, as shown in the photos. With the point of the knife, prick a hole in the center of the Pithiviers and at the border, to allow steam to escape.

Begin baking in a hot oven at 230° to 240°C (450° to 475°F) until the Pithiviers starts to brown, then lower the oven to 200° to 210°C (375° to 400°F) to finish. The Pithiviers will be golden brown on the top and the sides will appear cooked through when baking is complete.

Finishing

At the end of baking, lightly sprinkle the Pithiviers with confectioners' sugar and return the piece to the hot oven to caramelize it and glaze the top.

Storage

Pithiviers can be stored for 24 hours at room temperature. They freeze well unbaked, and can be stored for several weeks. Baked, they can be stored frozen for only a few days.

Variations

Pithiviers can also be glazed by brushing on sugar syrup at 1260 D as soon as they come out of the oven. The syrup may crystallize if the Pithiviers are not served soon after baking. For pieces that are overbaked or too dark, it is best to use the sugar syrup, as no further baking is required. This method is also faster than using confectioners' sugar.

Pains Complets ou Pithiviers Hollandais
(Dark Bread or Dutch Pithiviers)

For the pains complets (this pastry resembles whole-wheat bread, which is how pains complet translates), place a large cutter (or Pithiviers form) on the dough. Its circumference should be smaller than that of the first piece. This will serve as a guide for cutting the border. Cut off the excess dough around the cutter, holding the paring knife at an angle to the cutter to create a narrow border with a beveled edge. Turn the piece over and place it on a moistened (preferably blue steel) round sheet pan. Press around the border with the palm of the hand to finish and thin the border, to give the piece a dome effect. Lightly flute the edge if desired. Rest the piece in the refrigerator for at least 1 hour. Prepare the topping by combining 50 g (1.5 oz.) almond powder, 50 g (1.5 oz.) hazelnut powder, 1 egg white, and a few drops of red food coloring. Cover the

Composition

Puff pastry trimmings, almond cream, almond powder, hazelnut powder, raw egg white, red food coloring (optional), confectioners' sugar, egg wash

Puff pastry trimmings work well in this dessert. After making Pithiviers, vol-au-vents, or bouchées, making this pastry puts the leftover trimmings to good use.

Procedure

Roll out two rounds of puff pastry (from trimmings), approximately 2 mm (1/16 in.) thick or cut two circles from a sheet of rolled-out trimmings with a large cutter approximately 24 cm (9.5 in.) in diameter; this will serve 8.

Brush the border of one of the two circles of dough with egg wash. Place approximately 250 g (9 oz.) of almond or frangipane cream in the center with a pastry bag or metal spatula, forming a dome as for a Pithiviers.

Cover the piece with the second circle, and press on the border firmly to seal and thin it.

top of the pastry with a layer of topping, using a small metal spatula.

Generously sprinkle confectioners' sugar on top and mark the serving portions with the tip of a pastry horn, drawing it gently from the center of the piece to the bottom.

Do not dig deeply into the dough. Prick the piece lightly to allow steam to escape.

Rest the piece for approximately 30 minutes in the refrigerator.

Baking

Bake the pain complet at 180° to 200°C (350° to 375°F) maximum. Allow from 40 to 50 minutes for one piece of 8 portions.

It is best to cook the pastry fully, until it is slightly dry; it can fall after baking if not fully cooked.

Storage

Pains complet can be stored for 4 to 5 days in the refrigerator. They freeze well: unbaked for several weeks, baked for 1 week maximum.

Variations

Pain d'amandes (almond bread): The procedure is the same as for pain complet, but sliced almonds are sprinkled on top after glazing, before baking.

Galette Fourrée à la Crème d'Amandes ou Frangipane
(Galettes Filled with Almond Cream or Frangipane)

Composition

Puff pastry with four or five turns, almond cream or frangipane, egg wash for glazing, sugar syrup at 1260 D, 1 fava bean

A pâton of puff pastry weighing 1.5 kg (53 oz.) yields 6 galettes, 4 servings each; allow 250 g (9 oz.) of puff pastry dough for each galette.

375 g (13.5 oz.) of puff pastry dough yields 4 galettes, 6 servings each.

500 g (17.5 oz.) puff pastry dough yields 3 galettes, 8 servings each.

The amount of filling needed can vary. In general, allow 15 to 25 g (1/2 to 1 oz.) of filling per serving.

Procedure

Cut the puff pastry dough as needed. Cut each piece in half and roll each half into a ball. Gently flatten the ball of dough slightly to form a thick disk and place the pieces in the refrigerator to rest for at least 30 minutes.

Shaping

Roll out the two flattened balls of dough 2 mm (1/16 in.) thick, and turn them over so the smooth sides are facing the marble.

Filling

Lightly moisten the border of one disk of dough with water or egg wash.

With a pastry bag, pipe out the almond cream or frangipane onto one of the disks of dough, leaving a 2-cm (3/4-in.) border. Even out the cream with a metal spatula.

Placing the Fava Bean

The fava bean is placed inside the cream, 1 to 2 cm (3/8 to 3/4 in.) in from the edge of the cream.

Cover the piece with the second sheet of dough, turning it over before positioning it. Seal the two pieces of dough together by pressing on the border.

Fluting (see vol-au-vent, page 184)

Flute the border, then turn the galette over onto a sheet pan lightly moistened with water.

Resting

Rest the galette for approximately 30 minutes in the refrigerator.

Scoring

The galettes can be decoratively scored with any design.

Baking

Prick the top of the dough in just a few places to allow steam to escape. Bake the filled galettes just as for the galettes des rois.

Note:

The galettes can be made by placing the first circle of dough directly on a lightly moistened round sheet pan. This procedure is easier for beginners.

To speed up the procedure, the dough for filled galettes is often rolled out with a sheeter. In this case, the two circles are cut out of a sheet of dough with large cutters. The procedure for making the galettes is then the same as for the preceding method. Trimmings of puff pastry can also be used when using a sheeter.

Certain pastry chefs will score galettes differently according to their weight, as a way of marking them. Other chefs weigh the galettes as they are purchased, in which case the weight of the galette does not determine how it is to be decorated. Still other chefs will score all plain unfilled galettes the same (regardless of size), and freely decorate filled galettes.

Dartois et jalousies (en bandes) (Filled puff pastry strips)

Dartois Strips

Composition

Puff pastry with five or six turns, almond cream, egg wash

Two dartois strips can be made from 1 pâton of puff pastry weighing 1.5 kg (53 oz.), yielding a total of 24 portions.

Procedure

From 750 g (26.5 oz.) of puff pastry with five turns, roll out a sheet 3 mm (1/8 in.) thick. From this sheet of dough, cut two strips of dough 12 cm (4.5 in.) wide (the width of a pastry cutter) and 60 cm (24 in.) long, which is the length of a standard blue steel sheet pan, 40 × 60 cm (16 × 24 in.).

Place one strip of dough on the sheet pan lightly moistened with water. Brush the edges of the strip of dough with egg wash or water and fill the middle with almond cream or frangipane using a pastry bag and plain no. 12 tip. Pipe three bands of cream onto the dough lengthwise. Be sure not to get any cream on the border.

Place the second strip of puff pastry dough (same size as the first) carefully centered over the cream. Press on the borders to seal the two dough strips together.

Flute the borders and glaze the entire surface of the top layer of dough with egg wash.

Allow the dartois to rest in the refrigerator for 20 to 30 minutes.

Baking

Glaze a second time and decorate the dartois by scoring it with the point of a small paring knife. Prick the piece in several places to allow steam to escape.

Bake the dartois for 35 to 45 minutes at 220° to 230°C (425° to 450°F).

At the end of baking, glaze the dartois as for apple turnovers and Pithiviers (see pages 193 and 195 to 196).

Storage

Dartois strips can be frozen, baked or unbaked, for several weeks.

Bande de Jalousies

Composition

Puff pastry with five or six turns, apricot or raspberry preserves (with seeds) or marmalade, almond cream, egg wash

Allow 600 to 700 g (21 to 24.5 oz.) of filling per strip.

Procedure

Roll out and cut two strips of puff pastry as for the dartois.

Filling the Jalousies

The jalousies can be filled with a thin layer of almond cream, topped with an equal amount of preserves or marmalade.

Preparing the Second Strip

Lightly flour the second strip, then fold it in half lengthwise. Along the fold (which is the center of the strip), cut thin strips with the heel of a chef's knife, leaving room for a border. Be careful not to cut the strips too wide or long, and do not cut into the border.

Place this cut strip over the garnished strip, make sure the fold is centered over the filling. Unfold the strip, keeping it centered. Seal the borders by pressing them, then flute the edges.

Glaze the strip with egg wash. Place it in the refrigerator to rest for 20 to 30 minutes.

Baking

Glaze the jalousies with egg wash a second time, score the borders, bake, and glaze as for dartois.

Variation

After baking, the edges of the jalousies can be brushed with apricot glaze; then sugar crystals, toasted almond slivers, or chopped almonds can be sprinkled on the apricot glaze, which will hold them in place.

Storage

Same as for dartois.

Conversations

Composition

Puff pastry with six turns, frangipane or almond cream, royal icing

Procedure (for large pieces)

Line a tart ring with a circle of puff pastry 2 mm (1/16 in.) thick (see volume 1, Lining Tart Rings, pages 37 and 38). Fold any excess dough down over the edge of the ring without cutting it off. Then place the ring on a round sheet pan (preferably blue steel).

Fill the dough two-thirds full with almond cream or frangipane.

Moisten the edge of the circle of dough with water or egg wash. Cover with a second thin circle of dough, the same thickness as the first but larger in diameter, so the ends overlap the tart ring. Roll over the piece with a rolling pin to cut off the excess dough, thus sealing the edges of the two layers together. Allow the piece to rest for 12 hours in the refrigerator.

With a metal spatula, spread a thin even layer of royal icing, to which a small amount of flour has been added, over the entire surface.

Over the layer of royal icing, place thin, narrow strips of puff pastry trimmings, 2 mm (1/16 in.) thick and 4 mm (1/8 in.) wide. The strips of puff pastry can be placed decoratively on the royal icing to form diamonds. Press the strips firmly at the edge of the ring to attach them securely.

Rest the conversation for 30 to 40 minutes in the refrigerator.

Baking

Bake the conversation in a moderate oven at 180° to 200°C (350° to 375°F) until the sides are golden brown and cooked through.

During baking, if a lot of the royal icing starts to melt and drip over the edge of the tart, increase the temperature of the oven for several minutes to set the icing, then lower the oven to finish baking.

Unmolding

Place the blade of a small paring knife between the tart and the tart ring and slide it around to loosen and free the tart from the tart ring. This procedure should be done carefully as the royal icing is very fragile and cracks easily.

To remove the tart ring, lift the tart by placing a large metal scraper underneath and raising the tart, letting the ring drop down.

Variation

The thin strips of puff pastry trimmings can be replaced with apricot preserves by piping out the preserves with a paper cone to create diamonds or other shapes to decorate the pieces.

Allumettes Glace Royale (Royal Icing Strips)

Composition

Puff pastry with five turns, royal icing
A pâton weighing 1.5 kg (53 oz.) yields 22 pieces.

Procedure

Roll out a sheet of puff pastry dough approximately 4 mm (1/8 in.) thick. Cut the dough into strips 10 to 12 cm (4 to 4.5 in.) wide, and place these strips on a sheet pan.

With a metal spatula, spread a thin layer of royal icing mixed with a little flour on the strips of puff pastry. The flour will prevent the royal icing from sliding off the pastry during baking.

Cut each strip into slices 4 cm (1.5 in.) wide.

Rest the pieces in a cool, dry area for 20 to 30 minutes.

Baking

Verify that the royal icing has formed a crust before baking the pieces.

Once the pieces are ready, bake them in a moderate oven, 180° to 200°C (350° to 400°F) with the vents open (if available) until the sides are golden

brown and cooked through.

If necessary, place the pieces in a hot oven for several seconds at the end of the baking time, to make it easier to trim off any excess icing that has dripped down the corners.

Pains complets (individual pieces) and Jésuites

Individual Pains Complets

Composition

Trimmings of puff pastry, almond cream, royal icing or pains complets topping

Procedure

For these pastries, round molds will be lined using the method known as *tamponnage* (tapping). To use this method, place tartlet molds in staggered rows, on the work surface, leaving some space between them. Lightly moisten them with water.

Roll out a sheet of puff pastry dough 1.5 mm (1/16 in.) thick (somewhat larger than the area of the molds so it will more than cover them).

Prick the sheet of dough with a roller docker and roll it onto the rolling pin.

Unroll the sheet of dough from the rolling pin over the molds, being careful not to stretch the dough while unrolling. Tap the dough gently with a pastry brush until it takes on the form of the molds.

Form a piece of dough, of the same size as the interiors of the molds, from an extra piece of dough. Tap on the

sheet of dough with this piece to push the dough gently and evenly into the molds.

Moisten the rims of the molds with a pastry brush and fill each mold halfway with frangipane or almond cream, using a pastry bag and tip, metal spatula, or spoon.

Roll out a second sheet of puff pastry dough 1.5 mm (1/16 in.) thick. Prick it with the roller docker and roll it onto the rolling pin as for the first sheet of dough.

Unroll the sheet of dough over the molds without stretching it.

Trim off the excess dough by rolling over the molds with the rolling pin.

Finish by spreading on the topping as for the large pains complets (see page 196).

Rest the dough for approximately 4 hours in the refrigerator.

Baking

The temperature is the same as for the large pieces, 180° to 200°C (350° to 375°F), but the baking time is shortened to approximately 20 to 25 minutes.

Jésuites

Composition

Puff pastry with five or six turns, almond cream or frangipane, apple compote, vanilla extract, royal icing, chopped or sliced almonds

A pâton of puff pastry weighing 1.5 kg (53 oz.) yields approximately 30 jésuites.

Procedure

Roll out half the pâton of puff pastry into a sheet approximately 25 cm (9.5 in.) wide, 2 to 3 mm thick (1/16 to 1/8 in.) thick, and 60 cm (23.5 in.) long (the length will be determined by the amount of puff pastry used.)

Lightly prick the sheet of dough with a roller docker. Moisten one of the long borders with water. Then spread a thin layer of batter, consisting of equal amounts of almond cream (or frangipane) and apple compote, flavored with vanilla extract, over half the strip, lengthwise. Be careful not to cover the moistened border with the filling. Fold the sheet of dough in half over the cream, lengthwise.

Brush off any excess flour, and gently push out any air bubbles trapped inside the fold by smoothing the dough with the hands. Be careful not to press on the dough.

Spread a thin layer of royal icing on the dough with a metal spatula. Then sprinkle sliced or chopped almonds over the middle of the strip.

Trim off the folded side of dough (optional).

Cut the strip into triangles with 10-cm (4-in.) bases, as long as the width of the strip.

Allow the royal icing to form a crust, about 20 to 30 minutes.

Baking

Bake the jésuites in a moderate oven at 180°C (350°F) with the oven door cracked open.

The puff pastry should be crisp and the icing golden when the jésuites are done.

Cornets et feuilletés à la crème
(Filled puff pastry horns and squares)

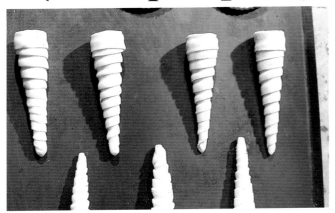
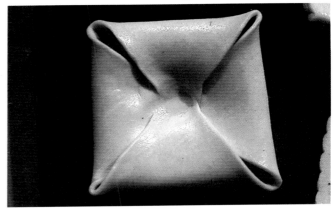

Cream-filled Horns

Composition

Puff pastry with six turns, egg wash, pastry cream, confectioners' sugar

Procedure

Butter the pastry horn molds. Roll out a sheet of puff pastry dough 2 mm (1/16 in.) thick and 30 cm (12 in.) long. Prick the dough with a roller docker, and brush off any excess flour. Trim the borders to even them out if necessary.

From the sheet of dough, cut narrow strips 2 cm (3/4 in.) wide and 30 cm (12 in.) long (the length of the dough).

Brush egg wash on the strips of dough; the side not glazed with egg wash will face the mold. Begin rolling the strips at the tip of the horn mold. Overlap the dough as it is rolled around the mold until the mold is completely covered.

Place the horns on sheet pans lightly moistened with water and rest the dough for a minimum of 20 to 30 minutes.

Baking

Glaze the horns a second time and bake them in a moderate oven at 220°C (425°F) until golden brown and cooked through.

Unmold the pieces as they come out of the oven.

Finishing

Fill the pastry horns with flavored pastry cream, using a pastry bag and tip.

Dip the top of the pastry cream in chocolate pieces or sprinkles or almond craquelées (sweet, roasted almonds).

Sprinkle either part or all of the horn with confectioners' sugar.

Storage

Filled pastry horns can be stored for up to 24 hours in the refrigerator.

Cream-filled Squares

Composition

Puff pastry with six turns, flavored pastry cream, almond cream or frangipane, confectioners' sugar

Procedure

Roll out a sheet of puff pastry dough approximately 3 mm (1/8 in.) thick. Do

not prick the dough. From the sheet of dough, cut 10- to 12-cm (4- to 4.5-in.) squares. Brush egg wash on each of the four corners.

Fill each square, using a pastry bag and tip or a spoon, with a spoonful of cream the size of a small plum. The cream should be placed in the center, equidistant from the corners. Bring the corners into the center of the square, pressing the tip of each one at the center with the thumb, so that all four corners are fastened together at the center of the square.

Rest the squares for 20 to 30 minutes in the refrigerator.

Baking

Bake the squares in a moderate oven at 230°C (450°F) until golden brown.

Finishing

After the pieces cool, generously sprinkle them with confectioners' sugar.

Cream-filled squares can be further decorated by lightly brushing strawberry, red currant, or other red jelly onto the corners of the pastries.

Storage

Cream-filled squares can be stored in the refrigerator for up to 48 hours. They also freeze well.

Mille-feuilles à la pièce (Individual napoleons)

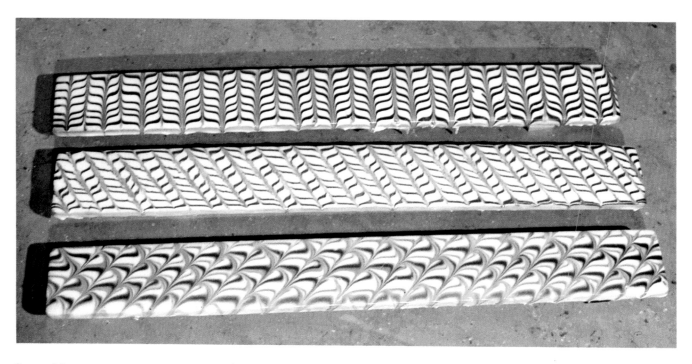

Composition

Puff pastry with six or seven turns or puff pastry trimmings, flavored pastry cream, fondant or confectioners' sugar

One sheet of puff pastry, weighing 750 g (26.5 oz.), filled with 750 g to 1 kg (26.5 to 35 oz.) of pastry cream yields 12 to 14 pieces.

Procedure

Roll out a sheet of puff pastry dough 40 by 60 cm (16 by 24 in.) and 2 mm (1/16 in.) thick. Prick the dough well with a roller docker. Roll the sheet of dough up on the rolling pin and unroll it onto a sheet pan (preferable blue steel) lightly moistened with water.

With the rolling pin or the back of a chef's knife, trim off any dough hanging over the sheet pan by rolling or scraping the dough against the edge of the pan (this can be done only with the low-sided blue steel sheet pans; if another type of sheet pan is used, cut the dough so it will fit inside the sheet pan).

Rest the dough for a long time, approximately 2 hours.

Baking

Bake the sheet of dough in a moderate oven at 200°C (375°F). Turn the sheet of dough over halfway through baking, when it begins to brown. Sprinkle confectioners' sugar on the dough at this point.

Avoid baking the puff pastry in an excessively hot oven. This can cause the dough to be undercooked and doughy in the middle, overdone on the surface. If the sheet of puff pastry is properly baked, the napoleons will be flaky and crisp, an even golden brown all over.

Examine the layers: if the middle section of the layers is very pale, return the pastry to the oven.

If, during baking, the sheet of dough buckles, cover it with a rack to keep it even.

Remove the rack and cool the dough after baking.

Assembling the Napoleons

Once the puff pastry is completely cool, the napoleons can be assembled.

Cut the baked sheet of puff pastry lengthwise into three equal bands. Trim the edges. Place one band of puff pastry dough on the work surface, then a layer of flavored pastry cream; repeat, and finish by placing the third band of puff pastry on top.

Advice for Assembling

Place the least attractive band of puff pastry in the middle. The best band should be reserved for the top and should be turned over so the smoother side is facing up. The band used for the bottom layer should be placed face up so the smoother side is supporting the piece.

Most often the borders of the puff pastry buckle most, which is why the middle strip of the pastry sheet is usually used for the top of the piece.

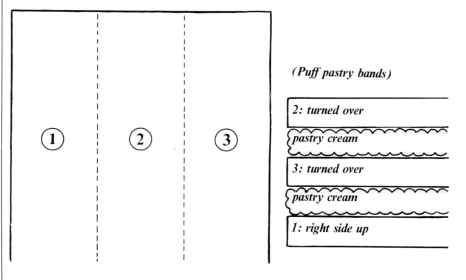

(Puff pastry bands)

2: turned over

pastry cream

3: turned over

pastry cream

1: right side up

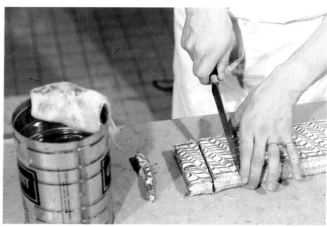

Press the piece somewhat firmly with a rack or wooden board reserved for this purpose, to secure the layers.

Trim the sides if necessary. Smooth a thin layer of cream around the sides using a metal spatula. The pastry cream can be flavored with rum, Kirsch, or Grand Marnier.

Glazing or Icing

Sprinkle with confectioners' sugar or smooth on a layer of fondant.

Marbling

A thin layer of apricot preserves, heated to boiling, can be spread over the surface of the top layer of puff pastry with a metal spatula. Once the preserves cool, smooth a thin layer of fondant, slightly warmed, over the top layer using a metal spatula.

With a paper cone filled with a different colored fondant, quickly draw

parallel lines spaced 1 to 2 cm (3/8 to 3/4 in.) apart lengthwise over the surface of the napoleon. Quickly drag the back of a small paring knife through the lines, on a bias or vertically.

Leave enough space between the verticals made with the knife in one direction (up to down) so that verticals can be made between them with the knife moving in the opposite direction (down to up).

This procedure of glazing and decoration is called *marbling*. It must be done very quickly before the fondant has time to set.

Trim off the ends of the napoleon and cut the piece into individual portions, which can be placed on a rack or sheet pan.

Storage

Napoleons can be stored for a maximum of 2 hours in the refrigerator.

Gros mille-feuilles (Large napoleons)

Procedure

Roll out a circle of puff pastry (trimmings or fresh dough) 2 mm (1/16 in.) thick. The dimensions depend on the size of the piece to be made.

Prick the circle of dough well with a roller docker. Cut out either three circles or squares of equal size. Place them on sheet pans lightly moistened with water.

Resting and Baking

Same as for individual napoleons (see page 202).

Assembling

In general, the assembly is the same as for individual napoleons.

Trim the baked puff pastry to fit a cardboard on which the pastry can be assembled.

Place a small dollop of pastry cream on the center of the cardboard and place the first layer on the cardboard. (Use the least attractive layer of puff pastry for the second, middle, layer of the napoleon.) The pastry cream will anchor the piece in place.

Finish assembling as for individual napoleons.

Marbling

After spreading a layer of slightly warm fondant over the top of the piece, with fondant of a different color, draw concentric circles spaced approximately 1 to 2 cm (3/8 to 3/4 in.) apart.

Quickly drag the tip of a small paring knife through the circles. Start at the center of the piece, dragging the knife to the edge. Leave enough space between the first set of lines to then drag the knife in the opposite direction, from the edge of the piece toward the center.

Trim the sides if necessary, and spread a thin layer of pastry cream around the sides using a metal spatula.

The sides of the napoleon can be decorated with grilled, chopped, or sliced almonds colored with green coloring (optional) or with crumbs of puff pastry.

The above description is a classic method of marbling napoleons, but there are various ways to decorate these pieces, according to the preference of the pastry chef.

Le Mille-feuilles Surprise (Surprise Napoleons)

Composition

Puff pastry with six or seven turns or puff pastry trimmings, génoise, flavored pastry cream, candied fruits or raisins, confectioners' sugar or fondant, flavored sugar syrup (1260 D)

Procedure

Roll out a sheet of puff pastry, and cut either two bands or two circles, as for the previous procedure. Place the bands or circles of dough on a lightly moistened sheet pan, prick, rest, and bake as indicated in the preceding procedure.

Assembly

Gather the following: two pieces of baked puff pastry, a layer of génoise (the same size as the puff pastry), and flavored pastry cream with candied fruits or raisins. Assemble the piece as for the classic napoleon, substituting the middle layer of puff pastry with the layer of génoise moistened with a flavored sugar syrup.

Decorating

This type of napoleon can be decorated according to personal taste. For examples, see the photo at the bottom of the page.

Storage

Napoleons can be stored in the refrigerator for up to 24 hours.

Mille-feuilles Royal (Royal Napoleons)

Composition

2 bands of puff pastry with 7 turns
1 band of vanilla sponge cake
red currant preserves
pastry cream
Chantilly cream
caramel
almond craquelées (sweet roasted almonds)

The procedure for making royal napoleons is the same as for the preceding napoleons; arrange the layers following the diagram at right.

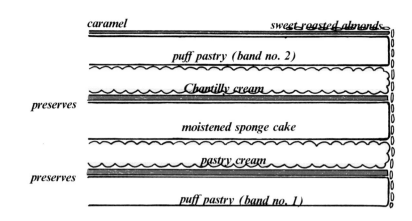

caramel — sweet roasted almonds
puff pastry (band no. 2)
Chantilly cream
preserves
moistened sponge cake
pastry cream
preserves
puff pastry (band no. 1)

Pommiers confiture (Apple-filled puff pastry)

Composition

Puff pastry with six turns plus trimmings, apple compote or marmalade, egg wash.

For one sheet of puff pastry 40 × 60 cm (16 × 24 in.), use approximately 750 g (26.5 oz.) fresh dough and trimmings.

Procedure

Roll out a circle of dough 2 to 3 mm (1/16 to 1/8 in.) thick (trimmings can be used). Place it on a sheet pan as for individual napoleons (see page 202). Lightly prick the dough with a roller docker, and moisten the borders with water.

Garnishing

Spread a 1-cm-thick (3/8-in.) layer of apple compote or marmalade (not too liquid or watery). Leave a 5-mm (1/4-in.) border if a tart ring is *not* being used.

Roll out a second sheet of puff pastry from 750 g (26.5 oz.) of dough, 2 mm (1/16 in.) thick. From this sheet, cut thin strips, approximately 5 mm (1/4 in.) wide. Place the strips on top of the apple filling, spacing them 5 mm to 1 cm (1/4 to 3/8 in.) apart. Lightly moisten the strips with water. Place a second row of strips over the first to form a criss-cross. (Another way of decorating can be seen in the photos on this page.)

Glaze the criss-crossed strips of dough with egg wash.

Let the piece rest for 1 1/2 to 2 hours in the refrigerator. After resting, glaze again with egg wash.

Baking

Bake the pastry in a hot oven, 240° to 250°C (475° to 500°F). Finish baking by lowering the oven to 200°C (375°F).

Finishing

Toward the end of baking, liberally sprinkle on confectioners' sugar and return the pastry to a hot oven to glaze it. The tart can also be glazed by brushing on apricot preserves, using a pastry brush, after baking is completed.

Tips

The same presentation can be obtained

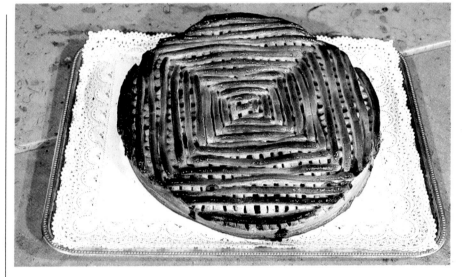

using a special roller made for this purpose, which cuts even strips of dough to the size needed and saves a great deal of time. Another way of speeding up this procedure is to place a whole sheet of puff pastry on top of the apple filling, without cutting strips. After resting in the refrigerator and applying the second glaze of egg wash, score the pastry with a criss-cross design. The scoring can also be made so as to define individual servings, making the tart easier to cut after baking.

Variations

Replace the apple compote or marmalade with apricot preserves.

Following the same procedure as above, the dough (with either filling) can also be cut into circles and used to line a tart ring.

Cutting and shaping pâte à brioche

When pâte à brioche is ready for cutting and shaping, it should be turned out onto a lightly floured pastry marble or work surface. Treat it gently and avoid working it unnecessarily.

Gently press on the dough with the hands held flat in order to push out any accumulated carbon dioxide.

This also flattens and tightens the dough slightly, making it easier to shape and mold.

Cut the dough into strips, which can then be shaped into elongated sausages. Be careful not to overwork the dough at this point.

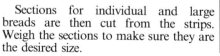

Sections for individual and large breads are then cut from the strips. Weigh the sections to make sure they are the desired size.

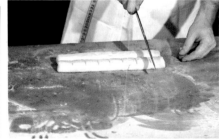

Petites brioches tête (Miniature round brioches)

Composition

Pâte à brioche, egg wash

500 g (17.5 oz.) of pâte à brioche will yield from 12 to 16 miniature brioches, depending on their size.

Equipment

Molds, sheet pans, brush (for flour), chef's knife, pastry brush

Procedure

Cut a 500-g (17.5-oz.) strip of dough and lay it out on a lightly floured pastry marble. Cut it in two lengthwise.

Form the two strips into sausage shapes, with diameters of 2.5 to 3 cm (1 to 1.5 in.). Cut each of the sausages into twelve to sixteen equal parts. Weigh to make sure all the pieces are the exact

same size before rolling them into balls.

Take a piece of the dough and roll it in a circular motion on the work surface with the palm of the hand. Work quickly, without pressing down on the balls. When the balls are finished, make sure

that any wrinkles or folds are on the bottom.

Cover the balls with a damp towel or plastic wrap to protect them from air and let them rest for 10 minutes.

The pieces of brioche dough are then divided into top and bottom sections. The small ball, which forms the top, should use about one-third of the dough, and the

bottom, two-thirds. Roll the balls of dough with the side of the hand using a back-and-forth motion to mark the division (do not actually divide).

Place the shaped dough into a buttered brioche mold, holding the top between three fingers dusted with flour. Without letting go of the top part of the dough, press the three fingers halfway into the dough, to form three holes.

Rotate the mold while pressing the edges of the top ball onto the base with the forefinger.

Brush the brioches with egg wash. Be careful that no excess egg wash runs between the dough and the sides of the mold. This would cause the dough to adhere to the mold and rise poorly. It would also make the brioches difficult to remove.

Final Rising

Place the brioches in a proof box or warm place, 38°C (100°F), to rise. Make sure the brioches are protected from drafts, which would cause the dough to form a crust and inhibit rising. If the brioches start to form a crust, be sure that the proof box is humid enough. If not, place a pan of hot water on the bottom to increase the humidity.

The length of time needed for the final rising depends on the size of the brioches, the amount of yeast used in preparing the dough, and the temperature of the proof box.

A degree of experience is necessary to judge if the dough is ready for baking or if a longer rising period is needed.

Generally, miniature brioches are ready to be baked when they have doubled in volume and rise above the edge of the molds.

Baking

Brush the brioches a second time with egg wash, taking the same precautions as noted above. Place them on hot sheet pans.

Cook in a very hot oven, 240° to 250°C (475° to 500°F) for 8 to 10 minutes.

Removing from Molds

Twist the brioches around in the molds when they first come out of the oven.

Once they have cooled somewhat, transfer them to cake racks.

Serving the Brioches

Brioches are best served warmed, up to 12 hours after they come out of the oven.

Once the brioches have been baked, they do not freeze well. They are always best when served fresh.

Grosse brioches tête (Large round brioches)

Composition and Equipment

Same as for miniature round brioches.

The weight of large round brioches can range from 100 g to 1 kg (3.5 to 35 oz.), but they are usually not smaller than 125 g (4 oz.) or larger than 750 g (26.5 oz.).

Procedure

Cut the brioche into the appropriate-sized sections. Divide each of the sections of dough in two, one-third for the tops and two-thirds for the bases.

Lightly flour the work surface and the hands. Gently press on the larger pieces of dough (the bases) with the palm of the hand to force out the carbon dioxide. Gently press on the sides of the pieces to form them into balls.

Place the balls of dough on the work surface with any seams or wrinkles facing down and the smooth surfaces facing up.

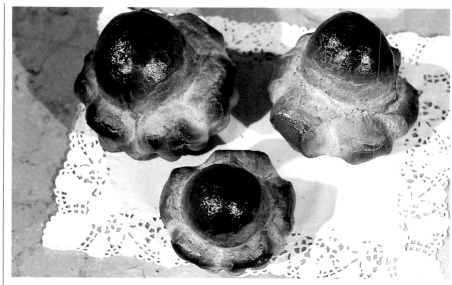

Prepare the smaller sections for the tops in the same way.

Roll the small, top sections into cone shapes with the side of the hand, shaping them like miniature brioches, by making an indentation in the dough that indicates the top and the base.

Place the brioches in the molds. Hollow a hole in the middle of the base with the tips of the fingers, to form a funnel shape.

Gently roll them between the palms of the hands until they are smooth and perfectly round.

Push the top of the brioche into the base by placing the small ball of the top into the funnel-shaped hole of the base and gently pressing the top into the base. A lip should form around the bottom of the top section.

Press this lip into the hole in the base with the tips of the fingers, which should be coated with flour. Make sure the top is firmly attached to the base.

Carefully brush the brioches with egg wash and allow them to rise. Follow the same precautions described for miniature round brioches.

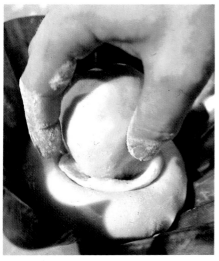

Baking

Brush a second time with egg wash. Make 1- to 1.5-cm-deep (3/8- to 5/8-in.) cuts around the outer edges of the brioches using a pair of sharp, pointed

scissors dipped in cold water (the water keeps the scissors from sticking to the dough).

Bake the brioches in a medium oven, 200° to 210°C (400°F); about 25 minutes of baking is needed for a 250-g (9-oz.) piece.

Removing from Molds and Serving

Same as for miniature round brioches.

Variations

Luncheon-style Miniature Brioches

Use 500 g (17.5 oz.) pâte à brioche, divided into 28 pieces.

Petit Four Brioches

Use 500 g (17.5 oz.) pâte à brioche, divided into 42 pieces.

These can be prepared in the same way as miniature round brioches, or they can be shaped and placed directly on sheet pans.

Brioche Nanterre (Brioche loaves)

Composition

Pâte à brioche, egg wash

Equipment

Loaf pans, knife or pastry cutter, scissors, flour brush, pastry brush, sheet pans.

Choose loaf pans based on the amount of dough being used:
- 18 × 8 × 7 cm (7 × 3 × 2.5 in.) loaf pans for 300 g (10.5 oz.) of brioche dough
- 25 × 8 × 7 cm (10 × 3 × 2.5 in.) loaf pans for 400 g (14 oz.) of brioche dough

Procedure

Butter the insides of the loaf pans and lightly flour the work surface.

When baking a 400-g (14-oz.) section of dough, divide it into four equal parts of 100 g (3.5 oz.) each. Form each of these parts into balls.

After letting the balls rest for 5 minutes, form them gently with the palm of the hand into oval shapes. Place the sections into the loaf pans, making sure that any seams or wrinkles face down. Space them as evenly as possible. Brush them carefully with egg wash.

Final rising: follow the instructions for miniature round brioches.

Generally, the loaves should be allowed to rise until the dough reaches the top of the loaf pan.

Once the dough has risen, brush it a second time with egg wash. Cut a cross or a lengthwise incision into the top of each ball with a pair of sharp scissors that have been dipped in cold water.

Bake the brioche loaves in a medium oven, 200°C (400°F) for about 30 minutes (for a 300-g [10.5-oz.] loaf).

Remove the loaves from the molds as soon as they are finished baking.

Variation

Loaves of brioche can be made with twice the number of balls (a total of eight for a 400-g [14-oz.] loaf). In this case, two balls should be placed side by side in the loaf pan. The dough can also be braided and baked as a loaf.

Brioche couronne (Crown-shaped brioches)

Composition

Pâte à brioche, egg wash

Equipment

Sheet pan, flour brush, pastry brush, knife or pastry cutter, scissors

Procedure

Lightly coat the work surface and the hands with flour.

Cut the dough into 250 to 500 g (9 to 17.5-oz.) sections. Roll the sections into balls as for brioche loaves. Flatten them slightly.

Cover the sections with plastic wrap to protect them from air and let them rest for 10 minutes. Keep any folds or wrinkles on the bottom. Dust with flour.

Sprinkle a little flour in the middle of each section and make a hole in each with the elbow or the tips of the fingers.

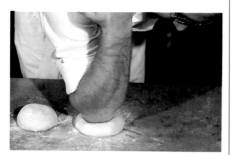

As the dough relaxes, pull the sides of the dough away from the center hole. This process can be repeated several times as the dough relaxes. Continue the process until the dough is stretched to the correct size.

Place the dough on sheet pans or round baking pans that have been buttered or covered with parchment paper.

Brush with egg wash.

Final rising: proceed in the same way as for miniature brioches. Avoid letting the brioche rise in too warm an area. The brioche is ready to bake when it has doubled in volume.

Baking

When the dough has doubled in volume, brush it a second time with egg wash.

Make cuts in the sides of the brioche with a sharp pair of scissors dipped in cold water. The bottom blade of the scissors should be poked into the dough about 1 cm (3/8 in.) from the inside edge. Drag the tip through the dough to a depth of from 1 to 2 cm (3/8 to 3/4 in.). This bottom tip serves as a guide for making the cuts with the top blade of the scissors. The cuts should be arranged to form a sunlike shape.

Bake the brioches in a medium oven 210° to 220°C (400° to 425°F); allow about 15 to 20 minutes for a 250-g (9-oz.) crown. Place the crowns on cake racks as soon as they are baked.

Brioche tressée ou natte (Mats and braided brioches)

Composition

Pâte à brioche, egg wash

Equipment

Sheet pans, medium-size knife, flour brush, pastry brush

Procedure

Lightly dust the work surface and the hands with flour.

Cut rectangular sections of brioche weighing 250 to 400 g (9 to 14 oz.) each.

Divide each of the sections lengthwise into three or four even ropes, all having the same length and width.

Braids

Use three ropes for each braid. Two methods can be used:
A. Start braiding at one end and finish at the other.
B. Start braiding in the middle and finish at each end.

Method A

Place the three ropes next to each other. Stand with the ends of the three ropes facing you.

Take one end of the rope on the left and place it in the middle, next to the rope on the right. Leave the other end in place.

Take the same end of the rope on the right and place it in the middle, next to the rope on the left. Again, leave the other end in place.

Take the rope on the left and place it in the middle next to the rope on the right. Continue until the whole loaf is braided.

Method B

Place the three ropes next to one another, leaving space between each.

Holding the middles of all three ropes gently with one hand, use the other hand to take the half-rope in the center and lift it over the rope on the left.

Take the half-rope in the center and lift it over the rope on the right.

Take the half-rope in the center and lift it over the the rope on the left.

Continue braiding in this way all the way to the end. Turn the braided dough around and finish the other half in the same way.

Mats

Use four ropes for mats. Arrange them in a cross shape, attached at the center.

Take the rope to the left in the left hand and the rope to the right in the right hand. Place the right rope where the left-hand rope was and vice versa. The left hand should pass over the right hand.

Repeat this operation with the two other ropes, which are vertical. The left hand should pass under the right hand.

Continue folding in this way until all the dough has been used. Be careful to alternate the hands consistently so that

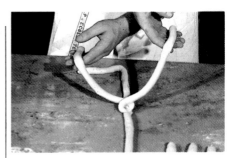

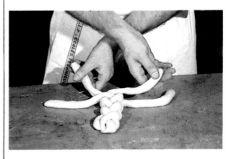

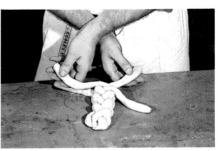

the left hand passes first under the right hand and then over the right hand.

Be sure to seal the ends of the ropes together at the end.

For the final rising and baking of braids and mats, proceed in the same way as for the preceding brioche recipes.

Brioche mousseline (Brioche cylinders)

Composition

Pâte à brioche, egg wash

Equipment

Cylindrical mousseline mold, medium-size knife or pastry cutter, parchment paper, flour brush, pastry brush, scissors

If cylindrical molds are not available, tin cans can be used.

Procedure

Brush the entire inside surface of the mold with butter. Cover the inside with a sheet of parchment paper. The parchment paper should protrude from the top by about one-third. Brush the inside of the paper with butter, including the section that sticks out of the mold. Form a ball of dough that fills the mold halfway, and place it in the bottom of the mold, with any folds or wrinkles facing down. Flatten the ball slightly to eliminate any accumulated carbon dioxide.

Delicately brush the dough with egg wash.

Follow the recommendations for miniature round brioches (pages 207 and 208) for the final rising.

Baking

Bake the brioche when the dough has risen to the top of the mold.

Brush the surface of the dough a second time with egg wash. At this point, the surface may be cut with scissors poked 1 to 2 cm (3/8 to 3/4 in.) into the dough, for decoration (optional). Bake in a medium oven, 200°C (400°F); allow

about 30 minutes for a 250-g (9-oz.) piece of dough. Remove the brioche from the mold as soon as it is baked.

Storage

Brioche cylinders can be frozen and used sliced for canapés and toasts. They can also be cut lengthwise into four slices, buttered and sprinkled with confectioners' sugar, and toasted under the broiler.

Brioche Mousseline "Enroulée" (Rolled Brioche Cylinders)

Roll out a strip of brioche about 4 to 5 mm thick and 30 cm long (1/4 by 12 in.).

Coat the surface of the brioche strip with butter that has been worked until creamy. Roll the sheet of brioche over itself to create a sausage with a slightly smaller diameter than the mold. Place the cylinder of brioche in the mold and press gently so that it is evenly distributed. Glaze, let rise, bake, and cool in the same way as for regular brioche mousseline.

Brioches Hollandaises (Dutch-style brioches)

Composition

Pâte à brioche, tant pour tant (equal parts almonds and sugar ground together—see volume 1, pages 88 to 90) or almond paste, raw egg white, confectioners' sugar, candied oranges or melon (decoration)

Equipment

Sheet pans, knife, flour brush, metal spatula, scissors

Procedure

Lightly flour the hands and the work surface.

Cut the brioche dough in squares weighing from 150 to 500 g (5 to 17.5 oz.), depending on desired final size. Form each section into a ball, and place on the work surface with any folds facing down. Press lightly on the balls to flatten them. Let the balls rest for several minutes and then proceed as for preparing brioche crowns (page 210). Dutch-style brioches are pierced with a knife.

Place the flattened sections of dough on sheet pans or on round baking pans, with any folds facing down. Press the surfaces gently with the palm of the hand to flatten them.

Prepare a sheet of almond paste, thinning it slightly with egg white and flavoring it with vanilla. One brioche serving 8 to 10 people requires about 100 g (3.5 oz.) of almond paste thinned with half an egg white. Tant pour tant can be moistened with egg white in the same way and used instead of the almond paste. The coating of almond paste or tant pour tant should be quite firm. Spread it over the surface of the dough with a metal spatula.

Final Rising

Allow the dough to rise slowly in a proof box or warm area until it has doubled in volume.

Baking

Bake in a 180° to 190°C (350° to 375°F) oven with the door ajar, for approximately 20 minutes.

The brioche should double in volume after baking. Sprinkle the brioche liberally with confectioners' sugar.

Decoration

After baking, decorate with the candied melons and oranges.

Variation: Pain Hollandais (Dutch-style Bread)

Procedure

Form the brioche dough into balls and let them rest. Shape the balls into short loaves (see volume 1, The Shaping of Leavened Dough, pages 164 to 165).

Place the loaves on sheet pans brushed with butter and coated with parchment paper. Press them gently with the palm of the hand.

Spread a layer of almond paste or tant pour tant over the surface of each loaf in the same way as for Dutch-style brioche.

Final Rising and Baking

Follow the procedure for Dutch-style brioche. To make sure the Dutch-style loaves look like bread loaves, make diagonal slashes on the surfaces of the loaves, as when baking regular bread. These loaves may be decorated with candied fruits or crystallized sugar.

Brioche de Saint-Genix (Brioche with candied pralines)

Composition

Pâte à brioche, pink or red candied pralines, egg wash

Equipment

Sheet pan, knife or pastry cutter, flour brush, pastry brush

Procedure

Lightly dust the hands and the work surface with flour. Divide the brioche dough into 150- to 500-g (5- to 17.5-oz.) sections, depending on the desired final size. Work the candied pralines into each section of dough, using about 20 g (1 oz.) of almonds per 100 g (5 oz.) of dough. The pralines can be broken up first.

Form each section of dough into a ball and flatten slightly with the palm of the hand. Place the balls of dough on the sheet pan, with any folds facing down, and brush them carefully with egg wash.

The final rising is the same as for miniature brioches.

Baking

Once the dough has risen, brush it a second time with egg wash. Press some candied pralines into the surfaces of the balls for decoration. The surfaces can also be decorated making cross- or sun-shaped incisions with scissors and inserting the pralines into these.

Bake in a moderate oven, about 200°C (400°F) for approximately 15 minutes.

Individual-sized pastries can be prepared by shaping ten to fourteen pieces from a 500-g (17.5-oz.) section of brioche dough.

Brioche Suisse (Swiss-style brioche)

Composition

Pâte à brioche (about 400 g [14 oz.] for one mold serving 8 people), rum-flavored pastry cream or frangipane cream, rum-macerated chopped candied fruits, egg wash

Equipment

Génoise mold, rolling pin, flour brush, metal spatula, knife, plastic pastry scraper, whisk, pastry brush

Procedure

Butter the génoise mold (these can have different shapes) and coat the inside with a thin layer, 1.5 to 2 mm (1/16 in.), of pâte à brioche. About 150 g (5 oz.) of dough is required to line one mold.

Coat the dough with a 2-mm (1/16-in.) layer of either pastry cream or frangipane cream. Roll out the rest of the dough including the trimmings (it should total about 300 g [10.5 oz.]) into a sheet about 3 mm (1/8 in.) thick and 20 to 30 cm (8 to 12 in.) wide.

Cover the surface of the rolled-out dough with a 3-mm (1/8-in.) layer of pastry cream or frangipane cream, using a metal spatula.

Sprinkle the sheet of dough with 100 g (3.5 oz.) of the macerated candied fruits.

Roll the sheet of dough into a tight

sausage shape. Cut the roll into 2.5-cm (1-in.) slices.

Filling the Génoise Pan

Place one of the slices in the middle of the lined génoise pan and place the others

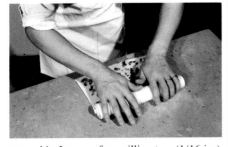

around it. Leave a few millimeters (1/16 in.) of space between the slices.

The slices can also be slightly over-lapped. For this method, it is best to start from the outside edges and work toward the middle. Thinner, 1-cm (3/8-in.) slices should be used.

Brush lightly with egg wash.

Final Rising

Place the constructed brioche in a proof box at a medium temperature. Let

it rise until it reaches the top of the mold. Brush it a second time with egg wash before baking.

Baking

Bake in a medium oven, 180° to 200°C (350° to 400°F) for 30 to 40 minutes, either on a sheet pan or directly on the floor of the oven if a bread oven is being used. Remove from the mold as soon as it is baked and brush the top surface with rum-flavored sugar syrup at 1260 D or with plain rum, using a pastry brush.

These brioches may be presented either plain or decorated.

Decoration

Brush the surface of the brioche with apricot preserves or hot apricot glaze. The edges may be coated with crystallized sugar and the surface may be glazed with rum-flavored fondant.

Regardless of the type of glaze used, the brioche should be placed in a hot oven for a short time to fix the sheen.

The top of the brioche may also be sprinkled with toasted slivered almonds or chopped almonds that have been dyed green.

Storage

Swiss-style brioche can be stored for 24 hours in a cool place.

Variation

The macerated candied fruits may be replaced with preserved oranges or macerated raisins. Swiss-style brioche can also be prepared in individual-sized portions by filling miniature molds with single slices of the rolled dough.

For the final decoration, the brioche may simply be brushed with apricot glaze or sprinkled with confectioners' sugar.

Brioche Noisette (Hazelnut Brioche)

Composition

Pâte à brioche, frangipane cream, praline paste, coarsely chopped, toasted hazelnuts, egg wash

Equipment

Same as Swiss-style brioche

Procedure

Butter the génoise mold and line it with brioche in the same way as for Swiss-style brioche. Cover the bottom of the brioche with a thin layer of praline-flavored frangipane cream. Sprinkle the cream with the chopped hazelnuts.

Proceed in the same way as for Swiss-style brioche, but replace the pastry cream in the rolled brioche with the praline-flavored frangipane.

The final rising and baking are the same as for Swiss-style brioche.

The hazelnut brioche may be served plain or sprinkled with confectioners' sugar.

Produits finis à base de pâte au lait (Milk-based breads and pastries)

Individual Milk-based Rolls "Fougasses"

Composition

Pâte à pain au lait (milk bread dough), egg wash, crystallized sugar (optional)

500 g (17.5 oz.) of bread dough yields 10 to 14 individual rolls.

Equipment

Sheet pans, medium-size knife, flour brush, pastry brush, scissors (optional)

Procedure

The procedure is the same as for miniature round brioches (see pages 207 to 208) up through the stage where the dough is formed into balls.

Roll each of the balls of dough into

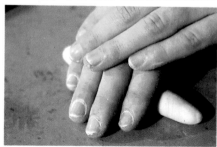

oval shapes. Do this twice to make sure the ovals are perfectly smooth.

Place the ovals on lightly buttered sheet pans with any folds or wrinkles facing down. Press them lightly to flatten them.

Brush the ovals with egg wash.

The final rising of the dough is the same as for miniature round brioches.

Baking

Brush the risen ovals a second time with egg wash. Bake in a hot oven, 240°C (450°F) for 8 to 10 minutes.

Serving and Storing

Serving and storage are the same as for miniature round brioches.

Variation

Milk-based raisin rolls: Add 50 to 60 g (about 2 oz.) macerated dark or light raisins to 500 g (17.5 oz.) of milk bread dough.

Milk-based walnut rolls: Add 50 to 60 g (about 2 oz.) chopped walnuts to 500 g (17.5 oz.) of milk bread dough.

Milk-based hazelnut rolls: Add 50 to 60 g (about 2 oz.) chopped and peeled hazelnuts to 500 g (17.5 oz.) of milk bread dough.

The procedure for making these variations is the same as for plain rolls. Decorative incisions may be cut lengthwise in the tops of the rolls with scissors. The incisions can then be sprinkled with crystallized sugar.

Miniature Milk-based Rolls

500 g (17.5 oz.) of pâte à pain au lait (milk bread dough) should yield 20 to 28 miniature rolls.

The procedure is the same as for

individual-sized rolls except that the miniature rolls should be baked in a hotter oven, 250°C (475°F), for approximately 6 to 7 minutes.

Bite-sized Milk-based Rolls

500 g of pâte à pain au lait (milk bread dough) should yield 48 to 56 bite-sized rolls.

The procedure is the same for the larger milk-based rolls, except that these small rolls should be glazed a second time with egg yolk instead of whole eggs and cooked in an extremely hot oven, 250° to 260°C (475° to 500°F) for about 5 minutes.

Avoid baking bite-sized rolls too slowly, or they will dry out.

Round Sweet Rolls

Composition

Pâte à pain au lait (milk bread dough), crystallized sugar, egg wash

500 g (17.5 oz.) of bread dough should yield 10 to 16 rolls.

Equipment

Sheet pans, medium-size knife, flour brush, pastry brush, scissors

Procedure

Follow the procedure for preparing miniature round brioches (see pages 207 and 208).

Place the balls, with any folds or wrinkles facing down, on lightly buttered sheet pans. The final rising should be carried out in the same way as for miniature round brioches. After the dough has risen, brush it a second time with egg wash and cut the tops with scissors. Sprinkle the incisions with crystallized sugar.

Bake the rolls in a hot oven in the same way as for miniature milk-based rolls.

Variation

The rolls may be flattened or elongated slightly before baking. The rest of the procedure is the same as above.

Brioche-style Loaves

Composition

Pâte à pain au lait (milk bread dough), egg wash.

Use loaf pans of the following sizes:
- 18 × 8 × 7 cm (7 × 3 × 2.5 in.) loaf pans for 300 g (10.5 oz.) of dough
- 25 × 8 × 7 cm (10 × 3 × 2.5 in.) loaf pans for 400 g (14 oz.) of dough

Equipment

Loaf pans or other shaped molds, medium-size knife or pastry cutter, flour brush, pastry brush

Procedure

The procedure is the same as for brioche loaves (see page 209). The only difference is that these loaves are not cut into balls before being placed in the loaf pans—the surface should remain smooth and even.

Variations: Raisin, Walnut, and Hazelnut Bread

Roll the bread dough into a sheet 4 mm (about 1/8 in.) thick. The width of the sheet of dough should equal the length of the loaf pan.

Sprinkle the surface of the dough with a mixture of walnuts, raisins, and/or hazelnuts. Use about 20 g (1 oz.) of this mixture per 100 g (5 oz.) of dough. Roll the nut/raisin mixture lightly with the rolling pin to hold it in place.

Roll the dough into a sausage shape and place it in the loaf pan with the fold facing down.

Brush the dough with egg wash.

Let the dough rise in a proof box, away from drafts.

The bread is ready to be baked when the dough begins to rise over the top of the loaf pan.

Bake 300-g (10.5-oz.) loaves in a medium oven, 200°C (400°F), for 20 minutes. Remove the loaves from the pans as soon as they come out of the oven.

Gâteau Lorrain (Lorraine-style Cake)

Composition

Pâte à pain au lait (milk bread dough) or fougasse, Kirsch-flavored pastry cream, egg wash, confectioners' sugar Allow about 50 g (1.5 oz.) of dough per serving.

Equipment

Sheet pans, rolling pin, flour brush, metal spatula, plastic pastry scraper, stainless steel bowl, whisk

Procedure

Form the dough into a ball and let it rest for about 10 minutes. Roll the ball out with the rolling pin to create a disk 3 to 5 mm (about 1/4 in.) thick. Place the round of dough on a sheet pan, with any folds or wrinkles on the bottom, and brush it with egg wash. Let the dough rise until it has doubled in volume.

Baking

After the dough has risen, give it a second coating of egg wash and bake it in a medium oven, 210°C (400°F), for approximately 15 minutes. When it is finished baking, place it on a cake rack to cool.

Filling

Slice the cake into two layers. Coat the bottom with a layer of Kirsch-flavored pastry cream 3 to 5 mm (about 1/4 in.) thick. Place the second layer over the cream filling. Press it lightly so it stays in place.

Decoration

Sprinkle the top of the cake with confectioners' sugar. Sometimes this preparation is sold by the piece. If so, each piece should be sprinkled separately after it has been sliced.

Variations

The surface of the cake may be coated with apricot glaze and the sides sprinkled with crystallized sugar.

The surface may also be glazed with sugar syrup and decorated with candied fruits. It is also possible to add macerated raisins to the cream filling.

Galette Normande (Normandy Galette)

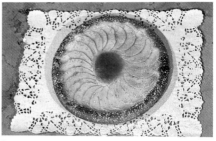

Composition

Pâte à pain au lait (milk bread dough) or fougasse, apples, Grand Marnier– or Kirsch-flavored pastry cream, egg wash, confectioners' sugar. Allow about 50 g (1.5 oz.) of dough per person.

Equipment

Rolling pin, flour brush, tart ring or génoise mold, paring knife

Procedure

Butter the appropriate-size tart rings or génoise molds and place them on sheet pans. Roll the dough out into a circular shape, as for gâteau lorrain (see instructions at left). The diameter of the dough should be slightly less than the inner diameter of the mold or tart ring. Place the ring of dough in the mold or tart ring. Brush the dough with egg wash and place it in a proof box until it has doubled in volume.

Baking

After the dough has risen, brush it a second time with egg wash. Peel and slice an apple and overlap the slices over the edges of the risen dough. Make a rosette shape with apple in the center of the galette. Bake the galette in a medium oven, 220°C (425°F), for approximately 15 minutes. Once baked, remove it immediately from the mold and let it cool on a cake rack.

Decoration

Once the galette has completely cooled, slice it into two layers. Coat the bottom layer with Grand Marnier– or Kirsch-flavored pastry cream. Place the second layer over the cream filling.

Brush the apples on the surface with apricot glaze and sprinkle with confectioners' sugar.

Variation

Cubes of apple that have been sautéed in butter can be added to the pastry cream.

Pains composés (Filled leavened breads)

Polonaises
(Polish-style Brioches)

Composition

Stale miniature round broches, rum-flavored sugar syrup at 1120 D, chopped candied fruits macerated in Kirsch or Grand Marnier, pastry cream flavored with the liqueur used to macerate the fruits, Italian meringue, slivered almonds

Equipment

Sheet pans, aluminum foil or paper muffin cups (or shells made from basic pie dough [pâte à foncer] or puff pastry [pâte feuilletée] trimmings), hotel pan or tray with rack for draining brioches (as for babas and savarins), mixing bowls, whisk, metal spatula, plastic pastry scraper

Procedure

Preparation

Prepare the rum-flavored sugar syrup. Set up the hotel pan or tray with the rack for draining the brioches.

Chop the candied fruits into cubes and combine them with the flavored pastry cream.

Trim the brioches and cut off their caps. Slightly hollow out the centers.

Prepare the Italian meringue.

If preparing pastry shells, roll them out and bake them blind. They should be slightly wider than the brioches (the brioches will be placed inside them).

Constructing the Polonaises

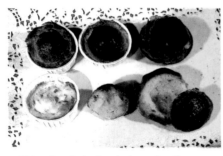

Dip the brioche halves in the rum-flavored syrup and drain them on the

rack placed over a tray. At this point they may be sprinkled with more rum or another liqueur.

Place the bottom halves of the brioches in the tart shells.

Fill the hollows in the brioche bottoms with the flavored pastry cream/candied fruit mixture. Use a spoon or a pastry bag.

Place the caps on the filled brioches. Press gently to hold them in place. Cover the surfaces of the brioches with the Italian meringue, using a metal spatula.

Sprinkle the meringue with raw slivered almonds. Finish by sprinkling with

confectioners' sugar.

Pipe a rosette of Italian meringue in the middle of each polonaise with a pastry bag. Place a candied orange or other candied fruit in the center.

Baking

Place the polonaises in a very hot oven, 240° to 250°C (450° to 500°F) for several minutes to dry the meringue slightly and brown the almonds.

Note

The Italian meringue can be applied to the polonaises with either a pastry bag with a fluted tip or entirely with a metal spatula (see photo at the bottom of page 217).

Variation

Large Polonaises

See photo at bottom of page 217. The procedure for making large polonaises is the same as for individual sizes.

Depending on the size of the polonaise being prepared, the brioche can be cut in three to four slices. The slices can be toasted before being soaked in the syrup.

Construct the polonaises on large aluminum pie tins.

Cover the surface in a decorative way with Italian meringue.

The final baking is the same as for individual polonaises.

Bostoks

Composition

Day-old large brioche cylinders, rum- or Grand Marnier–flavored sugar syrup at 1260 D, almond or frangipane cream, slivered almonds, confectioners' sugar

Equipment

Sheet pans, bread knife, metal spatula, plastic pastry scraper, mixing bowl, pastry brush

Procedure

Trim the brioche and cut it into 1-cm (3/8-in.) slices.

Brush each slice with warm rum- or Grand Marnier–flavored sugar syrup.

Coat the top of each syrup-soaked slice with a layer of the almond or frangipane cream about 3 mm (1/8 in.) thick.

Sprinkle each of the slices with raw slivered almonds and confectioners' sugar.

Bake in a hot oven, 240°C (450°F) for about 10 minutes.

Storage

Bostoks can be kept for a maximum of 24 hours.

Pêches (Peaches)

Composition

Pâte à pain au lait (milk bread dough), pastry cream, sugar syrup at 1140 D flavored with apricot preserves and either Kirsch, rum, Grand Marnier, or vanilla, granulated sugar, marzipan.

Equipment

Sheet pans, flour brush, medium-size knife, paring knife, plastic tub with rack, pastry brush, aluminum foil cups, cake rack

Procedure

Divide a 500-g (17.5-oz.) piece of dough into twenty-four to twenty-eight pieces.

Form each of the pieces into a ball. Place the balls in staggered rows on buttered sheet pans, with wrinkles and folds facing down. Brush lightly with egg wash.

Let the balls rise until they double in volume.

Baking

Bake in a hot oven, 250°C (475°F) for 8 to 10 minutes. Transfer the balls to a cake rack as soon as they are finished baking.

Constructing the Peaches

After the balls of baked dough have cooled, hollow out the bottom of each with a paring knife.

Brush the hollowed-out sides of the rolls with the flavored syrup and place on a rack over a plastic tub to drain.

Fill the hollows with pastry cream flavored in the same way as the syrup.

Press the bottoms of pairs of balls together so they adhere.

Decoration

Brush the surfaces of the peaches with boiling apricot glaze that has been colored either pink or yellow.

Gently roll the peaches in granulated sugar and place them in the aluminum foil cups.

Decorate the peaches with stems or peach leaves made with green marzipan. Normally one leaf per peach is sufficient.

Storage

These peaches will keep for 24 hours maximum in the refrigerator, 5°C (40°F).

Variations

The balls of bread can also be soaked in warm light sugar syrup at 1140 D. Drain them well on a rack and sprinkle them with a liqueur or liquor in the same way as when preparing savarins (see pages 220 and 221).

The balls are then filled with pastry cream from a pastry bag, by inserting a plain tip directly into the flat side of the ball. The two balls are then attached with apricot preserves.

The tops should then be colored with red or green food coloring to imitate peaches. They can then be finished with apricot glaze as explained above.

Pains aux Raisins (Raisin Rolls)

Composition

Pâte à pain au lait (milk bread dough), rum-flavored pastry cream, light or dark raisins macerated in rum, egg wash

Equipment

Rolling pin, flour brush, metal spatula, plastic pastry scraper, mixing bowl, whisk, medium-size knife, sheet pans, pastry brush

Procedure

Method A

Roll out a sheet of dough to a thickness of 3 to 5 mm (about 1/4 in.) and a width of 20 to 24 cm (8 to 9.5 in.).

Spread the surface of the dough with a thin layer of rum-flavored pastry cream and sprinkle it with the raisins.

Fold the sides of the pastry in toward

the middle, as when turning puff pastry, to obtain a long, narrow strip.

Method B

Roll out the dough in the same way as for method A.

Brush one of the long edges of the dough with egg wash with a pastry brush, to the width of the brush.

Spread the center of the strip with the flavored pastry cream and sprinkle it with the macerated raisins.

Pull the side that has not been brushed with egg wash in toward the center of the strip. Fold over the egg-washed side of the dough so that it overlaps the other side by 2 to 3 cm (about 1 in.).

Gently press the strip with the palms so that it holds its shape.

For Both Methods

Slice the strips of dough to the desired lengths, usually 4 to 5 cm (1.5 to 2 in.), using a medium-size knife. Place the raisin rolls onto sheet pans with the folds on the bottom. Brush each with egg wash.

Final Rising

Place the rolls in a proof box and let rise until almost doubled. Finish the rising at room temperature, being sure to protect the dough from drafts.

Baking

Brush the rolls a second time with egg wash. Bake in a medium oven, 210° to 220°C (400° to 425°F), for approximately 5 to 8 minutes.

Decoration

Serve plain or glaze with sugar syrup at 1260 D or confectioners' sugar.

Variations

Walnut Rolls

Use rum-flavored pastry cream and chopped walnuts instead of raisins.

Hazelnut Rolls

Use rum-flavored pastry cream and chopped toasted hazelnuts instead of raisins.

Candied Fruit Rolls

Use Kirsch-flavored pastry cream and chopped candied fruits macerated in Kirsch.

Galette aux Fruits Confits et aux Raisins (Candied Fruit and Raisin Galette)

(sometimes called Galette Bordelaise)

Composition

Pâte à fougasse
Kirsch-flavored pastry cream
Candied fruits macerated in Kirsch

Procedure

Follow the procedure for gâteau lorrain or galette normande (see page 215).

Decoration

Brush the surface of the galette with apricot glaze and decorate with candied fruits. It can also be glazed with sugar syrup.

Escargots ou Schnecks (Snails)

Composition

Pâte à brioche or fougasse; filling: almond cream, frangipane cream, or apricot preserves; macerated light or dark raisins and/or chopped candied fruits; egg wash

Equipment

Rolling pin, flour brush, sheet pan, metal spatula, medium-size knife, plastic pastry scraper, mixing bowl, whisk, pastry brush

Procedure

Roll the bread dough into a strip 3 to 5 mm (about 1/4 in.) thick and 25 to 30 cm (10 to 12 in.) wide. The length of the strip will, of course, depend on the amount of dough being used.

Brush one long side of the dough with egg wash to help seal after folding (optional).

Spread the surface of the dough with a thin layer, 3 mm (1/8 in.), of the chosen

filling. Leave a thin uncovered border around the edges of the dough.

Sprinkle the surface of the filling with the macerated raisins or candied fruits. A mixture of the two may also be used.

Roll the sheet of dough into a fairly tight sausage shape. Begin rolling with the unglazed side so that the roll can be

sealed with the edge that has been coated with egg wash.

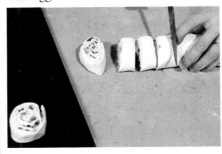

Slice the roll of dough into slices 2.5 cm (1 in.) thick.

Place the slices of dough on the sheet pan and brush them with egg wash.

Final Rising

Place the slices in a proof box. They are ready to bake when they have doubled in volume.

Baking

Brush the rolls a second time with egg wash. Bake in a medium oven, 220°C to 230°C (425° to 450°F), for approximately 5 to 7 minutes.

Decoration

Glaze the surfaces of the rolls with sugar syrup at 1260 D or sprinkle with confectioners' sugar.

Variations

These rolls may also be prepared with walnuts or hazelnuts.

Different Shapes

Proceed as above up to the point where the sheet of dough is rolled.

At this stage, instead of rolling the dough from one end only, roll both ends toward the middle.

Slice this double roll in the same way as for the single roll.

The slices can be placed flat on the sheet pans or can be twisted slightly in

the center.

Brush with egg wash.

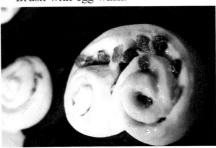

The final rising, baking, and decoration are the same as for the single rolls.

Soaking and final decoration of savarins

The final soaking of savarins, babas, and other similar preparations is simple and requires little or no experience. There are certain precautions, however, that must be closely followed. If the soaking is carried out incorrectly, the effect can be extremely detrimental to the finished product.

Be especially careful to use a sugar syrup with the correct density, at the correct temperature.

Preparing the Syrup

Prepare a syrup with a density of 1120 D, which contains about 450 g sugar per liter of water (16 oz. sugar per 34 fl. oz. water). This syrup should be heated to 90°C (195°F). It is best for soaking day-old savarins.

Depending on the type of pastry being soaked, the density of the syrup can range from 1110 to 1160 D.

Examples

Individual-size fresh savarins: 1140 D

Individual-size stale savarins:
1110 to 1115 D

Miniature stale brioches: 1120 D

Miniature day-old brioches: 1160 D

If the sugar syrup is too dense, it will not penetrate the pastries adequately and will leave hard, crusty sections.

If the syrup is too light, it penetrates the pastries rapidly but tends to drain out once the pastries are taken from the syrup. The pastries will then be too dry.

Temperature and Density of the Syrup

Remember that the density of the syrup should be measured when it is at the temperature at which it will be used.

Savarins that are cold or stale should be soaked in hot syrup, 90°C (195°F). Warm syrup is suitable for savarins that are relatively fresh.

Soaking the Pastries

Two methods can be used to soak the pastries in sugar syrup.

1. Immersion

Submerge the pastries in the sugar syrup, which should be at the right temperature and density.

Use a skimmer or spider to push the pastries into the syrup with their porous sides (the side that was in the mold) face down. The syrup should quickly penetrate the pastries.

Turn the pastries over and soak the firmer sides in the syrup. This takes somewhat longer, but eventually the syrup will soften the hard base. This process continues as the savarins are being drained. The syrup passes through the hard base as the excess drains out (see sketch on page 221).

2. Pouring the Syrup

This method involves pouring the syrup directly over the pastries with a ladle or saucepan. This method takes longer than the immersion method and is used only for pastries that are too large or are considered too fragile to be soaked.

When immersing large pastries, place a rack in the bottom of the pan or tray so that the pastries can be more easily removed.

Whichever method is used, be sure to pinch the pastries with the tips of the fingers to make sure that no hard sections remain.

Once the pastries are soaked, they should be drained over a tray with a cooling rack placed over it.

During the soaking and draining process, the pastries should double in volume. Wait until the pastries have cooled to sprinkle them with the appropriate liquor or liqueur. If they are too hot, the liquor will evaporate.

When sprinkling the pastries with liquor, be careful to add the same amount to each one. Be careful not to sprinkle some twice and others not at all.

Note

Any remaining syrup, including syrup that drains from the savarins, can be used again. First, strain the syrup to remove any crumbs; then heat it to a boil, to improve storage. The syrup can be stored in the refrigerator for up to 48 hours.

Before reusing the leftover syrup, add fresh syrup and heat the mixture to a boil. Check the density and add water or reduce as necessary.

Glazing

After the pastries have been sprinkled with liquor or liqueur, they should be brushed with apricot glaze.

Smaller pastries may be dipped directly into the hot, dissolved apricot glaze and turned out onto aluminum foil or plastic.

Large pastries should be glazed with a pastry brush. It is sometimes necessary to apply several layers of glaze to obtain an appealing sheen.

The pastries can be filled with pastry cream, mousseline cream, Chantilly cream, or fruit.

The pastries can be decorated with candied fruits, slivered almonds, candied mimosa flowers, candied violets, or other appropriate garniture.

Storage

Finished savarins will keep for 24 hours in a cool place.

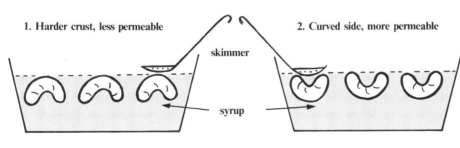

1. Harder crust, less permeable **2. Curved side, more permeable** **3. Drainage**

skimmer

syrup

high-sided sheet pan and rack

Step 1: fairly brief immersion, with softer, curved side down

Step 2: longer immersion, as the firmer crust needs more time to absorb the syrup

Step 3: allow the excess syrup to drain; it can be reused

Pains au chocolat et croissants amandes (Chocolate rolls and almond croissants)

Composition

Pâte à croissant (croissant dough) with 2.5 or 3 turns; chocolate strips *or* almond paste, raw egg whites, vanilla, apricot glaze, rum-flavored sugar syrup, and slivered almonds: egg wash

Equipment

Rolling pin, flour brush, medium-size knife, sheet pans, pastry brush

Chocolate Rolls

Procedure

Roll the pastry into a sheet 2.5 to 3 mm (about 1/8 in.) thick. Cut it into strips 10 cm (4 in.) wide. Then cut these strips into rectangles 8 × 10 cm (3 × 4 in.). Place a chocolate strip on each pastry rectangle about 2 cm (3/4 in.) from the edge. A second chocolate strip may be added after the first fold. Fold one side of the pastry and then the other

over the chocolate. Place the pastries on sheet pans with the folds on the bottom. Brush with egg wash. For rising and baking, see volume 1, Cutting and Baking Croissants, pages 182 to 185. Brush

a second time with egg wash before baking in a hot oven.

Almond Croissants

Procedure

Roll the pastry into a sheet 2 to 2.5 mm (about 1/8 in.) thick. Cut into 12-cm (5-in.) strips. Cut each of these strips into triangles with bases of 14 cm (6 in.)—slightly larger than regular croissants. Lightly brush the edges of the triangles with egg wash.

Using a pastry bag, pipe out strips of almond paste that has previously been thinned with egg white and flavored with vanilla onto the triangles. Frangipane or

almond cream can also be added to the almond paste.

Fold the pastry over the strip of almond paste and then roll up as for regular croissants.

Place the croissants on sheet pans. They can be shaped in the classic crescent shape or left straight. Brush lightly with egg wash.

The almond croissants should be left to rise and baked in the same way as regular croissants (see volume 1, pages 182 to 185). Once the croissants have been baked, brush them with apricot glaze and then with rum-flavored sugar syrup. Sprinkle with toasted slivered almonds or chopped almonds that have been dyed green to imitate pistachios.

Almond croissants can be served in the same way as regular croissants. They are best served warm and very fresh.

Variation

Replace the almond paste with fruit preserves and follow the same procedure.

Etoiles, triangles et gâteaux fantaisies à base de pâte à croissants (Stars, triangles, and special shapes made from croissant dough)

Etoiles (Stars)

Roll the croissant dough into a sheet 2.5 to 3 mm (about 1/8 in.) thick. Cut the dough into squares 10 to 12 cm (4 to 5 in.). Stack five of the squares and make a cut from each corner toward the center, as if forming triangles. Do not cut through the center. Spread the cut squares on the pastry marble.

Brush the surfaces of the squares with egg wash, using a pastry brush. With a spoon or pastry bag, place a dollop of almond paste thinned with egg white and flavored with rum or vanilla in the center of each square. Fold every other triangle corner into the center and attach to the almond paste filling. The final rising, brushing with egg wash, and baking are the same as for almond croissants.

Triangles

Cut triangles from a sheet of croissant dough as for preparing regular croissants.

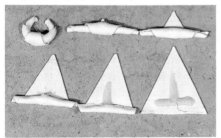

Brush the surface of the triangles with egg wash and sprinkle with chopped almonds. Gently roll over the surface of the triangles with a rolling pin to attach the almonds.

After baking, slice open the triangles and fill them with fruit preserves.

Bredzels ou Lunettes (Pretzels or Spectacles)

Roll croissant pastry to a thickness of 2.5 to 3 mm (about 1/8 in.) and cut it into thin strips 40 cm (15 in.) long and 2 cm (3/4 in.) wide.

Twist the strips of pastry over themselves to form pretzel or eyeglass shapes. Let the dough rise slightly; then fill in the hollow areas with pastry cream. Bake in a medium oven, 220°C (425°F), for approximately 8 minutes.

When the pastries have cooled, brush them with fruit preserves.

Schnecks ou Escargots (Snails)

Composition

Pâte à croissant (croissant dough) with 2.5 to 3 turns, pastry cream or frangipane cream, macerated candied fruits and/or raisins, egg wash

Procedure

Follow the procedure for snails made with milk bread dough (see page 219).

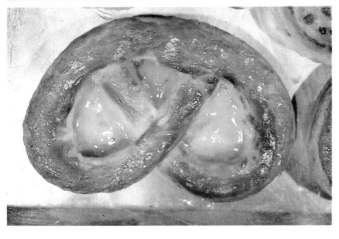

Molding and finishing kouglofs

Composition

Pâte à kouglofs (kouglof dough), egg wash, slivered almonds, confectioners' sugar

Procedure

Divide the dough into sections of the desired size. This, of course, depends on the size of the molds.

Form the sections of dough into balls and let them rest for about 10 minutes before shaping and molding. This makes it easier to shape the dough without tearing it.

While the dough is resting, butter the kouglof molds and sprinkle with the slivered almonds.

Baking

Bake the kouglofs in a medium oven, 180° to 200°C (350° to 400°F), for 20 to 40 minutes, depending on their size.

Remove the kouglofs from the molds as soon as they come out of the oven.

Decoration

Once the kouglofs have completely cooled, sprinkle them liberally with confectioners' sugar.

Shaping the Dough

Shape the dough in the same way as for brioche crowns (see page 210). Make only a hole in the center of the dough just large enough that it will slide easily into the mold.

Place the ring-shaped pastry in the kouglof mold and let it rise in a proof box until it rises slightly above the rim of the mold—no more than 2 cm (3/4 in.).

Glossary

Abaisse (sheet of dough)
A thin sheet of pastry dough that is rolled out with the aid of a rolling pin or electric rolling mill (sheeter) to the desired thickness.

Abaisse

Abaisser (to roll out)
To roll out a sheet of pastry dough to the desired thickness with a rolling mill (sheeter) or rolling pin.

Abaisser

Abricoter (to glaze or coat with jelly or preserves)
To coat a tart, a génoise, mille-feuilles, or other pastries with a thin coat of jelly or preserves using a pastry brush or metal spatula. Its purpose is to:
● give a sheen to finished pastries
● reinforce the fruit flavor already in the pastry
● protect a finished product from air (as for tart Chantilly)
● act as a base layer before glazing with other products such as fondant.
See also **napper.**

Abricoter ou napper

Alcooliser (to add liquor)
To add liquor or liqueur to syrups, sauces, creams, or doughs.

Alcooliser

Appareil (mixture)
Various ingredients that have been combined for a particular preparation but have not yet been baked, glazed, turned into ice cream, or otherwise treated. The term is used not only in pastry but in candy making, ice cream making, and other areas. Examples are "appareil a crème pâtissière" (pastry cream mixture) or "appareil à génoise" (génoise batter).

Appareil

Apprêt (final rising)
The final rising of a leavened dough from the time it is shaped or molded to the time it is baked.

Aromates (flavorings)
Refers specifically to natural flavorings that are used in sauces and other mixtures. Examples include bouquet garni and vanilla beans.

Aromates

Aromatiser (to flavor)
To add flavoring to a mixture, sauce, or cream. Examples are adding vanilla beans and bouquet garni.

Arroser or asperger (to add liquid)
To pour or sprinkle liquid such as water, liquor, or syrup, in a steady stream over a preparation to moisten, soften, or flavor it. Examples are moistening génoise or a baba with syrup.

Aromatiser

Assaisonner (to season)
To season a preparation with pepper, salt, vinegar, nutmeg, or other spices.

Assaisonner

Assouplir (to soften)
To soften butter or shortening to make it more malleable, using a rolling pin or the hands. To render less firm.

Bain-marie, cuisson au (cooking in a water bath)

Cooking method. See **cuire**

Assouplir

Battre (to whip or beat)
To beat a mixture or a preparation such as egg whites or whipped cream with a whisk or electric mixer in such a way as to incorporate air into the mixture and lighten it.

Battre

Beurrer (to butter)
To coat a mold or sheet pan with melted or softened butter with a pastry brush, in order to prevent a preparation from sticking during baking. To coat the inside of tart rings with butter, with the fingers, to help line them with dough and to prevent it from sticking. This facilitates removal of the tart after baking. To add butter to a dough or batter such as feuilletage or croissant dough.

Beurrer

Beurre (butter)
Clarified. See **clarifier**
Manié. See **manier**
Pommade. See **pommade**
Malaxé. See **malaxer**

Beurre noisette (brown butter)
Butter that has been cooked in a saucepan until the milk solids caramelize slightly. Characterized by a hazelnut-like odor.

Beurre noisette

Blanchir (to blanch)
1. To beat together egg yolks and sugar with a whisk until the mixture is white and frothy.
2. To cook a product, starting in cold water, bringing the water slowly to a boil. The length of time depends on the product being blanched.
3. To plunge fruits in boiling water. Certain dried fruits, vegetables, and even meats are blanched in order to soften them before the final cooking.

Certain foods, such as almonds and apricots, are blanched so that their skins can be removed more easily.

Blanchir

Bloquer/débloquer (to stiffen/to loosen)
Often used to describe the various stages in tempering chocolate. Chocolate is said to *bloque* when it sets up after being melted and then congeals. It is said to *débloque* when it is slightly overheated and becomes liquid. If it reaches this stage, chocolate must be tempered again before it can be used for molding or dipping. Certain mixtures are loosened by adding liquids before mixing with other, lighter ingredients, as in soufflés and ladyfingers.

Bloquer/débloquer

Bouler (to roll into balls)
Method of working dough with the palm of the hand, using a circular motion, to obtain even balls used for a variety of preparations.

Bouler

Bouquet garni
A packet of herbs, such as parsley, thyme, and bay leaf, that are tied together and used to flavor stocks, soups, and the like.

Brosser (to brush)
To brush the excess flour or sugar from a sheet of rolled-out pastry. To brush liqueur-flavored candies or fondant to remove cornstarch. To clean the work area with a brush.

Broyer (to grind)
To grind nuts with the use of a special grinder in order to obtain a fine powder or paste.

Bouquet garni

Brûler (to burn)
To burn or overcook. Used also to describe egg yolks that have been allowed to sit too long with sugar or a boiling liquid such as milk. Also said of a dough that is too dry and tends to break apart and remain brittle.

Buée (water vapor)
Water vapor released by baking pastries or boiling liquids. Steam specially introduced into the oven before baking certain leavened doughs, sometimes in an oven specially designed for this purpose.

Broyer

Brûler

Candir (to sugar-coat)
To submerge certain candies (for example, fruit-based or almond paste) in a concentrated sugar syrup called *sucre candi* to coat them with a shiny protective layer of crystallized sugar.

Candir

Canneler (to groove decoratively)
To cut decorative grooves in lemon and orange skins using a special tool called a *canneleur*. To decorate almond paste with a special grooved roller.

Canneler

Caraméliser (to caramelize)
To coat the interior of a mold with a thin layer of caramel.

To add caramel, cooked sugar, or diluted caramel to a cream, sauce, or mixture.

To coat the surface of certain pastries (mille-feuilles, polkas, puits d'amour) with confectioners' sugar and to burn or caramelize the surface with a heating element (caramélisateur) designed for this purpose.

To coat almonds or hazelnuts with cooked sugar or caramel.

Caraméliser

Casser un oeuf (to break eggs)
See *Breaking and Separating Eggs* in the text.

Chapelure (cake crumbs or breadcrumbs)
Breadcrumbs or génoise crumbs that have been dried in the oven and passed through a drum sieve.

Charger/décharger (to weight/to remove weights)
To place weights (cherry pits, dried beans) on unfilled pastry dough covered with parchment paper to hold it down during a preliminary baking, referred to as baking blind (à blanc).

Décharger: to remove weights after baking.

Casser un œuf

Charger/décharger

Chemiser (to line, coat)
To line a chilled mold with ice cream. To line a mold or sheet pan with parchment paper or flour. To line the sides and bottom of a mold with cooked sugar or jelly.

Chemiser

Chinoiser (to strain)
To strain liquids through a fine strainer (china cap) to eliminate certain substances (egg shells or lumps, for example).

Chinoiser

226

Chiqueter (to flute)
To make indentations or incisions on the side of certain uncooked pâte feuilletée preparations with the back of a knife. This is decorative and facilitates even rising of the pastry.

Chiqueter

Ciseler (to incise)
To make light incisions on certain pastries with the tip of a knife to help heat penetrate the interior and to prevent them from bursting open. Also, to dice parsley, lettuce, chervil, or other herbs finely.

Clarifier (to separate/to clarify)
To separate eggs.
   To melt butter slowly so that it separates into whey (skimmed off the top), butter fat (stays in the middle), and milk solids (fall to the bottom). Remove the butter fat (which is the clarified butter).
   To clarify a syrup, stock, or jelly by adding beaten egg whites to the liquid and bringing the mixture slowly to a boil for several minutes. Once the whites have floated to the surface, the liquid should be completely clear. The eggs can then simply be strained or skimmed off.

Clarifier

Coller (to thicken)
To add gelatin that has been softened in cold water and drained, to give a mixture added consistency. See also **gommer.**

Coller

Colorer or teinter (to color/to dye)
To color a mixture (sauce, cream, dough, cooked sugar) with either an authorized artificial food coloring or a natural ingredient: To color certain pastries in a hot oven.

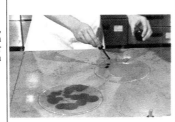
Colorer ou teinter

Concasser (to chop coarsely)
To crush or chop coarsely, as for walnuts, hazelnuts, and coffee beans.

Concher (to smooth)
To work chocolate to make it smooth and homogeneous.

Confire (to preserve in sugar)
To submerge fruits in sugar syrup to preserve them or for the preparation of fruits confits (candied fruits).

Congélation and surgélation (to freeze and deep-freeze)
To freeze at an extremely low temperature to preserve and solidify foods.

Corner (to scrape)
To scrape the sides of a mixing bowl or other container with a rubber spatula or pastry scraper so as to prevent waste. A well-scraped container should have no remaining matter.

Concasser

Corner

Corps (body)
A dough is said to have developed body when it has become elastic after successful kneading. Working a dough develops its body by activating the gluten to obtain elasticity, smoothness, and malleability.

Corps

Coucher or dresser (to pipe out)
To place batter on a sheet pan or in a mold using a pastry bag with a plain or fluted tip. Examples are *coucher des éclairs* or *dresser des choux.* Piping batter with the pastry bag at an angle is called *coucher.* If the bag is held straight up and down, piping is *dresser.*

Coucher ou dresser

Couler (to mold liquids)
To fill molds or embossed sheets with a liquid or semisolid either with a special funnel designed for this purpose (fondant) or mechanically for candy making.

couler

Couper or découper (to cut)
To slice a génoise or other cake in two or three layers with a serrated knife in order to fill it. This is done as follows :
● Mark the sides of the cake with the knife in order to cut it evenly.
● Cut around the sides of the cake in order to obtain even slices.
   Also, to cut pastries such as cakes, tarts, or ice creams with a knife.

Couper ou découper

Couvrir (to cover)
To protect a preparation from air by covering with plastic wrap, aluminum foil, a wet towel, etc. To cover a preparation during baking to prevent it from browning excessively.

Cracher (to split open)
1. The splitting open of a decorative incision made in a pastry in an appealing way when baked. Examples are Pithiviers, turnovers, and other feuilletée pastries.
2. The opening of an incision of any type because of heat.

Crémer (to cream)
To work a mixture so that it has a creamy consistency. To combine butter with sugar and eggs until it has a creamy consistency, either by hand or in the electric mixer.

Couvrir

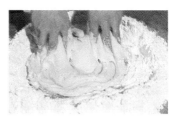
Crémer

Cribler (to roll)
To roll a mixture or substance inside a drum sieve, in order to separate particles. Hazelnuts are treated in this way to remove their skins.

Cristalliser (to crystallize)
To roll pastry or candy (fruits and fruit pastes) in crystallized sugar to coat them. To cook certain syrups to the stage where they crystallize. See also **candir.**

Cribler

Croûter (to crust)
To form a crust through exposure to air. Used to describe dough or creams that have been exposed to air and have dried and formed a thick, dry crust. The formation of a crust is caused by too low a humidity or a sudden change in temperature. To avoid this, doughs and creams should be covered at all times with plastic wrap or aluminum foil. The humidity can also be increased (for example, by putting water in a proofing oven).

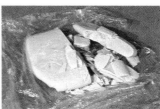
Croûter

227

Cuire (to cook)
Different cooking methods:

au four (in the oven): The temperature of the oven and the baking time are both functions of the size of the pastry being cooked.

sur le feu (on the stove): To cook in a saucepan, crêpe pan, frying pan, or other vesicle in direct contact with the flame. Used, for example, for cooked sugar, creams, and crêpes.

au bain-marie (in a water bath): To cook in a container (bain-marie) half-filled with hot water maintained at a temperature of 80° to 95° C (175° to 200° F). The water in the water bath must never boil. For certain delicate preparations, such as custards, diplomates, and terrines, the bain-marie is used directly on the stove.

à blanc (baking blind): Method of pre-baking tart and pie shells for which the fruit or cream used in the filling cannot be baked (crème Chantilly, raspberries, red currants). The method consists of first lining the raw dough with parchment paper, filling it with something to weigh it down (such as cherry pits or dried beans) and baking it ahead of time. The weights prevent the dough from swelling during this initial baking. If the procedure is performed correctly, the tart or pie shell should be an even, pale brown color. For best results, the weights should be removed about 5 to 8 minutes before baking is finished.

pre-cuisson à blanc (half-baking blind): This method is the same as for full à blanc baking, but as the name implies, it consists of cooking the tart or pie shells only halfway. The weights should be removed 5 to 10 minutes into the baking. The shell should then be filled with the appropriate mixture and the baking continued. Examples of preparations requiring this method are tart alsacienne and quiche.

Culotter (to scald)
To scald a mixture in a saucepan by cooking on too high a heat in such a way that the mixture adheres to the sides of the pan and burns.

Décanter (to pour off)
To pour liquids carefully to separate liquids from solids. Melted butter is clarified using this technique. When decanting liquids, pour into another container with great care in order to separate the elements.

Décercler (to remove tart rings)
To remove a ring from a tart, either during baking or as soon as the tart has been placed on a cake rack to cool. The term is also applied to miniature cakes and mousses.

Cuire   au four

au bain-marie

à blanc

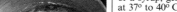
Culotter

Décanter

Décercler

Décorer (to decorate)
To decorate with a variety of ingredients (including cocoa powder, royal icing, chocolate nougatine, sugar, or almond paste) to make the appearance of a preparation more appealing. Decorating requires good taste, dexterity, cleanliness, and professional experience. In this area the professional may freely use his or her imagination.

Décortiquer (to shell/to shuck)
To remove the shell or peel from a fruit, nut, etc.

Décrouter (to remove crust)
To place warm water over the surface of fondant to eliminate the crust that has formed. This operation should precede the working and tempering of the fondant.

Décuire (to reverse cooking)
To add a certain amount of water to a cooking sugar syrup or fruit jelly to lower its temperature. To bring down the temperature once the optimum temperature has been exceeded.

Défourner (to remove from the oven)
To take from the oven, sometimes using a special paddle designed for this purpose.

Déglacer (to deglaze)
In French pastry, this term refers specifically to the removal of caked-on sugar from a copper sugar pan by dissolving it with boiling water. It is also possible to deglaze a hot sugar pan by brushing it with water and a pastry brush.

Dégourdir (to warm)
To warm a liquid, such as water, eggs or a syrup, gently. To temper a liquid, at 37° to 40° C (98° to 104° F).

Déguiser (to fill fruits with marzipan)
To fill certain types of petits fours, made with fruits, with marzipan.

Délayer (to mix with liquid)
To combine dry ingredients with liquids. Examples are powdered milk and water or flour and milk for soufflés.

Décorer

Décrouter

Décuire

Déglacer

Dégourdir

Déguiser

Délayer

Démouler (to unmold)
To remove a hot or cold preparation carefully from a mold. Examples are génoise, savarin, and molded ice creams.

Démouler

Dénoyauter (to pit)
To remove the pits from certain fruits using a special pitter. Examples are plums, cherries, and olives. Also, to remove the pits from certain fruits such as prunes and dates by opening them with a paring knife.

Dénoyauter

Denteler (to indent or scallop)
To cut the edge of a Pithiviers in a decorative scallop shape using a paring knife.

Denteler

Dessécher (to dry)
To dry a mixture by working it over the stove with a spatula to cause the moisture to evaporate. Pâte à choux (cream puff pastry batter) is an example. It is dried out over the stove before the eggs are added. To place certain preparations in an oven or proofing oven to dehydrate them.

Dessécher

Détailler (to section)
To divide dough into several chunks or pieces; for example, dividing a 500-g (17.5-oz.) piece of dough into 14 small balls, rolling out dough and cutting out turnovers, Pithiviers, or other pastries using a pastry cutter. Also, to cut a sheet of pastry dough using a knife; for example, cutting a strip of rolled-out pastry dough to form croissants.

Détailler

Détendre (to thin)
To thin a mixture (a dough, cream, batter, or other liquid or semiliquid) by adding liquid ; for example, thinning heavy cream by adding milk.

Détendre

Détrempe
A mixture of flour, water, salt, butter, and sometimes sugar or yeast used in the preparation of pâte feuilletée (puff pastry dough) or croissants.

Détrempe

Développer (to rise)
The rising of a dough or mixture caused either by heat or fermentation.

Développer

Dissoudre (to dissolve)
To dissolve ingredients such as salt and sugar in a liquid such as water or milk.

Dorer (to glaze)
To brush the surface of certain pastries with glaze (such as egg wash), to prevent the formation of a crust, to give a sheen, to help form a finer crust, or to develop an appealing brown appearance. Glazing is also used to attach two pieces of pastry dough during baking and to avoid the misshaping of certain preparations in the oven.

Dorure (glaze)
Mixture of beaten eggs that have been strained. Different types of glazes are used for different preparations : whole beaten eggs that have been salted and strained, whole eggs combined with yolks and milk or water, egg yolks combined with milk or water. Also, a mixture of milk and sugar or salt. A colored glaze contains caramel or coffee extract (as for sablées).

Doubler/tripler (to double or triple sheet pans)
To bake on a doubled or tripled sheet pan to help prevent the bottom of a pastry from browning too rapidly. This protects the pastries from the heat of the oven floor.

Dresser (to plate)
To place a preparation on a platter or plate for final presentation to the customer. Also, to arrange raw pastries such as croissants on a sheet pan in an orderly way. See also **coucher.**

Ebarder (to trim)
To trim the edges of cooked sugar preparations or molded chocolates with scissors or a paring knife.

Ebouillanter or échauder (to plunge in boiling water)
To plunge nuts or fruits in boiling water to facilitate the removal of the skin or shell. Examples are almonds and tomatoes.

Ecaler (to shell)
To remove the shell or skin from fruits and nuts such as walnuts and hazelnuts. To remove the shell from hard-cooked eggs.

Ecraser (to crush/to smash)
To force fruits (peeled and blanched if appropriate) through a drum sieve with a pastry scraper to turn them into pulp or puree.

Ecumer (to skim)
To remove froth and scum from the surface of a simmering liquid such as syrup or jelly, using a skimmer or spoon.

Effiler (to slice thinly)
To cut almonds, pistachios, or other nuts into thin slices using a paring knife or a special machine designed for this purpose (*effileuse* or *râpe à effiler*).

Egaliser (to trim/to smooth)
To trim certain pastries before their final assembly so the surfaces are even and flat. Used for génoises and meringues.

Egoutter (to drain)
To put a substance in a colander, strainer, china cap, drum sieve, etc., to drain off excess liquid.

Dissoudre

Dorer

Ebarder

Ebouillanter ou échauder

Ecaler

Ecraser

Ecumer

Egaliser

229

Emincer (to slice)
To slice pears, apples, peaches, onions, mushrooms, and other fruits and vegetables thinly.

Emincer

Emulsionner (to prepare an emulsion)
To make a mixture of butter, oil, or other fats and egg yolks. The particles of fat are held in suspension by forming a liaison with the egg yolk (as in mayonnaise).

Enfourner (to put into the oven)
To place in the oven, sometimes using a special paddle designed for this purpose.

Emulsionner

Enrober (to coat)
To cover a preparation completely with a protective and decorative layer of chocolate, cooked sugar, fondant, or other coating.

Enrober

Envelopper (to seal)
To enclose butter or shortening within a détrempe for the preparation of croissants or pâte feuilletée (puff pastry dough).

Epaissir (to thicken)
To thicken a cream or other mixture by adding a thickener such as starch or flour.

Eplucher (to peel/to trim)
To remove the peel from a fruit or vegetable. To remove what is spoiled or unusable.

Envelopper

Equeuter (to stem)
To remove the stem from washed and drained fruits.

Etaminer (to filter)
To filter a liquid through a fine-mesh strainer or through cheesecloth.

Equeuter

Etuver (to warm or to cook covered)
To place certain preparations in a warm oven or proofing oven to dry them or protect them from humidity. Examples are fruit pastes, liqueur candies, and nougatine. Also, to place certain types of dough in a proofing oven in order to encourage rapid fermentation. Also, to cook certain ingredients slowly in a covered pot or saucepan.

Etuver

Evider (to hollow)
To remove the cores of apples, pears, and other fruits. To remove the inside pulp of a fruit while leaving the outer peel intact, as for oranges and lemons.

Evider

Façon (preserving fruit)
Method of preparing preserved fruits (fruits confits) by submerging them in sugar syrups whose density is increased every 24 hours.

Façonner (to shape/to form)
The process of shaping a dough or preparation. An example is the shaping of dough into individual breads or braided breads. Also, to carve a block of ice or shape pastillage.

Façonner

Farcir (to stuff)
To fill the inside of a fruit, pâté, fowl, meat, etc., with a stuffing.

Farcir

Farder (to tint/to dye)
To tint lightly the surface of a substance, such as almond paste, cooked sugar, or pastillage, with food coloring.

Farder

Fariner (to flour)
To flour the work surface (table, marble) or dough lightly to prevent dough from sticking. To flour a mold or sheet pan that has been buttered. This leaves a film, which prevents batters and dough from running over the surface of the mold or sheet pan and also prevents them from sticking.

Fariner

Ferrer (to burn and stick)
A preparation that has accidentally burned on the bottom and thus sticks to the mold or sheet pan. An example is a génoise that has burned and is sticking to the cake pan. Bread that is burned on the bottom and sticks to the floor of the oven is also referred to as being ferré.

Feuilleter (to make into leaves)
To prepare a pastry by enclosing butter or shortening in a layer of dough and folding and rolling the dough to form thin layers or "leaves." Examples are pâte feuilletée (puff pastry dough) and croissants.

Feuilleter

Filtrer (to filter)
To strain a liquid through a fine-mesh china cap, cheesecloth, fabric, or filter paper in order to separate solid particles held in suspension in a liquid. Examples are to filter sugar syrup for babas and savarins and to filter coffee extract.

Filtrer

Flamber (to flambé/flame)
To coat a preparation with liquor that has been preheated to ignite the alcohol vapors. This technique is used for bananas, crêpes, baked alaska (omelettes norvégiennes), and other preparations.

Fleurer (to flour)
See **Fariner.**

Flamber

Foisonner (to whip)
To beat a mixture vigorously with a whisk so that it expands in volume, as in the whipping of cream mixtures.

Foisonner

Foncer (to line with pastry)
To line a tart mold, ring, or baking sheet with a layer of dough so that it holds firmly in the mold.

Foncer

Fonds (pastry bases or stocks)
1. Layers or rings composed of a wide variety of batters and dough, which enter into the final composition of a finished pastry. Examples are fonds de succès, fonds de génoise, meringues, and fonds de tart.
2. Stocks—veal stock, chicken stock, fish stock, etc.—used for the making of sauces and soups. See also **aromatiser.**
3. Roux.

Fonds

Fontaine (flour well)
A hollow space made in the center of flour which has been measured out for the preparation of a dough. The well in the middle is used to hold the liquid ingredients, which are gradually mixed with the flour using the fingertips.

Fontaine

Fouetter (to whip/to beat)
To beat a sauce, mixture, or cream vigorously either by hand or with the electric mixer to smooth it and make it homogeneous. Cream is whipped to incorporate air and make it lighter. See also **foisonner.**

Fouetter

Fournée (pastries for the day)
All of the pastries to be prepared for a particular day. Also, a particular batch of pastries that go into the oven at the same time.

Fourrer (to fill/to stuff)
To fill the inside of certain preparations with creams, mousses, or other mixtures, as for fond de succès (succès base), génoise, meringue, fond de tart (a tart base), and pâte à choux (cream puffs, eclairs).

Fourrer

Fraiser or fraser (to crush dough)
To crush a dough against the work surface or in a mixing bowl to make it smooth and homogeneous without overworking it. It is important that the different components in a dough be well incorporated at this point. To do this, the dough is broken up into sections and either pushed or pulled with the palm of the hand or with a pastry cutter. This method is used for pâte à foncer, sablée, sucrée, and other preparations.

Fraiser ou fraser

Frapper (to chill suddenly)
To cool liquids rapidly by placing them in a freezer or deep-freeze or by plunging them in crushed ice.

Frapper

Frémir (to simmer)
To heat liquid so that its surface trembles, barely simmering, not boiling. Simmering liquid is used for poaching. This simmering stage can be maintained with the help of a bain-marie (water bath).

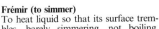

Frémir

Frire (to deep-fry)
To cook submerged in hot fat or oil. This method is used for beignets and bugnes.

Frire

Garnir (to garnish/to fill)
To fill a tart shell with filling or garniture such as creams or fruits. To fill pâte a choux (eclairs, cream puffs). To fill a mold or a pastry bag.

Garnir

Givrer (to frost)
To produce frost, for decoration, on the surfaces of pastries, fruits, etc., that have been placed in the freezer. Frost sometimes resembles confectioners' sugar. The term is also applied to fruits such as lemons and oranges that have been filled with sorbet.

Givrer

Glacer (to glaze)
To give a sheen or glaze to the surface of a pâte feuilletée (puff) pastry by first sprinkling it with confectioners' sugar and then placing it in a very hot oven long enough for the sugar to caramelize. The Pithiviers is an example of this.
To coat the surface of pâte feuilletée with sugar syrup (density 1260), using a pastry brush, as soon as it comes out of the oven, to give it an appealing sheen.
To cover certain pastries such as pâte à choux (eclairs, religieuses, glands) and petits fours with fondant, confectioners' sugar, or chocolate.

Glacer

Glucoser (to add glucose)
To add glucose to a sugar syrup, fruit preserves, or other mixtures.

Gommer (to thicken)
To put a gelatinous substance into a preparation to thicken it. Examples are gelatin added to a crème anglaise or pastillage or pectin added to fruit preserves. See also **coller.**

Glucoser

Grainer or grener (to become grainy)
To produce a grainy texture in incorrectly beaten egg whites, in a sugar syrup that crystallizes, in a fondant that has been overheated and the crust not removed before cooling, or in a crème anglaise that has been overcooked.

Grainer ou grener

Gratiner (to prepare au gratin)
To form a light crust on the surface of a preparation by placing it in an oven or under a salamander. An example is the croque-monsieur.

Gratiner

231

Griller (to grill/to toast)
To color almonds, hazelnuts, or other nuts by roasting in the oven. The nuts are placed in a mold on the floor of the oven, directly on a sheet pan, or in a tart mold placed on a sheet pan.

Griller

Hacher (to chop)
To chop into small pieces, sometimes using a chef's knife (*couteau de tour*) designed for this purpose. In French pastry the term is usually applied to chopping preserved fruits, almonds, pistachios, and other nuts.

Hacher

Homogénéisation (to homogenize)
Method of breaking up minute particles of fat contained in certain mixtures to work the fat evenly throughout (milk, ice cream mixtures). This operation is performed either mechanically using pressure or with a centrifuge. To make homogeneous.

Huiler (to oil)
1. To coat with a fine film of oil to prevent substances from sticking.
2. Badly worked almond paste or praline that has an oily feel and appearance.
3. A leavened dough that is too warm and has taken on an oily appearance.
4. A pâte à choux (cream puff pastry) that has been incorrectly dried.

Huiler

Hydrater (to moisten)
To add liquid to a solid ingredient in order to combine them. An example is water or egg being absorbed by flour.

Imbiber (to moisten)
To moisten with a liquor and/or sugar syrup to give a moist texture and provide flavoring. An example is to moisten a génoise with liquor-flavored sugar syrup.

Imbiber

Inciser (to cut/to make an incision)
To make a cut in a pastry with a sharp knife. An example is to make a cut in a puff pastry galette to put in a dried bean (for children to find during holidays).

Incorporer (to incorporate)
To combine two mixtures to lighten such as folding beaten egg whites into a soufflé, or to carefully fold one mixture into another in order to maintain airyness such as flour into beaten egg and sugar to prepare génoise.

Inciser

Incorporer

Infuser (to infuse)
To cook a substance in a liquid to add its aroma and flavor to the liquid. An example is heating milk with vanilla, coffee beans, cinnamon, or lemon zest.

Infuser

Intérieur (inside)
The inside of a pastry or mixture, which may contain a cream or other filling. Sometimes the interior is glazed with covering chocolate, fondant, etc. Frequently used to describe a wide variety of candies.

Inverti or intervertir (to invert)
To break down complex sugars into simple ones through hydrolysis. An example is turning sucrose into trimoline (invert sugar).

Intérieur

Laminer (to roll out with a machine)
To roll out dough using a machine called a sheeter, designed for this purpose. The machine has two cylinders that roll the pastry.

Laminer

Laver (to wash)
Refers specifically to washing the inside of a copper sugar pan using clean water and a pastry brush. Also cleaning sugar by dissolving it, bringing it to a boil, and skimming off the impurities that rise to the surface with a skimmer. To brush the walls of the sugar pan continually with a pastry brush during the cooking of a sugar syrup to prevent the formation of crystals.

Laver

Levain (a sponge or yeast starter)
A mixture of flour and water that contains either wild or manufactured yeasts and is used to inoculate and initiate the fermentation of leavened dough.

Lever (to rise)
The rising of a leavened dough as a result of fermentation.

Levain

Lier (to bind/to thicken)
To bind a substance with thickeners such as flour, egg yolks, or cornstarch. When using egg yolks, the temperature must never exceed 90° C (195° F), unless flour or starch has been added, or the mixture will coagulate.

Lier

Lisser (to smooth)
To beat a cream or a sauce with a whisk to smooth its texture.
· To make the surface of a cake or pastry smooth or flat using a metal spatula or palette.
To sand the surface of a piece of pastillage or almond paste.
To smooth out starch in a high-sided pan in order to make imprints for liquor candies.

Lyophiliser (to freeze-dry)
Method of dehydrating frozen products by evaporating the crystallized moisture in a vacuum.

Lisser

Macérer (to macerate)
To soak fresh or preserved fruits in a liquid (syrup, liquor, liqueur) to flavor or preserve them. During the maceration, the fruit becomes saturated with the liquid.

Macérer

Malaxer (to work/to mix)
To work or knead butter or shortening to soften and give it an even consistency. To work fondant between the hands to soften and warm it. To work a marzipan to make it soft and malleable.

Malaxer

Manier (to work)
To work together butter or shortening either by hand or in an electric mixer to form a smooth mixture.

Marbrer (to marble)
To give a cake or pastry that has been glazed with fondant the appearance of marble. To obtain this effect, lines of different-colored fondants are applied to the surface of the glazed pastry using a paper cone. The lines are then immediately streaked with a small knife so that they merge with the glazed surface. It is important that this be done rapidly so that the fondant does not have time to form a crust.

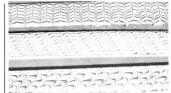
Marbrer

Mariner (to marinate)
To place pieces of fish or meat in a flavored liquid to preserve and flavor them. See also **aromatiser.**

Masquer (to mask/to coat)
To coat a preparation with a cream, a sauce, marzipan or jam using a pastry brush or a spatula in order to form a preliminary coating that will serve as a base for the final decoration. This preliminary coating is often applied before the final glazing of a pastry. A sheet of marzipan can be rolled out and placed over a cake to mask and decorate it. Masking a pastry also helps keep its texture and flavor intact.

Masquer

Masse (mixture)
A combination of several ingredients that form the basis for a finished product. See also **appareil.** The insides of candies are often referred to as the masse.

Masse

Masser (to form/to solidify)
The crystallization of a sugar syrup. Also, the cooked sugar that recrystallizes during or after cooking and becomes cloudy. To work cooked sugar from a liquid and transparent state to a solid, opaque paste (fondant). This may be done in the electric mixer or on a marble by hand.

Masser

Maturation (to ripen/to develop)
Technique used in ice cream making in which a pasteurized dairy product is allowed to ripen at a low temperature so that it develops a better flavor. This process may continue for up to 72 hours.

Meringuer (to stiffen egg whites)
To add a small quantity of sugar to egg whites near the end of beating to stiffen them and prevent them from becoming grainy. To coat a preparation with meringue and glaze it in a hot oven.

Meringuer

Mesurer (to measure)
To measure a liquid using a measuring cup.

Mix (mixture)
Primarily in ice cream making, a mixture to be used in a final preparation.

Modeler (to shape/to form)
To work or knead a substance, such as marzipan, nougatine, or pastillage, to give it texture and eventually a shape. To work one of these materials into a decorative shape.

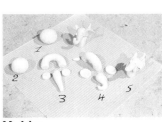
Modeler

Monder (to peel)
To plunge fruits and nuts into boiling water and then rinse them so that the peel can be more easily removed.

Monder

Monter (to beat/to construct)
To beat egg whites with a whisk or electric mixer to increase their volume. Also, assembling a finished cake, such as a moka, in preparation for its final decoration. Also, to construct a finished pastry such as presentation pieces or croquembouche.

Monter

Mouiller (to moisten)
To moisten a sheet pan before placing a preparation on it to be baked. To add liquid (eggs, milk, water) to a mixture. To add water to sugar in order to prepare a sugar syrup or cooked sugar.

Mouler (to mold)
To place a batter or other mixture in a mold so that it takes on the desired form when baked, as for génoise, pâte à cake, nougatine, pastillage, or chocolate. Frozen mixtures such as sorbets, parfait, and ice cream can also be molded.

Mouler

Mousser (to froth/to foam)
To work a sauce or mixture too much, so that it becomes frothy or covered with foam.

Napper (to coat)
To coat a spoon with crème anglaise to check its doneness. To coat a finished preparation with either a cold or hot sauce using a spoon, ladle, or metal spatula. To put the final coating on a cake or tart using a pastry brush or metal spatula. See also **abricoter.**

Napper

Paner (to bread)
To coat a preparation with breadcrumbs after first dipping it in egg glaze (beaten eggs).

Parer (to trim)
To trim the edges of cakes, cookies, génoise, or mille-feuilles before applying the final coating of glaze or before assembling a finished cake.

Parer

Parfumer (to flavor)
To add a flavoring to a preparation. See also **aromatiser.**

Parfumer

Pasteuriser (to pasteurize)
To heat a mixture to a certain temperature :
● for low-temperature pasteurization, the mixture should be heated to between 60° and 65° C (140° and 150° F) for 30 minutes and then quickly cooled to 6° C (43° F).
● for high-temperature pasteurization, the mixture should be heated to between 80° and 85° C (175° and 185° F) for 3 minutes and then quickly cooled to 6° C (43° F).
Pasteurization is used to kill harmful bacteria without altering the flavor or destroying the nutrients in a mixture.

Pasteuriser

Pâton (block of puff pastry dough)
A block of puff pastry dough or croissant dough after the butter has been folded into the détrempe to form an envelope. Section or piece of dough cut to the size of a piece of pastry to be prepared.

Pâton

Peser (to weigh)
To weigh the raw ingredients called for in a preparation. It is important to weigh all needed materials carefully before beginning to work. Also, to measure the density of a sugar syrup using a hygrometer.

Pétrir (to knead)
To work or knead a dough either to work together the various ingredients or to activate the gluten for leavened dough.

Pétrir

Piler (to grind/to crush)
To grind to a powder or paste with a mortar and pestle, as for almonds, hazelnuts, and walnuts.

Pincer (to pinch)
To pinch the edges of a tart or pâté with a pair of pastry pinchers or with the fingers to create a decorative border.

Pincer

Piquer (to prick)
To poke a sheet of dough (such as pâte feuilletée, pâte à foncer) with a fork or a roller docker to produce small holes. The purpose is to prevent dough from puffing irregularly or from shrinking during baking.

Piquer

Pocher (to poach)
To cook in a simmering (not boiling liquid) so that the substances being cooked hold their shape. Examples are fruits (poached in syrup), eggs, and quenelles. Also, a method of cooking certain fragile preparations that must not come into contact with direct heat, such as lemon curd or egg custard.

Pointage (rising/fermentation)
The rising of a fermented dough, which occurs between the kneading and the final shaping and molding of the dough.

Pocher

Pommade (creamed butter or shortening)
Butter, shortening, or a cream that has been creamed to the consistency of a pomade or ointment. Examples are pâte à cake, pâte à quartre-quarts, and creamed butter used for buttering molds and sheet pans.

Pommade

Pousse (rising/expansion)
The expansion of a fermented dough caused by yeast during rising. Also, the puffing of a whipped rising batter caused by baking powder during baking.

Praliner (to coat with cooked sugar)
To coat pieces or whole almonds or hazelnuts with cooked sugar.

Presser (to squeeze/to press)
To squeeze a mixture or fruit to extract liquid. Often a special squeezer or juicer is used especially for fruits.

Praliner

Puncher (to soak)
To soak sections of cake, biscuit, or other baked products with a liquor-flavored syrup.

Quinconce (to stagger rows)
To place batter on baking sheets in staggered rows. Each new row is started one-half space after the one preceding it. This helps the pieces of batter to cook evenly. The spaces between the pastries must be determined based on the anticipated expansion of the batter during baking.

Quinconce

Rabattre (to fold over)
To fold a risen leavened dough over itself in such a way as to force out the accumulated carbon dioxide. See also **rompre.**

Raffermir (to stiffen)
To solidify a dough or other preparation by placing in a cold place (refrigerator or freezer), as when placing a cake in a cold place before the final glazing.
   Also to stiffen a mixture by adding a solid ingredient. An example is adding confectioners' sugar to a glace royale (royal icing).

Rabattre

Rafraîchir (to cool/to refresh)
To add fresh fondant to fondant that has already been used and the crust removed. This is done each time the fondant is to be used. Also, to chill a preparation by placing it in the freezer or refrigerator.

Râper (to grate)
To grate certain substances, such as lemon, orange, nutmeg, or cheese, using a grater.

Rafraîchir

Rayer (to score)
To make decorative indentations or lines in pastry using a paring knife. This should be done after glazing with egg wash but before baking. This method is used for Pithiviers and chaussons (turnovers).

Rayer

Réduire (to reduce)
To reduce a mixture by cooking it down to eliminate excess liquid through evaporation. Used to concentrate the flavor and at times to thicken a final preparation.

Réduire

Relâcher (to soften or liquefy excessively)
Refers to a dough, sauce, or cream that loses its texture by liquefying or softening abnormally. This sometimes happens after kneading or during baking.

Repérer (to mark)
Method of marking the pieces used in the assembly of a final preparation in order to fit them together evenly. This method is used to mark the edges of cakes such as génoise so that they can be reconstructed evenly.

Retomber (to fall)
A preparation that falls in the oven after rising because of a sudden drop in oven temperature, excessive beating, or incorrect baking. Examples are a génoise that falls if the oven is opened prematurely or egg whites that fall if they have been overbeaten. Pâte à choux may also fall if it is taken out of the oven too soon.

Rioler (to decorate with strips of dough)
Method of decorating tarts or pies by placing strips of dough over the surface in a diagonal, lozenge pattern. Refers also to a similar pattern made from jelly piped from a paper cone on such preparations as tarts and tartlets.

Rognures (trimmings)
Trimmings of pâte feuilletée that are left after cutting the pastry for particular preparations. These trimmings may be used for other preparations such as napoleons or tarts. Trimmings that result from preparations made from the rognures are called second rognures. Also, sometimes used to refer to trimmings from cakes and meringues.

Rompre (to push down)
To push down a leavened dough to its original volume after it has risen, by folding it several times over itself. This technique eliminates carbon dioxide that has accumulated in the dough. It also helps stimulate the yeast cells by working additional oxygen into the dough, and it contributes to the final consistency of the dough.

Ruban (ribbon)
Method of measuring the consistency of a batter or preparation by seeing how it falls when lifted with a wooden spoon or whisk. A mixture is said to form a ribbon when it flows evenly off the whisk or spoon and folds over itself and also rests on the surface of the remaining batter. This technique is used most frequently in the preparation of génoise.

Sabler (to break up)
Method used in the preparation of pâte brisée, pâte à foncer, and pâte sucrée, in which the butter and flour are worked together with only the tips of the fingers or by rolling them in between the palms of the hands in such a way as to cause the mixture to break up into little beads or chunks. Also, to recrystallize sugar used in the preparation of praline almonds.

Saisir (to seize/to heat)
To expose certain preparations to intense heat either on the stove or in the oven for short periods of time. This method is usually used at the beginning of baking, before the final baking at a lower temperature.

Retomber

Rioler

Rognures

Rompre

Ruban

Sabler

Salpicon (chopped fruit filling)
A mixture of several types of fresh, preserved, or canned fruits that are cut into even cubes and added to certain preparations such as fruit cakes or diplomates. Also, any preparation that contains a mixture of elements that have been cubed and bound together with a sauce.

Sangler (to freeze)
Freezing ice creams and sorbets by placing crushed ice and salt around a mold filled with the preparation in a container or ice cream machine in order to freeze it. Crème anglaise, cream, and fruit syrups are converted into ice cream or sorbets by using an ice cream machine or sorbetière.
     Also, to place a mold in the freezer before coating the inside with ice cream or sorbet.

Sauce (sauce)
A flavored liquid that can be made from a variety of bases. Many different sauces are used in French pastry, usually as accompaniments to finished pastries, ice creams, etc.

Saupoudrer (to powder/to sprinkle)
To cover the surface of a preparation or work surface with a powder such as chocolate, confectioners' sugar, or flour, to decorate finished pastries or (on work surfaces) to prevent sticking.

Sentir (to smell)
To recognize, appreciate, or judge the quality of a raw ingredient or finished product through smell.

Serrer (to stiffen/to tighten)
To beat certain preparations quickly by making a circular motion with a whisk to obtain a perfectly smooth mixture, as for crème Chantilly and light cream. To stiffen egg whites through a final beating with sugar.

Singer (to flour/to bind)
To add flour to a mixture during cooking in order to thicken or bind the final sauce. It is important to avoid the formation of lumps.

Siroper (to soak in syrup)
To add flavored syrup to a preparation in order to soften, moisten, or flavor it.

Souder (to attach)
Method of attaching two sheets of dough with either water or egg wash. The first sheet of pastry is brushed with a thin layer of egg wash. The second sheet is placed over the first and the two are pressed gently on the outer edges with the fingers.

Stériliser (to sterilize)
To eliminate bacteria from a substance or material by killing them using heat, ultraviolet radiation, or an antiseptic such as household bleach or alcohol.

Salpicon

Sangler

Saupoudrer

Serrer

Souder

Suinter (to sweat/to ooze)
A dough or other preparation in which fat or liquid works out from the inside and coats its surface.

Tabler or mettre au point (to temper)
Method of working melted couverture (covering) chocolate to cool it, using a metal spatula or a triangle. This process is best carried out on a refrigerated pastry marble or other cool surface until the chocolate begins to thicken but not harden or set, before it is brought to the correct temperature for use (such as for molding and dipping).

Tabler ou mettre au point

Tamiser (to sift)
To sift a powder or mixture, usually through a drum sieve, to remove lumps and impurities. This method is most often used for flour, confectioners' sugar, and nut powders. Also, to crush or grind mixtures and to strain them in order to separate different-sized grains. To strain fruits to obtain purees.

Tamiser

Tamponner (to press/to tamp)
To tamp down the surface of a dough-lined mold with a piece of dough in order to press the dough firmly against the inside surface of the mold.

Tamponner

Tempérer or tiédir (to temper/to warm)
To warm a mixture gently without overheating. To warm a mixture to the same temperature as the preparation or mixture to which it is to be added.

Tirer (to pull)
To pull and refold sugar over itself. This operation is repeated until the sugar has a satinlike texture and appearance.

Tirer

Tolérance (tolerance)
The ability of a certain preparation, especially a leavened dough, to tolerate errors in its preparation, such as insufficient fermentation or overrising.

Tourer (to turn)
To give turns to pâte feuilletée or croissant dough by rolling the dough into a strip three times as long as it is wide and folding it in thirds or quarters.

Tourner (to turn/to shape)
To give the final shape to leavened dough before baking. Used most often with breads such as pain de mie (white bread) and pain de campagne (country-style bread).

Tourner

Travailler (to work)
To work or beat a mixture energetically, either by hand or in the electric mixer, to make it smooth, light, and homogeneous.

Travailler

Tremper (to soak)
To soak pastries such as babas or savarins in sugar syrup. Also, to coat certain types of candies with a thin layer of couverture (covering) chocolate, fondant, or cooked sugar.

Tremper

Turbiner (to churn/to turn)
To turn a liquid mixture in an ice-cream maker to convert it into ice cream or sorbet.

Upériser (to sterilize)
To sterilize (not pasteurize) milk by heating it to a very high temperature, 140° to 150° C (285° to 300° F) for 2 seconds, followed by immediate cooling.

Vanner (to stir/to whisk)
To stir a cream, sauce, or other mixture with a wooden spatula or whisk to keep it smooth and to prevent the formation of a film or skin on the surface during cooling.

Venue (raw ingredients)
The specific types and quantities of raw ingredients needed for a particular preparation.

Venue

Videler (to form a border)
To form a border on a tart or pie by folding the dough over itself on the edge with the fingers. This adds a decorative effect and also helps hold the filling within the borders.

Videler

Viennoiserie (Viennese pastries)
Richer leavened pastries. In France, these are usually eaten at breakfast or served at teas. Examples are pâte à brioche, croissants, pâte à pain au lait (milk bread), chaussons (turnovers), and carrés feuilletés (filled puff pastry squares).

Viennoiserie

Voiler (to veil)
To surround a finished pastry or ice cream with a net or veil of spun or pulled sugar. The technique is used for presentation pieces.

Zester (to zest)
To remove the thin, colored zest from a citrus fruit, using either a zester, a tool especially designed for this purpose, or a small paring knife. It is important to remove only the zest and none of the white pith, which tends to be bitter. The purpose of zesting is to extract the flavor from the zest. Also, to grate the zest of a citrus fruit with a small grater.

Zester

Glossary cross references: English / French

add decorative strips : rioler
add glucose : glucoser
add liquid : arroser/asperger
add liquor : alcooliser
attach : souder
bake : cuire, au four
bake blind : cuire, à blanc
balls, to roll into : bouler
beat : battre ; fouetter ; monter
bind : lier ; singer
blanch : blanchir
body : corps
boiling water, to plunge into : ébouillanter/échauder
borders, to form : videler
bread : paner
breadcrumbs : chapelure
break eggs : casser un œuf
break up : sabler
brush : brosser
burn : brûler
burn and stick : ferrer
butter (v) : beurrer
butter (n) : beurre
butter, brown : beurre noisette
butter, creamed : pommade
cake crumbs : chapelure
caramelize : caraméliser
chill suddenly : frapper
chop : hacher
chop coarsely : concasser
churn : turbiner
clarify : clarifier
coat : chemiser ; enrober ; masquer ; napper
coat with cooked suger : praliner
coat with jelly or preserves : abricoter
coat with sugar : candir
color : colorer/teinter
construct : monter
cook : cuire
cook covered : étuver
cool : refraîcher
cover : couvrir
cream : crémer
crumbs, cake or bread : chapelure
crush : écraser ; piler
crush dough : fraiser
crust : croûter
crust, remove : décrouter
crystallize : candir ; cristalliser
cut : couper/découper ; inciser
decorate : décorer
decorate with dough strips : rioler
decorate with grooves : canneler
deep-freeze : congélation/surgélation
deep-fry : frire
deglaze : déglacer
develop : maturation
dissolve : dissoudre

double/triple sheet pans : doubler/tripler
dough sheet : abaisse
drain : égoutter
dry : dessécher
dye : colorer/teinter ; farder
eggs, to break : casser un œuf
emulsion, to prepare : emulsionner
expansion : pousse
fall : retomber
fermentation : pointage
fill : fourrer ; garnir
fill fruit with marzipan : déguisser
filter : étaminer ; filtrer
final rising : apprêt
flambé : flamber
flavor : aromatiser ; parfumer
flavorings : aromates
flour : fariner ; fleurer ; singer
flour well : fontaine
flute : chiqueter
foam : mousser
fold over : rabattre
form : façonner ; masser ; modeler
freeze : sangler
freeze-dry : lyophiliser
frost : givrir
froth : mousser
fruit filling, chopped : salpicon
fruit preserve technique : façon
garnish : garnir
glaze (v) : dorer ; glacer
glaze (n) : dorure
glaze with jelly or preserves : abricoter
glucose, to add : glucoser
grainy, to make : grainer/grener
grate : râper
grill : griller
grind : broyer ; piler
groove decoratively : canneler
hollow : évider
homogenize : homogénéïsation
incise : ciseler ; inciser
incorporate : incorporer
indent : denteler
infuse : infuser
inside : intérieur
invert : inverti/inverterir
jelly, to glaze with : abricoter
knead : petrir
leaves, to make into : feuilleter
line : chemiser
line with pastry : foncer
liquefy excessively : relâcher
liquid, to add : arroser/asperger
liquid, to mix with : délayer
liquid, to mold : couler
liquor, to add : alcooliser
loosen : bluquer/débloquer
macerate : macérer

marble : marbrer
marinate : mariner
mark : repérer
mask : masquer
measure : mesurer
mix : malaxer
mix with liquid : délayer
mixture : appareil ; masse ; mix
moisten : hydrater ; imbiber ; mouiller
mold : mouler
mold liquids : couler
oil : huiler
ooze : suinter
oven, put into : enfourner
oven, remove from : défourner
pasteurize : pasteuriser
pastries for the day : fournée
pastry, to line with : foncer
pastry bases : fonds
peel : éplucher ; monder
pinch : pincer
pipe out : coucher/dresser
pit : dénoyauter
plate : dresser
plunge in boiling water : ébouillanter/échauder
poach : pocher
pour off : décanter
powder : soupoudrer
preserve in sugar : confire
preserved fruit technique : façon
preserves, glaze with : abricoter
press : presser ; tamponner
prick : piquer
puff pastry dough block : pâton
pull : tirer
push down : rompre
raw ingredients : venue
reduce : réduire
refresh : refraîcher
remove crust from : décrouter
remove from oven : défourner
remove tart rings : décercler
reverse cooking : décuire
ribbon : ruban
ripen : maturation
rise : développer ; lever
rising : pointage ; pousse
rising, final : apprêt
roll : cribler
roll into balls : bouler
roll out : abaisser
roll out with a sheeter : laminer
sauce : sauce
scald : culotter
scallop : denteler
score : rayer
scrape : corner
seal : envelopper
season : assaisonner
section : détailler
seize : saisir
separate : clarifier
shape : façonner ; modeler ; tourner
sheet of dough : abaisse
sheet pans, to double or triple : doubler/tripler
shell : décortiquer ; écaler

shortening, creamed : pommade
shuck : décortiquer
sift : tamiser
simmer : frémir
skim : écumer
slice : émincer
slice thinly : effiler
smash : écraser
smell : sentir
smooth : concher ; égaliser ; lisser
soak : puncher ; tremper
soak in syrup : siroper
soften : assouplir
soften excessively : relâcher
solidify : masser
split open : cracher
sprinkle : saupoudrer
squeeze ; presser
stagger rows : quinconce
stem : équeter
sterilize : stériliser ; upériser
stiffen : bloquer ; raffermir ; serrer
stiffen egg whites : meringuer
stir : vanner
stocks : fonds
strain : chinoiser
streak : rayer
strike with heat : saiser
stuff : farcir ; fourrer
sugar, to preserve in : confire
sugar, cooked, to coat with : praliner
sweat : suinter
tamp : tamponner
tart rings, to remove : décercler
temper : tabler/mettre au point; tempérer/tiédir
thicken : coller ; épaissir ; gommer ; lier
thin : détendre
tighten : serrer
tint : farder
toast : griller
tolerance : tolérance
trim : ébarder ; égaliser ; éplucher ; parer
trimmings : rognure
turn : tourer ; tourner ; turbiner
unmold : démouler
veil : voiler
Viennese pastries : viennoiserie
warm : dégourdir ; étuver ; tempérer/tiédir
wash : laver
water bath, to cook in : cuire, au bain-marie
water vapor : buée
weigh : peser
weight/remove weights : charger/décharger
whip : battre ; foisonner ; fouetter
whisk : fouetter
whiten : blanchir
work : malaxer ; manier ; travailler
yeast starter : levain
zest : zester

Acknowledgments

Translators Rhona Poritzky-Lauvand and Jim Peterson would like to thank the following people: Pastry chef, consultant, and friend Jean-Noel Bechamps and pastry chef Jean-Marie Guichard, for answering many questions; Paula Borden for small conversions and enormous support; Monica Yates; Rémi Lauvand and Tibi Fish for immeasurable encouragement and love.

Much gratitude to our meticulous editor, Linda Venaton, and conscientous associate editor, Cindy Zigmund, and to Judy Joseph, Executive Editor, and the rest of the staff at VNR, who appreciate how special this series is.

We would also like to thank the students who helped test recipes, and we dedicate this series to all those who make this work rewarding.

About the Translators

Rhona Poritzky-Lauvand trained professionally in the culinary arts in Paris, France, working as apprentice in such restaurants as the Michelin two-star Jacque Cagna and Gerard Panguad.

Ms. Lauvand returned to New York and worked in several restaurants, where her talent for instruction became evident. In 1986 she joined the staff of the French Culinary Institute in New York City, the sister school to Le Ferrandi in Paris. Ms. Lauvand currently heads up the pastry department at the French Culinary Institute and has contributed significantly to the development of the pastry curriculum there. In addition to her own professional activities as a pastry chef and free-lance pastry specialist, Ms. Lauvand seriously studies music in New York City.

Jim Peterson trained in the culinary arts as an apprentice in several restaurants in Paris and the French countryside, including Le Vivarois in Paris and Chez La Mère Blanc in Vonnas, both three-star Michelin restaurants.

In 1979, Mr. Peterson returned to the United States where he opened Le Petit Robert in New York to critical acclaim.

Since 1984, Mr. Peterson has taught French cooking for the French Culinary Institute, where he is also writing a comprehensive curriculum for the school. Mr. Peterson also writes professionally and consults. He has a bachelor's degree in chemistry from the University of California at Berkeley.

Index